YUE-MAN YEUNG

CHANGING CITIES OF
PACIFIC ASIA

A SCHOLARLY INTERPRETATION

The Chinese University Press

ISBN 962–201–480–1

THE CHINESE UNIVERSITY PRESS
The Chinese University of Hong Kong
SHATIN, N. T., HONG KONG

Printed in Hong Kong by Ko's Arts Printing Co., Ltd.

To
Norton Ginsburg
and
the loving memory of my parents

Contents

PART V. THEMATIC PERSPECTIVES

Preface

My initial interest in cities was first cultivated by James Simmons who taught me and supervised my Master's dissertation when I studied at the University of Western Ontario between 1964 and 1966. This interest, however, took a sharp regional focus on Asia when I pursued doctoral studies at the University of Chicago between 1967 and 1969. I studied primarily under Norton Ginsburg, but I also benefited tremendously from intellectual stimulation and insights of Brian J. L. Berry, Philip Hauser, Harold Mayer, Peter Goheen and many of my colleagues. At this time, I also began to correspond and be associated with Terry McGee who was teaching at the University of Hong Kong and came to be positively influenced by his research on Southeast Asian cities. We later became collaborators in two projects on hawkers in Southeast Asian cities and participatory urban services.

At the University of Chicago it was Norton Ginsburg who effectively steered my geographical focus from China, on which it was still extremely difficult to base doctoral research at the contemporary level for lack of available data, to Southeast Asia. A teaching position at the University of Singapore from 1969 to 1975 provided me with not only the opportunity to complete my dissertation on public housing and the marketing system in Singapore, but also a convenient base from which to gain a first-hand understanding of regional problems in Southeast Asia through travelling, reading and interaction with local scholars.

My understanding of Southeast Asian cities was greatly deepened by participation in two projects funded by the International Development Research Centre (IDRC) in the early 1970s, focussed on hawkers and vendors, and low-cost housing in Southeast Asia. Participation in these two regional research networks took me to many parts of Southeast Asia, where I was able to develop an appreciation of the complexities of development and the ineffectiveness of some of the public policies.

Between 1975 and 1984, I worked for IDRC, initially as its social science representative in Asia based in its Asia Regional Office in Singapore and later in its head office in Ottawa directing a Third World urban policy programme. During that period I further deepened my understanding of development problems in developing countries as frequent travels brought me to different parts of the world, in particular to developing countries where I was in contact with planners, policy-makers, researchers and people affected by certain development policies. I covered Pacific Asia especially thoroughly and visited most countries and their metropolitan centres where most universities and research centres were located.

In 1984 I returned to live and work in Hong Kong, where at The Chinese University of Hong Kong I continued to develop and expand my interest in Asian cities. The collection of my personal works in this volume has been prompted by many favourable responses to my recent writings. It is believed that their assembly in a convenient form will facilitate reference to an important subject. Several of the papers have not been properly published or published only for limited circulation, both of which cases would be helped by this collection.

Over the years I have learned from and have been guided by the wise counsel and advice of many friends in the pursuit of my research on Asian cities. It is not possible to thank every one of them but I wish to single out Norton Ginsburg, Terry McGee, Aprodicio Laquian, Francois Belisle, William Lim, Kamal Salih and Fu-chen Lo. I am indebted to Norton Ginsburg, C. P. Lo, D. W. Drakakis-Smith and Francois Belisle for their willingness to allow reproduction of some co-authored pieces in this volume. It is hoped that publication of this volume will contribute to our common quest for a better understanding of the ever-changing cities of Pacific Asia and improved policies for the solution of urban problems.

February 1990

Acknowledgements

Sincere and grateful thanks are extended to the publishers, editors and co-authors that are listed below for their permission to reprint copyright material in this volume.

PART I. GENERAL STATEMENTS

1. "A World in Cities." *The IDRC Reports*, Vol. 12, No. 4 (1984), pp. 4–6.
2. With Norton Ginsburg, "Pacific Basin Cities of the Eighties." Closing Session Report in *Proceedings of the Fourth Inter-Congress*, *Pacific Science Association* (1–5 September 1981), pp. 47–55. Singapore: Singapore National Academy of Sciences, 1983.

PART II. EASTERN ASIA

3. "Great Cities of Eastern Asia." In *The Metropolis Era: A World of Giant Cities*, ed. Mattei Dogan and John D. Kasarda, pp. 155–86. Newbury Park: Sage Publications, 1988.
4. "Controlling Metropolitan Growth in Eastern Asia." *The Geographical Review*, Vol. 76, No. 2 (1986), pp. 125–37.

PART III. SOUTHEAST ASIA

5. With C. P. Lo, "Introduction." In *Changing South-East Asian Cities: Readings on Urbanization*, ed. Y. M. Yeung and C. P. Lo, pp. xv–xxiv. Singapore: Oxford University Press, 1976.
6. "Southeast Asian Cities: Patterns of Growth and Transformation." In *Urbanization and Counterurbanization*, ed. Brian J. L. Berry, pp. 285–309. Beverly Hills: Sage Publication, 1976.
7. "The Urban Environment in Southeast Asia: Challenge and Opportunity." In *Geography and the Environment in Southeast Asia*, ed. R. D. Hill and J. M. Bray, pp. 17–33. Hong Kong: Hong Kong University Press, 1978.

I also wish to express my appreciation to Jane Wan, Janet Wong and Frankie Tsang for their secretarial and typing support, and to Too See Lou for his cartographic services. They have taken on the additional work with their usual cheerfulness and care.

Introduction

As we enter the last decade of the twentieth century, the emergence of the countries around the western Pacific rim economically, demographically and in terms of urbanization relative to other regions of the world is widely recognized, a pattern that is likely to persist into the next century. This part of Asia located on the eastern part of the continent stretching between Korea and Indonesia is called Eastern Asia, a term used synonymously with Pacific Asia.

Thus defined, Pacific Asia includes three subregions: Southeast Asia (Indonesia, Singapore, Malaysia, Burma, Thailand, the Philippines and Brunei), East Asia (South Korea, Taiwan and Japan), and centrally planned Asia (China, North Korea, Vietnam, Kampuchea and Laos). Consequently, Pacific Asia encompasses the world's dominant economic power of Japan, the four newly industrialized countries of Asia (sometimes called the four Little Dragons, i.e., South Korea, Taiwan, Singapore and Hong Kong), the awakened giant of China anxious to pursue modernization and economic growth, and the emerging regional bloc of the Association of Southeast Asian Nations (ASEAN). This is one of the most ancient, dynamic and heterogeneous regions of the world worthy of attention and study.

Between 1960 and 1980, Pacific Asia experienced a demographic growth of 463 million, 195 million of which can be classified "urban." In both 1960 and 1980, Pacific Asia's share of the world population stood consistently at thirty-two per cent. The saliency of urbanization in Pacific Asia is underlined by the fact that whereas in 1970, altogether seventy-two cities in the developing world were in excess of one million inhabitants, by 1980 Pacific Asia alone had sixty "million" cities. According to statistics recently released by the United Nations, five of the top twenty, or ten of the top forty megacities (that is, cities with a population of at least four million each) in the world were located in Pacific Asia in 1985. By 2000, ten of the world's twelve largest cities will be in developing countries. This pattern of development, in particular the emergence of megacities sometimes as world cities fueled by the internationalization of production, has vital implications for urbanization policy and development within the region and for its differential impact on systems of cities.

Although there have been many books and articles that deal with urbanization and cities within individual Pacific Asian countries, relatively little attention has been paid to these cities as a group. For Southeast Asia, McGee's treatise of *The Southeast Asian City* has been influential, and Yeung (1976), Yeung and Lo (1976), and Leinbach and Ulack (1983) have written on cities in Southeast Asia. For cities of East Asia, Williams (1983) distinguished himself with the only piece. Yeung has written two recent papers on cities of Eastern Asia (Chapters 3 and 4) but the most comprehensive and thorough treatment of urbanization and urban policies in Pacific Asia is provided by a recent book edited by Fuchs, Jones and Pernia (1987). Dogan and Kasarda (1988) also published a volume on the theme of giant cities of the world, in which Eastern Asian cities are a subject of individual and collective study.

SHIFTING PERSPECTIVES ON ASIAN URBANIZATION

Although urbanization has been a salient component of development in postwar Asia, the subject has not received systematic or widespread scholarly attention until the 1960s. Over the past three decades, the study of Asian urbanization, not unlike that of the Third World as a whole, has reflected notable shifts in theoretical perspectives. It is instructive to outline some of these shifts, however brief this might be, and to anticipate changes in the future.

For the first publications dealing specifically with Asian urbanization, one must cite Hauser (1957) and the companion volume by Textor (1956). South Asia, in fact, was more actively studied than other subregions of Asia, and in the 1960s, such studies as *India's Urban Future* (Turner, 1962), *Urbanization and Urban India* (Sovani, 1966), and many others were published. For Pacific Asia, as noted earlier, there have been very few regional studies on urbanization but national and individual studies of cities have been appearing with increasing frequency.

In the early studies of Asian urbanization, it may be noted that the correlates of the process, namely, demographic, social, economic, political and institutional factors were emphasized and analyzed. There was an overriding concern for urban form, structure and pattern, a focus that was more than justified when so little was known about Asian cities and the way they had come about. By the 1960s, however, students were beginning to probe the development process of urbanization and attempted to relate it to the larger process which was at work in changing the country and society at large. T. G. McGee's (1967) pioneering study, with its thesis of pseudo-urbanization, created much interest in the subject. Together with Warwick Armstrong, McGee expounded a theory of urban involution on the conceptual basis of economic dualism, a model that Clifford Geertz originally employed to describe the dual economy of an Indonesian town (Armstrong and McGee, 1968). The dualistic framework was found to be of service in the study of urban planning and regional planning (McGee, 1970), and retail distribution (Yeung, 1973).

Since 1972, when the World Bank began a major onslaught on urban poverty through development assistance in developing countries, there followed a period of searching for links between urbanization and development processes in general, and between urban and other sectoral development in particular. Examples of the latter may be found in regional and national studies of low-cost housing (Yeh and Laquian, 1979) and hawkers and vendors in Southeast Asia (McGee and Yeung, 1977). The influence of the International Labour Office in its World Employment Programme launched in 1969 to alleviate mass poverty and unemployment in developing countries was also pervasive. It popularized the concept of the formal and the informal sectors. In Pacific Asia, studies stemming from this conceptual basis have been undertaken in housing, transport and food distribution (Rimmer, Drakakis-Smith and McGee, 1978). Dissatisfied with the available models to explicate uneven development and evolving rural-urban relations, Lo, Salih and Douglass (1978) developed a basic macro-spatial model in which are embedded three dualistic relationships, viz. North-South, urban-rural and formal-informal. Under this model, country and regional differences in resource endowments, technology, demography and development ideology can be taken into account before regional types are identified. For Pacific Asia, a separate model type is applicable to East and Southeast Asia.

By the early 1980s, it became increasingly clear that the Pacific rim was destined to play an even greater role in terms of economic growth, urban development and world affairs. The intensification of the international production process had to be recognized in the urbanization of the region. Towards this end, Gilbert and Gugler (1982) delineated a paradigm shift, in which contemporary Third World cities, including those in Pacific Asia, had to be viewed as part of the global economy. They used the world system framework to situate dependent urbanization, peripheral capitalism, deepening inequality and regional disparity in developing countries, phenomena that are applicable to different degrees to Pacific Asia. Discarding their earlier conceptual positions based on the dualistic economy, Armstrong and McGee (1985) perceived, in like vein, cities in developing countries as theatres of surplus (capital) accumulation. Asian cities were cast in an encompassing framework derived from interweaving global capitalism and the international division of labour. The international dimension of contemporary Asian urbanization can be understood and explained in these two recent volumes.

In the 1980s, too, there have been more organized attempts to study, understand and analyze changing Asian urbanization on an institutional basis. At least two such concerted efforts are noteworthy. The first is the Working Group on Urbanization in Developing Countries under the auspices of the International Geographical Union that existed between 1980 and 1988. The Working Group published newsletters, organized meetings in many regions of the world, ran urban training workshops at Universiti Sains Malaysia in Penang in 1984 and 1985, and contributed to the literature (Drakakis-Smith, 1986; Yeung and Zhou, 1987, 1989). Secondly, the Asian Urban Research Association was established after its first and highly successful meeting at the University of Akron in 1985. Out of this meeting, several publications have already appeared, including two special issues in *Urban Geography* (July–August 1986) and *The Geographical Review* (April 1986) and two special volumes (Costa *et al.*, 1988, 1989).

The above attempt to describe the shifting perspectives on Asian urbanization is inevitably sketchy and incomplete. It does, however, convey the sense of an important mission and a growing enterprise. In looking ahead to the 1990s, where are the research frontiers and what are the urban challenges? As a preliminary attempt, I have identified the following.

THE URBAN CHALLENGES

The first challenge is related to what may be ascribed to the international impact of urbanization on Asian countries. Continued improvements in transportation and telecommunication have enabled urban development, at least that part directly related to capital formation, labour force mobility and economic growth, to be increasingly linked to a world system of development. As economic growth becomes more interdependent among nations, cities in national systems begin to articulate across national boundaries with specific functional complementaries, which are as important as those within particular space-economies. The spatial effects of this international production process are a tendency of footlooseness and a willingness of host countries to facilitate such production to occur within their administrative jurisdiction. The development of export processing zones in many Asian countries is a positive response to this changing pattern of production. The international impact of urbanization is felt throughout the urban hierarchy in Asia, but most clearly in the large cities. In fact, some of them have grown to be world cities with vital functional links outside their countries. Capital, intelligence and labour freely flow among countries. Along the Pacific rim, it has been observed that real estate, trade and capital markets in major urban centres are connected with Chinese investment (Goldberg, 1985). Three possible policy responses may flow from this pattern of world economic interdependence. One is to take into account of this international factor in national urbanization policy if there is any. Another is the attempt to control metropolitan growth which I try to show through the successes and failures in Eastern Asia (Chapter 4). The third is the need to devise measures to encourage and support the growth of secondary urban centres.

Secondly, a phenomenon that is peculiarly Asian is occurring in many longstanding and rich agricultural regions centred around a number of large cities. A process called Kotadesasi (town and village in intense interaction) by McGee (1987) aptly describes urbanization of the countryside where rural folks do not have to change residence or move to the cities. Simple transport modes like the bus have been effectively extending the ambit of the cities to as far as one hundred kilometres around them, with the increasing saliency of rural non-farm jobs as a source of employment and income and with substantial circular migration between city and countryside. This process has been noted to occur in Java, Taiwan, China, India and probably other regions in Asia. The process of rural-urban transition is creating new roles for surrounding rural regions of some megacities of Asia and is something that should be encouraged to happen in order to save the already large cities from further unwanted growth. The second challenge is therefore to find ways and means to consolidate this development process that apparently works well for some regions of Asia.

A third urban challenge in Asia is that despite efforts at the national and international levels to combat poverty, many cities are still saddled with grinding poverty, glaring inequality and poor services. Whatever economic growth in these cities has not been accompanied by expected redistribution. Issues of income distribution are often skirted. Jobs for the poor are scarce, urban services are lacking and deteriorating, and the vicious cycle of poverty is yet to be broken. Some of these problems stem from the uneven relationship between the central and municipal governments, in which the former exerts an overarching influence on the latter, particularly in the sphere of finance. Intentions to improve urban services and livelihoods of the poor are often bedevilled by limited municipal finance raised by a narrow tax base, to be supplemented by heavy central government subsidy. For example, only four kinds of taxes (house and land tax, land development tax, signboard tax and animal slaughter tax) come under the Bangkok Metropolitan Administration. It is now increasingly recognized that macroeconomic policies aimed at creating employment or mega urban projects fail to touch the lives of the urban poor. In the coming decade we have to do better.

Still another challenge is a direct result of accelerated urbanization in Asia, in particular the growth of megacities. By the year 2000, one-fifth of the world's population will be living in megacities. The Asian landscape is becoming an urban landscape, with grave implications on the natural environment to provide large concentrated urban populations with land, water and air. Excessive concentration of population and economic activities has already posed serious problems for the environment. Water pollution, acid rain, disappearance of fertile arable land, over utilization of underground water resources ... are some of the problems that many Asian cities have to deal with. Visitors to Shanghai would remember that Su River which feeds into Huangpu River stinks (although the World Bank has helped by funding to clean up) and more often than not, lovely sandy beaches in Hong Kong are closed in the summer because of water pollution. A challenge in the years ahead thus is to help raise among urban inhabitants and policy-makers their level of consciousness on the environment and to ensure that the environment is not unduly fouled up in the process of economic development pursued by the cities. Resource-conserving cities provide one of the options that offer some inviting possibilities.

Finally, given the peculiar setting within which Asian urbanization is developing, another urban challenge is to search for indigenous urban innovations to come to terms with problems of the cities. These innovations may not even have to be technological in nature; they can be management innovations involving new ways of deploying resources to tackle old problems. The Area Licensing Scheme in Singapore, implemented since 1975, is one example. Another example is the new institutional framework of Metro Manila to deal with the same situation but in a more effective manner, minimizing overlapping and fragmented organizations. In this connection, the potential contributions of non-governmental organizations (NGOs) should not be taken lightly as they do work with the people and often with good results.

ORGANIZATION AND SELECTION

This volume is put together for the purpose of better understanding the cities of Pacific Asia with an accent on constant change. The papers are derived entirely from my publications over the last decade but most notably during the last few years. The papers are organized in five parts, conceptually from the general to the specific.

Part I provides two statements highlighting, respectively, urbanization in the Third World and new challenges it presents to development, and a perspective on Pacific Basin cities in the eighties, the theme of the Pacific Science Inter-Congress held in Singapore in 1981.

Part II consists of two important papers on great cities of Eastern Asia that attempt firstly, to analyze the trends of urban growth, key urban problems, and attempted solutions and policies in the period 1960–1980, and secondly, to review for some of these cities during the same period, several strategies to restrain growth under the headings of physical control, regional planning and social policy. Both papers point to the increasingly pivotal roles that are being played by megacities of the region.

Four papers focussed on cities in Southeast Asia constitute Part III, offering different perspectives and insights. Chapter 5 emphasizes the need for a theory of Third World urbanization before the cities in Southeast Asia may be conceptually situated, followed by a review of the historical development of these cities. The theme of rapid change recurs in the study of Southeast Asian cities. Chapter 6 is an important review of salient urban growth patterns between 1960 and 1975, of development policies and strategies, and of aspects of the urban transformation of Southeast Asian cities. There is a conscientious attempt to review all major scholarly works on the subject as of the mid-1970s. Innovations in the management of urban problems is the focus of Chapter 7, in which a range of policy responses of large Southeast Asian cities are described and evaluated. Lessons may be drawn from some of these policy measures for other cities in the developing world. Chapter 8 is an essay about the growth and decay of Southeast Asian cities, with more emphasis on the former than the latter. It ends with a plea for a more careful examination of the roles of cities in the development process of the region.

Part IV deals with the special urban setting of the city-states of Hong Kong and Singapore, both equally noted for their rapid economic growth and efficient urban management. Specifically, Chapter 9 touches on several aspects of urban management, with an emphasis on the planning process and the urban environment. It is concluded that lessons for planning for high-density urban centres may be drawn from the urban development experience of Hong Kong and Singapore. Chapter 10 probes the factors behind their urban policies, employing public housing and urban transportaion as examples to illustrate urban efficiency. The study shows that 1984 was an important year for both city-states in different ways.

Part V represents an assembly of papers on eclectic themes having to do with urban Asia. In fact, Chapter 11 has its geographical purview of the Third World, outlining the scope of urbanization in these countries and the responses of international development agencies to it. The specific role of the International Development Research Centre in this response has been summarized as of 1984. The phenomenon of travelling night markets was a thriving economic and social institution in Singapore until its demise in the late 1970s. Chapter 12 provides the most comprehensive account of this now historical occurrence, which is not only of nostalgic interest to old-timers of Singapore but of theoretical import to the study of periodic markets and of practical relevance to other cities still finding night/periodic markets a useful mechanism for the distribution of goods and services. Chapter 13 addresses the critical yet little researched subject of urban agriculture in Asia. It is a systematic review of problems of urban agriculture, present production patterns, specific case studies, policy issues and implementation strategies. The chapter ends on the optimistic note that increased food production in Asian cities is a realizable goal but there are daunting obstacles to overcome. The last two chapters revolve around the theme of the urban poor in Asia. Chapter 14 draws findings from a five-country study on participatory urban services in Asia and shows that, when basic services are not adequately provided by the government, the poor have devised a host of mechanisms to improve their immediate living environment. Finally, Chapter 15 reviews briefly the contributions of the informal sector in absorbing surplus labour and of intervention at the international, national and city levels to alleviate urban poverty and increase employment opportunities. It is argued that more positive measures can be undertaken by metropolitan governments to improve the livelihoods of the urban poor.

REFERENCES

Armstrong, W. R. and T. G. McGee. 1968. "Revolutionary Change and the Third World City: A Theory of Urban Involution." *Civilizations*, 58(3): 353–78.

——. 1985. *Theatres of Accumulation: Studies in Asian and Latin American Urbanization*. London and New York: Methuen.

Costa, Frank, Ashok Dutt, Lawrence Ma and Allen Noble, eds. 1988. *Asian Urbanization: Problems and Processes*. Stuttgart: Gebruder Borntraeger.

——. 1989. *Urbanization in Asia: Spatial Dimensions Policy Issues*. Honolulu: University of Hawaii.

Dogan, Mattei and John D. Kasarda, eds. 1988. *The Metropolis Era: A World of Giant Cities*. Newbury Park: Sage Publications.

Drakakis-Smith, David, ed. 1986. *Urbanization in the Developing World*. London: Croom Helm.

Fuchs, Roland J., Gavin W. Jones and Ernesto M. Pernia, eds. 1987. *Urbanization and Urban Policies in Pacific Asia*. Boulder and London: Westview Press.

Gilbert, Alan and Josef Gugler. 1982. *Cities, Poverty, and Development: Urbanization in the Third World*. London and New York: Oxford University Press.

Goldberg, Michael A. 1985. *The Chinese Connection: Getting into Pacific Rim Real Estate, Trade and Capital Markets*. Vancouver: University of British Columbia Press.

Hauser, P. M., ed. 1957. *Urbanization in Asia and the Far East*. Calcutta: UNESCO Research Centre.

Leinbach, Thomas R. and Richard Ulack. 1983. "Cities of Southeast Asia." In *Cities of the World: World Regional Urban Development*, ed., Stanley D. Brunn and Jack F. Williams, pp. 371– 407. New York: Harper and Row.

Lo, Fu-chen, Kamal Salih and Mike Douglass. 1978. "Uneven Development, Rural-Urban Transformation, and Regional Development Alternative in Asia." Paper presented at Seminar on Rural-Urban Transformation and Regional Development Planning, 31 October–10 November. Nagoya, United Nations Centre for Regional Development.

McGee, T. G. 1967. *The Southeast Asian City*. London: G. Bell and Sons.

———. 1970. "Dualism in the Asian City: The Implications for City and Regional Planning." *The Third International Symposium on Regional Development*, pp. 34–47. Tokyo: Japan Centre for Asia Development Centre.

———. 1987. *Urbanisasi or Kotadesasi? The Emergence of New Regions of Economic Interaction in Asia*. Working Paper, Environment and Policy Institute. Honolulu: East-West Center.

McGee, T. G. and Y. M. Yeung. 1977. *Hawkers in Southeast Asian Cities: Planning for the Bazaar Economy*. Ottawa: International Development Research Centre.

Rimmer, P. J., D. W. Drakakis-Smith and T. G. McGee, eds. 1978. *Food, Shelter and Transportation in Southeast Asia and the Pacific*. Canberra: Research School of Pacific Studies, Australian National University.

Sovani, N. V. 1966. *Urbanization and Urban India*. Bombay: Asia Publishing House.

Textor, R. B. 1956. *The Social Implications of Industrialization and Urbanization in Southern Asia*. Calcutta: UNESCO Research Centre.

Turner, Roy, ed. 1962. *India's Urban Future*. Berkeley: University of California Press.

Williams, Jack. 1983. "Cities of East Asia." In *Cities of the World*, ed. Brunn and Williams, pp. 409–50.

Yeh, Stephen H. K. and A. A. Laquian, eds. 1979. *Housing Asia's Millions: Problems, Policies, and Prospects for Low-Cost Housing in Southeast Asia*. Ottawa: International Development Research Centre.

Yeung, Yue-man. 1973. *National Development Policy and Urban Transformation in Singapore: A Study of Public Housing and the Marketing System*. Research Paper, No. 149. Chicago: Department of Geography, University of Chicago.

———. 1976. "Southeast Asian Cities: Patterns of Growth and Transformation." In *Urbanization and Counterurbanization*, ed. Brian J. L. Berry, pp. 285–309. Beverly Hills: Sage Publication. (Included in this book as Chapter 6.)

Yeung, Yue-man and C. P. Lo. 1976. "Introduction." In *Changing South-East Asian Cities: Readings on Urbanization*, ed. Yeung and Lo. Singapore: Oxford University Press. (Included in this book as Chapter 5.)

Yeung, Yue-man and Zhou Yixing, eds. 1987. *Urbanization in China: An Inside-Out Perspective. Chinese Sociology and Anthropology*, 14 (3–4).

———, eds. 1989. *Urbanization in China: An Inside-Out Perspective* (II). *Chinese Sociology and Anthropology*, 21(2).

PART I

General Statements

1. A World in Cities

Juanita is a vegetable vendor in Manila. She moved to the city from a rural *barrio* (village) ten years ago. Juanita and her husband work seven to nine hours a day to earn five pesos (less than US$1). The money goes quickly to support her family of five children. The family lives in one small rented room, part of a converted market building now partitioned to house about one hundred people near the public market where she works. There is no toilet, bath, or water. The residents use toilets in the market, and drinking water is some twenty metres away. The family possesses the barest of essentials, but poverty does not quell their hopes for a better future than education for the children might bring.

Calcutta, founded in 1690, grew by successive waves of in-migration and natural increase to be the largest city in India. Over nine million people live in a city built for 250,000. Calcutta is severely short of the basic facilities of drainage and sewerage, water supply and housing. Garbage is dumped indiscriminately and collected irregularly. Over the last fifty years, the amount of filtered water available per person has dropped by over half. More than three-fourths of the city's population live in overcrowded tenement and *bustee* (slum) quarters. At least 100,000 people without *any* proper shelter live on the pavements.

Once a thriving trading and commercial centre, Calcutta has been stagnating and deteriorating, both economically and physically, in recent decades. It has acquired the dubious reputation of being the worst city in the world.

One urban dweller and one city, Juanita and Calcutta epitomize, each in their own way, the urban phenomenon that has been rapidly unfolding in many parts of the developing world since the end of the Second World War. Although Calcutta may be an example of extreme urban breakdown, there are many Juanitas and many Calcutta-like cities in the world. What is worse, their numbers continue to grow.

In 1970, there were 84 cities with populations in excess of one million in the developed regions, compared with 72 in the developing regions. By the end of this century, it is projected that of the 425 "million" cities, 149 may be found in the developed countries, compared with 276 in the developing countries. Looked at differently, of the 30 largest cities in the world in 1970, 19 were situated in the Third World (14 in Asia). By 1990, 23 of the 30 largest cities will be in the less-developed countries; Asia alone will have 16. Among the "top ten" in 1990, the developed regions will be represented only by Tokyo and New York. All of these ten largest cities will be gargantuan urban agglomerations of many millions each.

The figures underline the fact that Third World urbanization has been rapidly accelerating. By the year 2000, more than half of the world's population will be living in urban areas, with a majority in developing countries. The implications for the provision of services and well-being of the millions of inhabitants of Third World cities are as serious as they are challenging, for policy-makers in these countries, and for international development specialists alike.

CRISIS AT HAND

Cities in developing countries have grown rapidly under circumstances quite different from those of developed countries. Urbanization in the Third World has not been accompanied by industrialization and the creation of abundant job opportunities. The process has also been telescoped: the complex institutions that normally evolve over time to tackle increasingly demanding and complicated tasks have not appeared. Meanwhile, urban populations continue to grow by massive natural increase as well as incessant rural-urban migration. For the first time in history, Third World cities are confronted with enormous and seemingly intractable problems of huge populations, pervasive poverty, and limited resources. Urbanization in this environment is characterized by gross economic inefficiencies and social inequities, and an extraordinary imbalance between population and the demand for basic urban services. The litany of urban problems is now familiar to many administrators and researchers. The challenge is to find solutions within the financial, technological, and institutional constraints of these countries. An urban crisis is said to be at hand.

There are no tested solutions from developed countries that can be applied with efficacy to Third World urban problems. At the cost of time and lost opportunities, it has been discovered all too often that ready-made Western formulas have not produced the expected results in Third World cities. The basic conditions are simply too different, indigenous solutions, particularly of a low-cost type, will have to be found. Trial and error may often be the method.

Despite unmistakable signals of mounting development problems in the early 1960s, the international assistance community refused to address head-on the issues associated with rapid Third World urbanization. Assistance programmes of the United Nations system of organizations and private foundations had their emphasis squarely on the rural areas, or on development in specific sectors that may have included partial support for urban activities. It was not until 1972, when the World Bank began to provide development assistance directly to urban projects, that the international assistance climate appeared to take a more favourable turn. The urban projects supported by the World Bank stressed low-cost and effective means of delivering urban services and a broad application of results. They have measurably strengthened the management of urban growth. By the end of 1981, the World Bank had sixty-two projects in the fields of shelter, urban transport, integrated urban development, and regional development in different parts of the developing world at various stages of implementation.

Apart from the World Bank, the Asian Development Bank, the United States Agency for International Development (USAID), the United Nations Centre for Human Settlements (Habitat), United Nations Children's Fund (UNICEF), the International Labour Office (ILO), and the United Nations Environment Programme (UNEP), among others, have been active in supporting infrastructure or social improvement of livelihoods in Third World cities. There is, however, a conspicuous need of *indigenous* research designed to seek better means or policies to cope with urban problems.

The International Development Research Centre (IDRC) tries to meet the demand for policy-relevant research in the Third World by encouraging indigenous specialists to study their own problems. Within the general concern for the welfare of the rural poor, IDRC has, since 1980, provided more support for urban research in developing countries. An Urban Policy Programme within the Centre's Social Sciences Division actively works with Third World researchers in the design and implementation of urban projects.

Where the other assistance agencies have provided technical assistance and capital investment, IDRC has encouraged policy-relevant research. Projects synthesize existing knowledge of urban development policies, diagnose important urban problems and suggest solutions, or evaluate completed and on-going urban strategies and programmes. A major focus of the programme is on urban services—particularly in improving the delivery, access to, and effectiveness of, these services for the urban poor.

In order to assist developing countries to seek more practical solutions to their problems of shelter, IDRC has supported a number of studies in low-cost housing. An eight-country study in Asia in the 1970s yielded useful data and information upon which existing housing policies were improved and new ones proposed. In addition to providing research data, the project promoted cooperation among participating agencies that continues well beyond the completion of the project.

A strain on urban services has caused some governments to extend basic services (water, sewerage, roads, electricity) to peripheral urban land in order to encourage squatters and slum dwellers in the city centre to move there and build their own housing through mutual and self-help efforts. In conjunction with the World Bank, IDRC supported a four-country study on the evaluation of "sites-and-services" projects to determine the extent to which the goals of the projects are being achieved, assess the impact of the project on the people living in them, and develop information that would help in the efficient execution of such projects in future, and help formulate policies within the cities and countries. It was a most worthwhile experience, for when the projects were launched in 1975, there was hardly any prior experience on which one could depend. It was a case of "learning by doing" for all concerned, and the research has yielded lessons and insights which are extremely useful for later projects to be developed. More recently, in 1981, IDRC supported a seminar in Indonesia in which more recent approaches to low-cost housing provision in Asia were critically reviewed and compared. A recent publication, *A Place to Live*, highlighted some of these approaches.

FOOD AND TRANSPORTATION

Support of research on food distribution and markets in urban areas began with a three-country, six-city study of hawkers and vendors in Southeast Asia. A comprehensive study of food markets in Mexico City followed, and two similar projects are underway in Bangkok and Manila. These projects examine the role of food markets in the supply, dependability and price of food for the poor. Other research in Egypt, Malaysia, India and Zimbabwe will further define the problems of providing food in the city.

Low-cost transport is another sector of urban activities to which IDRC has lent research support. Not unlike similar projects IDRC supported in the 1970s, a four-country comparative study produced a wealth of data and recommendations in Manila (Philippines), Yogyakarta and Bandung (Indonesia), Chiang Mai (Thailand) and Istanbul (Turkey), and has had a measure of success in galvanizing public attention and debate on ways to improve low-cost transport facilities within these cities. Even more effectively, the recently completed study of *matatu* taxi-buses in Nairobi (Kenya), has been able to bring policy-makers and *matatu* drivers together to discuss and evaluate research. Low-cost travel modes in Kathmandu (Nepal), Dhaka (Bangladesh) and Trivandrum (India) are being investigated. At the core is a concern for the relationship of these diverse types of travel modes to the urban community, development plans, and the lives of the urban poor in these cities.

INSTITUTIONS

One key factor in the inability of many urban governments in developing countries to respond effectively to rapid urbanization is the lack of appropriate institutions. A network of five countries in Asia have completed their investigation of largely self-help mechanisms to deliver basic urban services (see Chapter 14). Researchers have been able to show that, with the government's failure to provide minimum basic services for low-income populations, the inhabitants have been able to evolve rather effective low-cost mechanisms to meet at least some of their own most urgent needs.

The issues surrounding urban-regional relations, such as the role of cities in national and regional development, policies affecting urban growth and regional development, and the flow of capital, goods and services between city and countryside are real concerns for many Third World administrators and planners. Teams of researchers in Indonesia and the Philippines are trying to unravel the effects of circular and short-term migration of population on employment in medium-sized cities in the Sumatra and Mindanao regions of the two countries. Similarly, studies on the influence of medium and small towns on urban growth (in Nepal) and another seeking a more rational industrial and regional development pattern consistent with re-source allocation (in Egypt) have recently been approved.

Urban change entails constant economic and social adaptation by individuals and household, especially the urban poor and recent in-migrants. Households exchange food and other goods so as to cope with exigencies as they arise. The theme of a study soon to be completed in Papua New Guinea examines how interhousehold transfers in urban areas have served vital redistributive ends.

In addition to these broad themes of support, the urban programme has funded exploratory studies, such as those on urban waste management in Korea, central area revitalization in several cities in Latin America, and urban food and fuel in Kenya. New initiatives on possible studies on urban agriculture in Asian cities (see Chapter 13) and on urban land policies and land needs in the South Pacific are being reviewed.

The urban projects supported to date are by no means exhaustive. Instead, they indicate the kinds of urban concerns that are considered to be most in need of research and policy guidelines.

As the present century comes to an end, the saliency of Third World urban problems and urban poverty will likely become more pronounced. If these problems are not to worsen, adequate resources must be made available within the international assistance community for work in the urban sector. Within this common goal of lessening, if not banishing, urban malaise in developing countries, IDRC's contribution will continue to help developing countries to seek innovative ways to come to grips with their ever-daunting problems.

2. Pacific Basin Cities of the Eighties*

PART I

The choice of urbanization as the main theme of this Pacific Science Inter-Congress is especially appropriate and timely given the recent population projections from sources of the United Nations. In less than twenty years or at the end of this century, the Pacific Basin will possess some of the largest cities in the world—Mexico City and Tokyo—and will also have several cities in the ten million class—Shanghai, Beijing, Manila, Bangkok and Jakarta. Levels of urbanization will continue to increase and overall urban policy and development will loom increasingly large in the national development of the countries in the Pacific Basin.

An urban conference on such a scale in the Pacific Basin is not only timely but also overdue. In the 1970s we witnessed a radically different global situation in the emergence of a new economic order, an energy crisis triggered by the quadrupling of oil prices, in 1973, international migration of population and labour force on a massive scale (refugee exodus from Vietnam and Asian guest workers to the Middle East), and continued saliency of transnational corporations in national development in Asian countries. All these factors are beginning, and will continue, to bear on urban growth and development in Pacific Basin countries. The last two times we had an urban conference on the present scale in Asia were both in the 1960s—The Pacific Conference on Urban Growth in 1967 in Honolulu the memory of which now lies faintly in the summary volume, *The Urban Debate*, and 1969 in Hong Kong at the conference entitled The City as a Centre of Change in Asia—a book bearing the same title appeared in 1971. The 1976 United Nations Habitat Conference did address many issues related to urban development, but we have waited for more than a decade to

---

*Part II of this chapter is attributable to Norton Ginsburg.

take stock of the past and chart a course for the urban future.

Given the large number of papers presented in this Congress, even a combined effort between Professor Ginsburg and myself cannot do them justice in any attempt to synthesize the materials. What we would propose is for me to raise a number of specific topics and comment on them, leaving issues of a more conceptual and general nature for Professor Ginsburg. In other words, I will attempt to draw what may be called a research agenda for the 1980s, however tentative and preliminary it may be, making incidental references to the papers if possible. Professor Ginsburg will amplify the significance of these and put them in a developmental context.

When the issues of urbanization in the Pacific Basin were first publicly discussed in the fifties and sixties, considerable concern was centred around the characteristics of Asian urbanization and the differences and similarities it had with urbanization in developed regions at similar stages of development. By now the parameters and correlates of Asian urbanization are more or less better delineated. The recent emphasis of urban research appears to be more concerned with practical matters of urban governance, of inequality and, of uneven rural/urban development. The urban debate still continues, but it is presently carried out within government circles as well as in academic forums.

Indeed, the urban debate presently revolves around the urban dilemmas in which city governments have found themselves. In a sense, these are, as Kamal Salih argued, policy dilemmas. He raised three questions. How should the government avoid the question of urban bias in resource allocation and development and maintain a more even pattern of development between the rural and urban sectors? What should be the policy choice and balance between formal and informal sector development, between growth and redistribution? What strategies and approaches should be adopted in the improved access and delivery of urban services? We can extend this list of questions by drawing attention to other dilemmas which are confronting many governments. For example, the increasing importance of the international dimension of national urban development, the role of cities in development (especially the relative roles of development by city size, the perennial debate of the relative merits of large city vs. small city), policies relating to the growth of urban population and movement of people and the labour force.

As cities are generally agents of change and funnels along which foreign goods, capital and ideas are directed, national urban systems have always been subjected to external influences. What indications have crystallized over the past several years, however, is that the international dimension of national urban development will likely become more prominent in the 1980s as papers by Logan, A. Scott, and Connell and Curtain suggest. Partly as a result of continual improvement in transportation and telecommunication, urban development, at least that part directly related to capital formation, labour force mobility and economic growth, is more and more linked to a world system of development. As economic growth has become more interdependent among nations, cities in national systems begin to articulate across national boundaries with specific functional complementarities. In some cases these transnational functional linkages are as important as those within particular national space-economies. The growth of transnational corporations, the relative ease of capital flows, and the wage level and skill differential between countries have contributed to the ascendancy of this international dimension of urbanization in the Pacific Basin. Quite clearly, resulting from this pattern of recent development, studies on trade flows, capital flows, labour force migration, kinship networks between cities across national boundaries will elucidate the nature of these relationships and assist national governments to devise policies best suited to their interest.

Germane to the international dimension of urbanization is a growing phenomenon of international migration from several Pacific Basin countries to the Middle East since about 1975, a topic not addressed in any of the papers. Nonetheless, this development has vital policy implications for the countries concerned since the migration is noticed to be temporary with the well-nigh certainty of reverse flow, affecting the most active stratum of the labour force, of single male population etc. The implications, both positive (such as remittances, relief to unemployment) and negative (such as creating certain skills shortage, family dislocation and adjustment), are yet to be fully understood in countries such as the Philippines, Korea, Thailand, Malaysia in the Pacific Basin, and India, Pakistan, Bangladesh in South Asia.

Perhaps viewed as a parallel conceptual and policy development to the international dimension just adumbrated is the recent resurgence of interest in research about the role of small towns. No doubt the debate of the relative roles of large and small cities in national development continues, but the latest convergence of development and research interest in small towns may be seen in part as a renewed skepticism of the ability of large Pacific

Basin cities to provide the same or improved quality of life with available financial resources at their disposition. The need to examine alternative policy options is necessary in view of the already strained urban services provisions in many of these large cities and the somewhat alarming population projections for these cities in the years ahead.

This Congress has heard the results of preliminary investigations of the research on small towns in almost the entire geographic purview of the Pacific Basin from China, through Southeast Asia, to the South Pacific. T. McGee called for a radical rethinking for the role of small towns, pointing to the danger of their being bypassed with technological development. Peter Rimmer and H. Dick strongly cautioned that large-city policy solutions must be carefully scrutinized before they are applied to small cities. The implication to be drawn from this series of studies is that the subject of small towns will likely continue to be a subject of continued academic curiosity and policy interest. However, to be able to break new ground, these studies will have to be seen in a more specific developmental context, with more purposefully collected data which can reflect their functional niches in the urban hierarchy and in relation to the immediate rural areas.

While a better understanding of small cities is being sought, the large cities in the Pacific Basin will strive to be better planned and managed. The experience of management of the primate cities of Southeast Asia since the 1900s has been such that Rimmer and Drakakis-Smith called it one of taming "the Wild City!" Whether these large cities have indeed become "wild" depends on one's personal predilection, but they have certainly grown rapidly in physical, material and population terms, at least in Southeast Asia. There has been no lack of innovative approaches in an attempt to plan and manage these large cities. Singapore's national development policy of decentralization through public housing and successful traffic control by adoption of the Area Licensing Scheme, Jakarta's closed-city policy, Metro-Manila's administrative amalgamation, Bangkok's decentralization policy, and Kuala Lumpur's ethnic-oriented urban developments are examples. This is not the place to evaluate the success or failure of these innovations, but they do reflect a serious concern of policy-makers in their endeavour to improve the efficiency and management ability of these cities.

In the Pacific Basin cities, more particularly in the large ones, the problem of urban services has come to the fore consequent, on the one hand, to the large gap between demand and supply and, on the other, to a revolution of rising expectations and greater concern about economic inequality and social injustice. Papers by K. K. Khatu and Nancy Chen, among others, address different facets of urban services. In the 1970s national development programmes and international capital assistance contributed in no small measure to the improvement of the infrastructure and urban services in many selected cities in the region. The problem of access and delivery, in particular their institutional and organizational aspects, is in need of research and evaluation. The need to explore innovative approaches of delivery, with an emphasis on self-help mechanisms, is real in view of the continuing lack of financial and technical resources in most governments to bring about material improvements within present institutional and fiscal constraints. The critical services in need of support and improvement include housing, food supply, water supply, waste disposal, fire protection, child care, etc., many of which have been the topics of papers at this Congress.

Finally, the complex of relationships between population and employment was highlighted by many papers in this meeting. With the population explosion in the postwar period being translated into a labour force explosion, many countries in the Pacific Basin are faced with the problem of how to keep unemployment at bay without a structural economic transformation. Formal sector employment will unlikely provide greatly expanded employment opportunities in the next two decades. The informal sector will therefore be increasingly expanded and encouraged as a realistic response to the situation. A fruitful line of enquiry can thus be an exploration and elaboration of the linkage between formal and informal sector employment, which at present is only vaguely understood.

Rural-urban transfers mediated by migration of population and flows of capital and goods will continue to be an important facet of national development. These interactions will be affected by policies that have been adopted for spatial investment of economic activities, regional development, and fiscal allocations of national budgets. By now the dynamics and socioeconomic correlates of population migration between rural and urban areas are broadly known. Future research on these issues should thus focus on clearly defined migration streams related to labour market segmentation in the cities and to policy interventionist strategies whereby these streams may be channelled in such a manner as is in keeping with development priorities of the countries concerned. The research on small towns earlier mentioned will, like this emphasis on specific population migration, be aimed at an improved understanding of rural-urban relations and consequent policy measures to rectify uneven developments.

I have attempted, perhaps vainly and not entirely successfully, to draw together some themes which I personally consider worthwhile to be on the agenda of urban research in the Pacific Basin in the eighties.

To do so is only to raise more questions than to provide answers. It is not the aim of the organizers of this Congress that answers to the complex and perplexing questions of urbanization in the region are to be found within the deliberations of this week. Certainly to my mind many of the significant questions have been posed and reformulated. I would now like to invite Professor Ginsburg to add on to the research agenda and to address certain fundamental questions of definition and development which I have deliberately avoided.

PART II

Dr. Yeung has set us well on the way towards defining a future research agenda on the nature and problems of Pacific Basin cities in the 1980s. Let me continue along the same vein, but perhaps on a somewhat broader scale. I propose to discuss three major issues which might be added to our research agenda: the idea of the city, urbanization and development, and food for the city and its relation to development strategies. First, a problem of definition!

The Idea of the City

Commonsensically we all know what the city is, but in fact there is far from complete consensus about its definition. You recall Professor Glass, for example, objecting to Professor Meier's reference to the city as "it," though I'm sure she appreciated the fact that *some* pronoun needs to be used when referring to the city, and "he" and "she" will not do. What then is "it"?

The city is an artifact. Its nature is determined by the culture of the society which calls it into being. The city thus may be likened to an American Indian arrowhead, or a Japanese sword. It has both purpose and substance. It also is culturally and temporally relative in structure and function.

The city differs from the arrowhead, however, in three significant ways:

first, it is not only functional and material; it is also societal and organizational, in that it is composed both of people and of social institutions. Second, it is multi-functional. All cities in fact are multi-functional; some are simply more specialized than others. It comes into being to serve a variety of purposes, not merely one. Third, it is characterized by inertia; it cannot readily be altered or discarded and replaced. To be sure, this is in part a function of size, but it also is a consequence of its vast complexity. Cities are indeed complex systems; and they are here to stay. Though not necessarily impossible to change, city-systems have a dynamic of their own, which makes induced change difficult.

Let me explore some of the implications of these propositions briefly.

The fact that the city is culturally relative means that both its functions and its structure may differ from society to society, and from time to time for that matter. Although cities may resemble each other in many respects, they need not be designed to serve identical functions, they may develop differing spatial and social structures, they may display problems that vary, both in kind and in intensity from those of other cities, and those problems might not be amenable to solution in the same ways. At this Congress, much discussion has, not improperly, emphasized the homogeneity of the urban phenomenon. I would urge that its *heterogeneity* be both borne in mind and carefully examined. After all, we would not expect all governments to be alike, and *they* are cultural phenomena. Why should we expect all cities to follow the same trajectory and life cycle? In fact, of course, they don't.

Being as complicated as they are and possessed of a high degree of inertia, especially with regard to physical forms, cities have the capacity to both direct their futures—at least in part—and to influence what goes on around them. In the current systems analysis jargon, they possess both "feed-forward" and "feed-back" capabilities. Once established and operative, they also place constraints on the choices for change confronting the decision-makers who determine policy. This is true of all social "going concerns," to use Halford Mackinder's phrase, and the city *is* a going-concern.

This reference to policy leads to yet another basic consideration—cities as multifunctional entities are not only physical, social and economic systems, they also possess a political function. By a political function, I mean not only that they may perform symbolic roles. Of course, Paul Wheatley is correct in pointing to a fundamental urban characteristic when he refers to "The City as Symbol," that is, symbol of State and Society, but there is more to it than that, even in the capital cities of Asia. The city is, *inter alia*, a political system in the sense that what goes on in it and how it relates to other entities outside it are determined through the practice of *politics* whereby, as Harold Lasswell put it long ago, "who gets what, when, and how." To Lasswell's list we must, of course, add the word "where," since the urban ecosystem has a strong geographical dimension. To be sure, some apparent "decisions" are made through the marketplace, but that depends on what sort of political organization exists in a given country. The study of the political economy of cities, then, needs to be high on the list of our research priorities. We need to know much more than we do about urban politics in the Pacific Basin.

Unlike the arrowhead, too, the city operates within a complex environment wherein a variety of forces impinge on it, as well as are influenced by it. There is nothing new about this, to be sure. It has been true from the beginnings of civilization, which means, literally, since the beginnings of cities. These forces are *both* domestic and foreign. Therefore, we are right in emphasizing the need for the examination both of the relations between cities and the broader national systems of which they are part, and of the international forces which may impinge especially on the larger and more cosmopolitan of them.

Among those forces are those of technological change, to which we have paid too little attention at this meeting, but which, as Jacques Ellul so forcefully has reminded us, possesses an imperative of its own. C. C. Chandrasekhara pointed out at the 1969 conference in Hong Kong on Asian cities to which Yue-man Yeung has referred that many of the cities in Asia appear to be "a collection of period pieces." By this he meant that the various functional areas in those cities reflect not only functional differences but also different percepts over time about what functions ought to have been performed and how; they also reflect the technologies of the times when decisions about them were being made. One of the major problems of Pacific Basin cities today, then, is adapting to the new transport, communications and energy-related technologies which have become available since they were founded and developed in their present forms. This can be a difficult and expensive matter, in real terms, and it will take time, given the inertia in the urban systems. This means that careful consideration needs to be given to, in a phrase, the recycling of old forms and structures in keeping with news percepts, new demands and new opportunities.

The problem of adaptation and modification, however, is not simply a matter of land-uses, housing, local transport and the provision of services. It is much more a matter of adapting the existing urban centres and hierarchies to the current and future needs of the countries and peoples of the region. Given the history of most cities in Asia and the Pacific as "alien towns," introduced to the area as a result of the expansion of Europe and the imposition of European-based colonialism, it is not strange that they might seem to ill-serve the purposes of new nations and post-colonial societies. On the other hand it is all too easy to deride the colonial cities as inappropriate barriers to progress. It is far more challenging to regard them for what I, at least, think they are, great resources which need to be put to different and better uses than before. Another great problem, then, of the Pacific Basin cities, particularly those in Southeast and East Asia, is a reconciliation of formerly colonial urban and transportation networks with the needs of the developing countries.

It is worth noting, however, that this challenge assumes very different forms in different countries. In China, for example, a great urban hierarchy existed long before the impact of the West through the Treaty Ports and of Japan in Manchuria became important. The Chinese have recently come to recognize that the cities and transportation facilities of the pseudo-colonial period are major resources upon which to build a new society, much out-moded rhetoric to the contrary. In contrast, Malaysia for example, also inherited a considerable urban system from the colonial period, which no one could responsibly suggest be discarded, but pre-colonial Malaysia had no urban system. Would a national urban system have developed in Malaya had the Europeans—and the Chinese—not appeared and "done their thing" when they did? On the evidence of both the Sri Vijaya maritime Empire and the short-lived Melaka Sultanate which followed it, the answer would have to be, "no." In the modern world, perhaps a foreign-stimulated urban pattern is preferable to none.

What then of our second theme?

Urbanization and Development

This subject has underlain, as a partly hidden agenda, a large part of this important conference, but the question of the nature and intensity of the relationship has been skirted. Is development, meaning a substantial improvement in the welfare of peoples and nations, possible without concomitant urban development? If not, how much urban development is appropriate and necessary? What kinds of cities do their jobs best? These are almost intractable questions, to be sure, but that does not mean that they should not be clearly borne in mind.

Yue-man Yeung has referred to the Pacific Conference on Urban Growth held in Honolulu in 1967, at which sixteen ministers from Asian countries were present. So were several of us at this meeting. The conference concluded that rapid and substantial urbanization was a necessary prerequisite for accelerated economic development. Moreover, it endorsed the idea that large cities might well be the *sine qua non* for such development, in a world that "primacy" might be the preferred condition of city-size ranking. All this was against the received wisdom of the time. Apparently that would still be true today, judging from views implicit in several papers at this Congress. In any event, until such times as it becomes possible to develop cost-benefit techniques for measuring and evaluating the effectiveness for development of larger versus smaller cities, something economists say cannot be done, the question of the "large and the small" and "balanced versus unbalanced hierarchies" in developmental strategy formation and implementation must remain moot. Nonetheless, there is much evidence that the large, despite many problems, are more efficient than the small if development is the objective. For this reason the Chinese have now apparently decided, having rejected the assignment of top priority to smaller places, to adopt a new great-city strategy for national development, although they have not, to be sure, abandoned the small city "leg" of their over-all strategy.

Fascinating as this topic is, time requires that we move on to other matters. One of these concerns Singapore itself as a model for development strategies elsewhere in Asia. When that possibility has arisen in these discussions, the tendency has been to dismiss it. After all, Singapore is a city-state and unique in the world. But let us think about this a little more. Let us, for example, assume that Singapore were to have a hinterland of, say, one hundred miles radius, and therefore a land area of some thirty thousand square miles. Let us assume too that a fourth of this area was agriculturally productive and that, with a rural population density of about two hundred per square mile, it contained a population of about six millions, making the total population of this hypothetical state about nine millions. Then what? Would Singapore, under its present management, be better or worse off? Surely it would be better off. It could feed itself in all probability, and labour would be available for agriculture, industry and services. In fact, it would resemble Taiwan, at least in terms of food self-sufficiency. Imagine now a map of Asia with areas of 100-mile radius drawn around every city of half a million and more. What percentage of Asia's billions would be incompassed by those circles—30 per cent, 50 per cent, 70 per cent? Such an exercise would be meaningful only in eastern and southern Asia, among all the underdeveloped areas, because, for the most part, arable land and urban populations coincide so well there, unlike the case in Latin America and Africa. In any event, would such a multiplicity of Singapores-cum-hinterlands be worth thinking about? It might though it would stretch our imaginations!

When we speak of urban hinterlands, we think almost at once of the third problem.

The Problem of Food for the City

Can the burgeoning cities be fed, and how? This question has been one of the major issues discussed at this Congress, and deservedly so, although the provision of other material needs—especially water and energy supplies—deserves equal attention. Nearly thirty years ago Rhoads Murphey published his Harvard doctoral dissertation on Geography in Shanghai. In a chapter entitled, "How the City Is Fed," he demonstrated that Shanghai in the 1930s, then a city of about three million, was fed almost exclusively from grain and vegetables grown within one hundred miles of the metropolis under traditional forms of agriculture and transported to the city by pre-modern riverine transport. Moreover, the rural areas within that hinterland were among the more prosperous in China, so well did the symbiosis between city and country operate in times of peace and stability. I underscore this last clause because of its great importance. Without peace and stability and effective government, the system could not have operated, and Shanghai would have had to import goods. In fact, under those circumstances, it often did. But in general it was *not* a drain on its hinterland. Quite the contrary!

Why is this example important? It is important for two quite different reasons. In the first place it helped disprove the assumption widely held by demographers that very large cities could only be products of the modern era, that is, of global industrialization and modern technology.

That should interest us here a lot, but the second reason for its importance might be even more interesting because of its implications for the cities of Asia at the present time. If Shanghai could be fed then that way, why not now? And why not the other large cities of Asia blessed with productive agricultural hinterlands? One answer is that Shanghai is indeed largely fed in this way today, though not because of any miracles wrought by the Peking authorities. So are many other Chinese cities. However, when one attempts to deal with other Asian cities, one runs into difficulties, for agricultural productivity is so low in most Southeast and South Asian countries, with or without the so-called "Green Revolution." Paddy yields per unit area in Lower Siam, for example, are only about forty per cent of those in the Yangtze lowlands, and only about a third of those in Japan. But it is not necessarily nature that is at fault, but man. As Satyesh Chakraborty has pointed out in his analysis of the food problems of West Bengal and Calcutta, there are a number of scenarios as to what might be done, all of which depend upon—let us not avoid the word—*politics*, and the ideologies that inform it. In strictly biological terms, there is no doubt that all the cities of Asia can be fed almost exclusively from domestic resources (except for Singapore and Hong Kong), given the proper mix of government policies. Rural development clearly is essential in dealing with problems of urban development.

Obviously, the distribution of food is yet another matter, but in a better Asian world, composed of a multiplicity of Singapores, perhaps it may yet prove to be a lesser problem than it now appears to be.

These remarks may seem somewhat frivolous, at least those that refer to a "multiplicity of Singapores." I plead guilty to some measure of frivolity, but put forward the defense that it might be justified at the end of so successful and arduous a conference as the one which is now about to close. But my—and our—intentions are serious. The current history of the Pacific Basin countries is being writ upon an increasingly urban landscape, and the future is obscure. It is proper to indulge in an exercise in retrospective futurology to stretch our imaginations, if that exercise might suggest ways to deal with the policy and practical dilemmas that concern their cities. And we need to become better informed; but how?

It is said in the Confucian *Analects* [Book 1, Chapter X]:

Tzu-ch'in asked Tzu-kung: "When the Master arrives in a state, he invariably gets to know about its government. Does he seek this information? or is it given him?"

Tzu-kung said, "The Master gets it through being cordial, well-behaved, respectful, frugal and deferential. The way the Master seeks it is, perhaps, different from the way other men seek it."

A far cry indeed from the way in which enquiries are made by ordinary men today.

PART II
Eastern Asia

3. Great Cities of Eastern Asia

Eastern Asia, broadly defined as that part of the western Pacific rim between Korea and Indonesia, is one of the fastest growth regions in the world in the postwar period, economically, demographically and in terms of urbanization. As a reflection of the remarkable economic upsurge experienced in many of the countries under review, Japan, Hong Kong and Taiwan witnessed a 13-, 11- and 14-fold increase, respectively, in per capita gross national product in the two decades prior to 1980. Demographically, approximately 463 million people have been added to the region from 1960 to 1980, although in relation to the world population, Eastern Asia's share stood consistently at 32 per cent in 1960 and 1980 (see United Nations, 1982:Table 4). Over the same period, the region's urban population was augmented by some 195 million. While in 1970, the entire developing world had 72 cities with more than one million inhabitants, by 1980 Eastern Asia alone had 60 "million cities." Many were gargantuan urban agglomerations of many millions (Fig. 3.1).

Rapidly urbanizing Eastern Asia has engendered, particularly in the great cities, a myriad of problems which planners and policy-makers are still having to come to terms with. The term *great city* follows conventional use as first employed by Ginsburg (1955) in his landmark statement on the phenomenon of functional dominance of primate cities in Southeast Asia. This chapter focuses on one of the critical dimensions of development in Eastern Asia in the period from 1960 to 1980 by examining trends of urban growth, salient problems faced by the cities, and attempted solutions and

Author's note: I am grateful to my many friends in the cities studied for counsel and providing data and reference material. I especially appreciate the timely research assistance of Yvette Luke Ying at the Centre for Contemporary Asian Studies. Margo Monteith, International Development Research Centre, Ottawa, helped graciously with repeated bibliographic searches.

Figure 3.1: The Million Cities of Eastern Asia, c. 1980

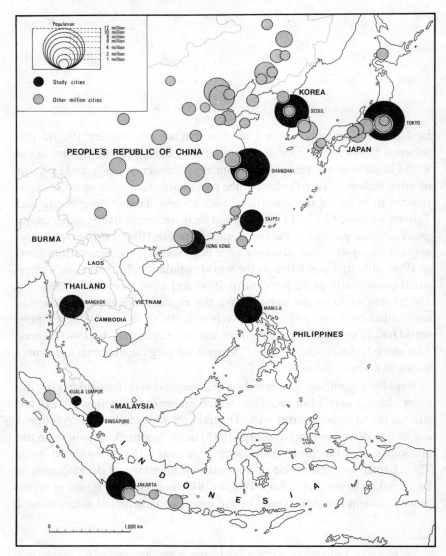

policies. I then discuss policy options open to the cities before concluding with tentative constructions of urban scenarios to the end of this century.

To capture the heterogeneity and diversity of Eastern Asia, ten large cities—Shanghai, Hong Kong, Tokyo, Seoul, Taipei, Jakarta, Kuala Lumpur, Manila, Singapore and Bangkok—were selected for analysis. Each represents the largest urban agglomeration of the countries under study and can, therefore, best personify the urban problems confronting the region. The diversity of the region is underlined by the inclusion of socialist and huge China, laissez-faire and city-state Hong Kong, several culturally Confucian countries, and the heartland of the Malay world. The study of urban problems and policies must heed this diverse background in one of the most culturally rich, historically ancient and economically vibrant regions of the world.

URBAN GROWTH PATTERNS

Measured by levels of urbanization, Eastern Asia can be roughly divided into two subregions. East Asia, represented by countries north of Hong Kong, is characterized, with the obvious exception of China, by a higher-than-world-average level of urbanization. This pattern was already clear in 1960, merely accentuated in 1980 (Table 3.1). The doubling of South Korea's level of urbanization during this period is most noteworthy, mirroring the circumstances that led to its extraordinary urban and economic growth since the end of the Korean War. By contrast, Southeast Asia, save for the city-state of Singapore, may be depicted as one of the least urbanized regions, consistently below world average, even developing country average, in both 1960 and 1980. As I have maintained elsewhere (1976), an urban transformation has not taken place in this part of Asia.

Levels of urbanization, however, leave unspecified the magnitude of change of the urban population. Substantial urban growth can occur if the urban population grows in tandem with the total population, leaving the level of urbanization relatively unchanged. Singapore aside, this situation did happen in all countries in Southeast Asia, which saw a doubling of the urban population in the two decades since 1960 (Table 3.2). The urban population has been growing slightly faster than the total population, but an urban transition as defined by Davis (1965) has not been in progress in Southeast Asia. In East Asia, on the other hand, the most dramatic has been the tripling of South Korea's urban population in the 1960–1980 period, from 6.9 million to 21.1 million, an increase of 204.1 per cent. Equally important, one should note that twice as many people in China lived in urban places in 1980 compared with 1960. Despite a modest increase in the level of urbanization, 128.5 million inhabitants were added to the Chinese cities.

TABLE 3.1
Levels of Urbanization—
Eastern Asia and the World, 1960–2000 (in percentages)

Place	1960	1970	1980	1990	2000
China	18.7	21.7	25.7	31.5	39.1
Hong Kong	89.1	89.7	90.3	91.4	92.6
Japan	62.5	71.4	78.3	83.0	85.9
North Korea	40.2	50.1	59.7	67.4	72.9
South Korea	27.7	40.7	54.8	65.2	71.4
Taiwan	58.4	62.4	66.8	—	—
Indonesia	14.6	17.1	20.2	25.2	32.3
Malaysia	25.2	27.0	29.4	34.2	41.6
Philippines	30.3	32.9	36.2	41.6	49.0
Singapore	77.6	75.3	74.1	75.0	78.5
Thailand	12.5	13.2	14.4	17.5	23.2
World	33.9	37.4	41.1	45.8	51.2
More developed regions	60.3	66.4	70.6	75.6	77.8
Less developed regions	21.4	25.2	29.4	36.8	40.4

Sources: United Nations (1982:Table 1); for Taiwan, Liu (1983:3).

At still another level of data aggregation, Table 3.3 portrays population profiles of the ten cities included in this study. Because of highly varied definitions of metropolitan areas, both population and density figures must be read with extreme care. Overall, the figures should be seen as indicative of the magnitude of change and comparative reading of density figures must be duly qualified. Even then, one may note that while Kuala Lumpur and Jakarta have more than doubled their populations, Seoul, Taipei and Bangkok tripled theirs. Of the ten cities, Seoul grew the fastest, with an increase of 126 per cent in the decade of the sixties, whereas Kuala Lumpur vastly expanded in the succeeding decade with a 108 per cent growth. With respect to population density, all cities except Kuala Lumpur increased. Expansion of metropolitan area accounted for the decrease. In other cities population density increase sometimes is quite marked. As cautioned earlier, at first glance density figures could be misleading. For example, inclusion of sizeable rural areas in the metropolitan area of Shanghai resulted in incredibly lower density figures compared with other cities. In reality, Shanghai and Hong Kong are two of the most densely populated cities in the world. In 1983, Hong Kong and Shanghai recorded in their urban areas an overall density of 28,000 and 27,762 persons per square kilometre, respectively, and the highest density in Shamshuipo of Hong Kong reached 165,000 persons per square kilometre, while the Nanshi district of Shanghai similarly recorded 101,500 persons per square kilometre.

Rapid population increases in several study cities were accompanied by extensive boundary expansion with net gains of people and area. By annexing three areas in 1963 and two in 1973, the Seoul administrative area reached its present size of 627 square kilometres. Similarly, Taipei quadrupled its city area to 272 square kilometres in 1968, with corresponding expansion of its metropolitan area, both of which have since remained unchanged. The most recent areal redefinition occurred in Kuala Lumpur in 1974 when its area was more than doubled to 243 square kilometres as it became the Federal Territory. Just prior to the study period, in 1958 Shanghai also gained about ten times its area to reach its present size by acquiring jurisdiction over ten adjacent counties. This expansion was the last of a series of administrative boundary changes affecting that urban complex since 1949.

Hand in hand with these areal expansions have been important changes in the internal structure of some cities. In almost every case, there has been very large extension of built-up areas. Tokyo may be considered an extreme case in which the daily commuting distance reached as far as forty kilometres in 1970 (Hall, 1977:229). This distance was extended by a further ten kilometres in 1984. In part as a result of the successful development of commuting transport links, the daytime and nighttime populations in the central parts of Tokyo have become highly imbalanced. In 1980 the daytime population in the three central wards of Chiyoda, Chuo and Minato exceeded the nighttime population by 6.8 times (TMG, 1984b:26). In Seoul, imbalanced development of another type has occurred. Because of its relative proximity to the Demilitarized Zone and North Korea, the area north of the Han River in Seoul has developed more slowly in recent years.

TABLE 3.2
Total Urban and Largest City Populations, Growth Rates and Share of Urban Population in Largest City—Eastern Asia, 1960–2000

Country/city	Country					Largest city							
	Urban population (millions)			Growth rate[a] (percentages)		Population (millions)			Growth rate[a] (percentages)		Share of urban population (percentages)		
	1960	1980	2000	1960–80	1980–2000	1960	1980	2000	1960–80	1980–2000	1960	1980	2000
China/Shanghai	127.5	256.0	491.9	100.7	92.2	7.7	15.0	25.9	94.8	72.7	6.0	5.9	5.3
Hong Kong	2.7	4.6	6.5	68.4	40.0	—	—	—	—	—	—	—	—
Japan/Tokyo	58.8	91.3	111.1	55.3	21.7	10.7	20.0	23.8	87.6	19.0	18.2	22.0	21.4
North Korea/ Pyongyang	4.2	10.7	19.9	152.4	86.0	0.6	1.3	2.2	102.0	74.6	15.0	12.0	11.3
South Korea/Seoul	6.9	21.1	36.2	204.1	72.0	2.4	8.5	13.7	254.4	61.2	34.1	40.3	37.9

City												
Taiwan/Taipei	6.3	11.9	—	88.2	—	1.1	2.2	—	102.1	—	17.5	18.8 —
Indonesia/Jakarta	14.3	29.9	64.1	109.9	114.3	2.9	7.0	14.3	141.4	104.3	20.3	23.4 22.3
Malaysia/ Kuala Lumpur	2.1	4.1	8.8	100.5	114.1	0.4	1.1	2.6	198.9	130.7	18.0	26.9 28.9
Philippines/ Manila	8.5	17.8	37.8	109.3	112.0	2.3	5.7	10.5	147.6	84.2	26.9	31.8 27.8
Singapore	1.3	1.8	2.3	39.6	31.5	—	—	—	—	—	—	— —
Thailand/Bangkok-Thonguri	3.4	6.8	15.9	98.5	135.2	2.2	4.9	9.9	126.4	102.0	65.1	72.0 62.3

Sources: United Nations (1980:Table 48; 1982:Tables 2 and 8); for Taiwan, Liu (1982:4; 1983:3).

a. Computed from source tables, not from rounded figures presented here.

TABLE 3.3
Population Profiles of Selected Great Cities—
Eastern Asia, 1960–1981

| City | Year | Population (millions) | Growth Rates | | Area (km²) | Population Density (per km²) |
			Decadal (%)	Annual (%)		
Bangkok	1960	1,577	+ 37	+ 3.2	—	—
	1970	2,157	+ 118	+ 8.1	—	—
	1980	4,697			1,565	3,001
Hong Kong	1961	2,668	+ 30	+ 2.6	184	14,499
	1971	3,457	+ 23	+ 2.1	197	17,547
	1981	4,241			198	21,418
Jakarta	1960	2,907	+ 56	+ 4.6	—	—
	1970	4,546	+ 43	+ 3.6	604	7,527
	1980	6,503			656	9,914
Kuala	1967	450	+ 0.3	+ 0.03	93	4,839
Lumpur	1970	452	+ 108	+ 7.6	93	4,857
	1980	938			243	3,860
Manila	1960	2,462	+ 61	+ 4.9	636	3,879
	1970	3,976	+ 49	+ 4.1	636	6,237
	1980	5,926			636	9,317
Seoul	1960	2,445	+ 126	+ 8.5	268	9,125
	1970	5,536	+ 51	+ 4.2	613	9,032
	1980	8,367			627	13,344
Shanghai	1962	10,225	+ 1	+ 0.2	5,895	1,735
	1970	10,368	+ 5	+ 0.5	—	—
	1980	10,889			6,059	1,797
Singapore	1960	1,646	+ 26	+ 2.3	582	2,828
	1970	2,074	+ 16	+ 1.5	586	3,539
	1980	2,414			618	3,906
Taipei	1960	1,546	+ 79	+ 6.0	884	1,749
	1970	2,769	+ 58	+ 4.7	1,070	2,588
	1980	4,381			1,070	4,095
Tokyo	1960	9,684	+ 18	+ 1.7	2,023	4,787
	1970	11,408	+ 2	+ 0.2	2,141	5,328
	1980	11,618			2,156	5,389

Source: Variously derived official statistics.
Note: Wherever possible, metropolitan areas were used in constructing profiles.

Consequently, accelerated development south of the Han River resulted in a doubling of the population in the six years between 1973 and 1979, as opposed to a stable or declining population north of the river (Kwon, 1981a:320). Over the past twenty years, some study cities have developed mass rapid transit systems, leading to improved areal and functional integration within their administrative territories. In this respect, the opening of a subway system in Hong Kong on 1 October 1979, along with the vital cross-harbour tunnel open since 3 August 1972, has greatly assisted in integrating what previously had been a fragmented and complex urban structure (Lo, 1972). In Seoul, too, the opening of a subway system in 1974 has progressively improved travel times and the general traffic situation.

Finally, the study cities have grown by natural increase as well as rural-urban migration. Nowhere is the latter phenomenon more poignant than in Seoul, where urbanward migration accounted for 82 per cent of the total population increase in the period from 1966 to 1970. Since then, the contribution of migration has been much reduced, thanks to a host of population diversion and decentralization strategies (Kwon, 1981b:80). In Taipei in-migration accounted for 51 per cent of the total population increase between 1968 and 1973 (Tsay, 1982:23). However, the migration factor has become less significant as a component of population increase since 1970, so much so that, by 1977, net migration contributed only 8 per cent of Taipei's population increase (Hsu and Pannell, 1982:29). Elsewhere, there were also signs that the cities under review grew more by natural increase than in-migration in recent years. Tokyo's is probably the only case where since 1967, population outflow has exceeded inflow. In 1980, Tokyo was the only prefecture recording a population decrease (TMG, 1984a:68).

Whatever the sources of growth dynamism, the cities studied are, and will remain, the most important urban centres in their respective countries. Their pivotal roles nationally and internationally in spearheading development are clearly evidenced in their disproportionate share of the total urban population in their countries. Greater Bangkok and Seoul, for instance, constituted 72 and 40 per cent, respectively, of their total urban population in 1980 (Table 3.2). Dominance of the study cities over the economic, social, political and other spheres in their countries is brought home vividly in the random indicators compiled in Table 3.4. While their importance in national life is indisputable, they have, as well, a greater-than-usual share of urban problems. Concentrated development and population have

magnified many of these problems to crisis proportions, which the next
section addresses.

TABLE 3.4

Selected Indicators of Functional Dominance in Great Cities—
Eastern Asia, 1972–1984

City		Measures of centrality
Shanghai	Accounted for	12.5% of national industrial output
		11.0% of national heavy industrial output
		14.0% of national light industrial output
		5.8% of state industrial staff and workers
		10.3% of new state industrial investment
	Produced	30% of China's television sets and wristwatches
		50% of China's cameras
	Conducted	23% of China's foreign trade
	Had	48 universities and higher educational institutions with
		70,000 students and 250 research centres with about
		240,000 scientific and technical personnel
Tokyo	Accounted for	60% of Japan's top business leaders
		60% of total invested capital
		33.3% of deposited banking accounts
		33.3% of university graduates
		21% of tertiary industry income
		27% of retail and wholesale sales
		15% of sale of manufactured products
		15% of working population in secondary industry
		33.3% of department store sales
		25% of entertainment admissions
		20% of Japan's universities
		50% of university students
		60% of heads of industrial and commercial enterprises
Seoul	Housed	78% of headquarters of business firms
		90% of large business enterprises
	Accounted for	28% of the nation's value added by manufacturing
		25% of the nation's total manufacturing employment
		32.3% of all manufacturing establishments
		65% of all loans and deposits
		55% of all colleges and universities
		50% of all medical doctors and specialists
		50% of the national wealth
		27.9% of South Korea's GNP (1977)

TABLE 3.4 (Continued)

City		Measures of centrality
Bangkok	Accounted for	26.8% of Thailand's GNP
		77.7% of Thailand's banking
		48.8% of transport and communication installations
		33.3% of the country's manufacturing industry
		33.3% of the country's construction industry
		33.3 of foreign trade
		34% of all motor vehicles
		56.5% of electricity consumed
		74% of telephones installed
		8 of Thailand's 12 universities

Sources: For Shanghai, *Business China* (1982:44) and Henderson (1984:43); for
Tokyo, Honjo (1972:12; 1975:346) and Tokyo Metropolitan Government
(1984a:31); for Seoul, Chu (1980:438); for South Korea (1982:28) and Kwon
(1980:35; 1981b:74–75); for Bangkok, Kanjanaharitai (1981:203–4).

A MOSAIC OF URBAN ILLS

The litany of problems in the great cities of Eastern Asia is highly similar to
that in other parts of the Third World: chronic housing shortages, traffic
snarls, deteriorating basic services, increasing social inequality, omnipresent squatter settlements and slums, widespread poverty, limited employment opportunities and so on. As each of the study cities differs in the
extent and details it suffers from these afflictions, what follows will be
synopses of each urban situation.

Shanghai

The largest socialist city in the world, Shanghai epitomizes the contradic-
tions inherent in the development of Chinese cities since 1949. It suffers
from acute housing shortages, poor infrastructure and public services, and
environmental pollution (Wu, 1984). About half the population lives in lane
housing—usually of two or three storeys, lacking basic facilities, and
located in alleys or small lanes (*China Daily*, 1984), and another 16 per cent
live in slums built of temporary materials. Average per capita housing
space was 4.3 square metres in the early 1980s, only a minor improvement
on living conditions in 1949. Shanghai is probably the most crowded city in

China, with only 24.6 square metres per person in the central city area (Lee *et al.*, 1983). The housing crisis is exacerbated by uncontrolled and indiscriminate industrial development. Between 1962 and 1980, about 1.6 million square metres or 15 per cent of the total residential floor area was lost to factories (Tao, 1981). This unfortunate situation resulted from the long-accepted policies of "production first, livelihood second" and "construction where there is room."

Similarly, the ideological bias against investment in "nonproductive sectors" since 1949 has led to the sad neglect of infrastructure development. Only 16 per cent of the population in the urban districts is served by sewers, another 16 per cent by septic tanks, the rest by night soil collection. Extreme traffic congestion resulted in the average traffic speed being halved from thirty kilometres per hour in 1949 to fifteen in 1979 (UNDP, 1979).

Serious cases of water, air and noise pollution have also been reported. In the central city, daily industrial waste and domestic sewage amount to 500,000 tons, the majority of which is discharged into the Huangpu River untreated (Yan and Tang, 1984:71–72). Measured by sulphur dioxide, nitrogen dioxide and suspended particulates, the standard acceptable air quality standards have all been exceeded. Poor air quality is not confined to the urban area as acid rain is known to affect large parts of the surrounding rural area (Yan and Tang, 1984).

Finally, some 200,000 youngsters leave middle schools every year, in addition to returned youths from the rural areas. Because of the limited absorptive capacity of the economic structure, many have to wait for years before jobs are assigned.

Hong Kong

Situated at the doorstep of China as a borrowed place on borrowed time, Hong Kong is a prime example of laissez-faire capitalism. Its remarkable postwar economic growth has been matched to a certain degree by significant progress in urban management and infrastructure development. Public housing, for example, accommodated over 2.4 million inhabitants or 45 per cent of the total population in 1984. Each year close to 180,000 people are allocated new public housing. These massive efforts still lag behind demand, for even in 1984, there was still an estimated total of 500,000 living in squatter colonies, as opposed to 275,000 in 1973 when the Ten-Year Housing Programme was launched (Hong Kong Housing Authority, 1984).

In the peak 1978–1979 property boom, the annual rate of price increase for various sizes of private housing was in the region of 70 per cent (Kwok, 1983:335).

Planners and administrators find themselves in a quandry, for carefully drawn up plans are often overtaken by events beyond their control. In particular, successive waves of legal and illegal immigrants from China have rendered many development plans short of meeting targets. Nevertheless, over the years substantive improvements have been made in basic service provision which are no longer critical issues in most areas. A recent four-district study showed that it was largely for improving the quality of life that local leaders organized themselves (Lau et al., 1983).

Extremely high population densities in the urban area separated by the harbour imply thorny traffic problems. Between 1966 and 1981, the number of cars registered soared from 93,000 to 310,916. In the period from 1976 to 1981 private cars increased by 13 per cent per year but road mileage increased by only 2 per cent (Fong, 1984; C. K. Leung, 1984). Although the population is heavily dependent on public transport, extensive car ownership has created problems for transportation planners. In land-scarce Hong Kong, the price of land until recently rose precipitously.

Finally, in recent years Hong Kong has been plagued by a rising incidence of crime, drug addiction and other social problems symptomatic of a progressively sophisticated urban society.

Tokyo

By certain definitions, Tokyo is arguably the largest city in the world. It occupies 1 per cent of Japan's land and constitutes about 10 per cent of its population. Described as a city of paradoxes, Tokyo is a symbol of Japan's postwar economic miracle, with by far the highest per capita gross national product in Asia and every evidence of high-technology urban sophistication. Yet its inhabitants do not generally enjoy the same level of amenities available in lesser Asian cities.

Tokyo is probably the most innovative with urban solutions, but many could not be implemented for lack of funds (Blair, 1974:34; Hall, 1977). Housing, commuting, traffic and pollution rank as the major problems besetting the city. Ten years ago, some 28 per cent of the families lived in substandard, overcrowded houses and 34 per cent complained about housing problems (Honjo, 1975). The existence of over one million wooden rental apartments reflects the gravity of the housing situation (TMG, 1984a:26). Overcrowding and high land prices have been pushing home-seekers farther from the city, causing rapid suburbanization and large-scale commuting.

Fantastic advances have been made in mass transport but planners cannot solve traffic jams caused by three million automobiles (1980). Every day over 2.2 million people commute from neighbouring prefectures to offices and schools in Tokyo. Concomitant to this pattern of development is the "emptying out" of the central city area at night.

In 1981 only 76 per cent of the population was served by a sewerage system. Population of every type remained serious, although air pollution caused by sulphur dioxide concentrations gradually decreased after peaking in the mid-1960s (TMG, 1984b:155).

After the disastrous fire of 1923, planners in Tokyo have been very conscious of how vulnerable the city is to natural disasters. Yet not a great deal has been accomplished in this direction. The biggest challenge to the city is to lure more people away from Tokyo so that the feared paralysis of basic services will not materialize.

Seoul

Richard Meier once described Seoul as the product of the most intense and compressed process of urbanization in the world, with continuous in-migration flooding the city for sixteen years. Some 22 per cent of South Korea's population lived in Seoul in 1982, compared with 5 per cent in 1955 (Kwon, 1981b:73). Unabated urban growth has led to intolerable population and traffic congestion, serious industrial pollution, environmental deterioration, housing shortages and inadequate public services (Kim, 1980; Kwon, 1981a). As a measure of crowding, there were 2.51 persons per room in Seoul in 1975, hardly an improvement on the 1970 figure of 2.67 (Kwon, 1981a:308). *Panjachon* or squatter settlements predominate the hills surrounding Seoul. One reason for the difficulty in housing provision is the astronomical increase in land prices that skyrocketed by almost twenty-eight times from 1963 to 1979 (Kwon, 1980:38).

Being a monocentric city with a high concentration of activities within the Central Business District (CBD), Seoul has the problem of unbalanced provision of public services in different parts of the city. This imbalance is further aggravated by the uneven development, since 1970, across the northern and southern part of the Han River. Considerable residential relocation to the south of the river has taken place, unaccompanied by the provision of community and basic facilities (Kwon, 1980, 1981a).

One inevitable consequence of growth has been separation of home and work place. In the area within two kilometres of the CBD, daytime population is more than four times the resident population. This situation has brought further strains on the transport system which has to move 500,000 people daily in and out of Seoul (Kwon, 1981a:318). The opening of the subway system since 1974 has helped mobility but a threefold increase in automobiles since then has counteracted any improvement made in urban traffic. Between 1975 and 1983 the number of automobiles soared from 83,661 to 253,647 (SMG, 1983:88).

Taipei

In Taipei one thorny problem has been the speculative land price rise. Between 1952 and 1976, the average land price increased 4.3 per cent in Taiwan, as contrasted with a 265-fold spiral in Taipei. During the same period, the average commodity price increased by 3 times in Taiwan versus 76 times in Taipei (Tang, 1982). The increase in land price, far surpassing that in commodities, has been the result of primarily speculative investment and improper planning control. Far worse, the government has no mechanism to capture part of the land price increase, thus providing an impetus to land speculation. Another problem is restriction on land-use conversion. For example, the government permits conversion only of low-grade agricultural land to other uses, but restricts similar conversion of high-grade arable land. Even then, in the period from 1956 to 1967, some 628 hectares of vacant or arable land, constituting 9.5 per cent of Taipei's land area, was converted to residential, commercial, or industrial uses (Hsu and Pannell, 1982:32). Consequently, average land price already accounts for over half of housing value (Chen, 1984:166). This situation has led to a very tight housing situation saddled with problems of insufficient supply, concentrated ownership, and a deteriorating living environment. In 1975, the total housing stock in Taipei was owned by 5.6 per cent of its inhabitants, with 11,187 each owning at least three dwelling units accounting for at least 48,999 dwelling units (Tang, 1982). Public housing is negligible, totalling merely 31,794 units in 1981.

The hodgepodge of urban development has also given rise to a confused transport situation in which road construction has lagged far behind the growth of motorized vehicles. Between 1960 and 1980 the number of automobiles exploded from 5,506 to 179,106, while that of motorcycles soared from 6,704 to 350,921. The proliferation of small vehicles since the mid-1950s has been a real problem. Widespread vehicle ownership has contributed directly to air pollution, particularly that of suspended particulates and sulphur dioxide. The reported incidence of water and noise pollution has also been high. In a recent survey in Taipei, 82.4 per cent of the respondents regarded noise pollution as very serious (Tang, 1982).

Jakarta

Often described as a vast conglomeration of *kampungs* (villages), Jakarta is a city with monumental obstacles to overcome. It sorely lacks infrastructure, housing, jobs and a sound tax base. Within the urbanized area of the city, as much as 70 per cent of the residential space is occupied by *kampungs*, providing shelter for some 80 per cent of the total population (Erni and Bianpoen, 1980). Most of the housing units within this residential environment are temporary or semipermanent structures. Various sources have estimated that around 60,000 new dwelling units would be required annually to meet demands, whereas the Jakarta Office of Public Works approved in a year only 5 per cent of this number of new housing units (Sethuraman, 1976:33–34).

The sad state of urban services is revealed by 80 per cent of all dwelling units having no electricity and 70 per cent having to depend on private or public wells, as opposed to 30 per cent using piped water—part of which may be purchased from vendors. A recent survey showed that residents cited supply of drinking water, access to telephones, family planning services and recreational facilities as highly unsatisfactory. Less dissatisfying were waste disposal, sewers and street lighting, while shopping facilities, public transport and religious services fared better (Krausse, 1982:61).

Economically, Jakarta is ill-prepared to provide employment for its hordes of rural immigrants. One study found that nearly 43 per cent of the economically active population was employed in the informal sector where low requirements of capitalization, skills and education permit the employment of many (Moir, 1978). The continual influx of these migrants has not been welcomed by planners and administrators. Some measures they adopt, such as becak-free zones where muscle-powered transport is forbidden and banning hawkers in certain busy areas, are directly inimical to the livelihood and existence of low-income groups.

Finally, despite its status as the National Capital Special Region, Jakarta has a narrow tax base to carry out most of the needed urban functions. Although the central government's contribution to Jakarta's revenue increased markedly by the early 1970s, in the final analysis those who make the laws and design development policies will have to agree to tax themselves at a higher rate if local fiscal power is to increase (Specter, 1984b:27).

Kuala Lumpur

Called the "superlinear" city, Kuala Lumpur has witnessed progressive and intensive expansion westward towards Port Klang, some thirty-five kilometres away, over the past three decades. The Klang Valley is now strewn with "dormitory suburbs" with Kuala Lumpur acting as the heart of the conurbation. Rapid and less-than-careful development has increased the risks of erosion, flooding and water pollution, the last two phenomena especially affecting Kuala Lumpur (Aiken and Leigh, 1975).

The city has since the Japanese Occupation period had to deal with a squatter problem. In 1979, 240,000 inhabitants—22 per cent of the population—lived in squatter settlements (Leong, 1981:273). About 40 per cent of these squatters were Malays and 77 per cent of them were in-migrants. This situation has given a different complexion to Kuala Lumpur, which is beginning to tip in favour of *bumiputras* (Malays) in population composition, government spending and urban redevelopment. Since its implementation in 1970, the effects of the New Economic Policy are most clearly seen in the Federal Territory with increasing Malay participation in every facet of life. Some local politicians even went so far as to assert that government development plans were transforming Kuala Lumpur into a city in which the Chinese majority was becoming a minority (Specter, 1984a:24). Low-cost housing is being provided by the government but during the Third Malaysia Plan (1976–1980), only 58 per cent of the plan target was met. Although the government still takes full responsibility for providing low-cost rental housing, it has encouraged the private sector to assume a greater role in providing low-cost dwellings for sale at a maximum price of M$25,000 (US$10,800).

Traffic congestion is most serious in Kuala Lumpur's older areas with the doubling of automobile ownership between 1973 and 1980. Despite only 30 per cent of the population is being dependent on public transport, the government is committed to the twin transit system of aerobus and light rail transit to solve its traffic problems (Specter, 1984a).

Manila

Metropolitan Manila, created in 1975 to cover an area of 636 square kilometres consisting of four cities and thirteen municipalities, has been a bold management innovation in the Philippines in attempting to come to grips with problems this primate city faces. The official diagnosis of major problems besetting the city is as apt today as a decade ago when this list was compiled:

- Scattered indiscriminate subdivision and urban development;
- Serious traffic and transport bottlenecks and congestion;
- Inadequate and uncoordinated transport services;
- Coexistence of very high densities in core areas with haphazard low-density sprawl in the suburbs;
- Deficient water supply, sewage and drainage systems;
- Extensive annual flood damage (1972 was the most disastrous);
- Land and housing shortages reflected by formidable slums and squatter areas;
- Lack of community facilities, open spaces and recreational areas;
- Environmental pollution;
- High land values and inordinate land speculation. (NEDA, 1973)

Identifying problems is one thing; solving them is quite another. Basic service needs of the population outstrip the capability of government agencies to supply them. In sewer facilities, for instance, 46 per cent of Manila is served by an antiquated system installed in the early 1900s. Much of the sewage is being discharged untreated into waterways that eventually drain into Manila Bay. Flooding and drainage also still pose serious problems despite government programmes in flood control. A recent study of low-income communities in Metro Manila found only 15.2 per cent of surveyed households had water directly piped into their houses and 17 per cent depended on water peddlers for their supply (Aquino, 1983). The National Housing Authority designed different programmes to improve housing for the poor but 28 per cent of the population still lived in squatter settlements (Viloria, 1981:287).

Singapore

Widely known as the garden city of Asia, Singapore had by the early 1980s, solved many of its urban problems. In 1983, 75 per cent of the total population lived in public housing, unemployment was negligible, basic services were available to the vast majority of the population, and the economy was healthy. As the population becomes more affluent, problems of a social nature take a higher priority. These include ways to provide for an ageing population, better recreational facilities and community participation.

There is, by and large, general acceptance of the high-rise, high-density environment, despite critics' questioning the pace of development (Soon, 1969). The gradual disappearance of the old Chinatown west of the Singapore River, for example, has been lamented by many Singaporeans as well as romanticized foreign visitors. In place of the former shophouses and low-rise, tile-roofed structures, the new environment is one of all, modern, glass-façaded office buildings, hotels and apartments.

The only major problem the city faces is that of ever-increasing traffic caused by the rapid rise in car ownership. Between 1961 and 1975 automobile ownership more than doubled. Since 1975, when a congestion price scheme was put into practice, the situation has much improved. Overall, Singapore is perhaps the one city in which the usual problems afflicting the other cities are within the most manageable dimensions.

Bangkok

Finally, although Bangkok is endearingly named the city of angels, its citizens have to fight daily battles with horrendous traffic jams, a polluted environment and poor housing. Traffic jams in Bangkok are arguably among the worst in Asia. During peak hours cars run at twelve kilometres per hour and buses at nine. It has been estimated that costs of traffic congestion were 30 million baht per day in 1978 (Medhi Krongkaew and Trongudai, 1983:39–40; also Kanjanaharitai, 1981). It was also estimated that if congestion could be reduced to half, savings on gasoline alone could amount to at least 750 million baht a year. A 1975 survey showed that some of the main roads had air pollution levels more than twice the standard danger limits (Muqbil, 1982).

Water and noise pollution are also serious, while waste disposal is no less easy for a city of almost five million. Existing facilities can handle half of the waste.

About 25 per cent of the population lives in squatter settlements, the biggest of which is in Klong Toey. Moreover, in 1982 the National Housing Authority identified 410 slum areas involving 551,000 inhabitants—12 per cent of the total population. Planning controls in Thailand are very weak, so that the Bangkok City Planning Department can only advise rather than implement. It takes an individual act of parliament to obtain land for a specific public purpose (Kanjanaharitai, 1981:218). Consequently, development in Bangkok is practically free from any planning intervention, but is guided by the alignment of public infrastructure, land values and private initiative. The resultant pattern of land-uses is highly mixed, lacking definable areas of special activities. Related to this style of planning is the increasing monopolization of the land market by real estate developers and professional land speculators (Tanphiphat, 1982).

Most serious of all, Bangkok is a sinking city of its own making. The excessive use of deep artesian wells, drawing about 1.15 million cubic metres per day, has caused soil subsidence by as much as 0.6 metres in the southeastern parts of the city and 0.4 metres in the central areas. The introduction of multistorey buildings of heavy construction also contributes to this land subsidence threat. Because Bangkok lies virtually at sea level, the smallest rate of sinking could result in catastrophe (Donner, 1978:771; Kanjanaharitai, 1981).

URBAN STRATEGIES AND INNOVATIONS

A generalization that may be drawn from the foregoing paragraphs is that the large cities of Eastern Asia have grown too quickly and too big, not out of any deliberate urbanization policy but as the consequence of population movements and dynamics over which the cities did not have full control. In this section I review briefly the important urban strategies that have been implemented, with an emphasis on those considered innovative in the region. Rather than follow a city-by-city format, urban policies will be discussed comparatively across cities.

Decentralization Policies

The metropolitan governments under study have for years been vexed at their rapid growth and have devised variants of decentralization policies to slow, divert and control future growth (Simmons, 1979). First, we note two rather radical policies adopted in China and Jakarta, with quite different results.

In China a policy called *hsia-fang*, literally the sending down of second-ary school graduates to rural areas, provides the first example of govern-ment-sponsored, large-scale population transfer from urban to rural areas. Throughout China this movement involved ten to fifteen million individu-als in the period from 1969 to 1973 (Prybyla, 1975). The movement could only be successful given the Chinese government's strong administrative controls (travel permits and ration cards), massive media propaganda, and political exhortation. Shanghai was an active participant in this movement, a decision that no doubt accounted for stabilization of its population in the region of ten million since 1959.

Even more desperate has been Jakarta's declaration, in August 1970, of a "closed city" policy to new jobless settlers. Immigrants are required to show evidence of employment and housing accommodation before they are issued residence permits. They are further required to deposit with the city government for six months the equivalent of the return fare to their point of origin. The drastic measure was intended primarily for its psychological impact rather than physically to prevent people from coming to Jakarta (Critchfield, 1971). Evidence to date indicates that the policy has produced mixed results. On the one hand, Suharso *et al.* (1975) have suggested that there has been no noticeable diminution of the rate of growth from migration. An average of 648 migrants continued to enter Jakarta every day. On the other hand, Papanek (1975) has found that since a high "price" is attached to the residency card, the lowest income groups tend to ignore the regulation altogether, whereas others who need it contribute towards bribery and corruption.

Relocation

In terms of actually decentralizing metropolitan growth, at least four strategies may be cited. First is the sequence of structural, land-use, and industrial relocation plans adopted by Seoul since 1964 to decentralize growth in the metropolis. Each plan was found wanting in fully meeting the targets of controlling growth, to be succeeded by more encompassing designs, culminating in the Capital Regional Plan adopted in 1981 for ten years. The plan involved thirty local and provincial governments in the Capital Region affected by the regional land-use plan, but the absence of a single metropolitan government may present a real obstacle in implementation (W. Kim, 1983).

In 1973, in desperation to slow the tide of in-migration, new industries in Seoul were subject to a "new citizen tax." Property and acquisition taxes payable by new firms were several times higher than those for established industries. In addition, differential school fees and new college entrance examinations for candidates outside the Seoul area were introduced (Hwang, 1979:8). Furthermore, as most migrants have been attracted by jobs provided by industries, an active industrial relocation has been pursued with vigour since 1977. Relocatable industries were identified by size of firms, type of production, interindustry linkages, labour availability and other factors. It was reasoned that spatial rearrangement of manufacturing is a precursor to population dispersal (Kwon, 1981b). Consequent upon these decentralization strategies, Seoul's population growth slowed to 4 per cent per year by 1975, as compared with 7.3 per cent in the period from 1960 to 1966. Likewise, Seoul's share in the number of industrial firms and employees, university enrollment, and gross regional product has declined appreciably (Hwang, 1979:12–13).

New Towns

Second, several study cities have chosen to develop new towns, satellite towns and small/medium towns to divert metropolitan growth to these areas. Seoul's first attempt at decentralization through a satellite town was the establishment of Sungnam, 25 kilometres to the south, in the late 1960s to relocate squatters from the city. However, the new town did not have sufficient industries to provide jobs, with the result that many squatters moved back to or commuted to Seoul. Realizing Sungnam as a financial drain, Seoul quickly imposed the new town on the neighbouring province of Kyonggi in 1973 (Kwon, 1981a:324). The satellite town approach, nevertheless, was not forsaken, for in the basic guidelines for the capital region in 1971, the development of ten satellite towns was proposed in areas within a radius of 30 kilometres from Seoul. More recently, in 1978, five medium-sized cities with populations between 200,000 and one million were designated as priority investment centres to provide alternative migration destinations to Seoul (S. U. Kim, 1980:66).

In Shanghai, too, a policy of satellite towns, designed as balanced and self-contained communities, has been in practice since 1958 in efforts to disperse population and industries. As conceived by Shanghai's planners, the optimal distance between the central city and satellite settlements lies between 20 and 70 kilometres, far enough from being absorbed by Shanghai and near enough to retain needed mutual coordination. These towns range in population between 50,000 and 200,000 (Fung, 1981:289–90). Similarly in Tokyo, satellite towns were planned at distances 17 to 45 miles from central Tokyo to absorb decentralized population and employment, but these did not develop for the most part into self-contained communities without large-scale commuting (Hall, 1977:232–35).

On a smaller scale, the city-states of Hong Kong and Singapore have also decentralized population and employment from congested core areas through development of new towns since the early 1960s. In both cases public housing has been a salient component in this development and responsible for improving living conditions in these communities. By 1981, 18.7 per cent of Hong Kong's population lived in the new towns (W. T. Leung, 1983:211). While these new towns allow room for new physical and structural designs, estate management has become more challenging and complex (Fung, 1983; Lim et al., 1983).

New Capitals

Third, there have been proposals to build brand new capital cities, much along the model of Brasilia, Canberra and Islamabad, to relieve pressure on existing ones. During the reign of President Park Chung Hee in South Korea, for example, a plan was broached to establish a new capital city to reduce Seoul's sociopolitical attraction by removing from it central administrative and executive functions. After the abrupt turnover of political leadership in 1979, the idea of a new capital city no longer received political support (Kim, 1981:68). The latest proposal for twin cities came surprisingly from Malaysia, where the prime minister recently revealed plans for constructing a new city at Janda Baik, at present a quiet retreat 30 kilometres from Kuala Lumpur. Initially the new city will be under the administration of Kuala Lumpur but will grow fast to become a city of 100,000 by 1990 and 500,000 by the year 2000 (Specter, 1984a: 24–25).

Green Belts

Finally, if construction of new urban communities is viewed as a positive strategy to channel new growth, designation of green belts may be regarded as a measure to restrict uncontrolled metropolitan sprawl. Several cities under review have adopted this strategy to limit undesirable growth. In Tokyo a seven-mile wide green belt was delineated in the 1956 development plan right beyond the defined built-up area of ten miles in all directions from the Tokyo Central Station. This belt was abandoned a decade later as it was unable to hold development, and was replaced in 1965 by a new suburban development area extending beyond 30 miles from the city centre (Hall, 1977:236). In Seoul the green belt was formally instituted in 1972 through revision of the City Planning Act to contain its physical growth. By 1982 the total area amounted to 369.5 square kilometres, out of which 66.5 per cent was development-restricted (Park, 1981:35; SMG, 1983:50). Likewise in Bangkok, green belts covering agricultural land 12 kilometres wide along the eastern and western flanks of Bangkok's built-up areas were specified in 1981 prohibiting any building more than 100 metres from either side of existing roads (Tanphiphat, 1982:36).

Somewhat different in purpose but not in function has been the preservation of a vegetable production belt around the central city and satellite communities in Shanghai (Fung, 1981:292–94). Food production for the city has thus been successfully safeguarded. In 1959 Shanghai produced three-quarters of the fruits and 97 per cent of the vegetables its inhabitants consumed (White, 1981:260).

Policies for Urban Well-being

Having reviewed macroantimetropolitan growth policies, I now shift attention to some of the more important policies designed for improving urban well-being.

Shelter

With respect to shelter—one of the intractable problems evidenced by the data presented earlier—it has been maintained elsewhere that the 1970s was the most important decade insofar as policy innovations and physical construction in Asia are concerned (Yeung, 1983). Following the lead provided by Singapore, Hong Kong (1972), Thailand (1973), Indonesia (1974) and the Philippines (1974) established unified housing bodies, thus minimizing many of the difficulties of overlapping responsibilities and competition for scarce financial resources arising from multiagency delivery of low-cost housing.

While Singapore and Hong Kong have accomplished impressive success in public housing, most other countries have adopted a combination of slum upgrading, sites and services, and core housing approaches. True, most of these approaches were not innovated in the region, but they have been adjusted and adapted to suit local circumstances, such as the Kampung Improvement Programme (KIP) in Indonesia, and the Zonal Improvement Programme (ZIP) and Bagong Lipunan Sites and Services Programme (BLISS) in the Philippines. Many of these programmes receive outside funding, notably from the World Bank, Asian Development Bank and United Nations organizations.

Nonetheless, it is probably the large-scale public housing developments in Singapore and Hong Kong which are unparalleled in any city of the world and which have the most to offer in terms of experience and innovations for other similar situated metropolitan areas. To a limited degree, Seoul and Taipei have also adopted this high-rise, high-density mass housing to provide shelter for the low-income population.

Transport

Over the past two decades, many study cities have taken steps to strengthen transport systems and improve traffic. Most basic to the former has been construction of expressways, elevated roadways, ring roads and other design measures to achieve mode separation, higher speed and direct connection. External factors such as Tokyo's hosting the Asian and Olympic Games and the same games hosted by Seoul in 1986 and 1988 have been instrumental in speeding construction of transport and other infrastructural facilities.

With urban traffic becoming ever-congested, the region has witnessed in the past ten years several cities adopting mass rapid transit systems of different kinds. Most notable were subway systems opened in Seoul in 1974 and in Hong Kong in 1979. Both systems are still being expanded. Singapore, Kuala Lumpur and Manila are also committed to rail-based mass transit systems which are under construction. Shanghai is the only mega-city in the world without a mass transit system; the situation may change soon as the city is assessing the feasibility of constructing one.

As new systems are being developed, roles of intermediate transport systems will have to be defined. For example, the electric, elevated metrorail system being developed in Metro Manila will compete directly with the present system dominated by jeepneys. Both systems run along Taft Avenue, one of Manila's busiest thoroughfares to the central station (*SCMP*, 1984). In Jakarta and Bangkok traditional low-cost travel modes will likely continue to play an important role, given no immediate plans for any mass rapid transit system (Ocampo, 1982). In light of China's new economic policy allowing for individual initiative, intermediate transport modes appeared to have become quite active in Shanghai. Along with advances in physical transport provision have been noteworthy innovations in improving traffic. Bus lanes, air-conditioned buses and one-way traffic systems are some of the recent experiments carried out in Singapore, Hong Kong, Bangkok and Kuala Lumpur.

To curb automobile ownership, Singapore and Hong Kong are two cities that have adopted the most comprehensive car restriction policies through substantial increases in registration fee, road tax, fuel prices and parking charges. These measures were only partly effective, leading to the adoption, since 1975, in Singapore of the first area licensing scheme in the world. Cars are restricted in entry to the central city area of Singapore in the morning peak hours between 7:30 and 10:30 A.M. unless they meet requirements of car pooling or payment of a daily or monthly fee. From all accounts results have been highly successful (Watson and Holland, 1976). Towards the same end, Hong Kong tested an electronic road-pricing system which charged motorists selectively at times and places where congestion needed reducing. The scheme would require some two hundred toll sites, fitting vehicles with electronic number plates, and installing enforcement cameras (Fong, 1984). Completed in June 1985, the pilot test was technically successful, but the scheme was socially unacceptable and has been shelved temporarily.

Other Strategies

This overview of urban strategies and innovations is intended to be indicative rather than comprehensive. Equally important, Eastern Asian cities have made praiseworthy contributions in other spheres, such as the enlightened package of policies for assisting the informal sector in Kuala Lumpur, successful and systematic urban renewal in Singapore, metropolitan growth management in Manila, collective enterprises as a means to cope with youth unemployment in Shanghai and pollution abatement measures implemented in Seoul, Shanghai and Tokyo. Unfortunately, space does not allow further discussion of these subjects.

POLICY ISSUES AND OPTIONS

Underlying most of the strategies and measures reviewed above are some critical policy issues and options. It will be instructive to recount some of these insofar as they pertain to most of the cities studied. Discussion of these issues should bear in mind the varied socioeconomic contexts in which the cities are set.

City Size

First is the question of city size. Pervading many decentralization policies reviewed earlier was accepting that the city had grown too large. At its peak, Seoul grew at 7 to 9 per cent annually and Tokyo's population rose by an average of 329,000 per year from 1955 to 1960 (Hall, 1977:225; Hwang, 1980:34). Bangkok also grew to forty times the size of Thailand's next largest city, Chiengmai. There was no prescription of optimal size of the city in each case but a good sense of pragmatic governance prevailed to the extent that the cities could not go on growing at those rates without severely compromising the quality of life or level of basic services. Indeed, the urban environment in some of the cities studied has visibly deteriorated over time, a development that added urgency to the need to control and divert future urban growth. For this reason, the anti-big city philosophy was enthusiastically embraced by several of the cities represented, particularly Shanghai, Tokyo, Seoul, Bangkok and Jakarta, which have already become, or are on the way to becoming very large cities in Eastern Asia. Although there is theoretically no size limit to growth, more rapid growth than a city is prepared for invariably results in urban diseconomies. It is therefore common practice for cities to plan development according to a population target over a certain period, but such a target is more often than not exceeded by events not foreseen in the plan.

Cities and Development

The next issue is the city's role in national and international development. Here the cities represented differ the most as they are informed by varied ideologies. The choice of making Shanghai a productive instead of a consumer city led, inter alia, to uncoordinated growth of industries at the expense of infrastructure construction, emphasis on self-sufficiency in fruits and vegetables in the city region, and assumption of a critical position in spearheading the industrialization of China (Fung, 1981:283). Similarly, accelerating Malay urbanization has taken place in Kuala Lumpur since implementation of the New Economic Policy in 1970 designed to eradicate poverty and restructure the economy. A different urban ecology, with an accent on Malay participation, is emerging and the cultural role of Kuala Lumpur as a centre of Malay urbanism is being promoted (Specter, 1984a; Yeung, 1982). These cities are two examples of how very different policy options have led to varied functional roles and spatial patterning of activities within cities.

Other cities, notably Hong Kong and Singapore, play very pivotal roles in regional and international economies. As an aspiring global city, Singapore offers many types of professional services to surrounding countries, as well as being used as a base for some types of regional activities like oil exploration.

With the adoption of an increasingly open economic policy in China, Hong Kong's contribution to China's modernization programmes, in particular development of special economic zones, will increase. As the third largest financial centre and third largest container port in the world, Hong Kong's role in international development is clearly underlined. In fact, Hong Kong, Singapore, Bangkok and Kuala Lumpur, with their large overseas Chinese communities, are becoming a genre of world cities where circuits of capital are not geographically restricted, giving rise to a changing economic order around the Pacific rim. Overseas Chinese investment in real estate in and across cities in the region is a momentous phenomenon (Goldberg, 1984).

Viewed from another perspective, development of many of the study cities through transnational corporations has produced other effects. It is argued that unequal terms of exchange within the international economy have led to further increases in urban primacy, distortion in previous patterns of urban hierarchy, and increasing centralization of activities within cities (Walton, 1982). It would appear that Bangkok and Manila, and to a degree, Jakarta, Taipei and Seoul, are prime candidates that fit this description of development.

Food and Fuel

As Eastern Asian cities continue to grow and as their surrounding rural area is being encroached upon, the issues of food and fuel will be of increasing concern. On one hand, there is the question of changing food demand structures with increasing affluence. On the other hand, the extent of domestic production versus foreign imports of food has to be rationalized and decided upon. Generally speaking, foodgrains for the cities under study are brought in, either from within the country or abroad, but cities are to different degrees self-sufficient in vegetables, fruits, eggs, poultry and the like. Singapore and Hong Kong, for example, have concentrated their efforts on certain types of food and have become efficient producers for their needs. In other cases, the city has not formulated clearly defined development plans, resulting in loss of arable land and hence food production. Urban agriculture in Asian cities is a little-studied subject that given proper attention is likely to yield tangible benefits.

Meeting fuel requirements for Eastern Asian cities entails careful analysis of the sources of supply, fuel alternatives and relative costs before any energy policy can be designed.[1] Such a policy is not in place in any of the cities reviewed despite lingering memory of the energy shocks of the 1970s.

Finances

In terms of the administration of cities, one of the dilemmas confronting planners and decision-makers is lack of funds. Even Tokyo could not carry out many of its public projects for this reason. During the boom years prior to the early 1970s, economic buoyancy was sufficient to carry many of the ambitious projects through. Strains quickly developed and, by 1976, Tokyo was said to be in a financial crisis (Hall, 1977:237). More glaring in

---

[1]Two parallel research groups are interested in urban food and fuel issues in Asia. One group was to be organized by the Resource Systems Institute at the East-West Center which jointly organized with Nihon University a May 1984 Tokyo meeting to mount a multicountry research project. Another, coordinated out of Urban Resource Systems in San Francisco, tried to organize a similar research network focussed on urban agriculture in Asia. A meeting with International Development Research Centre funding was held in Singapore in mid-1983. Both networks are yet to get off the ground.

inadequate budgetary provision is the case of Jakarta. In 1959 Jakarta had a municipal budget less than 10 per cent of Singapore's, for a population twice as large (Hanna, 1961:5–6). Bangkok's fiscal powers are not much stronger as property, land and cars are grossly undertaxed. Only four taxes[2] come under the Bangkok Metropolitan Administration. In 1981 the average revenue of the city government was 741 baht per person, one-third the national average (Medhi Krongkaew and Tongudai, 1983).

Lack of financial resources often bedevils well-intentioned plans. The experience of the National Housing Authority (NHA) in Thailand, formed in 1973, is illuminating. The Five-Year Plan drawn up in 1976 called for construction of 120,000 dwelling units at a rate of 24,000 units a year. The high cost of this conventional approach quickly led to its being down-graded, complemented by a much heavier emphasis on slum upgrading as something that would benefit most people and at costs the government and the poor could afford. In the Fifth Plan Period (1982–1986), NHA no longer provides for rental housing; only sites and services projects and slum upgrading will be pursued (Kanjanaharitai, 1981:214–17; Tanphiphat, 1982:45–46).

In contrast to the above-cited cities, greater fiscal autonomy is realized in Hong Kong and Singapore by virtue of their power to tax and acquire land. Not surprisingly, their ability to carry through public works projects is correspondingly higher.

Services

The inability of the cities to provide needed basic services raises the next policy dilemma: Who is responsible for service provision—the government or the people? When a city government is financially hamstrung in providing essential services, people often organize themselves to improve the situation. In several cities included in this study, participatory urban services premised on people's initiatives and resources have been successfully carried out.[3] In

---

[2]These taxes are house and land, land development, signboard and animal slaughter. They constitute a small faction of the total revenue of the Bangkok Metropolitan Administration which is heavily supported by the central government.

[3]The International Development Research Centre supported a five-country project in Eastern Asia on this subject involving South Korea, Hong Kong, the Philippines, Malaysia and Indonesia. The project has been completed and publication of the findings is in progress.

Seoul the *Saemaul Udong* (new village movement) initiated in rural areas was extended to urban slum communities. In low-income communities in Manila and Jakarta similar mechanisms of self-help delivery of urban services exist to alleviate the hardship of life in these communities. Leadership is a critical variable which means success or failure of these people-based efforts (Yeung and McGee, in press).

The Poor

Finally, the remarkably economic growth experienced in Eastern Asian cities has not been equally shared. A large proportion of the population remains mired in poverty and will likely remain so in the foreseeable future. Many policy options taken in the cities do not have the interests of urban poor taken into account. Hyung-Kook Kim (1981:70) thus criticized Seoul's population dispersal plans as being pursued in their own right without the welfare of the urban poor or in-migrants taken into account. Uneven distribution of basic services in high-income versus low-income areas is also a common feature in Eastern Asian cities. At a more general level, development plans within a city are not always compatible with interests of the urban poor. For example, a new shopping centre may be constructed at the expense of relocating existing vendors, a new express-way can be constructed only if certain slum housing is demolished, and modernization of urban transport may mean phasing out traditional modes of transport. Each policy alternative affects the livelihood of the urban poor, and good policy decisions must take into consideration conflicting interests of different income groups and strike a balance among them. Most cities, however, do have some policies geared towards improving the lives of the urban poor. Poverty redressing policies in Manila (Viloria, 1983), Kuala Lumpur and Seoul are noted for their concerted efforts to combat poverty[4] and are mostly organized by sectors rather than being location-specific.

FATHOMING URBAN FUTURES

A decade ago Hicks (1974:3) introduced her study of large world cities with this assessment:

---

[4]The International Development Research Centre has supported research on this subject in the three cities mentioned. See Viloria (1983) for a summary of the Philippine results.

All over the world the great cities are in trouble. The problem of how to deal with the large urban concentrations of the modern world has not yet been solved. It is a problem which besets not only the advanced countries, but afflicts all areas with dense populations and consequently large cities. The troubles seem to be particularly severe (if one can particularize) in Japan, India and the U.S.A.; very likely also in China....

This diagnosis of the problem is still accurate for the large cities of Eastern Asia not only today but also likely to the end of this century.

According to population projections of the United Nations, the developing countries will loom exceptionally large in the share of very large cities by A.D. 2000. Of the 25 largest urban agglomerations in the world, 18 will be in Asia alone. Eight Eastern Asian cities will be in this class, including Shanghai (25.9 million), Tokyo/Yokohama (23.8), Jakarta (14.3), Seoul (13.7), Manila (10.5) and Bangkok/Thonburi (9.9) covered in this study (United Nations, 1982:Table 8). However, there are some comforting signals from the United Nations statistics. They show a slowdown of urbanization in developing countries as a whole, giving rise to speculation that an urban turnaround in these countries is possibly afoot. For East Asia and South Asia, 34.2 and 36.8 per cent, respectively, of the total population will reside in urban places by the year 2000, still below the less developed regions' average and world average of 40.4 and 48.2 per cent, respectively. Between 1980 and 2000, cities in East Asia and South Asia will grow at 1.0 and 1.9 per cent, respectively. There are also signs that migration patterns have turned towards smaller urban places rather than large metropolises (United Nations, 1983).

Along with the robust economic forecast for Eastern Asia, there is little doubt that the cities under review will continue to play vital roles in their national and international economies. Hofheinz and Calder's speculation (1982:251) well sums up the thoughts of many regarding sustained growth of the region:

But it is one thing to doubt whether Eastasia can continue to grow at the same phenomenal rate, and quite another to believe that its fortunes will be reversed. Short of a world war or some other cataclysmic event that interrupts the flow of commerce and raw materials, it is hard to conceive of a dramatic decline in Eastasia growth and performance, and the possibility exists of a considerable and sustained upward thrust. Given the deep-seated ills of Western societies, Eastasia may gain against the West even if, in comparison with past performance, it only stands still.

With such an optimistic outlook, officials of most large Eastern cities have envisioned their futures to the end of this century. Tokyo (TMG, 1984a), Seoul (W. Kim, 1980) and Kuala Lumpur (Dewan Bandaraya, 1982), to cite only three examples, have approached the subject by preparing an official perspective view of the future, an academic discussion and a formal development plan, respectively. Certain common elements can be distilled from these urban futures.

First, there is an increasing realization that problems of the great Eastern Asian city cannot be solved within the context of the metropolis. The metropolitan area will become a large, integrated regional complex, with the central city being its core. Beyond the regional complex, a national urbanization policy should be in place in which other spatial components should be articulated with the metropolitan region. The futility of the approach of metropolitan growth management divorced from national urban development goals is widely accepted. At least on paper and with a vision, the great Eastern Asian city should strive to create what W. A. Robson and D. E. Regan idealized—an ordered, coherent, decentralized metropolitan region.

Second, within the metropolitan-regional framework rural-urban migration will probably be moderated, given the likelihood of an urban turn-around alluded to earlier. Assuming continued rapid economic development, rapid technological, social and functional change will impinge on every aspect of metropolitan life. With concomitant growing affluence and persistent poverty, administrators and planners will forever be torn by the trade-off between efficiency and equity goals. Notwithstanding political rhetoric to the contrary, the interests of the urban poor are by and large not incorporated into existing plans.

Third, despite the application of comprehensive private car restraint programmes in some cities, the general tendency is towards a continuing and greater emphasis on the automobile. Even bicycle-dominated Shanghai is changing in this direction. At the same time, within the next fifteen years, mass rapid transit systems of some sort will probably be installed in Shanghai, Taipei, Kuala Lumpur, Singapore and Manila. While the former will aggravate the already serious condition of traffic congestion, the latter will improve mobility within these cities.

At the industrial city level, a few remarks of special interest on future development may be of interest. In view of China's recent more open and relaxed economic policy and the signing of the joint Sino-British accord,

Shanghai and Hong Kong are destined to play more vital roles in China's development. Shanghai has been designated one of the fourteen open cities along the coast of China, signalling probably the beginning of a period of rapid growth for the coastal areas of the country, and then beyond. With its excellent harbour, strategic location and infrastructural facilities, Shanghai can be catalytic in ushering in a new period of economic growth to that part of China. Similarly, Hong Kong is expected to bring its development experience to bear on assisting China's modernization programmes through the special economic zones and open coastal cities to speed progress. Barring any unforeseen political twists and turns in China, Hong Kong's contribution to China's economic development goals can only be enhanced towards 1997 and beyond.

Concerning future needs for social institutions and physical structures in the great Eastern Asian cities, Tokyo may well be the most pressed. By the year 2000, Tokyo will have 12 per cent of its population aged 65 and above, as compared with 7 per cent in 1984. Tokyo is already making plans to cope with its ageing population with adjustments in welfare service, employment structure, medical care, and so on in light of changing needs (TMG, 1984a:11–14). By the end of this century, tertiary industries will employ over 70 per cent of the labour force, vertical land-use zoning will operate in the inner city where land values are high, and disaster prevention living areas will have been designed.

Both Seoul and Taipei will develop multiple-core city structures to decentralize development. Urban renewal will have begun in Taipei, with anticipation of improved infrastructural facilities. However, water supply may be a difficult problem to deal with. One perspective of Seoul by the year 2000 is to predict the ascendancy of transactional metropolitan development. The central city will be dominated by abstract, information-oriented functions that operate in offices and in skyscrapers that form the skyline (Corey, 1980:66).

Much along the orientation of the metropolitan region, Jakarta has developed a master plan which will link it to three other neighbouring cities, Bekasi, Bogor and Tangerang. Called Jabotabek, it will have a projected population of 25 million as it enters the twenty-first century. During Repelita IV (1984–1988) almost Rps 900 million (US$904.5 million) is earmarked for expenditure on Jabotabek. The central government has committed to provide 75 per cent of the funds, a decision which indirectly means increased taxes to finance the plan (Specter, 1984a:26–27).

Kuala Lumpur of A.D. 2000 will look substantially different from what it is today. It will be more modern, Malay-dominated and densely developed. Government policies since 1970 have consistently promoted Malay urbanization focussed on the Federal Territory, which is gradually witnessing a population shift in favour of Malays. Increasing *bumiputra* (Malay) participation is most notable in the development and redevelopment of the central planning area where, by virtue of the established policy, there must be 30 per cent participation by Malays in ownership and operation of most economic activities. By administrative fiat and contrived change, an ethnically and functionally different city is being shaped.

The urban scenarios that have been lightly touched on are for the most part purposeful vistas with which to perceive the future in Eastern Asia. Their realization, like any development plan, depends on the interplay of a complex of political, economic, human and fiscal factors. Given the special administrative status of many of the cities studied and their growing importance in national and international economies, the outlook of their ability to fulfil their respective urban futures is moderately sanguine.

REFERENCES

Aiken, S. Robert and Colin H. Leigh. 1975. "Malaysia's Emerging Conurbations." *Annals of the Association of American Geographers*, 65:546–63.

Aquino, Rosemary M. 1983. *The Delivery of Basic Services in Three Selected Philippine Urban Centres: Implications for a Participatory Management Model.* Manila: Integrated Research Centre, De La Salle University.

Blair, Thomas L. 1974. *The International Global Crisis.* New York: Hill & Wang.

Business China, 8(31 Mar. 1982):44–45. "Shanghai—Up Close."

Chen, S. H. 1984. "Problems of Urban Development" (in Chinese). In *Social Problems in Taiwan*, ed. K. S. Young and C. C. Yeh, 2nd ed. Taipei: Che-Liu.

China Daily (26 July 1984):3. "Shanghai Housing Shortage Studies."

Chu, Chong-Won. 1980. "Issues on Housing and Urban Development in Seoul." In *The Year 2000*. See W. Kim (1980).

Corey, Kenneth E. 1980. "Transactional Forces and the Metropolis: Towards a Planning Strategy for Seoul in the Year 2000." In *The Year 2000*. See W. Kim (1980).

Critchfield, Richard. 1971. "The Flight of the Cities: Dakarta—The First to 'Close'." *Columbia Journal of World Business*, 6(4):89–93.

Davis, Kingsley. 1965. "The Urbanization of the Human Population." *Scientific American*, 213(3):41–53.

Dewan, Bandaraya. 1982. *Kuala Lumpur Draft Structure Plan*. Kuala Lumpur.

Donner, Wolf. 1978. *The Five Faces of Thailand: An Economic Geography*. New York: St. Martin's Press.

Erni, L.L.M. and Bianpoen. 1980. "Case Study: Jakarta Indonesia." In *Politics toward Urban Slums*. Bangkok: United Nations Economic and Social Commission for Asia and the Pacific.

Fong, Peter K. W. 1984. *The Electronic Road Pricing System in Hong Kong*. Hong Kong: Centre of Urban Studies and Urban Planning, University of Hong Kong.

Fung, Kai-iu. 1981. "The Spatial Development of Shanghai." In *Shanghai, Revolution and Development in an Asian Metropolis*. Contemporary China Institute Publications. Cambridge: Cambridge University Press.

Fung, Tung. 1983. "Public Housing Management in Hong Kong's New Towns." In *A Place to Live*. See Yeung (1983).

Ginsburg, Norton S. 1955. "The Great City in Southeast Asia." *American Journal of Sociology*, 60:455–62.

Goldberg, Michael A. 1984. *Hedging Your Great Grandchildren's Bets: The Case of Overseas Chinese Investment in Real Estate around the Cities of the Pacific Rim*. Working Paper No. 22. Vancouver: Institute of Asian Research, University of British Columbia.

Hall, Peter G. 1977. *The World Cities*. 2nd ed. London: Weidenfeld & Nicolson.

Hanna, Willard Anderson. 1961. *Bung Karno's Indonesia: A Collection of 25 Reports Written for the American Universities Field Staff*. New York: American Universities Field Staff.

Henderson, J. V. 1984. "Urbanization: International Experience and Prospects for China." Department of Economics, Yale University, New Haven, CT. Mimeo.

Hicks, Ursula K. 1974. *The Large City: A World Problem*. New York: Halsted.

Hofheinz, Roy, Jr. and Kent E. Calder. 1982. *The Eastasia Edge*. New York: Basic Books.

Hong Kong Housing Authority. 1984. *A Review of Public Housing Allocation Policies: A Consultation Document*. Hong Kong.

Honjo, Masahiko. 1972. "Recovering the Tokyo Bay Coastal Area: The Choice for Balance." Background paper. Nagoya, Japan: United Nations Centre for Regional Development.

————. 1975. "Tokyo: Giant Metropolis of the Orient." In *World Capitals: Toward Guided Urbanization*, ed. H. Wentworth Eldredge. Garden City, N. Y.: Anchor Press/Doubleday.

Hsu, Yi-Rong Ann and Clifford W. Pannell. 1982. "Urbanization and Residential Spatial Structure in Taiwan." *Pacific Viewpoint*, 23:22–52.

Hwang, Myong-Chan. 1979. "A Search for Development Strategy for the Capital Region of Korea." In *Metropolitan Planning: Issues and Policies*, ed. Yung Hee Rho and Myong-Chan Hwang. Seoul: Korea Research Institute for Human

Settlements.

————. 1980. "Planning Strategies for Metropolitan Seoul." In *The Year 2000*. See W. Kim (1980).

Kanjanaharitai, Paiboon. 1981. "Bangkok: The City of Angels." In *Urbanization and Regional Development*, ed. Masahiko Honjo. Singapore: Maruzen Asia.

Kim, Hung-Kook. 1981. "Social Factors of Migration from Rural to Urban Areas with Special Reference to Developing Countries: The Case of Korea." *Social Indicators Research*, 10:29–74.

Kim, Song-Um. 1980. "An Overview of Recent Urbanization Patterns and Policy Measures for Population Redistribution and Resettlement in the Republic of Korea." In *Migration and Resettlement Rural-Urban Policies*, Vol. 2. Manila: Social Welfare and Development Centre for Asia and the Pacific.

Kim, Won. 1983. "Land Use Planning in a Rapidly Growing Metropolis: The Case of Seoul." *Asian Economies*, (Jan.):5–21.

————, ed. 1980. *The Year 2000: Urban Growth and Perspectives for Seoul*. Seoul: Korea Planners Association.

Krausse, G. H. 1982. "Themes in Poverty: Economics, Education, Amenities, and Social Functions in Jakarta's Kampungs." *Southeast Asian Journal of Social Science*, 10(2):49–70.

Krongkaew, Medhi and Pawadee Tongudai. 1983. "The Growth of Bangkok: The Economics of Unbalanced Urbanization and Development." Paper presented at the Annual Conference of the Association of Asian Studies, San Francisco, 25–27 March.

Kwok, Reginald Y. W. 1983. "Land Price Escalation and Public Housing in Hong Kong." In *Land for Housing the Poor*, ed. Shlomo Angel, Raymon W. Archer, Sidhijai Tanphipat and Emiel A. Weglen. Singapore: Select Books.

Kwon, Won-Young. 1980. "Metropolitan Growth and Management: The Case of Seoul." Seoul, Korea: Korea Research Institute for Human Settlements.

————. 1981a. "Seoul: A Dynamic Metropolis." In *Urbanization and Regional Development*. See Kanjanaharitai (1981).

————. 1981b. "A Study of the Economic Impact of Industrial Relocation: The Case of Seoul." *Urban Studies*, 18:73–90.

Lau, Siu-kai, Kuan Hsin-chi and Ho Kam-fai. 1983. *Leaders, Officials and Localities in Hong Kong*. Centre for Hong Kong Studies Occasional Paper No. 1. Hong Kong: Institute of Social Studies, The Chinese University of Hong Kong.

Lee, Chunfen, Yen Chungmin and Tang Jianzhong. 1983. "A Spatial Analysis of Shanghai's Economic Development." Guangzhou: Department of Geography, East China Normal University.

Leong, K. C. 1981. "Kuala Lumpur: Youngest Metropolis of Southeast Asia." In *Urbanization and Regional Development*. See Kanjanaharitai (1981).

Leung, Chi-keung. 1983. "Urban Transportation." In *A Geography of Hong Kong*, ed.

T. N. Chiu and C. L. So. Hong Kong: Oxford University Press.

Leung, W. T. 1983. "The New Towns Programme." In *A Geography of Hong Kong*. See Chi-keung Leung (1983).

Lim, Kok Leong, Chin Keim Hoong, Chin Koon Fun, Goh Leslie and Ong Sze Ann. 1983. "Management of Singapore's New Towns." In *A Place to Live*. See Yeung (1983).

Liu, Paul K. C. 1982. "Labour Mobility and Utilization in Relation to Urbanization in Taiwan." *Industry of Free China*, (May):1–12.

————. 1983. "Factors and Policies Contributing to Urbanization and Labour Mobility in Taiwan." *Industry of Free China*, (May):1–20.

Lo, C. P. 1972. "A Typology of Hong Kong Census Districts: A Study in Urban Structure." *Journal of Tropical Geography*, 34:34–43.

Moir, Hazel V. J. 1978. *Jakarta Informal Sector*. Monograph Series. Jakarta: National Institute of Economic and Social Research (LEKNAS-LIPI).

Mugbil, I. 1982. "The Poisoning of Bangkok." *Bangkok Post*, (13 June):24.

NEDA. See Philippines, National Economic Development Authority.

Ocampo, Romeo B. 1982. *Low-Cost Transport in Asia: A Comparative Report on Five Cities*. Ottawa: International Development Research Centre.

Papanek, Gustav F. 1975. "The Poor of Jakarta." *Economic Development and Cultural Change*, 24:1–27.

Park, Soo Young. 1981. "Urban Growth and National Policy in Korea." Paper presented at the Pacific Science Association 4th Inter-Congress, Singapore, 1–5 September.

Philippines, National Economic Development Authority. 1973. *Regional Development Projects: Supplement to the Four-Year Development Plan, FY 1974–77*. Manila.

Prybyla, Jan S. 1975. "*Hsia-Fang*: The Economics and Politics of Rustication in China." *Pacific Affairs*, 48:153–72.

SCMP. See *South China Morning Post*.

Seoul Metropolitan Government. 1983. *Seoul: Metropolitan Administration*. Seoul.

Sethuraman, S. V. 1976. *Jakarta: Urban Development and Employment. A WEP Study*. Geneva: International Labour Office.

Simmons, Alan B. 1979. "Slowing Metropolitan City Growth in Asia: Policies, Programmes, and Results." *Population and Development Review*, 5:87–104.

SMG. See Seoul Metropolitan Government.

Soon, Tay Kweng. 1969. "Housing and Urban Values—Singapore." *Ekistics*, 27(158): 27–28.

South China Morning Post (13 Sept. 1984). "Manilans Queue Up for Metrorail."

South Korea. 1982. *The Second Comprehensive National Physical Development Plan 1982–1991*. Seoul.

Specter, Michael. 1984a. "The 'Small Town' Big City." *Far Eastern Economic Review*, 125(27 Sept.):23–30.

————. 1984b. "A Sprawling, Thirsty Giant." *Far Eastern Economic Review*,

123(29 Mar.):23–30.

Suharso, *et al.* 1975. *Migration and Education in Jakarta*. Jakarta: National Institute of Economic and Social Research (LEKNAS-LIPI).

Tang, F. Z. 1982. *Research on Questions and Policies of Urbanization in Taiwan* (in Chinese). Taipei: Development Research Committee of the Executive Assembly.

Tanphiphat, Sidhijai. 1982. "Thailand Country Study: Urban Land Management Policies and Experiences." Paper presented at the International Seminar on Urban Development Policies, Nagoya, Japan, 13–18 October.

Tao, Z. J. 1981. "Examining Urban Construction and Urban Finance from the Perspective of the Urban Structure of Shanghai" (in Chinese). In *Zhongguo caizheng wenti*, ed. Zhongguo caizheng bu. Tianjin: Tianjin kexue jixue chubanshe.

TMG. See Tokyo Metropolitan Government.

Tokyo Metropolitan Government. 1984a. *Long-Term Plan for Tokyo Metropolis: "My Town Tokyo"—Heading into the 21st Century*. TMG Municipal Library No. 18. Tokyo.

——. 1984b. *Plain Talk about Tokyo: The Administration of the Tokyo Metropolitan Government*. 2nd ed. TMG Municipal Library No. 15. Tokyo.

Tsay, Ching-lung. 1982. "Migration and Population Growth in Taipei Municipality." *Industry of Free China*, (Mar.):9–25.

United Nations, Department of International Economic and Social Affairs. 1980. *Patterns of Urban and Rural Population Growth*. ST/ESA/SER.A/68. Population Studies No. 68. New York: United Nations.

——. 1982. *Estimates and Projections of Urban, Rural and City Populations, 1950–2025: The 1980 Assessment*. ST/ESA/SER.R/45. New York: United Nations.

United Nations, Population Division. 1983. "Urbanization and City Growth." *Populi*, 10(2):39–50.

United Nations Development Programme. 1979. "Project of the Government of the People's Republic of China: Municipality of Shanghai." Mimeo.

Viloria, Leandro A. 1981. "Manila: Creation of a Metropolitan Government." In *Urbanization and Regional Development*. See Kanjanaharitai (1981).

——. 1983. "Study of Poverty Redressal Programmes in Metro Manila." Report submitted to International Development Research Centre. Mimeo.

Walton, John. 1982. "The International Economy and Peripheral Urbanization." In *Urban Policy under Capitalism*, ed. Norman I. Fainstein and Susan S. Fainstein. *Urban Affairs Annual Review*, Vol. 22. Newbury Park, CA.: Sage.

Watson, P. L. and E. P. Holland. 1976. "Congestion Pricing—the Example of Singapore." *Finance and Development*, 13(1):20–23.

White, Lynn T. 1981. "The Suburban Transformation." In *Shanghai: Revolution and Development in an Asian Metropolis*, ed. Christopher Howe. Cambridge: Cambridge University Press.

Wu, C. T. 1984. "Coping with Urban Growth under Socialism: The Case of Shanghai." Department of Town and Country Planning, University of Sydney. Mimeo.

Yan, Z. M. and J. Z. Tang. 1984. "Urbanization and Urban Eco-Environment in Shanghai" (in Chinese). *Journal of East China Normal University*, 1:68–73.

Yeung, Yue-man. 1976. "Southeast Asian Cities: Patterns of Growth and Transformation." In *Urbanization and Counterurbanization*, ed. Brian J. L. Berry. *Urban Affairs Annual Reviews*, Vol. 11. Newbury Park, CA.: Sage. (Included in this book as Chapter 6.)

————. 1982. "Economic Inequality and Social Injustice: Development Issues in Malaysia." *Pacific Affairs*, 55(1):94–101.

————, ed. 1983. *A Place to Live: More Effective Low-Cost Housing in Asia.* Ottawa: International Development Research Centre.

Yeung, Yue-man and Terence G. McGee, eds. 1986. *Community Participation in Delivering Urban Services in Asia.* Ottawa: International Development Research Centre.

4. Controlling Metropolitan Growth in Eastern Asia*

Rapid urbanization characterized most of Asia from 1960 to 1980. The increase was differential, but by 1980 three subregions—East, Southeast and South—provided empirical evidence to support the often stated relationship between levels of economic development and urbanization. The level of economic development in these subregions is reflected in the gross national product (GNP) for each country. In 1980 the World Bank listed a per capita GNP of US$1,490 for South Korea, of US$710 for the Philippines and of US$310 for Pakistan. With the exception of China all Eastern Asian countries are urbanizing very rapidly and have attained a level of urbanization that is markedly above the average for developing countries. This article presents an examination of the methods with which some large cities in Eastern Asia, a collective term for East and Southeast Asia, have coped with recent population growth, changes in socioeconomic structures and resultant problems (Yeung, 1985).

Metropolitan growth has been widespread and rapid in Eastern Asia during the past two decades. Large cities have loomed increasingly important in many countries. The rate of urbanization can be suggested by the following statistic: in 1970 the developing countries of the world had seventy-two cities each with a population in excess of one million, but in 1980 Eastern Asia alone recorded sixty so-called "million cities." Equally significant, the share of the largest city in the total urban population of each country is so vast that much of the economic wealth, political power and service facilities are concentrated in these cities (Table 4.1). Bangkok, for example, with 72 per cent of the population of Thailand illustrates an extreme case of a primate city with virtually complete dominance over the economic, social, political and cultural activities of a country.

*Reprinted with permission of The American Geographical Society from *The Geographical Review*, Vol. 76, No. 2 (1986), pp. 125–37.

TABLE 4.1
Urban Growth in Eastern Asia, 1969–1980

Country	Urban population			Largest city					
	Population in millions		Growth rate (%)	Name	Population in millions		Growth rate (%)	% of urban pop.	
	1960	1980			1960	1980		1960	1980
China	127.5	256.0	100.7	Shanghai	7.7	15.0	94.8	6.0	5.9
Hong Kong	2.7	4.6	68.4	n.a.	n.a.	n.a.	n.a.	n.a.	n.a.
Japan	58.8	91.3	55.3	Tokyo	10.7	20.0	87.6	18.2	22.0
N. Korea	4.2	10.7	152.4	Pyongyang	0.6	1.3	102.0	15.0	12.0
S. Korea	6.9	21.1	204.1	Seoul	2.4	8.5	254.4	34.1	40.3
Taiwan	6.3	11.9	88.2	Taipei	1.1	2.2	102.1	17.5	18.8
Burma	4.3	9.6	123.6	Rangoon	1.0	2.2	123.4	22.8	22.9
Indonesia	14.3	29.9	109.9	Jakarta	2.9	7.0	141.4	20.3	23.4
Malaysia	2.1	4.1	100.5	Kuala Lumpur	0.4	1.1	198.9	18.0	26.9
Philippines	8.5	17.8	109.3	Manila	2.3	5.7	147.6	26.9	31.8
Singapore	1.3	1.8	39.6	n.a.	n.a.	n.a.	n.a.	n.a.	n.a.
Thailand	3.4	6.8	98.5	Bangkok	2.2	4.9	126.4	65.1	72.0

Sources: Department of International Economic and Social Affairs, *Patterns of Urban and Rural Population Growth* (New York: United Nations, 1980), Table 48; Department of International Economic and Social Affairs, *Estimates and Projections of Urban, Rural and City Populations, 1950–2025: The 1980 Assessment* (New York: United Nations, 1982), Tables 2 and 8; for Taiwan: Paul K. C. Liu, "Labor Mobility and Utilization in Relation to Urbanization in Taiwan," *Industry of Free China*, May 1982, pp. 1–12; and "Factors and Policies Contributing to Urbanization and Labor Mobility in Taiwan," *Industry of Free China*, May 1983, pp. 1–20.

Bangkok is not the only large Eastern Asian city whose overarching influence is felt widely in its country. Shanghai, Tokyo, Jakarta, Seoul and Manila exhibit the same tendency. Moreover, other large cities in the region share the same experience of growing too rapidly and too much without commensurate fiscal and physical provisions. The consequent problems afflicting these urban centres include chronic housing shortages, snarled traffic, deteriorating basic services, increased social inequality, omnipresent squatter settlements, widespread poverty and limited employment opportunities. To mitigate problems and to forestall further deterioration of the urban environment, several cities have experimented with numerous planning, policy and administrative strategies. These means to control, divert and decelerate future metropolitan growth are grouped in three categories for the analytical purposes of this study.

PHYSICAL CONTROL

The first category is developmental strategies intended to contain, restrain and control physical metropolitan expansion. One method is to design and build satellite towns in a wide regional context, so that they absorb population and economic activities associated with growth that would otherwise locate on the immediate outer limits of a metropolitan area. Satellite towns ideally are self-contained, balanced communities that are near enough to be influenced by a metropolis, but are distant enough to discourage commuting.

Proposals to develop new towns and growth poles outside Seoul were first advanced in a plan in 1964. However, it was not until the late 1960s, with the establishment of Sungnam approximately twenty-five kilometres south of Seoul that serious implementation of the proposal began. Intended primarily for relocation of squatters, Sungnam was ineffective in meeting the original objectives, because the lack of industrial employment opportunities forced residents to commute to the capital or to move back there. The administrative transfer of the new centre to the neighbouring province in 1973 did little to resolve the basic economic problems (Kwon, 1981a:324). The 1971 guidelines for the capital region proposed establishment of ten satellite towns within a radius of thirty kilometres from Seoul. In 1978 five medium-sized cities each with a population between 200,000 and 1,000,000 were designated as primary investment centres to provide alternative destinations for migration to Seoul. Because of the strong industrial economy in each of these centres, growth has been rapid, especially with groups of low-skilled, poorly educated youths (Kim, 1981:66).

Satellite-town development has been vigorously pursued around Shanghai since the late 1950s. The successful implementation, in part, explains the remarkable stability of the Shanghai population during the past twenty-five years. The metropolitan population numbered 11.8 million in 1982, a mere 9.6 per cent increase since 1964 (SSKY, 1983:1232). The satellite-town policy was adopted for Shanghai in 1958, when the area was expanded ten times its size to six thousand square kilometres. These towns are located twenty to seventy kilometres from the city and are expected to accommodate 50,000 to 200,000 inhabitants each (Fig. 4.1). It is envisaged that such distant satellites will not be absorbed by the parent city but will retain mutual advantages in industrial production and other functional linkages. Since 1957 construction of highways and other infrastructure has been concurrent with satellite-town growth. The success of the satellite communities around Shanghai is partly the consequence of their being self-contained, each with numerous separate independent neighbourhoods. Each neighbourhood is clustered around a factory or important commercial centre to minimize travel between home and workplace. Other essential services and facilities are found in a neighbourhood. Every satellite town in the region may be distinguished by its type of industrial production (Fung, 1981a:34).

Tokyo experienced rapid population growth in the postwar period. The pressure of congestion and inadequate services began to be felt in the late 1950s. The developmental plan for 1956 identified satellite towns as potential growth areas to accommodate decentralized population and employment opportunities. The towns were to be located twenty-seven to seventy-two kilometres from central Tokyo. Tama New Town, one of the more developed satellite centres, was planned and built by the metropolitan government in co-operation with the Japan Housing Corporation. Located in the Tama Hills to the west of the capital, the new town is a commuter centre with a projected population of 400,000. Two railroad lines link the satellite with the city centre. Construction of the town is expected to be completed by 1990 (Honjo, 1975). Partly because of the efficient transportation facilities, satellite communities around Tokyo have not become self-contained as they are around Shanghai. The commuting radius of Tokyo has progressively extended to some fifty kilometres (TMG, 1984a:33) (Fig. 4.2). The central-city area of Tokyo has a very low nighttime population in comparison with the daytime figure. Tokyo has been extending its sphere of influence rather than

Figure 4.1: The Shanghai Region

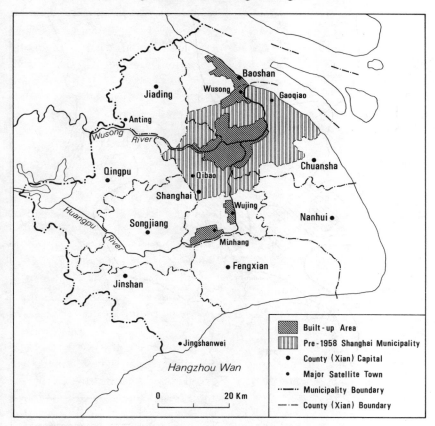

decentralizing population and economic opportunities beyond it.

The city-states of Hong Kong and Singapore, on a much smaller scale, have used satellite towns to decentralize population and economic opportunities from congested core areas since the early 1960s. Public housing has been a salient component of this development with resultant improved living conditions in the communities. The programme in Hong Kong has been earnestly pursued since 1972 with an ambitious ten-year schedule essentially through the establishment of new towns on the mainland. A measure of success can be observed in the relative shift of population. In 1971, 81.1 per cent of the

Figure 4.2: The Tokyo Metropolitan Region

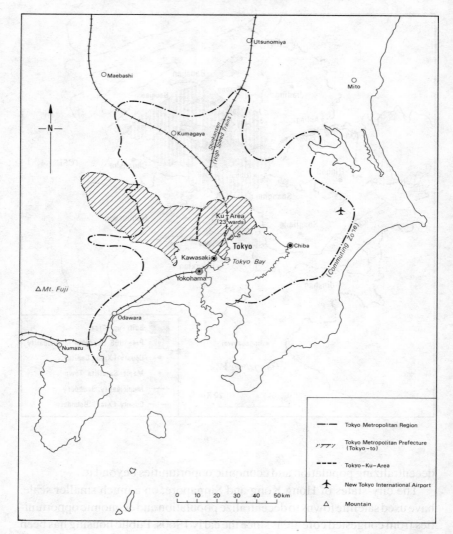

population lived in the main urban area; the proportion had dropped to 72.9 per cent in 1981. Conversely the population residing in the new towns rose from 9.8 per cent in 1971 to 18.8 in 1982 (Yeh and Fong, 1984:83).

The greenbelt, another widely applied planning strategy to contain metropolitan growth, has been adopted in several Asian cities. A greenbelt eleven kilometres wide was delineated in the 1956 plan for Tokyo to be located beyond the built-up area in all directions from Tokyo Central Station. The strategy was abandoned a decade later and replaced in 1965 by a new suburban-development area that was to begin forty-eight kilometres from the city centre (Hall, 1977:236). This growth area was physically contiguous to the existent urban area, but open space was retained wherever possible. The concept of distinguishing urban-promotion areas and urban-control areas was introduced in 1968. The former consisted of already urbanized places or ones that would be preferentially and systematically urbanized within ten or more years. The latter were to have restricted urbanization. This distinction is made in current plans for future development of Tokyo (TMG, 1984b:69).

A greenbelt for Seoul was formally instituted in 1972. The concept was later extended to thirteen other large urban areas in South Korea. By 1980 a total of 5,420 square kilometres had been designated as greenbelts, or 11 per cent of the total urban area of the country. For Seoul alone, 329 square kilometres were designated greenbelt, of which 66.5 per cent was development-restricted (SMG, 1983:50). Greenbelts covered agricultural land twelve kilometres wide along the eastern and western flanks of the Bangkok built-up areas. Construction was prohibited more than one hundred metres from either side of the existent roads. The preservation of a vegetable-production belt for Shanghai has been somewhat different in purpose, but not in function around the central city and satellite communities. Food production has been successfully safeguarded (White, 1981:260).

A third planning strategy that has not been widely adopted is construction of new capital cities to relieve functional pressures on existent ones. Among the 1976 proposals for dispersal and redistribution of Seoul's population was the suggestion of a new administrative capital for the country. A new capital not only would reduce the attractiveness of Seoul for migrants but also would be a symbol of postwar development and prosperity (Kim and Donaldson, 1979:671). However, the plan has been dormant since 1979. The government of Malaysia has considered this strategy, although Kuala Lumpur does not suffer the same degree of congestion and concentration that marks other large Eastern Asian capitals. The new capital is proposed for Janda Baik, a location thirty kilometres from Kuala Lumpur. Initially under its administration, Janda Baik is expected to reach a population of 500,000 by the year 2000 (Specter, 1984a:24–25).

REGIONAL PLANNING AND MANAGEMENT

Implicit in strategies to restrain growth is an awareness of spatial inter-dependency between a metropolis and the wide region of which it is a part. It is increasingly recognized that problems of metropolitan growth cannot be solved in a restricted geographical setting. A large region surrounding a metropolis must be incorporated into its planning and development, if growth is to proceed in an orderly manner along preconceived lines. This expansive tendency must be accounted for in metropolitan planning.

Tokyo was probably the first large Eastern Asian city to adopt a regional approach to planning in order to handle the remarkable postwar growth and expansion. The National Capital Region was proclaimed in 1956 to encom-pass planning for the Tokyo Metropolitan Government, three prefectures and parts of four others. This new metropolitan region included an area that extended 97 to 124 kilometres from central Tokyo. Over the years new laws were enacted to empower agencies to implement their plans; the adminis-trative structure was reorganized and streamlined; and regional decentral-ization was formulated. The principle of a regionwide approach to the manifold problems of the capital is contained in the plans for the remaining years of this century (Hall, 1977:233–37).

Similarly a City Region was established immediately after the massive an-nexation of territory in 1958 by Shanghai. A principal objective for that move was to allow a broad selection of locations for industrial development and new satellite towns. The method permitted planners to locate these facilities at optimal distances from the central city. Whenever possible the satellite towns were to be at existent villages, and industrial sites were to have easy access to water and rail transportation. To minimize the necessary invest-ment, preference was to be given to suburban units with a basic urban infra-structure. Intensification of agricultural land-uses and large-scale conversion of cropland on the urban fringe to market gardening accompanied the creation of the satellite towns. Shanghai has successfully contained its growth and de-velopment within manageable bounds by effectively dispersing people and activities to many preselected localities in the surrounding region.

Although decentralization was embodied in plans for the Seoul metro-politan area from 1964 onward, relentless population pressure and econom-ic growth augmented the unwanted size. Only in the late 1970s did growth rates on concentration indexes moderate. The Capital Region Plan, adopted in 1981, extends for a ten-year period. The plan covers a region of 12,489 square kilometres interacting spatially with Seoul. Interdependencies are especially important for land-uses, transportation, employment and housing, because the plan allows intraregional decentralization to have precedence over interurban dispersal.

The Capital Region has five subunits, each of which has a specific land-use plan and developmental strategy. The subunits are a zone of restricted development, a zone of controlled development, an area where development is encouraged, a zone for environmental conservation and a subregion for special development (Fig. 4.3). More than half of the region is reserved as open space for purposes of national security. Population growth will be accommodated in the second and third zones, which account for 45 per cent of the total region. The well-conceived plan requires coordination among thirty local and provincial governments, a factor that may be a formidable obstacle to implementation (Kim, 1983; Rondinelli, 1984). Ultimate success depends on strict preservation of the greenbelt around Seoul, stringent control of office developments and flourishing growth centres elsewhere in the country (Hwang, 1979:18).

Efforts to improve and enlarge metropolitan planning in Southeast Asia have been on a small scale. The most noteworthy administrative innovation has been the creation of the Metropolitan Manila Area, also known as the National Capital Region, in 1975. The area encompasses four cities and thirteen municipalities with 639 square kilometres and a population of 6,000,000 in 1980. An operational goal for the area is integrated planning and improved delivery of basic services to rectify the inefficiency of metropolitanwide services such as flood control, police and fire protection, traffic management and water supply. The 1976 structural plan provides for the relative location of activities, the spatial arrangement of functional areas and the desired pattern of metropolitan growth. The metropolitan region comprises an inner core of high-density development, an intermediate area of low-density residences and an outer area extending to fifty kilometres from the inner core (Viloria, 1981:295). Reorganization of metropolitan government in Manila is a first step in reducing bureaucratic excess and fiscal competition, but an assessment of the accomplishments of the new governance is overdùe.

Kuala Lumpur offers a case study that demonstrates time lags for legal provisions about metropolitan planning in face of rapid development. In 1974 the federal capital area was expanded by annexation to a total of 243 square kilometres, and the 1973 planning act for the city was applied to the newly annexed territory. But in the absence of a comprehensive plan for the

Figure 4.3: Development Zones in the Seoul Region

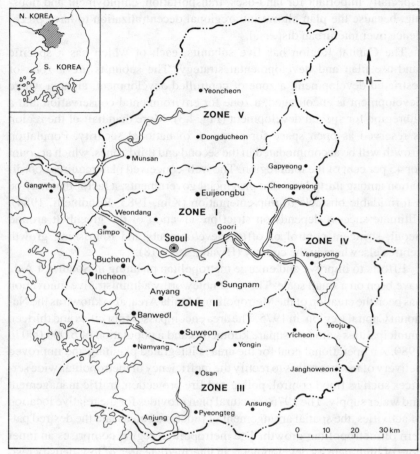

		Area (1977) (km²)	Manufacturing Employment Growth 1970–79
ZONE I	(Seoul)	627.1	83.5%
ZONE II	(Immediate South)	1,652.6	271.9%
ZONE III	(Outer South)	4,017.9	628.2%
ZONE IV	(Immediate North)	1,039.1	259.4%
ZONE V	(Outer North)	5,012.7	114.6%

entire territory, controls were piecemeal outside the city. An act in 1976 gave a new legal framework to planning and control on peninsular Malaysia outside the Federal Territory. This act emphasizes social, economic and physical factors as the bases for a comprehensive plan rather than one physically oriented. This emphasis was applied to the Federal Territory in 1982. A plan that is to be reviewed periodically envisages development of the capital region for the next twenty years (Dewan Bandaraya, 1982). It follows governmental economic guidelines, but it has been criticized for unduly favouring one ethnic group (Specter, 1984a).

There is a developmental plan for metropolitan Bangkok through 1990. The planning area includes the four municipalities of Greater Bangkok and a portion of the surrounding nonmunicipal land. The innovative feature of this plan is the recognition given to the influence of the large hinterland on the development of the city. An inner area of influence with a population of 2,800,000 measures 4,150 square kilometres. A middle area broadly corresponds to a zone encompassed by a circle with a radius of seventy-five kilometres centred on Bangkok. An outer area of influence consists of approximately fifty thousand square kilometres, with Chainat, Hua Hin, Kanchanaburi and Nakhon Nayok marking the limits of the city region of Bangkok (Donner, 1978:872–75).

The interminable north-south sprawl of Jakarta has led to such horrendous problems of providing services and of uncoordinated development that planners devised an innovative, alternative solution. Basically it extends the planning and developmental context of the city to a wide region that includes several adjacent urban centres. Named Jabotabek, this new region will include Jakarta, Bogor, Tangerang and Bekasi; the population for this region is projected to be 25,000,000 in 2003. In spite of a large commitment of governmental funds, implementation of many projects in the master plan rests on the ability of Jakarta and the associated cities to devise a new revenue structure to finance developments (Specter, 1984b). In the absence of adequate fiscal provisions, the new regional plan may merely diffuse the growth problems of Jakarta to a wider area.

SOCIAL POLICY

Several important policies are being used in Eastern Asia to control urban growth. Each policy emerged from an ideological and sociological context befitting a particular city. The first policy was the mass migration of Chinese urban dwellers to the countryside. To a degree, this movement contributed to stabilizing the size of the urban population in China. An example is the hovering of the figure for Shanghai around 10,000,000, as noted previously. One estimate placed the number involved in this exodus between 1961 and 1963 at 20,000,000 (Prybyla, 1975:153). The rustification programme that spanned approximately two decades beginning in the mid-1950s had several goals, both ideological and practical: to narrow differences between city and countryside and between physical labour and mental work, to alleviate the threat of urban unemployment and to use educated urban youths as catalysts for rural transformation. The movement generally succeeded in meeting its objectives through strong administrative controls, massive media propaganda and political exhortation. The programme encountered resistance and opposition from farmers, the rusticated youths and their families. It was abandoned after 1974.

Another, quite different policy affects only one city, not an entire country. The "closed city" policy for Jakarta was implemented in 1970 for new, jobless settlers. This drastic policy highlights the futility of other alternatives in stemming the tide of rural-urban migration. Under this policy each in-migrant is required to show evidence of employment and housing before being issued a residence permit. Furthermore, migrants must deposit with the city government for six months the equivalent of the return fare to the point of origin. The policy was intended to have a psychological effect rather than physically to prevent migration to the city (Critchfield, 1971). The evidence indicates mixed results. On the one hand, observers assert that there has been no noticeable drop in the growth rate from migration. On the other hand, the lowest-income groups tend to ignore the regulation, and others satisfy it by means that contribute to bribery and corruption (Suharso et al., 1975; Papanek, 1975).

Of the large cities in Eastern Asia, Seoul experienced the fastest growth between 1960 and 1980. Consequently this city perhaps best exemplifies the range of possible policy measures to curtail metropolitan growth. In 1960 Seoul had 2,400,000 inhabitants; twenty years later the total was 8,500,000, or a 254 per cent increase. Growth was particularly rapid in the 1960s when in-migration was the principal factor (Kwon, 1981b:80). The government recognized the gravity of the situation and applied a battery of policies that left untouched scarcely any facet of urban life. The primary intent was to check further uncontrolled growth by dispersing population and economic activities to other parts of the country.

By 1975 the population of Seoul had reached 6,800,000, or 41 per cent of the total urban population. There were few indications that the rate of growth was slackening. The government decided on a more systematic attack. A 1977 plan suggested redistributing population to other parts of the country over a ten-year period as well as short-term measures to achieve a reduced population for the city. Among the latter were restrictions on in-migration, encouragement of out-migration and accommodation of the dispersed groups in other regions. For the first time, the problem was viewed in a nationwide context and linked to industrial relocation and land-use plans. The plan was innovative for its preventive and development-oriented approach. A targeted population figure of 7,400,000 for 1986 was a source of dispute. The government proposed to stabilize the population at the 1977 level, but 4,000,000 inhabitants would have to be diverted to other places. Critics have viewed this policy as too extreme and jeopardizing the planned economic growth of the country (Hwang, 1979).

Concomitant with the planned redistribution was a strategy for industrial relocation to create employment opportunities in the outlying regions. Because most in-migrants come to Seoul in search of improved economic opportunities, industrial location is a key variable in designs to redistribute population. Experience to date suggests that relocatable industries are large pollution-causing enterprises, needing space for expansion, that may be classified as economically robust (Kwon, 1981b).

It is too early for full assessment of the various policy measures adopted with such determination by the South Korean government to control metropolitan growth. However, the annual average rate of 7 to 9 per cent population increase in previous years slowed to approximately 4 per cent by the late 1970s. During the past fifteen years the Seoul share of industrial employment and economic production has declined markedly on many indexes. Seoul accounted for 23.4 per cent of the firms on South Korean industrial estates in 1973; the proportion was 13.1 per cent in 1978 (Hwang, 1979:12–13). Nevertheless, a prime factor that runs counter to the decentralizing tendency has been the rapid growth of the service sector, particularly office development. This aspect must be restrained, if the decentralizing policy is to have a fair chance of attaining its goals (Hwang, 1980).

CONCLUSION

None of the macro strategies surveyed here has been entirely successful, but most have fulfilled to varying degrees the restraining or decentralizing objectives for which they were designed. Several factors seem to have a crucial role in determining success or failure for a strategy.

The need for coordination among implementing agencies is vividly illustrated by Seoul, where successive policies failed to achieve goals. Without effective plans for implementation, efforts to limit growth will be meaningless. The problem is especially acute where a metropolitan area is fragmented among competing administrative units.

Even the best-conceived plans for controlled growth cannot become reality without adequate funding. Tokyo, Jakarta and Bangkok have been unable to carry out some aspects of their plans because of fiscal constraints. On the other hand, much to the benefit of individuals, but to the detriment of the city, property, land and vehicles are grossly undertaxed in Jakarta and Bangkok. The central government consequently must provide a substantial portion of the city's expenditures with resultant deterioration of urban services.

This study supports the current planning philosophy that recommends inclusion of a large region for planning and operational strategies, if metropolitan growth-resistant policies are to succeed. This approach has been used in Shanghai, Seoul, Tokyo and Jakarta. To ensure success and integration of a large city with other urban centres and regions of a country, plans for city-region development should articulate a countrywide urbanization policy in order to relate them to both a regional and national context. Urbanization policies should be continually improved and refined.

REFERENCES

Critchfield, R. 1971. "The Plight of the Cities: Jakarta—The First to 'Close'." *Columbia Journal of World Business*, (6) 6(4):89–93.

Dewan, Bandaraya. 1982. *Kuala Lumpur Draft Structure Plan*. Kuala Lumpur.

Donner, Wolf. 1978. *The Five Faces of Thailand: An Economic Geography*. New York: St. Martin's Press.

Fung, Ka-iu. 1981. "Satellite Town Development in the Shanghai City Region." *Town Planning Review*, 52(1):26–46.

Hall, Peter. 1977. *The World Cities*, pp. 219–39. New York: McGraw-Hill.

Honjo, Masahiko. 1975. "Tokyo: Giant Metropolis of the Orient." In *World Capitals: Toward Guided Urbanization*, ed. H. W. Eldredge, pp. 340–87. New York: Anchor Press.

Hwang, Myo-chan. 1979. "A Search for a Development Strategy for the Capital Region of Korea." In *Metropolitan Planning: Issues and Policies*, ed. Y. H. Rho, and M. C. Hwang, pp. 3–32. Seoul: Korea Research Institute for Human Settlements.

————. 1980. "Planning Strategies for Metropolitan Seoul." In *The Year 2000: Urban Growth and Perspectives for Seoul*, ed. W. Kim, pp. 31–53. Seoul: Korea Planners Association.

Kim, Hyung-koon. 1981. "Social Factors of Migration from Rural to Urban Areas with Special Reference to Developing Countries: The Case of Korea." *Social Indicators Research*, 10:29–74.

Kim, Son-ung and Peter Donaldson. 1979. "Dealing with Seoul's Population Growth: Government Plans and Their Implementation." *Asian Survey*, 19(7):660–73.

Kim, Won. 1983. "Land Use Planning in a Rapidly Growing Metropolis: The Case of Seoul." *Asian Economies*, January:3–21.

Kwon, Won-yong. 1981a. "Seoul: A Dynamic Metropolis." In *Urbanization and Regional Development*, ed. M. Honjo, pp. 297–329. Singapore: Maruzen Asia.

————. 1981b. "A Study of the Economic Impact of Industrial Relocation: The Case of Seoul." *Urban Studies*, 18:73–90.

Papanek, G. V. 1975. "The Poor of Jakarta." *Economic Development and Cultural Change*, 24(1):1–27.

Prybyla, Jan S. 1975. "*Hsia-Fang*: The Economics and Politics of Rustication in China." *Pacific Affairs*, 48(2):153–72.

Rondinelli, Dennis. 1984. "Land Development Policy in South Korea." *Geographical Review*, 74:425–40.

Seoul Metropolitan Government (SMG). 1983. *Seoul: Metropolitan Administration*.

Shanghai shehui kexue yuan (SSKY), ed. 1983. *Shanghai jingji: 1949–1982* (The Economy of Shanghai, 1949–1982). Shanghai: Renmen chubanshe.

SMG. See Seoul Metropolitan Government.

Specter, Michael. 1984a. "The 'Small Town' Big City." *Far Eastern Economic Review*, 27 September:23–30.

————. 1984b. "A Sprawling, Thirsty Giant." *Far Eastern Economic Review*, 29 March:23–30.

SSKY. See Shanghai shehui kexue yuan.

Suharso, *et al.* 1975. *Migration and Education in Jakarta*. Jakarta: LEKNAS.

TMG. See Tokyo Metropolitan Government.

Tokyo Metropolitan Government (TMG). 1984a. *Long-Term Plan Tokyo Metropolis: "My Town Tokyo" Heading into the 21st Century*. TMG Municipal Library No. 18.

————. 1984b. *Plain Talk about Tokyo: The Administration of the Tokyo*

Metropolitan Government. 2nd ed. Tokyo.

Viloria, L. A. 1981. "Manila: Creation of a Metropolitan Government." In *Urbanization and Regional Development*, ed. M. Honjo, pp. 281–96. Singapore: Maruzen Asia.

White, Lynn T. 1981. "The Suburban Transformation." In *Shanghai: Revolution and Development in an Asian Metropolis*, ed. C. Howe, pp. 241–68. Cambridge: Cambridge University Press.

Yeh, Anthony G. O. and Peter K. W. Fong. 1984. "Public Housing and Urban Development in Hong Kong." *Third World Planning Review*, 6(1):79–94.

Yeung, Yue-man. 1985. *The Great Cities of Eastern Asia: Growing Pains and Policy Options*. Occasional Paper No. 69. Department of Geography, The Chinese University of Hong Kong.

PART III

Southeast Asia

5. Changing Southeast Asian Cities*

Among the events of the twentieth century, the astounding growth in world population together with its attendant concentration in urban places, will almost certainly be recorded as a revolutionary development in the history of mankind. As the population explosion in the Third World becomes increasingly serious, the ramifications and implications of accelerated urbanization in these countries have begun to attract increasing scholarly attention. Of those engaged in the task of evaluating urbanization in a developing region, Hauser (1957, 1961) was among the first to review the situation in Asia and the Far East, and in Latin America. His efforts were followed by Miner's (1967) and Beyer's (1967) studies of the urban situation in Africa and Latin America respectively. Breese (1966, 1969) broadened the geographic scope of enquiry by including all of the newly developing countries and, most recently, Dwyer (1972) addressed himself to Asian cities. Wheatley (1971) also has enlarged the stock of knowledge about city evolution and ancient urban genesis. At the same time substantive monographs on cities in individual developing countries have appeared with increasing rapidity (Turner, 1962; Hashim and Jones, 1967; Mabogunje, 1968; Lewis, 1971; Dwyer, 1971).

For the Southeast Asian region, McGee's pioneering treatise, *The Southeast Asian City*, was recently complemented by Jakobson and Prakash's (1971), which also included South Asia. In spite of the traditional research concern about cities by economists, sociologists, political scientists, planners, anthropologists, and geographers, there is an ironic dearth, at least for Southeast Asia, of these materials in any convenient form. Indeed, Alonso (1971:1) has drawn attention to the fact that the poverty of data is "an intrinsic condition of underdevelopment, not a happenstance." It is a modest attempt to present a multi-disciplinary perspective of cities in Southeast

---

*Co-authored with C. P. Lo.

Asia around 1970 that this volume was conceived. It is hoped that such a book will make available to the intending student a handy collection of papers which he can use as supplementary reading materials, to form the basis of seminar and tutorial discussions, and generally to further his understanding of cities in the region.

Southeast Asia, commonly defined geographically to include the peninsulas between India and China in addition to the Indonesian and Philippine archipelagos, is one of the least urbanized regions in the world. Only certain parts of Africa and Asia are characterized by a lower percentage of urban population, variously defined (Davis, 1972:191).[1] In 1970 (Fig. 5.1) only 20 per cent of the population in Southeast Asia lived in urban places, and 12 per cent in cities of 100,000 or more inhabitants.[2] Measured against the corresponding statistics of 14 per cent and 7 per cent in 1950, it is evident that in the post-war period rapid urbanization has been a characteristic of the region. In absolute terms, the urban population rose from 23.3 million in 1950 to 57.1 million in 1970. Although Southeast Asian countries are new and their cities few, the national modernizing process in many instances is closely linked to urban growth.

It would be ideal if one could relate urbanization in Southeast Asia to a body of theory. Unfortunately, no general theory of urbanization with wide applicability exists. Miner (1967:4) maintains that "it is the nature of the city, rather than the dullness of its students, which has so long precluded the discovery of a distinctive body of urban theory." One often has to be on guard against any wholesale application of Western-based theories to countries and situations with a vastly different societal setting. It is encouraging that many students of urbanization in the Third World, such as Miner (1967), Mabogunje (1968) and McGee (1971) have been in search of theoretical explanations to their studies. McGee's statements (1969a, 1969b, 1971) have been the most explicit of this objective for Southeast Asia, and he has extended the discussion elsewhere to the overall Third World situation (McGee, 1971).

---

[1]Davis indicated that of the twenty-two regions of the world, only five had in 1970 a smaller proportion of urban population than Southeast Asia. The five regions were South Central Asia, Western Africa, Middle and Southern Africa, Eastern Africa and Oceania.

[2]The data in the remainder of this paragraph are derived from Davis (1969:70).

While a formal theory of urbanization is still in the making, most of the research on Southeast Asia to date has been guided by hypotheses and concepts. This represents a more heuristic approach which attempts to discover generalities about these cities, leading hopefully in the end to theory formulation. Pioneering in this direction, Ginsburg (1955) made a general but important statement almost two decades ago, which drew attention to the functional dominance of one great city in each of the countries as a major characteristic of urbanization in Southeast Asia. Similarly, the colonial heritage and a comparable pattern of urban evolution were highlighted by Fryer (1953), Murphey (1966, 1969), Dwyer (1968), among others. Boeke (1953), Geertz (1963) and McGee (1970), moreover, have attempted to study aspects of urban development in a dualistic conceptual framework.

However, hypotheses and concepts are of uneven usefulness and utility. Indeed, the conceptual smog created by the application of some of these ideas is so dense that it will require a great deal of research and verification before the air is clear. One such example is the concept of "over-urbanization," originally introduced by Davis and Golden (1954) to describe those countries with a level of urbanization above a norm. The norm is a regression line obtained by correlating between the percentage of population living in urban areas and the proportion of the total labour force engaged in non-agricultural occupations for a large number of countries circa 1950. "Over-urbanization" was believed to be undesirable since it was supposedly caused by rural migrants being "pushed" rather than "pulled" into the urban areas by population pressure and rural poverty. Sovani (1964) has challenged, on the basis of contrary evidence, the soundness of the concept, but "over-urbanization" remains a common term in the lexicon of urban studies (e.g., Hauser, 1957; Ham, 1973). Allied to this is Breese's concept of "subsistence urbanization," underpinned by the notion of "shared poverty" (Wertheim, 1964). Applied specifically to Southeast Asia, McGee (1967) has employed still another concept, that of "pseudo-urbanization," to describe the process of city growth which has not been associated with a rate of growth of economic development fast enough to provide employment opportunities for rapidly increasing urban populations. Like other theses of urbanization, "pseudo-urbanization" must be carefully tested before it can be concluded with fairness whether it accurately depicts the Southeast Asian scene.

The basic assumption in the above concepts of urbanization is that urbanization is "true" only when it is accompanied by industrialization, in the manner that Western cities have developed. Generally speaking, employment becomes more plentiful in the wake of industrialization. As the development of manufacturing industries lags far behind urban growth in Southeast Asia, urbanization is, almost by definition, "subsistent," "pseudo," and at a level higher than what it should be. Considerable sectoral lags emerge, with different sectors of the economy developing at widely varying rates. Modern sectors, which are dependent upon building for the basic urban infrastructure, are slow in developing. One symptom of this pattern of development is the dominance of the tertiary sector, with "marginal" occupations exemplified by hawkers, becak drivers, porters and such like playing an unduly prominent role. Thus as a word of caution, tertiary employment must not be used as an index of a high level of economic development, in the way it can be applied in post-industrial societies. But the debate on the nature of urbanization is far from over. Laquian (1972b), Wittermans (1969) and Murphey (1966), for example, cast doubt on the fundamental premises of the above-mentioned hypotheses. Murphey (1966:12) is skeptical whether Western experience with the process of urbanization will be duplicated in Asia, or even whether urban growth will necessarily go as far. McGee (1969a:12) likewise questions the inevitability of the "urban revolution" in Southeast Asia.

On the other hand, there is the consensus that cities are funnels along which modernization and Westernization influences from the outside are directed in Southeast Asia. Modernization, according to Lerner (1967), should start with the plantation of urban life and the establishment of manufacturing industry, to be followed by the development of means of communication through mass media, culminating in the growth of political participation among a broad segment of the population. The modernization process seems to have taken a different course in Southeast Asia from what Lerner envisaged. Goodman (1973b:19–92), for example, argues that rapid urban growth has little impact on politics and that urban growth is not associated with the expansion of political participation. Nevertheless, it has become more common to view urban growth positively as an agent to stimulate national and regional development, a subject on which later paragraphs will refocus.

EVOLUTION OF SOUTHEAST ASIAN CITIES

Unlike East and South Asia, Southeast Asia in general does not have a strong urban tradition. The history of the pre-colonial era was essentially

Figure 5.1: The Urban Pattern in Southeast Asia, c. 1970

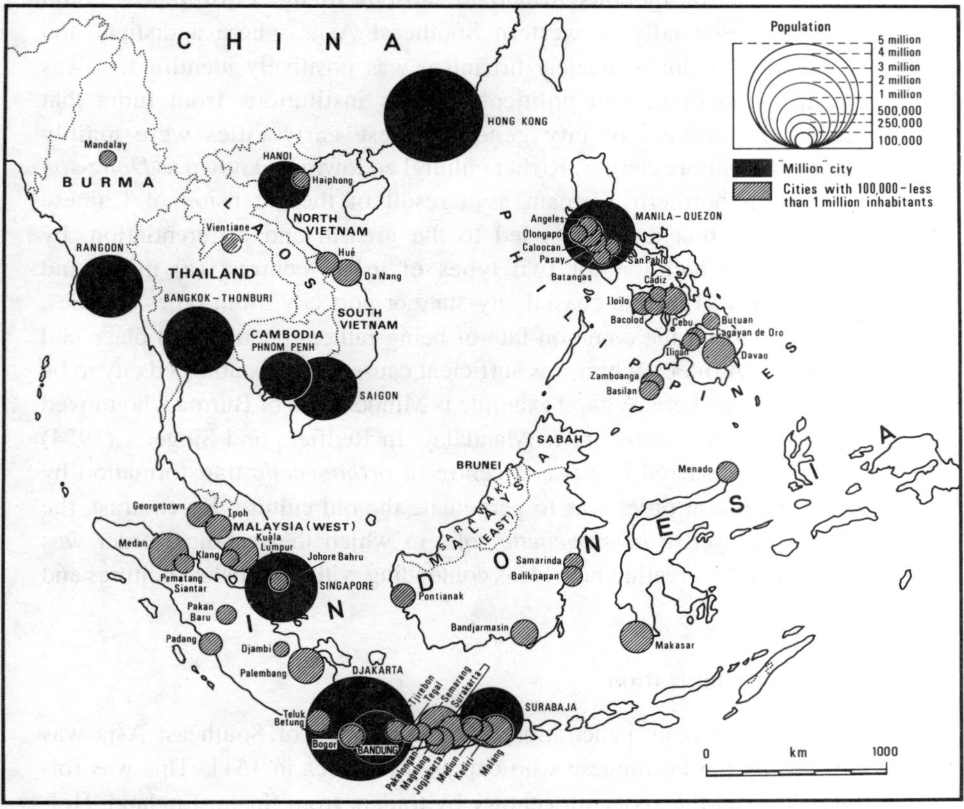

one writ on rural landscapes (Ginsburg, 1966); it was succeeded by a period marked by the founding of the great cities of Southeast Asia, created by European colonial powers. Generally speaking, three periods of urbanization may be distinguished.

Indigenous Urbanization

Evidence of indigenous urbanism, absent in the Philippines, could be found, especially in western Southeast Asia, where a distinct and independent realm of nuclear urbanism was positively identified; it was the diffusion of certain politico-religious institutions from India that started the process of city genesis. These early cities were mainly indigenous culture centres. Richer cultural endowment known as *Dong-son* came from northern Vietnam as a result of the extension of Chinese control into that area. This led to the growth and differentiation, by geographical location, of two types of urban centres: (a) the inland sacred city, and (b) the coastal city-state or port city. Both types of cities, however, shared the common fate of being rather ephemeral in place and prosperity. A ruler's whim was sufficient cause for an established city to be relocated elsewhere. A good example is Mindôn Min of Burma who moved his court from Amarapura to Mandalay. In Redfield and Singer's (1954) typology, the sacred city was a centre of *orthogenetic* transformation by which the moral order was to perpetuate the old culture. By contrast, the port city played a *heterogenetic* role, in which the technical order was responsible for creating new ideas contending with established cultures and civilization.

Colonial Urbanization

European economic penetration and colonization of Southeast Asia was initiated by the Portuguese who captured Malacca in 1511. This was followed later in the sixteenth century by traders from Spain, England, Holland and other European countries, thus ushering in a period of colonial urbanization in the region. Under foreign dominance, urban growth was accelerated after 1800 when the European powers adopted a policy of territorial and political imperialism (Murphey, 1969:73).

This phase of urbanization varied from one country to another according to the colonial policy of the European powers. Colonial urbanization in the

Philippines, for instance, revealed the great influence of the Church and the State more than any other country. The absence of a traditional urban system in the Philippines facilitated the Spaniards in establishing a hierarchy of settlements. As Doeppers (1972) observed, the Spaniards were not content to establish isolated trading posts or entrepôts, as other European colonial powers were. The economic policy of Spain at the early stage was to concentrate on the development of the galleon trade in Chinese goods and Indian cotton; these had to be collected in a single port for forwarding by galleon to Mexico and Spain. Manila, the foremost *barangay*, the basic political unit consisting of thirty to one hundred families, of the northern islands, was selected as the capital and port. Manila could therefore be regarded as an urban warehouse; and as the galleon exchange was firmly established, Manila became the foremost colonial capital in Asia by 1580. Notwithstanding this status, Manila remained a rather small centre of population when compared with cities developed in the nineteenth and twentieth centuries.

The change in Spanish economic policy came after 1764 when the galleon trade showed signs of decline as a result of competition by the British trade in the region. Spanish interest was thus diverted for the first time to develop the rich resources of the Philippines itself and to establish industries in the country, notably the manufacture of tobacco. In the 1790s Manila was opened to European and American vessels. Desires to develop other sectors of the colonial economy, especially in commerce, gave rise to a new policy of encouraging Chinese immigration so that after 1850 the Chinese population increased rapidly and penetrated most parts of the archipelago. Chinese-dominated central commercial districts henceforth became entrenched in all the large settlements. All these factors contributed towards the rapid growth of Manila. By the time when the Spaniards left the Philippines, Manila as the primate city dominated over other secondary centres in economy, culture and politics. Significantly, this pattern of urbanization in the Philippines appeared to be repeated in minor different shades in other countries in the region.

Manila may be viewed as the epitome of the colonial capital city of Southeast Asia. Sited invariably on a seaboard location for convenience of communications and transportation, these capital cities or "head links" (Spate, 1942) performed vital port functions. Much like Manila dominating over the Philippines, Rangoon, Bangkok, Singapore, Djakarta and Saigon-Cholon completely overshadowed lesser cities in their respective countries.

Ethnic segregation became a feature of the colonial city, because in pursuance of a policy by the colonial administrators to separate people of different cultural backgrounds, distinct ethnic quarters were a natural outgrowth. Immigrant groups, primarily from China and the Indian subcontinent, resided in demarcated areas, hence the beginning of Chinatowns and Indian quarters in these cities (Hodder, 1953). Coastal colonial cities became centres of heterogenetic transformation whereby new concepts and ideas came in through frequent outside contacts. Their role was analogous to that of the coastal city-state in the indigenous urbanization phase. However, since they were created to serve the needs of European colonial powers, the colonial cities should be more properly regarded functionally as parasitic instead of generative (Hoselitz, 1955). The pattern of development emerging under the Europeans was one which tended to emphasize the production of a few agricultural commodities and the exploitation of mineral resources for the international market. It was also a pattern of development which furthered directly the interests of the colonial powers, and only secondarily the Southeast Asian countries and cities which provided the resource base.

Post-colonial Urbanization

With decolonization and the rise of independent sovereign nations in Southeast Asia after World War II, the region entered a new phase of rapid urbanization which resulted in the further growth of the primate cities. However, the level of urbanization remains low. With the exception of the city-state of Singapore, in none of the countries does the urban population exceed 50 per cent of the total population.

In contrast to the phase of colonial urbanization when rapid urban growth stemmed in no small measure from considerable international migration of population, booming rates of urbanization in the present phase were fuelled by persistent high rates of natural increase in population on the one hand, and substantial rural-urban migration on the other. The "push-pull" model is often employed to account for migration motivations, although recent researchers tend to view it as over-simplified for the complex phenomenon of urbanward migration. Based on field work in the Kuala Lumpur area, McGee (1972) thus found the model inadequate to explain individual migrants' attitudes and social relations prior to the act of migration.

One of the consequences of large-scale rural-urban migration is the strains exerted on housing, schooling and other urban services. Overcrowding is conducive to illegal squatting by immigrants and residents who cannot afford other housing alternatives. Squatter encampments commonly take root in localities near the city centre where many squatter dwellers work, or in the city periphery, in preference, as McGee (1967:158) suggested, for more living space to urban amenities. In either case, Dwyer (1964) draws a warning of the detrimental effects if this form of migration is uncontrolled.

Building upon colonial foundations, modern Southeast Asian cities are dualistic in more than one sense. Dwyer (1968:354) has highlighted the dichotomy in physical form, the juxtaposition between the old and the new, Western and non-Western parts. The residential pattern is a hotchpotch of the poorest and the wealthiest elements, in both the city proper and the urban fringe. The urban economic base is differentiated by Geertz (1963) into a firm-centred sector and a bazaar sector, with widely varied functional roles and characteristics. These two sectors are always in competition for space and dominance. Depending on the stage of economic development, the penetration of the bazaar sector by the firm sector continues at different rates. Ethnically, the alien "fragments," notably of Chinese and Indian origin, prevail in certain spheres of the urban economy, but their participation in the political process is circumscribed (Goodman, 1971). The political vacuum left by the Europeans after independence was filled by a new elite, typically of indigenous stock and often schooled in Western institutions. The conciliation of potential conflicts of indigenous and alien ethnic communities ranks high on the agenda of most urban governments, as events in Kuala Lumpur in May 1969 and in Bandung in August 1973 serve as a constant reminder. The result of the above facets of dualism is an infinitely more complex ecological and cultural mosaic than the Western equivalent. To an untrained eye, Southeast Asian cities may even appear "chaotic."

At another level, counter-insurgency activities in certain Southeast Asian countries, such as Malaysia, the Philippines and South Vietnam in the early stages of independence, led to the growth of particularized urban forms and unwittingly induced urbanization. The common strategy adopted was to collect people from dispersed villages into a centralized, easily controlled settlement so that relocation would place them within the sphere of influence and protection of a government stronghold, such as a large city (Dow, 1965). During the emergency period in West Malaysia, a resettlement programme took the form of New Villages which were concentrated in the Kinta district, around Kuala Lumpur, and in the Johore districts of Segamat and Johore Bahru. One unforeseen result is that the pattern of New Villages tended to enhance the Chinese dominance of the urban sector and further compounded the traditional imbalance between the Chinese "fragment" and the Malays. In the Philippines, the resettlement programme was instituted in the early 1950s to counteract the insurgency of the Huk rebellion. The programme involved resettling the Huks who would lay down their arms in undeveloped land where government assistance would be given to develop agriculture. Finally, in South Vietnam counter-insurgency activities were in the guise of "Strategic Hamlets" which, forti-fied from existing settlements, were to provide homes for people within a radius of four or five kilometres. Not unlike the previous examples, it was a policy of consolidation.

THE NEXUS OF CHANGE

The foregoing account of Southeast Asian cities has underlined the theme of continual change to which the dynamics and consequences of the urban-ization process have been subjected from the very beginning. As the region is in the midst of a period of stirring changes, a complex of everchanging forces will continue to bear upon the urbanization process and shape the character of the end product. When the decade of the 1960s came to a close, McGee (1969b) was able to discern four distinct patterns of urbanization; rapid changes in many countries have led to more diversified developments.

One of the more notable results of the 1960s was the war-induced urban-ization in South Vietnam, where urban population increased from 22 per cent to 35 per cent in the decade 1960–1970 (Goodman, 1973a:9). As the Vietnam conflict came to an end, the consequences of this sharp rise in urban popula-tion have begun to be faced. Goodman (1973a), looking from the framework of migration, has indicated that Vietnamese urbanization, unlike the experi-ence in other Southeast Asian countries, was telescoped; that people migrat-ed to the cities less for fear of war than for insecurity; that urbanization has been a substitute for social change and political mobilization in the country-side; and that urbanization was a continuing phenomenon. Seltz (1969) further observed that urban services in Saigon, whose population increased by 45 per cent between 1960 and 1970, were strained to almost breaking point.[3]

In North Vietnam, the only communist nation in the region and the other major country affected by the Vietnam War, has adopted a military doctrine that "the villages and the cities advance together." Consequently, attempts have been made to improve the interaction between Haiphong and its nearby villages (Woodside, 1970). Lately, the declared goals have been geared to regional diversification and industrialization within the country and the government will embark on a programme of "urbanization of the villages."

The drive for change in Southeast Asia seems to be most clearly reflected in the changing roles of its cities, be these political, cultural, or economic. The cultural role which vacillated between orthogenetic and heterogenetic in the pre-colonial and colonial periods appears to swing after independence to the promulgation of indigenous cultures. Large cities, particularly the capital cities, are nurtured as symbols of national unity and national identity. However, in a plural society such as Malaysia, McGee (1963) has concluded that an orthogenetic role is not easily achieved, much as this is desired. The new urban roles, to summarize Murphey's (1969:72–73) thesis, are to act as the meeting grounds for the long-delayed confrontation between Asia and the West, between traditionalism and Westernization, the outcome of which is never a one-sided victory. But it is effectively through these urban gateways that the Southeast Asian countries see the world, and to a smaller extent, vice versa.

As seats of bureaucracies, financial and commercial headquarters, centres of modernization and bastions of Asian nationalism, Southeast Asian cities are committed to national development. It is from these urban beachheads that the impulses of economic development and modernization should be transmitted to the countryside and in the process uplift it (Goh, 1973). The strategy of operationalizing these objectives varies from one country to another. It is generally believed that an urban policy aimed at

---

[3]With the conclusion of the Vietnam War since April 1975, some redistribution of population must have occurred, especially with the southward influx of population into Saigon towards the end of the conflict. However, there are indications that the new government favoured a policy of returning in-migrants to their places of origin and that the pre-Communist urban structure of Saigon will continue to exercise its influence for a long period of time.

mitigating urban primacy is desired (Poethig, 1970), although Ginsburg (1972) cautions that for certain countries a "balanced urban hierarchy" need not necessarily be the only or even appropriate path to development. Whatever the choice, the need for a strategy of national urban development, connected to regional development and migration problems, seems universal (Laquian, 1972a). One can safely concur with Dwyer (1972; also Kaplan, 1968) that Southeast Asian cities, like other Asian cities, are centres of change. "However, in the context of Southeast Asia, it seems that a theoretical framework which regards the city as the prime catalyst of change must be discarded. Rather, the city must be seen as a symptom of processes operating at a societal level" (McGee, 1969a:18).

Indeed, the very concept of urbanization is going through changes. Jakobson and Prakash (1971:20) have stressed that urbanization is, in the context of South and Southeast Asia, no longer a simple process of urban growth; it is a process or an instrument of social change and development. This is indicative of not only a change in thinking about development itself but also a positive conviction that cities can be centres for generating development. Increasingly, urbanization is viewed as an independent variable which, when supported by a deliberate urban policy, promotes national development (Dotson, 1969; Friedmann, 1968). It is true that "urban villages" or "folk" conditions prevail in many Southeast Asian cities (Hauser, 1957:87), it cannot be denied that social change associated with city life is often nothing less than revolutionary.

While cities in Southeast Asia are changing and growing rapidly, the catalogue of urban problems continues to become longer. Fryer (1972) provides a summary of these problems, which included a chronic shortage of employment, continual rural-urban migration, shortage of housing, squatter settlements, inadequate facilities, among others. Countries and cities in the region differ markedly in their degree of success in grappling with these problems. The city-state of Singapore is often upheld as a model of success, especially in the provision of public housing, urban renewal and national development (Yeung, 1973). Many of Singapore's urban problems are typical of Southeast Asia, but the setting is not. In the quest for clues from the Singapore experience, one must not overlook the facts that it is an island-republic, in which many of the seemingly intractable urban problems, such as rural in-migration, are more manageable, and that it enjoys the second highest level of per capita gross national product in Asia after Japan.

Furthermore, one must consciously avoid uncritical transference of techniques or values in studying problems of cities in Southeast Asia. For instance, squatter colonies may appear to be from a Western point of view, a symbol of urban squalor, a health hazard and a problem area for law and order. Yet squatting may be regarded as positive evidence of the creative energy of the people, representing a substantial contribution to the national wealth (Alonso, 1971:4). In a similar vein, Laquian (1972:50) argued the need to distinguish between the "slums of hope" and "slums of despair," and warned against the danger of pronouncing "a blanket verdict of doom on many cities with varying characteristics."

REFERENCES

Alonso, W. 1971. *Planning and the Spatial Organization of the Metropolis in the Developing Countries*. Working Paper 153. Berkeley: Institute of Urban and Regional Development, University of California.

Beyer, G. H., ed. 1967. *The Urban Explosion in Latin America*. Ithaca: Cornell University Press.

Boeke, J. H. 1953. *Economics and Economic Policy of Dual Societies as Exemplified by Indonesia*. New York: Institute of Pacific Relations.

Breese, G. W. 1966. *Urbanization in Newly Developing Countries*. Englewood Cliffs: Prentice-Hall.

—————, ed. 1969. *The City in Newly Developing Countries: Readings on Urbanism and Urbanization*. Englewood Cliffs: Prentice-Hall.

Davis, Kingsley. 1969. *World Urbanization 1950–1970, Volume I*. Population Monograph Series, No. 4. Berkeley: Institute of International Studies, University of California.

—————. 1972. *World Urbanization 1950–1970, Volume II*. Population Monograph Series, No. 9. Berkeley: Institute of International Studies, University of California.

Davis, K. and H. H. Golden. 1954. "Urbanization and the Development of Pre-Industrial Areas." *Economic Development and Cultural Change*, 3:6–26.

Doeppers, D. F. 1972. "The Development of Philippine Cities before 1900." *Journal of Asian Studies*, 31:769–92.

Dotson, Arch. 1969. "Urbanization, Administration, and National Development: A Prolegomenon to Theory." *SEADAG Papers*. New York: Asia Society.

Dow, M. W. 1965. *Nation Building in Southeast Asia*. Boulder, Colorado: Pruett Press.

Dwyer, D. J. 1964. "The Problem of In-Migration and Squatter Settlement in Asian Cities: Two Case Studies, Manila and Victoria-Kowloon." *Asian Studies*, 2:145–69.

—————. 1968. "The City in the Developing World and the Example of Southeast Asia." *Geography*, 53:353–63.

—————, ed. 1971. *Asian Urbanization: A Hong Kong Casebook*. Hong Kong: Hong Kong University Press.

—————, ed. 1972. *The City as a Centre of Change in Asia*. Hong Kong: Hong Kong University Press.

Friedmann, John. 1968. "The Strategy of Deliberate Urbanization." *Journal of the American Institute of Planners*, 34:264–73.

Fryer, D. W. 1953. "The Million City in Southeast Asia." *Geographical Review*, 43:474–94.

—————. 1972. "Cities of Southeast Asia and Their Problems." *Focus*, 12.

Geertz, C. 1963. *Peddlers and Princes: Social Change and Economic Modernization in Two Indonesian Towns*. Chicago: University of Chicago Press.

Ginsburg, N. S. 1955. "The Great City in Southeast Asia." *American Journal of Sociology*, 60:455–62.

—————. 1966. "Urban Geography and 'Non-Western' Areas." In *The Study of Urbanization*, ed. P. M. Hauser and L. F. Schnore, pp. 311–46. New York: John Wiley.

—————. 1972. "Planning the Future of the Asian City." In Dwyer (1972), pp. 269–83.

Goh, Keng-swee. 1973. "Cities as Modernizers." *Insight*, August:46–50.

Goodman, A. E. 1971. "The Political Implications of Urban Development in Southeast Asia." *Economic Development and Cultural Change*, 20:117–30.

—————. 1973a. *The Causes and Consequences of Migration to Saigon, Vietnam*. Final Report to SEADAG. New York: Asia Society.

—————. 1973b. "The Political Consequences of Urban Growth Policies in Southeast Asia." Unpublished paper.

Ham, Euiyoung. 1973. "Urbanization and Asian Life-styles." *Annals*. American Academy of Political and Social Science, 405:104–13.

Hashim, S. H. and G. N. Jones. 1967. *Problems of Urbanization in Pakistan*. Karachi: National Institute of Public Administration.

Hauser, P. M., ed. 1957. *Urbanization in Asia and the Far East*. Calcutta: UNESCO Research Centre.

—————, ed. 1961. *Urbanization in Latin America*. Paris: UNESCO.

Hodder, B. W. 1953. "Racial Groupings in Singapore." *Malayan Journal of Tropical Geography*, 1:25–36.

Hoselitz, B. F. 1955. "Generative and Parasitic Cities." *Economic Development and Cultural Change*, 3:378–94.

Jakobson, Leo and Ved Prakash, eds. 1971. *Urbanization and National Development*. Beverly Hills: Sage Publications.

Kaplan, Milton. 1968. *The New Urban Debate*. Report of Pacific Conference of Urban Growth, A.I.D.

Laquian, A. A. 1972a. "The Need for National Urban Strategy in the Philippines." *SEADAG Papers*. New York: Asia Society.

—————. 1972b. "The Asian City and the Political Process." In Dwyer (1972), pp. 41–55.

Lerner, Daniel. 1967. "Comparative Analysis of Processes of Modernization." In Miner (1967), pp. 21–38.

Lewis, J. W., ed. 1971. *The City in Communist China*. Stanford: Stanford University Press.

McGee, T. G. 1963. "The Cultural Roles of Cities: A Case Study of Kuala Lumpur." *Journal of Tropical Geography*, 17:178–96.

————. 1967. *The Southeast Asian City*. London: G. Bell and Sons.

————. 1969a. "The Urbanization Process: Western Theory and Southeast Asian Experience." *SEADAG Papers*. New York: Asia Society.

————. 1969b. "Beach-Heads and Enclaves: The Urban Debate and Urbanization Process in Southeast Asia since 1945." First published in French in *Revue Tiers-Monde*, 12:115–44.

————. 1970. "Dualism in the Asian City: The Implications for City and Regional Planning." *The Third International Symposium on Regional Development*, pp. 34–47. Tokyo: Japan Centre for Asia Development Research.

————. 1971. *The Urbanization Process in the Third World: Explorations in Search of a Theory*. London: G. Bell and Sons.

————. 1972. "Rural-Urban Migration in a Plural Society: A Case Study of Malays in West Malaysia." In Dwyer (1972), pp. 108–24.

Mabogunje, A. L. 1968. *Urbanization in Nigeria*. London: University of London Press.

Miner, Horace, ed. 1967. *The City in Modern Africa*. London: Pall Mall Press.

Murphey, Rhoads. 1966. "Urbanization in Asia." *Ekistics*, 21:8–17.

————. 1969. "Traditionalism and Colonialism: Changing Urban Roles in Asia." *Journal of Asian Studies*, 29:67–84.

Poethig, R. P. 1970. "Needed: Philippine Urban Growth Centers." *Ekistics*, 30:384–86.

Redfield, R. and M. Singer. 1954. "The Cultural Roles of Cities." *Economic Development and Cultural Change*, 3:53–73.

Seltz, M. 1969. "Saigon 1969: Urbanization and Response, A Personal Memoir." *Journal of American Institute of Planners*, 36:310–13.

Sovani, N. V. 1964. "The Analysis of 'Over-Urbanization'." *Economic Development and Cultural Change*, 12:113–22.

Spate, O.H.K. 1942. "Factors in the Development of Capital Cities." *Geographical Review*, 32:622–31.

Turner, Roy, ed. 1962. *India's Urban Future*. Berkeley: University of California Press.

Wertheim, W. F. 1964. *East-West Parallels: Sociological Approaches to Modern Asia*. Chicago: Quandrangle Books.

Wheatley, Paul. 1971. *The Pivot of the Four Quarters: A Preliminary Enquiry into the Origins and Character of the Ancient Chinese City*. Chicago: Aldine.

Wittermans, E. 1969. "Urban Patterns of Indonesia: Variety and Change." Unpublished paper, Institute of Advanced Projects, University of Hawaii.

Woodside, A. 1970. "Decolonization and Agricultural Reform in North Vietnam." *Asian Survey*, 10:705–23.

Yeung, Yue-man. 1973. *National Development Policy and Urban Transformation in Singapore: A Study of Public Housing and the Marketing System*. Research Paper No. 149. Department of Geography, University of Chicago.

6. Southeast Asian Cities: Patterns of Growth and Transformation

INTRODUCTION

In the global perspective of population redistribution and spatial reorganization, the nineteenth century was noted for the remarkable urban transformation and attendant industrialization and rapid economic growth of the present developed countries rimming the North Atlantic (Weber, 1899; Lampard, 1955); the twentieth century may be distinguished by the phenomenal urban growth in developing countries. With cities in the Third World growing at an average annual rate of 5 per cent to 8 per cent, both Nelson (1970:393) and Davis (1965:49) observe that urban populations double every ten to fifteen years. Between 1950 and 1970, many large Southeast Asian cities indeed assumed such growth patterns. For instance, Djakarta, Bandung, Kuala Lumpur and Hanoi at least tripled their populations, while Surabaja, Medan, Rangoon, Manila and Saigon more than doubled theirs (Davis, 1969:197–99).

Despite these almost runaway growth rates of individual large cities, Southeast Asia remains one of the least urbanized regions in the world. Of the twenty-two regions delineated by Davis (1972:191), only five regions had in 1970 a proportion of their urban population smaller than that of Southeast Asia. In 1970 one person in five was regularly domiciled in urban places in Southeast Asia, a rate of population concentration comparable to that of the Dutch Netherlands and Britain in 1800 (Lampard, 1969:3). At the same time, with 12.1 per cent of the total population living in cities of 100,000 and over, the degree of urbanization was equivalent to that of Europe and North America between 1850 and 1900 (Lampard, 1965:548).

Author's note: This chapter was written before the recent political upheavals in Cambodia and before the radically different policies of the new regime with respect to Cambodia's major cities.

However, given the signs and portents of present trends, urbanization will almost certainly continue apace. Goldstein (1973:85) anticipates that by 2000, one-third of the region's population will live in cities and towns, and the urban population will increase by more than threefold from 60 million in 1970 to 203 million.

The foregoing brief account of urbanization trends in the region implies that urban growth may well be the mainspring of progress in Southeast Asia in the decades ahead. Tentative futuristic statements will thus be offered toward the end of the essay. The primary focus of this chapter, nevertheless, is to analyze the salient urban growth patterns since 1960, to evaluate development policies and strategies, and to examine aspects of transformation which urbanization, in the experience of developed economies, frequently entails.

URBAN GROWTH TRENDS

The survey begins here with regional trends (Davis, 1969:70). In the decade 1950–1960 the total population of Southeast Asia increased at an annual rate of 2.4 per cent, as compared with a 5.7 per cent increase in the urban population. The succeeding decade saw overall population growth accelerating at a rate of 2.8 per cent per year, while the annual increase of the urban population was slightly moderated at 5.0 per cent. Even at this reduced rate, the 1970 urban population will double itself in slightly over fourteen years.

That urban populations have been growing more rapidly than total populations is better illustrated in Table 6.1, which shows that all countries individually exhibit this pattern. Laos and North and South Vietnam, especially, had their urban population increasing in the last decade at rates at least two times the population increase as a whole. Table 6.1 bears out, in addition, the low degree of urbanization of individual countries. With the exception of Brunei, a tiny oil-rich British protectorate, and the city-republic of Singapore, none of the other countries had its urban population close to 40 per cent in 1970. It must be noted in this connection that the definition of "urban" widely varies, and in both Malaysia and the Philippines rather different census definitions of "urban" were applied in the 1970 census. Malaysia, for example, adopted in the 1970 census a threshold population of 10,000 for urban, instead of a threshold of 1,000 as in the 1947 and 1957 censuses (Ooi, 1975). Similarly, the Philippines used a more realistic but

TABLE 6.1
Urban Populations in Southeast Asia

Country	1960 Urban population in millions (1)	1960 Percentage of total (2)	1970 Urban population in millions (3)	1970 Percentage of total (4)	Annual growth rate 1960–1970 Urban (5)	Annual growth rate 1960–1970 Total (6)	GNP per capita (US$) (7)	Percentage of labour force in manufacturing industries (8)
Brunei	0.04	43.5	0.05	44.1	3.6	3.5[a]	1,793 (1971)[b]	4.3 (1971)
Burma	3.20	14.3	4.33	15.8	3.1	2.1	85 (1973)	—
Cambodia	0.55	10.1	0.88	12.8	4.8	3.2	130 (1970)	3.8 (1962)
Indonesia[c]	15.03	15.5	20.77	17.4	3.3	2.0	112 (1972)	7.4 (1971)
Laos	0.20	8.6	0.40	13.4	7.2	2.4	120 (1970)	—
Malaysia: West[d]	1.67 (1957)	26.5	2.53	28.7	3.3	2.6	391 (1972)	15.5 (1967)
East[e]	0.17 (1957)	14.0	0.26	15.8	3.3	2.4		6.6 (1960)
Philippines[f]	8.17	30.2	11.68	31.8	3.6	3.0	254 (1972)	14.5 (1967)
Singapore[g]	0.91 (1957)	63.1	1.25	60.1	2.5	2.4	1,780 (1973)	36.3 (1973)
Thailand	3.00	11.4	4.66	13.0	4.5	3.1	193 (1972)	6.0 (1966)
North Vietnam	2.29	14.2	5.28	23.9	8.9	2.8	100 (1970)	—
South Vietnam[h]	3.08	21.9	6.06	34.9	6.8	2.6	174 (1971)	5.0 (1966)

Sources: Columns 1 to 5: Davis (1969); Column 6: IBRD (1973); Column 7: UN (1973), IBRD (1973), FEER (1975), etc.; Column 8: ILO (1973), You and Yeh (1971), etc. unless otherwise indicated.

Notes: a. Davis (1969:151).

b. Chua (1975:22).

c. Milone (1966:3–4), Indonesia (1972).

d. Chander (1971), Ooi (1975), Saw (1973).

e. Chander (1969, 1970).

f. Mijares and Mazaret (1973:23).

g. Arumainathan (1973:231).

h. Goodman and Franks (1974:26).

more complicated set of criteria to define its urban population in the latest census. According to the new definition, 11.68 million people lived in urban places in the Philippines in 1970, which is almost 400,000 short if the old definition had been used (Mijares and Nazaret, 1973:23). In applying the new urban definitions, particularly in Malaysia, the level of urbanization may thus appear to be lower than reported in previous censuses. It should also be noted in Table 6.1 that the increase in the proportion of urban populations (columns 2 and 4) has, to varying degrees, been rather modest over the last decade; only Singapore recorded a reverse trend of a decreasing level of urban population, largely the result of a programme of successful decentralization of population through public housing construction (Yeung, 1973). On the other hand, the increment in urban populations (columns 1 and 3) between 1960 and 1970 has been rather substantial in most countries. This suggests, in the light of the generally modest increase in urbanization levels, that urban growth has proceeded in sympathy with the immutable trend of overall population growth.

When the survey is extended to individual countries, the available information is extremely uneven on the urban situation. Although little is known about the extent of population redistribution in the Indochina states, incessant warfare over decades has certainly been responsible for considerable induced migration towards the cities. It is therefore no accident that the two Vietnam states, Laos and Cambodia experienced the highest rates of urban growth in the last decade (Table 6.1). The high rate of urbanization in North Vietnam is rather surprising, since, at the height of the Vietnam conflict, American bombing was said to have caused massive evacuation from the cities. In South Vietnam the most dramatic population increases between 1960 and 1970 centred on small and middle-sized cities; cities in the 20,000 to 100,000 class increased from fifteen to twenty-eight, with a growth of 161 per cent in population, and cities in the 100,000 to 300,000 class jumped from two to six, recording a population inflation of 307 per cent (Goodman and Franks, 1974:26). Metropolitan Saigon escaped the major thrust of war-induced migration, its population having grown only by 26 per cent in the stated period, and the city developed, politically and administratively, more by decree than by evolution (Goodman, 1973:3).

Malaysia is another country which has witnessed guerilla war-induced urbanization. During the period of Emergency (1948–1960), as part of the strategy to combat guerillas, more than half a million inhabitants were moved from rural settlements to towns and New Villages in peninsular

Malaysia. More than seventy New Villages, each with a population of 2,000, were created (Lam, 1974; also Sandhu, 1964). This policy, while deployed with immense success against the insurgents, has had the unwitting effect of exacerbating the ethnic imbalance of the urban population further in favour of the Chinese, for most of the rural settlers involved in the programme were Chinese. In the period of 1957–1970, however, some of the rural folk, as Saw (1972:115) has observed, returned to their farms in the former terrorist infested areas, and the previous rural-urban drift was partly reversed. Consequently, the rate of growth of urbanization slowed down appreciably in the period 1957–1970, as compared with the previous intercensal period 1947–1957. From 1957 to 1970 there is evidence of migration up the settlement hierarchy, with thirteen settlements crossing the 10,000 threshold to become part of the forty-nine urban centres (Pryor, 1973; Ooi, 1975). However, the fastest growing urban places were the metropolitan areas of 75,000 and over, which experienced a 96.7 per cent increase in population (Lam, 1974). Of these centres, Kuala Lumpur has grown most rapidly, specifically in the direction of the Klang Valley towards Port Swettenham. So speedily had some of the large urban centres grown that by 1970, in eight of the nine largest cities, a substantial proportion of the population overspilled the urban boundaries; almost all these cities had become underbounded (Pryor, 1973:57). The expansion of the city area of Kuala Lumpur in 1974 from thirty-seven square miles to ninety-four square miles was in part motivated by this phenomenon of conurbation and metropolitanization (Ooi, 1975).

In another mainland Southeast Asian country, Thailand, which has one of the fastest growing populations in the region, there have been significant changes in the differential patterns of growth by city size and a tendency for urban development to permeate other regions outside the central region. Since 1960, while the primacy of Greater Bangkok remains unchallenged, the larger cities have accounted for the bulk of the urban population increase. Goldstein (1973:90) shows that, since 1947, the cities in the smaller size categories have been losing consistently their share of the total urban population to the larger centres. In 1947, for instance, almost one-half of the urban population lived in places under 20,000, but by 1967 the figure had declined to one-fifth. In a similar vein, Romm (1972:19) draws attention to the fact that in the decade 1960–1970 urban places with more than 20,000 people have grown at average annual rates greater than 7 per cent, whereas centres below that size category have grown more slowly than their natural rates of increase. Many smaller municipalities have in fact lost population by net outward migration. Romm further observes a trend towards equalization of the distribution of large urban centres among regions. In 1947, five of Thailand's ten largest municipalities were located in the central region. By 1970, the share of the other regions has increased significantly, indicative of perhaps the result of a policy of fostering economic and urban development in the other three regions in the north, northeast and south.

Within archipelagic Southeast Asia, the latest census results do suggest emergent trends of urban growth in Indonesia, by far the region's largest and most populous country. Between 1930 and 1971, the urban population grew at 4.7 per cent per year, while the overall population increased annually at 1.7 per cent (King, 1974:926). Table 6.1 indicates that the corresponding figures for the last decade are 3.3 per cent and 2.0 per cent. Like the Malaysian case, then, urban growth over the last decade has slowed down. More importantly, in comparing the growth rates of the twenty-seven cities of over 100,000 inhabitants in 1971 (22 in 1961), it is readily apparent that the decrease in their annual growth rate in the period 1961–1971 from the growth rate between 1930 and 1971 has been sharp (McNicoll and Mamas, 1973:47). In many cases, the recent growth rates are but a fraction of what they were in the earlier period. Only three cities maintained a higher rate than before. However, Djakarta still grew at a booming annual rate of 4.6 per cent over the last decade, which is a slight decline from the previous rate of 5.5 per cent. The other high growth cities are all located in Sumatra and Kalimantan, their high growth rates explanable by their late start and the fact that the age-old development policy to decentralize congested Java has lately been gaining some momentum. In spite of the slackened tempo of growth in the larger cities, Fisher (1967:183) maintains that

> in Indonesia it is the high density metropolitan core which is poverty stricken and in direct economic difficulty, whereas the more sparsely peopled and relatively unsophisticated outlying regions have enjoyed the highest standard of living and the brightest prospects for the future.

In a country as diverse as Indonesia, national averages often mask significant regional variations. Therefore, King (1974:927) has shown that, by region, Djakarta, Kalimantan, Sumatra and East Java have grown more rapidly in urban population in that descending order in the period 1961–1971.

Finally, in the Philippines, notwithstanding the small gain in the degree of urbanization between 1960 and 1970, the growth rate of the urban population has shown little signs of abatement (Mijares and Nazaret, 1973). In the period 1948–1960, the urban population grew at an average annual rate of 3.7 per cent, which declined only marginally to 3.6 per cent in the last intercensal period. Owing to the application of a unique set of definitional criteria for "urban" (including population density, size of settlement, and urban form and functions), the number of urban places in the Philippine urban system must rank among the highest in Southeast Asia. There was an increase of 807 urban places alone over the last decade, reaching a total number of 2,406 in 1970. The urban population is most unevenly distributed among the regions. In 1970, Manila and its suburbs, central Luzon, southern Luzon and adjacent islands, western Visayas and eastern Visayas together contained 76.8 per cent of the urban population. In other words, more than three-quarters of the urban population are concentrated in five of the ten regions. Not surprisingly, these five regions also reveal the highest degrees of urbanization. Aside from Manila and its suburbs, which may be regarded as totally urban, the most rapidly urbanized region in the decade 1960–1970 was southern Luzon and adjacent islands, where the level of urbanization increased from 33.9 per cent to 41.0 per cent, with an absolute increase of almost one million inhabitants living in urban places.

A BRIEF URBAN PROFILE

After a survey of trends of recent urban growth, it seems appropriate to summarize some of the salient characteristics of the product of the urbanization process and the urban dynamics before attention is turned to urban problems and strategies.

Although with the exception of the Philippines most of the present Southeast Asian countries had some form of cities before the advent of the Europeans, these urban phenomena were for the most part inland, ephemeral, "orthogenetic" cult entities which have been eclipsed by subsequent urban expansion. The pattern of contemporary urban development dates from European colonization of the region, beginning in the sixteenth century. Each of the Southeast Asian countries followed a pattern of development in which one city, almost invariably on a riverine or deltaic site for ease of external communications and transportation, was chosen to perform the main urban functions. These happened to be capital cities as well and soon developed to a size many times the size of the second largest city.

Many of these urban centres have grown to "million" primate cities, and their dominance has often been accentuated in the postcolonial period. In 1970 there were nine "million" cities in the region, which is an increase of four from the five studied by Fryer in the 1950s (Fryer, 1953). In step with the growth rate of the urban population, the growth of the primate cities was slightly slower in the period 1960–1970 than during the preceding decade. Djakarta's annual rate of growth declined from 10.8 per cent in the decade 1950–1960 to 4.6 per cent in the following decade, while the corresponding growth rates for Greater Bangkok decreased from 6.9 per cent to 4.8 per cent (Breese, 1969:78). However, even those growth rates are too large for the comfort of city administrators and policy-makers.

The pivotal role of the primate cities in the urban life of their countries can be easily gauged by the large proportion of the urban population they contain. These range from a low of 21.7 per cent for Djakarta to a high of 79.7 per cent for Phnom Penh. Classic examples of primacy are provided by Greater Bangkok and Metropolitan Manila, which completely overshadow the respective second largest cities of Chiengmai and Cebu. To illustrate the overwhelming dominance of Greater Bangkok, Romm (1972:7) maintains that it "contains 77 per cent of the nation's telephones and about half its motor vehicles, consumes 82 per cent of its electricity, generates 82 per cent of its business taxes and 73 per cent of its personal income taxes, holds 72 per cent of all commercial bank deposits, and absorbs 65 per cent of the annual investment in construction." A similar set of statistics can be assembled for Metropolitan Manila (Viloria, 1972). The predominance of Bangkok and Manila is so complete that one begins to question whether diseconomies of scale, agglomeration and centrality have set in.

Other important features of contemporary Southeast Asian cities pertain to the social and economic structures inherited from the colonial period. The urban population in most countries is ethnically diverse, with varying proportions of alien Asians, notably Chinese and Indians, who were recruited to help pioneer development under European colonialism. As later paragraphs will discuss, this multi-ethnic factor may pose a constraint to some development programmes. Another inherited feature is the dualistic economy, differentiated into a modern and a traditional sector, or in Geertz's (1963) terminology, into a firm-type sector and a bazaar-type sector, with little functional interaction between them. Yet both coexist. As a consequence, retailing outlets, transportation modes and industrial units are fragmented into a myriad of forms along two levels of operation.

Because of their easy entry, labour intensiveness and low visible productivity, bazaar-type functions are sometimes regarded as marginal and redun-
dant. Hawkers, pedicab drivers, domestic servants and shoeshine boys fall
into this category. However, in view of burgeoning urban populations in the
region, one must not underrate the role that these traditional occupations
(with their high labour-absorption capacities) contribute in employment
opportunities (Yeung, 1975a).

The dualistic urban structure throws into relief the nature of urbanization
in Southeast Asia. In contradistinction to the Western experience, urbanization in the region, as in much of the Third World, has not been accompanied
by industrialization and marked economic progress. Table 6.1 reaffirms that
the general economic well-being of the countries, as denoted by a low per
capita gross national product, is unsatisfactory and that the occupation
structure has not transformed itself to a relatively large manufacturing
work-force. Only Singapore and Malaysia are relatively advanced in economic terms. This condition of urban growth without commensurate expansion of economic opportunities has been variously termed "static expansion"
(Wertheim, 1964:216–17), "pseudo urbanization" (McGee, 1967) and
"urban involution" (Armstrong and McGee, 1968). As cities continue to
grow in the demographic sense without sufficient qualitative change, dualism persists, symptomatic of the underdevelopment of the countries at large.

What is the nature of urban dynamics which have been shaping contemporary Southeast Asian cities and the urbanization process? At least five
dynamic forces may be identified. Apart from the traditional sources of
growth arising from population dynamics and migration, there have been
significant changes in the urban population owing to warfare and insurgent
activities, city boundary expansion and census redefinition.

The demographic components of urbanization in Southeast Asia of
today and those in developed countries at a comparable stage of development are not exactly identical (McGee, 1971:164). In the developed countries concurrent high rates of births and deaths in their cities permitted
extensive rural-to-urban shift mediated by migration (Lampard, 1969:8).
Migration was the principal mechanism to attain their urban transformation,
for no evidence can be adduced to show that urban rates of natural increase
were higher than rural rates. Only in a few instances did the contribution by
natural increase outweigh that of migration (Lampard, 1973:13). On the
other hand, Southeast Asia is trapped in what Davis (1971) depicts as a
combination of pre-industrial fertility and post-industrial mortality. Crude

birth rates are generally over 40 per 1,000, but crude death rates are as low as less than 10 per 1,000 in Singapore and Malaysia (You *et al.*, 1974:460). Moreover, the data on differential annual growth rates between the urban population and the total population as presented in Table 6.1 appear to lend support to Davis's (1965) contention that the main factor in the rapid inflation of city population is derived from biological increase at an unprecedented rate rather than from rural-urban migration.

The prevailing patterns of population dynamics just described do not imply, nonetheless, that rural-urban migration does not contribute to overall urban growth. In fact, the ejective mechanism set in motion by lagging rural development and a progressively unfavourable man-land ratio has triggered a continual urbanward stream of population movement. The pressure felt by the primate cities is especially acute. In spite of the spotty evidence available for assessing the extent of rural in-migration to the primate cities, Sakornpan (1975:3; also Sternstein, 1974) indicates that of the 1.91 million native-born inhabitants in Greater Bangkok in 1960, one-quarter had been born in the provinces outside the metropolis. Similarly, almost half the residents in Manila had been born elsewhere (Hollnsteiner, 1976; also Dwyer, 1964), and about half of Djakarta's present annual growth results from migration (McNicoll and Mamas, 1973:33). In Malaysia, which has been pursuing the twin national goals of eradicating poverty and restructuring society—goals that underlie the Second Malaysia Plan (1971–1975)—indigenes have been encouraged to move into the cities. As a result, 14.9 per cent of the Malays lived in cities in 1970, as opposed to 11.2 per cent in 1957 (Ooi, 1975). As mentioned before, war-related factors have accounted for considerable migration of population from the rural areas to small and medium-sized urban centres in South Vietnam. However, the usual migration factors, including distance, are poor explanatory variables in the case of South Vietnam (Goodman, 1973).

Akin to the war-induced migration in Indochina was the reorganization of settlement forms stemming from counterinsurgency activities in the early stages of independence. These took place in Malaysia, the Philippines and South Vietnam and led to particularized urban forms. The common strategy was to collect people from dispersed villages into centralized, easily controlled centres. Malaysia's New Villages during the Emergency were an outgrowth of this strategy and have since then been integrated into the urban hierarchy. The Huk rebellion in the Philippines in the early 1950s was likewise calmed down by a resettlement programme which was geared to the rebels. Finally, in South Vietnam "Strategic Hamlets" were established and fortified out of existing settlements in order to counter-insurgency activities. All of these are policies of population consolidation and have unwittingly induced urbanization.

The remaining factors affecting urban change are city boundary expansion and new urban definitions used in the latest census, as alluded to before. Kuala Lumpur, for instance, extended in 1974 its city area by more than 150 per cent. When city-area redefinition of such a magnitude has taken place, sometimes the city takes on an entirely different name, such as Makasar in Sulawesi, which was recently renamed Ujung Pandang, to underscore its new entity.

URBAN PROBLEMS AND ISSUES

The galaxy of urban problems, such as housing shortages, inadequate jobs, insufficient infrastructural and social facilities, traffic jams, environmental deterioration and a high incidence of crimes, is by no means unique to Southeast Asian cities. Yet these problems bedevil particularly the primate cities which, from the standpoint of the total urban environment, are de-monstrably worse off than before. The urban situation is further aggravated in a generation of rising expectations, thanks to the success of the mass media and to the population and labour force explosions in the postwar period, the latter following on the heels of the former (Yeh and You, 1971). Needless to say, the primate cities differ greatly in their ability to cope with these problems. Singapore, perhaps more easily managed as a city-state, can be regarded as more successful in tackling its problems. The other larger cities are, unfortunately, hamstrung by a host of administrative, budgetary and organizational difficulties.

In the provision of public housing for the low-income groups, Singapore is without doubt far ahead of the other cities. Public housing construction, typically high-rise and large-scale, has been undertaken since 1960, not only as a programme to meet the initial housing shortage but as an agent for national development and nation-building as well (Yeung, 1973). With over 40 per cent of the total population residing in public flats in 1974, the impact that this form of development has had on the urban structure, political participation and the general way of life is indeed far-reaching (Yeh, 1975). Similar developments on a smaller scale have taken place in the larger urban places in Malaysia, such as Kuala Lumpur, Georgetown and Johore Bahru. Other cities, lacking adequate economic resources, have relied to a much smaller extent on high-rise residential development to meet housing shortages. Djakarta, Manila and Bangkok have adopted a sites-and-services approach, particularly in the more peripheral urban areas (Yeung, 1975b).

As a manifestation of prevailing housing shortages in Southeast Asian cities, at least one-quarter of the population in the primate cities live in squatter settlements (Hassan, 1972). Although most city governments are inclined to view squatter colonies as a passing stage of cities on the road to modernization, these urban elements figure prominently in the spatial patterning of contemporary Southeast Asian cities (Jackson, 1974). Laquian (1968), Hollnsteiner (1974), Poethig (1971) and Taylor (1973), among others, have recognized the positive contributions that squatters can make in nation-building. Laquian (1968, 1971) also demonstrates that slums and squatter areas are often stable and coherent economic and social entities bound by their own normative standards of social and functional relations.

Lack of employment opportunities is the compound of rapid population growth and sluggish economic development. The situation is particularly acute in the developing countries (Lewis, 1967), although Grant (1971) maintains that it is a global crisis. Singer (1970) has suggested that the international dualism in science and technology is in part responsible for the intensification of internal dualism in developing countries, where capital-intensive products and production methods are uncritically adopted, with attendant deleterious effects. Until the mid-1960s, unemployment even in relatively wealthy Singapore was higher than 10 per cent (Oshima, 1967); and in 1970 unemployment in metropolitan Malaysian areas reached 10.1 per cent, as compared with 5.4 per cent in the rural areas (Ooi, 1975). In order to prevent unemployment from becoming an explosive social issue, there is the need in many Southeast Asian countries to explore and expand labour-intensive technologies and to develop the informal sector.

Among the primary factors leading to a worsening urban environment is the horrendous increase in the number of automobiles. Most of the Southeast Asian cities, originally built for foot and hoof, are ill prepared for such demands as generated by the sixfold increase of automobiles in Greater Bangkok between 1957 and 1969 (Romm, 1972:87) or the threefold increase in Singapore over the same period (Yeung, 1973:101). Many city governments are now watching with interest how effective are some of the draconian measures that Singapore has brought to bear on curbing car ownership, including high road taxes and restricted entry to the central city area at peak hours. Additionally, crime rates reach their peak in the large cities, as for example in Greater Bangkok, where the incidence of crimes is seven times the country rate (Watanavanich, 1975:21) and in Metropolitan Manila, where it is sixty times higher than in the rest of the country (Laquian, 1972b:10). Lately, too, the problem of drug addiction has begun to affect some of the youthful population in the cities (Punahitamond, 1974). Broadly speaking, these observations are symptomatic of the pitfalls of the process of modernization and rapid social change, and before conditions can improve a number of basic issues with respect to the city's functional base and social priorities need to be resolved.

The first general issue has to do with the ecological relations between the city and the countryside. Notwithstanding contrary viewpoints, Keyfitz (1965) and other researchers propose that cities exist as part of a process that includes instituting a food surplus from the countryside. However, the size of the population of a city must be proportional to its productive capacity. When the productivity of secondary industries in the city remains low and other spheres of economic activities similarly fail to provide growth dynamism, the city may be considered to have grown beyond its productive means. They become "parasitic" and a burden to the country, as Reissman (1968:131) states:

> The countries ... where urban growth has progressed faster than industrial and middle class growth, are generally in a worse position than even the completely underdeveloped nations.

Under such conditions, frustrated individuals are likely to take on anomic and pathological attitudes and behaviour.

Second, widespread urban poverty, resulting from the lethargic economic transition, prevails in Southeast Asia. Income distribution in the primate cities is highly skewed, with only a fraction of the work force really able to sustain a relatively high standard of living. Eames and Goode (1973:256) make the pessimistic projection that the extent of material deprivation, unlike the Western experience, is likely to grow in developing Third World cities in default of a demographic transition and because of the legacy of colonial exploitation. In any event, despite the lack of a growing middle class to provide leadership for social change as in Western cities of the past (Murphey, 1954), issues of equity and wealth-sharing will probably become sharpened when a heightened sense of justice is acquired by the proletariat and the urban poor.

Insofar as considerable urban poverty persists, the indigenes are too ready to blame immigrant groups who often hold the economic reins of power in the cities. The Chinese in particular have become the target of a variety of nationalist policies, which range from harsh outright nationalization in Burma to benign toleration in Thailand (Golay *et al.*, 1969:452–459; Chang, 1973). In many countries concerned there was a clamor to extend the national revolution to the economy after the political battle with the European colonialists was over. According to Golay *et al.* (1969:455), the intensity of indigenism has been accelerated by urbanization, greater population mobility and the "nationalization" of the traditionally cosmopolitan capital cities. Thus, Dwyer (1972c:30; also Osborn, 1974) forewarns the possibility of a future urban-centred confrontation of formidable dimensions in Kuala Lumpur, to which rural Malay in-migration has continued rapidly. Herein also looms the uncertainty, as in other Southeast Asian cities, whether urban change is effected through radicalism or incremental change, through revolution or evolution.

Finally, much as they are desired, evolutionary changes are difficult to attain given the fragmented administrative structures and overlapping responsibilities in many metropolitan governments. Metropolitan Manila, for instance, is composed of five cities and twenty-three towns in four provinces, with twenty-eight separate and distinct administrative units (Hollnsteiner, 1974:105). With the present trend towards greater local autonomy, Laquian (1972a:643–44) also recognizes the obstacles in Metropolitan Manila to effective city governance and reform. Future accomplishments must await a restructuring of the governmental setup, with a view to establishing at least for some major urban services metropolitan-wide authorities.

DEVELOPMENT POLICIES AND STRATEGIES

If the present problems facing the large cities appear too daunting, it is hoped that an evaluation of development policies and strategies may provide some spots of optimism. It is fair to say that the will to develop is present in every Southeast Asian country, but the way to realize developmental goals in many cases is yet to be discovered. Unlike the struggle to win independence, which is readily targeted and terminable with victory, the struggle to achieve modernization and developmental change is a long and continuous process. It is also a complex process of mobilizing and organizing a country's total resources for the advancement of social and economic progress. In agrarian-based economies of the developing world, the key role that cities can play in the spatial diffusion of innovations and technologies is widely recognized by policy-makers and scholars (Goh, 1973; Mabogunji, 1973). It involves, in Friedmann's (1961) formulation, a social transformation in which there is a national integration of the social, political and economic space. This may take place via the spatial diffusion mechanism down the urban hierarchy and from urban centres to interurban peripheries. In the kaleidoscopic shifts of rulers and regimes in the region after World War II, one gains the impression that, as far as national integration of the space economy and planned developmental changes are concerned, successive governments are more dynastic than dynamic. Crook's (1971:253) characterization of the planning process in the Third World is certainly apt for Southeast Asia as well:

> Sectoral emphasis, especially at the national level, concentrates on economic change and has ignored physical and social dimensions. Environmental planning has frequently received a low priority and more often than not has been confined to the spatial arrangement of cities but not in context of regional urban systems or in the larger framework of the nation. Nations tend to view urbanization as a natural by-product of change and development rather than one of the components that ought to be manipulated as a means for achieving developmental goals.

However, the countries under review do provide a variety of developmental strategies which may vary in effectiveness but were born of the best intentions.

As indicated before, the preeminence of the primate cities is an outstanding feature of the urban systems in the region. Widely regarded as an unhealthy pattern of development, there has been no lack of alternative developmental strategies designed to alleviate primacy, to plan for decentralization and to develop a more "balanced" urban system. Bradley's (1971:181–82) statement summarizes this line of thinking:

> The sort of planned change likely to succeed in this heterogeneous region is one based on new urban centres to serve the large populations now remote from the cities. It requires devolution of decision making, education, business activity and cultural control away from the primate cities.... Irrespective of whether existing states remain intact, their present major cities will remain, for they already serve vital functions.

The need for urban dispersion is nowhere more urgently felt than in Bangkok, the region's classic primate city. Romm (1972:130–32) has reported a noticeable decentralization of industries with attendant employment opportunities and new housing construction beyond suburban Greater Bangkok. Towards the same end, plans are in the making for five major universities and other institutions of learning to resite or expand to new locations as far away as one hundred kilometres from the metropolis. Whether these policies will merely extend Bangkok's sphere of influence or be sufficient for secondary nodes of activities to sustain themselves remains to be seen. What is needed for Thailand is, in fact, not a Bangkok-related expansion of development, but rather policies aimed at a more "balanced" distribution of future urbanization and the formulation of a national urban strategy in which Bangkok is viewed in relation to the rest of the country and other urban centres are given enough opportunities to develop into important employment and cultural nuclei (Sakornpan, 1975:25).

In the Philippines, Laquian (1972b) also advocates the need for a national urban strategy. He recognizes that a national policy is embodied in the Philippine Four-Year Development Plan (1971–1974), but it has failed to spell out the way to overcome the spatial imbalance in which the agricultural sector has been lagging much behind the urban and industrial sectors. To translate development goals into reality, Laquian emphasizes, a national urban strategy is needed.

Other researchers have proposed for other countries more country-specific solutions. In a study of the development policy in Malaysia, for example, Osborn (1974:254) concludes that the most important problem for future development in that country is a reconciliation of the differing levels of income and opportunity between the rural rich and poor and between the urban rich and poor—most significantly between Malays and non-Malays. An alternative approach to current patterns of development is proposed, which calls for public capital investment and management in middle cities below the so-called "threshold of dynamism." Undynamic cities stagnate in the existing development policy which tend to be oriented towards Kuala Lumpur and the new towns. In a similar manner, were Indonesia to modernize itself effectively, Fisher (1967:185) prescribes the development of Java into a truly metropolitan region. This entails a three-pronged strategy of checking population growth in Java, of moving as many of the landless labourers from that island to useful construction work in the outer territories, and of expanding the industrial sector in Java itself.

In discussing the variety of urban strategies, it is necessary to stress the fact that population concentration is everywhere an *adaptive* process and urban tradition is country-unique (Lampard, 1965:539). The number and size of the cities in an urban system is the outcome of the interplay of four variables: population, environment, technology and organization (Lampard, 1965:522, 1969). The level of technological competence, the capacity for specialization and functional differentiation are crucial factors which will dictate (1) the fashion in which administrative, social and economic functions are articulated through the space economy and, indirectly, (2) the number, size and spacing of cities. So far, the theory and empiricism of the relationship between city-size distribution and economic development are at best conflicting (Berry, 1961, 1971; Hamzah, 1966; Böventer, 1973). Thus, city-size distribution per se must not be used as a policy tool in fashioning the course of economic development in a country. Despite the inordinate primacy of urban systems in most Southeast Asian countries, policies designed to create artificially or theoretically "balanced" urban hierarchies are certainly ill-founded (Ginsburg, 1972). While caution is needed to avoid planning and building a "balanced" city-size distribution for its own sake, the practical significance of national urban strategies, in conjunction with sectoral considerations, cannot be overemphasized. It should also be noted that in Southeast Asia, particularly in the archipelagic region, the extension of political-administrative authority from the capital city to the more distant regions is inhibited by distance and water bodies. As a result, the hold that Manila has upon Mindanao and that Kuala Lumpur has upon East Malaysia cannot realistically be said to be more than tenuous.

Apart from the urban development strategies reviewed above, regional development is often used as a policy instrument to improve urban-rural relations. At the present stage of development in most countries in the region, the underlying principles and rationale of regional development policies are more implicit than explicit. One way of inferring the implicit developmental strategies is to examine the pattern of allocation of public funds to different regions over periods of time, an approach which Osborn (1974) pioneered in Malaysia (also Unthavikul, 1970). With the general paucity of socioeconomic data in regional areal units in most of the countries, the approach is more often than not approximate and holds much scope for increasing sophistication and utility. Although growth centres may be identified only on the basis of one or two variables rather than from a host of variables which would allow pinpointing input-output linkages, lead or growth sectors and other critical levers of development, it is a step forward in reducing the dualistic pattern of development between the rural and the urban areas. Consequently, Poethig (1970) suggested that the rate of out-migration should be used as a criterion in the choice of growth centres, so that alternative points of attraction may be created to counteract the magnetic pull by Manila. Laquian (1973) also envisages growth poles to promote creeping urbanism which, used by Guyot (1969) originally, connotes a process of accelerating the spread of urban influence to the rural areas. Population migration is clearly linked to both of these strategies. More deliberate in dispersing the economic base is the suggestion by Tinker (1972:45; also Fryer, 1970:91) to build up small and medium-sized towns and industrial centres specializing in light and medium-scale industries.

These diverse approaches may suggest that while existing strategies in regional development are rudimentary, they do signify an awareness of the need to bridge the gap between the rural and the urban areas. Regional inequities in growth and resources complicate developmental priorities even in developed countries; and, where these are exacerbated by considerable urban-rural differences, it seems that some degree of efficiency will have to be compromised in order to narrow the gap between the rural and the urban sectors. This is a perennial debate of the dichotomy and trade-off between growth and equity. However, even a limited attack on the problem is an improvement on an otherwise helpless attitude to let development take its own course. As Onibokun (1973) has separately stated, the challenge of urbanization in developing countries is to evolve their own pragmatic comprehensive regional planning solutions. "Pragmatic" specifically implies selective actions, which are justified by scarce human and other resources at a country's disposal, but the decision- making must be preceded by a comprehensive endeavour to establish the interdependence of problems, with due regard to existing realities and constraints.

URBAN TRANSFORMATION CONSIDERED

The analysis so far of urbanization trends, problems and strategies has highlighted a range of experiences in Southeast Asian countries. It remains to examine the nature and extent of the urban transformation with its corollary changes in demographic, economic and social structures.

In the first place, a country may be said to be approaching an urban transformation when 40 per cent to 50 per cent of its population is concentrated in urban areas, or when from 25 per cent to 30 per cent live in large cities of 100,000 and over (Lampard, 1969:5–6). Judged by these yardsticks, no country except the city-state of Singapore in Southeast Asia is undergoing an urban transformation, as attested by the generally low proportion of urban populations (Table 6.1). On the basis of the second criterion of the percentage of the population living in large cities of 100,000 and over, the range is from no such population in Brunei to the highest of 17 per cent in West Malaysia (Davis, 1969:126–27). Nevertheless, the rate of population concentration or incremental urban share exceeds, to varying degrees, the rate of total population increase (Table 6.1). This means that urbanization is occurring in all countries and most rapidly in the battle-torn Indochina states. As Davis (1965) postulates, urbanization is a definite process for which there is a beginning and an end. For Southeast Asia there is no question that it is in the middle of accelerating urbanization, but, given the fact that urbanization already occurs ahead of economic development, it can be argued (Murphey, 1966) whether the region should for its own good allow unbridled urban growth to reach a level customarily considered the threshold of the urban transformation. In this sense, it is fortunate that the sustained rural-urban migration as witnessed in developed countries in the past has not been repeated in its full dimensions.

With the urban transformation only in its incipient stages, the accompanying changes in the economic and social structures also are short of a true transformation. Of course, many of these changes are mutually reinforcing. The ecological relations between the city and the countryside can be taken as an illustration. Countries in Europe and North America underwent the urban transformation at a time when the farming sector went through remarkable growth in productivity and output brought about by technological innovations and increasing commercialization. As a consequence, there was less demand for farm labourers, who migrated to the cities, which were able to sustain the urban majority because of the enlarged agricultural surplus (Lampard, 1969:14). These basic changes in agriculture are still eluding the farmers in Southeast Asia, where the Green Revolution over the last decade has not produced the much vaunted cornucopia (Jacoby, 1972; Brown, 1968). This also explains why the economy and the functional organization of industries or occupations have not significantly been modified from traditional norms. Agriculture at present engages by far the largest proportion of the labour force, ranging from a low of about 55 per cent in the Philippines and West Malaysia to a high of about 80 per cent in East Malaysia, Cambodia and Thailand, leaving Singapore out of this discussion (You and Yeh, 1971:526). In addition, little structural change of the economy is reflected in the continuing high share of agricultural earnings in the gross domestic product. Even in relatively prosperous West Malaysia, agriculture accounts for about 63 per cent of the GDP (Wikkra-matileke, 1972:484). The experience of the developed countries undergoing an urban transformation is such that as the gross national product grew, the proportion contributed by the agricultural output markedly and progressively decreased while nonagricultural sectors concomitantly gained their importance (Lampard, 1969:17). For lack of basic structural changes in the economy, Southeast Asian cities hence remain largely dualistic in character, marginal occupations abound and their populations grow despite restricted economic opportunities provided by limited industrialization.

Finally, considering the question of social change in Southeast Asian cities, revolutionary changes in life styles, behavioural patterns and social stratification have not yet affected the masses. McGee (1969:16) suggested that the persistence of pluralistic ethnic structures and a large bazaar sector have inhibited the kind of social change said to have occurred in Western cities. The normative standards of the Western "urban way of life" characterize a much smaller proportion of the urban population as compared with Western cities. Through the existence of squatter settlements and the bazaar sector, interlocking social and economic relations between city and rural folk continue. In fact, basic village forms of political and social organization prevail in these settlements (Laquian, 1971), and Hauser (1957) pointed to the persistence of "folk" conditions in many Southeast Asian cities. However, in view of the nature of urbanization in the region, Dwyer (1972c) has called attention to the city as a source of potential tensions, political conflict and extremist behaviour.

The far-reaching changes which went hand in hand with the urban transformation took more than a century to complete in Western cities. In the present period, when the aeroplane and the mule are put into use at the same time in the region, there are inevitably lags and overlaps between modernization and traditionalism. The period also provides an opportunity for these changes to be telescoped. Indeed, Hoan (1974:30) even argues for Southeast Asia that:

The region cannot afford the luxury of waiting for the slow transformations that accompanied urbanization in the West. It faces a grim future unless modernizing influences usually associated with urbanization can be made to operate in the rural context as well.

Some of the measures adopted by the countries concerned do suggest that they do not have the patience to wait for slow evolutionary changes; the urban policies employed sometimes smack instead of a touch of radicalism. One example is the "closed door" policy applied since 1970 in Djakarta, in an attempt to stem the tide of rural-urban migration. In-migrants are required to show evidence of employment and housing accommodations before they are issued residency permits. They are also required to deposit with the city government for six months the equivalent of return fare to the point of origin (Berry, 1973:100–101). The policy is only partially successful, for, as Petersen (1966:26–27) has observed, many sets of rules have been applied in the game to block urbanization in the developing countries; the goalkeepers have never won. Similarly, to implement the New Economic Policy under the Second Malaysia Plan, the Urban Development Authority has since 1971 carried out a number of urban renewal and other projects which specifically encourage Malay participation. The impact that these will have on spatial reorganization, ethnic patterning and relative economic roles is likely to be momentous and is being watched with care. Radical some of these changes may be, but change must come to effect progress. For Tinker (1969:116) has perspicaciously offered the comparison that, whereas in China, out of continuity will come change, out of change will emerge continuity in Southeast Asia.

FUTURE PROSPECTS

This essay should perhaps best be concluded by taking into account what future prospects should hold for Southeast Asian cities. The dramatic events that culminated in the ascendancy of Communist-led governments in Indochina in early 1975 have introduced new elements of uncertainty and political instability in the region, at least in the short run. Unquestionably, different development policies in which urban roles may be redefined will be adopted by the new governments. There is, however, little reason to believe that the Indochina states, guided by whatever political philosophies, would ignore the allomerative advantages inherent in the existing urban centres. In other words, Saigon, Phnom Penh and Vientiane will most probably continue as primate cities of their respective countries, but how these and other cities are related to one another and to overall developmental strategies can only be determined by later events.

The political and economic impact that the recent events in Indochina on other Southeast Asian countries remain to be assessed. However, it is clear from the high rates of growth of the primate cities discussed before that, barring dramatic declines in fertility rates or success in migration and population control, the majority of the primate cities will become gigantic urban agglomerations of ten million or more each by the year 2000 (McGee, 1972; Goldstein, 1973). Hamzah (1974) recognizes two opportunities in these huge urban regions: one, the integration of rural and urban occupations, thus effectively developing a viable domestic market and the other, the reduction of ethnic identification with certain economic activities. More broadly, however, futurism involving a long-term projection of socio-cultural change should be employed if the kind of developmental change being sought is forward-looking and realistic. After all, "the most important social change of our time is the spread of awareness that we have the ability to strive and deliberately to contrive change itself" (Berry, 1972:42).

A striking feature which emerges from this paper is that Southeast Asian cities are of greater relative poverty compared with Western cities. This condition is characteristic of other Third World countries too. If they are to follow the traditional approach to development, they would need to attain unrealizable rates of economic growth at 9 per cent to 11 per cent per year in the gross domestic product to achieve reasonable employment objectives (Grant, 1971:115). These rates, moreover, would absorb only the increase in labour force in nonagricultural jobs and would far exceed corresponding rates in developed countries at comparable stages of development. In comparison with Western cities, it would thus appear that a larger majority of urban poor and a larger marginal class will be with Southeast Asian cities for a long time. To cope with this persistent condition, Dwyer (1972b:52) advocates that "Cities for the poor will have to be consciously designed, rather than the poor fitted into cities basically designed for the convenience of the moderately wealthy and the rich." There is the need, for instance, to reorient urban planning and revise developmental strategies. One example, as suggested before, may be the development of the informal sector by virtue of its high labour absorption capacities. Another illustration is the question of transference of technology. In the face of current levels of development, it is probable that only medium-level and labour-intensive types of technology are appropriate for most Southeast Asian countries. Greater emphasis could conceivably be put on men rather than on machines, as Turner (1970:262) has summarized:

> By facing the fact that they cannot substitute machines for men, the developing countries may well show us how to use our own sophisticated tools in humane and genuinely constructive ways. Their only chance for development and survival, after all, is to use the few tools that they can afford to stimulate and support the initiative to the mass of the common people.

Furthermore, it is necessary to revise the expectations of economic growth for its own sake. Imitation of Western aspirations in pursuit of economic growth and social life styles would seem to lead inevitably to the same nightmarish visions of ecological and social malaise as in developed countries. Above all, population growth must be brought under control if real economic progress in the urban and rural sectors can be attained. In short, the countries in question must "aim for a pattern of economic development that ensures employment and equity instead of growth and dualism, and built cities that can offer adequate opportunities for personal development" (Hoan, 1974:34).

All these revisions of developmental goals imply that the planning style in general will have to shift from what Berry (1973:174) terms ameliorative problem-solving to allocative trend-modifying, that is, from planning for the present towards planning for the future. Whether and how soon the shift comes about depends on the speed at which present governments can tackle their problems and how realistically development is envisaged. At any rate, Southeast Asian cities of today and tomorrow must be viewed as a frontier of opportunity as well as a challenge to which the creative energies of the people may be harnessed to serve purposeful developmental ends.

REFERENCES

Armstrong, W. R. and T. G. McGee. 1968. "Revolutionary Change and the Third World City: A Theory of Urban Involution." *Civilisation*, 18:353–78.

Arumainathan, P. 1973. *Report on the Census of Population, 1970, Singapore*, Vol. 1. Singapore: Department of Statistics.

Berry, B.J.L. 1961. "City Size Distribution and Economic Development." *Economic Development and Cultural Change*, 9(July):573–87.

————. 1971. "City Size and Economic Development: Conceptual Synthesis and Policy Problems, with Special Reference to South and Southeast Asia." In *Urbanization and National Development*, ed. L. Jakobson and V. Prakash, pp. 111–15. Beverly Hills, Calif.: Sage.

————. 1972. "Deliberate Change in Spatial Systems: Goals, Strategies and Their Evaluation." *South African Geographical Journal*, 54(December):30–42.

————. 1973. *The Human Consequences of Urbanisation*. London: Macmillan.

Böventer, E. von. 1973. "City Size Systems: Theoretical Issues, Empirical Regularities and Planning Goals." *Urban Studies*, 10(June):145–62.

Bradley, J. 1971. *Asian Development Problems and Programmes*. New York: Free Press.

Breese, G., ed. 1969. *The City in Newly Developing Countries: Readings on Urbanism and Urbanization*. Englewood Cliffs, N.J.: Prentice-Hall.

Brown, L. R. 1968. "The Agricultural Revolution in Asia." *Foreign Affairs*, 46(July):688–98.

Chander, R. 1969. *Annual Bulletin of Statistics, Sabah, 1968–1969*. Kota Kinabalu: Sabah, Department of Statistics.

————. 1970. *Annual Bulletin of Statistics, Sarawak, 1972*. Kuching: Sarawak, Department of Statistics.

————. 1971. *1970 Population and Housing Census of Malaysia: Field Count Summary*. Kuala Lumpur: Malaysia, Department of Statistics.

Chang, D. W. 1973. "Current Status of Chinese Minorities in Southeast Asia." *Asian Survey*, 8(June):587–603.

Chua, W. 1975. "The Petroleum Industry of Brunei." Unpublished academic exercise. Singapore: Department of Geography, University of Singapore.

Crooks, R. J. 1971. "Planning for Developing Countries." *Journal of Royal Town Planning Institute*, 57(June):251–56.

Davis, D. 1965. "The Urbanization of the Human Population." *Scientific American*, 213(September):41–53.

————. 1969. *World Urbanization 1950–1970, Volume I*. Population Monograph Series, No. 4. Berkeley: University of California.

————. 1971. "The Role of Urbanization in the Developing Countries." Paper presented at Rehovot Conference.

————. 1972. *World Urbanization 1950–1970, Volume II*. Population Monograph Series, No. 9. Berkeley: University of California.

Dwyer, D. J. 1964. "The Problems of In-migration and Squatter Settlement in Asian Cities: Two Case Studies, Manila and Victoria-Kowloon." *Asian Studies*, 2(August):145–69.

————, ed. 1972a. *The City as a Centre of Change in Asia*. Hong Kong: Hong Kong

University Press.

————. 1972b. "Future (Urban) Shock." *Insight*, (May):49–52.

————. 1972c. "Urbanization as a Factor in the Political Development of Southeast Asia." *Journal of Oriental Studies*, 10:23–32.

Eames, E. and J. G. Goode. 1973. *Urban Poverty in a Cross-Cultural Context*. New York: Free Press.

Far Eastern Economic Review. 1975. *Asia 1975 Yearbook*. Hong Kong: Far Eastern Economic Review.

Fisher, C. A. 1967. "Economic Myth and Geographical Reality in Indonesia." *Modern Asian Studies*, 1:155–89.

Friedmann, J. 1961. "Cities in Social Transformation." *Comparative Studies in Society and History*, 4(November):86–103.

Fryer, D. W. 1953. "The Million City in Southeast Asia." *Geographical Review*, 43(October):474–94.

————. 1970. *Emerging Southeast Asia*. London: Philip and Sons.

Geertz, C. 1963. *Peddlers and Princes: Social Change and Economic Modernization in Two Indonesian Towns*. Chicago: University of Chicago Press.

Ginsburg, N. 1972. "Planning the Future of the Asian City." In *The City as a Centre of Change in Asia*, ed. D. J. Dwyer, pp. 269–83. Hong Kong: Hong Kong University Press.

Goh, K. S. 1973. "Cities as Modernizers." *Insight*, (August):46–50.

Golay, F. H., *et al.* 1969. *Underdevelopment and Economic Nationalism in Southeast Asia*. Ithaca, N.Y.: Cornell University Press.

Goldstein, S. 1973. "The Demography of Bangkok: The Case of a Primate City." In *Population, Politics and the Future of Southeast Asia*, ed. W. H. Wriggins and J. F. Guyot, pp. 81–119. New York: Columbia University Press.

Goodman, A. E. 1973. *The Causes and Consequences of Migration to Saigon, Vietnam: Final Report to SEADAG*. New York: Asia Society.

Goodman, A. E. and L. M. Franks. 1974. "Between War and Peace: A Profile of Migrants to Saigon." *SEADAG Papers*. New York: Asia Society.

Grant, J. P. 1971. "Marginal Man: The Global Unemployment Crisis." *Foreign Affairs*, 50(October):112–24.

Guyot, J. 1969. "Creeping Urbanism and Political Development in Malaysia." In *Comparative Urban Research: The Administration and Politics of Cities*, ed. R. T. Daland, pp. 124–61. Beverly Hills, Calif.: Sage.

Hamzah, S. 1966. "City Size Distribution of Southeast Asia." *Asian Studies*, 4(August):268–80.

————. 1974. "Trends in Urban Development, with Special Reference to Southeast Asia." Speech read at the Annual Conference of the Asia Foundation, Penang.

Hassan, R. 1972. "The Problem of Squatter Relocation in Southeast Asia." *Asia Research Bulletin*, 11(April):756–57; 12(May):843–43.

Hauser, P. M., ed. 1957. *Urbanization in Asia and the Far East*. Calcutta: UNESCO Research Centre.

Hauser, P. M. and L. F. Schnore, eds. 1965. *The Study of Urbanization*. New York: John Wiley.

Hoan, B. 1974. "Cities the Poor Build." *Insight*, (June):28–34.

Hollnsteiner, M. 1974. "The Case of 'The People Versus Mr. Urbano Planna y Administrator'." In *Development in the '70s*, ed. J. Hoyt, pp. 84–111. Manila.

————. 1976. "The Urbanization of Metropolitan Manila." In *Changing South-East Asian Cities*, ed. Y. M. Yeung and C. P. Lo. Kuala Lumpur: Oxford University Press.

ILO. see International Labour Office.

Indonesia, Republic of, Central Bureau of Statistics. 1972. *Indonesia, 1971 Population Census: Population by Province and Regency/Municipality*. Djakarta: Central Bureau of Statistics, Republic of Indonesia.

International Bank for Reconstruction and Development. 1973. "World Bank Atlas." *Finance and Development*, 10(March):26–27.

International Labour Office. 1973. *Year Book of Labour Statistics, 1973*. Geneva: International Labour Office.

Jackson, J. C. 1974. "Urban Squatters in Southeast Asia." *Geography*, 59(January):24–30.

Jacoby, E. H. 1972. "Effects of the 'Green Revolution' in South and Southeast Asia." *Modern Asian Studies*, 6:63–69.

Jakobson, L. and V. Prakash, eds. 1971. *Urbanization and National Development*. Beverly Hills, Calif.: Sage.

Keyfitz, N. 1965. "Political-economic Aspects of urbanization in South and Southeast Asia." In *The Study of Urbanization*, ed. P. M. Hauser and L. F. Schnore, pp. 265–309. New York: John Wiley.

King, D. Y. 1974. "Social Development in Indonesia: A Macro Analysis." *Asian Survey*, 14(October):918–35.

Lam, T. F. 1974. "Urban Land Use Policy and Development with Reference to Malaysia." Paper presented at the International Seminar on Urban Land Policy, Singapore.

Lampard, E. E. 1955. "The History of Cities in the Economically Advanced Area." *Economic Development and Cultural Change*, 3(January):81–102.

————. 1965. "Historical Aspects of Urbanization." In *The Study of Urbanization*, ed. P. M. Hauser and L. F. Schnore, pp. 519–54. New York: John Wiley.

————. 1969. "Historical Contours of Contemporary Urban Society: A Comparative View." *Journal of Contemporary History*, 4(July):3–25.

————. 1973. "The Urbanizing World." In *The Victorian City: Images and Realities* (Vol. 1), ed. H. J. Dyos and M. Wolf, pp. 3–57. London: Routledge and Kegan Paul.

Laquian, A. A. 1968. *Slums Are For People*. Manila: DM Press.

————. 1971. "Slums and Squatters in South and Southeast Asia." In *Urbanization and National Development*, ed. L. Jakobson and V. Prakash, pp. 183–203. Beverly Hills, Calif.: Sage.

—————. 1972a. "Manila." In *Great Cities of the World: Their Government, Politics and Planning* (3rd ed., Vol. 2), ed. W. A. Robson and D. C. Regan, pp. 605–44. London: Allen and Unwin.

—————. 1972b. "The Need for a National Urban Strategy in the Philippines." *SEADAG Papers*. New York: Asia Society.

—————. 1973. "Urban Tensions in Southeast Asia in the 1970s." In *Population, Politics, and the Future of Southeast Asia*, ed. W. H. Wriggins and J. F. Guyot, pp. 120–46. New York: Columbia University Press.

Lewis, W. A. 1967. "Unemployment in Developing Countries." *World Today*, 23(January):12–22.

Mabogunji, A. L. 1973. "Role of the City in the Modernization of Developing Countries." *Canadian Geographer*, 17(Spring):67–76.

McGee, T. G. 1967. *The Southeast Asian City*. London: G. Bell.

—————. 1969. "The Urbanization Process: Western Theory and Southeast Asian Experience." *SEADAG Papers*. New York: Asia Society.

—————. 1971. "Catalysts or Cancers? The Role of Cities in Asian Society." In *Urbanization and National Development*, ed. L. Jakobson and V. Prakash, pp. 157–81. Beverly Hills, Calif.: Sage.

—————. 1972. "Man and Environment in Southeast Asia: Ecology or Ecocide?" Unpublished paper. Partly published as "Urban Ecocide," *Insight*, (June):29–31.

McNicoll, G. and S.G.M. Mamas. 1973. *The Demographic Situation in Indonesia*. Papers of the East-West Population Institute, No. 28. Honolulu: East-West Population Institute.

Mijares, T. A. and F. V. Nazaret. 1973. *The Growth of Urban Population in the Philippines and Its Perspective*. Technical Paper No. 5. Manila: Republic of the Philippines, Bureau of the Census and Statistics.

Milone, P. D. 1966. *Urban Areas in Indonesia: Administrative and Census Concepts*. Research Series No. 10. Berkeley: Institute of International Studies, University of California.

Munson, F. P. 1968. *Area Handbook for Cambodia*. Washington, D.C.: U.S. Government Printing Office.

Murphey, R. 1954. "The City as the Centre of Change: Western Europe and China." *Annals of the Association of American Geographers*, 44:349–62.

—————. 1966. "Urbanization in Asia." *Ekistics*, 21(January):8–17.

Nelson, J. 1970. "The Urban Poor: Disruption or Political Integration in Third World Cities?" *World Politics*, 22(April):393–414.

Onibokun, A. 1973. "Urbanization in the Emerging Nations: A Challenge for Pragmatic Comprehensive Regional Planning." *Planning Outlook*, 13(Autumn):52–66.

Ooi, J. B. 1975. "Urbanization and the Urban Population in Peninsular Malaysia, 1970."

Journal of Tropical Geography, 40(June):40–47.

Osborn, J. 1974. *Area, Development Policy, and the Middle City in Malaysia*. Research Paper No. 153. Chicago: Department of Geography, University of Chicago.

Oshima, H. T. 1967. "Growth and Unemployment in Singapore." *Malayan Economic Review*, 7(October):32–58.

Petersen, W. 1966. "Urban Policies in Africa and Asia." *Population Review*, 10(January):24–35.

Poethig, R. P. 1970. "Needed: Philippine Urban Growth Centers." *Ekistics*, 30(November):384–86.

———. 1971. "The Squatters of Southeast Asia." *Ekistics*, 183(February):121–25.

Pryor, R. J. 1973. "The Changing Settlement System of West Malaysia." *Journal of Tropical Geography*, 37(December):53–67.

Punahitamond, S. 1974. *A Preliminary Study of the Problem of Narcotic Drugs and Related Issues in Thailand*. Bangkok: Social Science Research Institute, Chulalongkorn University.

Reissman, L. 1968. "Urbanization: A Typology of Change." In *Urbanism in World Perspective: A Reader*, ed. S. F. Fava, pp. 126–44. New York: Crowell.

Roberts, T. D. *et al.* 1969. *Area Handbook for Laos*. Washington, D.C.: U.S. Government Printing Office.

Romm, J. 1972. *Urbanization in Thailand*. New York: Ford Foundation.

Sakornpan, C. 1975. "The Social Aspects of Low-Cost Housing." *IDRC-supported Low-Cost Housing, Thailand Monograph*. Bangkok.

Sandhu, K. S. 1964. "Emergency Resettlement in Malaya." *Journal of Tropical Geography*, 18(August):157–83.

Saw, S. H. 1972. "Patterns of Urbanization in West Malaysia, 1911–1970." *Malayan Economic Review*, 17(October):114–20.

Singer, H. W. 1970. "Dualism Revisited: A New Approach to the Problems of the Dual Society in Developing Countries." *Journal of Development Studies*, 7(October):60–75.

Sternstein, L. 1974. "Migration to and from Bangkok." *Annals of the Association of American Geographers*, 64(March):138–47.

Taylor, J. L. 1973. "The Slums and Squatter Settlements of Southeast Asian Cities." In *Kuala Lumpur Forum*, pp. 175–89. Kuala Lumpur: Edinfo Press.

Thailand, Republic of, National Statistical Office. 1973. *1970 Population and Housing Census*. Bangkok: National Statistical Office, Republic of Thailand.

Tinker, H. 1969. "Continuity and Change in Asian Societies." *Modern Asian Studies*, 3:97–116.

———. 1972. *Race and the Third World Today*. New York: Ford Foundation.

Turner, J.F.C. 1970. "Squatter Settlements in Developing Countries." In *Toward a National Urban Policy*, ed. D. P. Moynihan, pp. 250–63. New York: Basic Books.

United Nations. 1974. *Yearbook of Statistics, 1973*. New York: United Nations.

Unthavikul, P. 1970. "Regional Planning and Development: Thailand." *Ekistics*, 180(November):416–23.

Viloria, L. A. 1972. "The Mileños: Significant Elites in Urban Development and Nation-building in the Philippines." In *The City as a Centre of Change in Asia*, ed. D. J. Dwyer, pp. 16–28. Hong Kong: Hong Kong University Press.

Watanavanich, P. 1975. "Urbanization of the Bangkok Region: A Study of the Relations of Crime and Other Social Factors." Unpublished paper. Bangkok: Thai University Research Associates.

Weber, A. F. 1899. *The Growth of Cities in the Nineteenth Century*. New York: Macmillan.

Wertheim, W. F. 1964. *East-West Parallels: Sociological Approaches to Modern Asia*. Chicago: Quadrangle Books.

Wikkramatileke. 1972. "The Jengka Triangle, West Malaysia: A Regional Development Project." *Geographical Review*, 62(October):479–500.

Wriggins, W. H. and J. F. Guyot, eds. 1973. *Population, Politics, and the Future of Southeast Asia*. New York: Columbia University Press.

Yeh, S., ed. 1975. *Public Housing in Singapore: A Multi-disciplinary Study*. Singapore: Singapore University Press.

Yeh, S. and P. S. You. 1971. "Labour Force Supply in Southeast Asia." *Malayan Economic Review*, 15(October):25–54.

Yeung, Y. M. 1973. *National Development Policy and Urban Transformation in Singapore: A Study of Public Housing and the Marketing System*. Research Paper No. 149. Chicago: Department of Geography, University of Chicago.

————. 1975a. "Hawkers and Vendors: Dualism in Southeast Asian Cities." Paper presented at the Annual Meeting of the Association of American Geographers, Milwaukee.

————. 1975b. "Locational Aspects of Low-Cost Housing Development in Southeast Asia." Paper presented at the IDRC-supported Low-Cost Housing Conference, Tagaytay City, Philippines.

Yeung, Y. M. and C. P. Lo, eds. 1976. *Changing South-East Asian Cities*. Singapore: Oxford University Press. (Included in this book as Chapter 5.)

You, P. S. and S. Yeh. 1971. "Aspects of Population Growth and Population Policy." In *ADB, Southeast Asia's Economy in the 1970s*, pp. 448–580. London: Longman.

You, P. S., *et al.* 1974. "Social Policy and Population Growth in South-East Asia." *International Labour Review*, (May):459–70.

7. The Urban Environment in Southeast Asia: Challenge and Opportunity*

INTRODUCTION

As a region, Southeast Asia is characterized by an overall low level of urbanization but also by a high degree of primacy. However, the increase in urban population has been outstripping the growth of the population as a whole. In the decade of the 1950s, the total population of Southeast Asia increased at an annual rate of 2.4 per cent, while the urban population grew at 5.7 per cent. In the succeeding decade the corresponding figures were 2.8 per cent and 5.0 per cent. Even at the latter reduced rate, the 1970 urban population of Southeast Asia will double in slightly over fourteen years and, according to one projection, its 1970 urban population of sixty million will multiply threefold by the year 2000 (Goldstein, 1973:85). Whereas one in five persons of the region lived in cities in 1970, one third of the total population will live there by the end of this century. The implication to be drawn from these growth trends is that the urban component of the population will loom increasingly large in the development of Southeast Asian countries in the future.

Within the urban sector the saliency of the primate cities, which are many times the size of the second largest cities, is readily apparent in the majority of the Southeast Asian countries (Table 7.1). Although the rate of population increase in some of these cities had slowed down in the decade 1960–1970 compared with the preceding decade, the growth rates as shown for most capital and/or million cities are still too large for the comfort of city administrators and policy-makers (Breese, 1969:78). At the present rate of growth, some cities will double their population in a little over ten

*Reprinted with permission of the publisher from R. D. Hill and J. M. Bray (eds.), *Geography and the Environment in Southeast Asia* (Hong Kong: Hong Kong University Press, 1978), pp. 17–33.

TABLE 7.1
Capital and/or Million Cities of Southeast Asia, 1970

City	Population in millions		Annual growth rate (1960–1970)	Percentage of urban population	Primacy index[a]
	1960 (1)	1970 (2)	(3)		
Rangoon	0.88	1.20	3.1	22.7	4.00
Phnom Penh	0.34	0.70	7.6	79.7	13.10[b]
Greater Jakarta[c]	2.97	4.58	4.6	21.7	3.44
Surabaya[c]	1.01	1.33	2.8	6.3	—
Bandung[c]	0.97	1.20	2.1	5.7	—
Vientiane	0.11	0.21	6.3	52.5	8.70[d]
Kuala Lumpur (metropolitan area)[e]	0.31 (1957)	0.45	2.8	17.8	1.67
Manila (metropolitan area)[f]	2.12	3.18	4.2	46.2	11.50
Singapore[g]	0.91 (1957)	1.25	0.7	60.1	—
Greater Bangkok[h]	1.80	2.92	4.8	62.7	34.90
Hanoi	0.64	1.40	8.1	26.5	2.33
Saigon (metropolitan area)[i]	2.29	3.32	1.4	69.2	8.60

Source: Columns 1 to 3, Davis (1969), unless otherwise indicated.
Notes: a. The ratio of the largest city to the second largest city.
        b. Munson (1968:33).
        c. Milone (1966:157); McNicoll and Mamas (1973:47).
        d. Roberts (1969:41).
        e. Saw (1972).
        f. Hollnsteiner (1976).
        g. Arumainathan (1973:231).
        h. National Statistical Office (1973).
        i. Goodman and Franks (1974:29).

years. The pivotal role that these primate cities play in their respective countries can be easily inferred from the very large proportion of the urban population which they contain. They range from a low of 21.7 per cent for Jakarta to a high of 79.7 per cent for Phnom Penh. Classic examples of primacy are provided by Greater Bangkok and Metropolitan Manila which completely overshadow their respective urban systems in economic, social and administrative terms (Romm, 1972:7; Viloria, 1972).

It is in the urban environment of these primate cities that the greatest challenge is posed to city administrations to provide enough jobs, decent housing, basic infrastructure, free-flowing traffic and, ideally, the machinery to transmit positive growth-generating impulses down the urban hierarchy and to the countryside. The urban environment in some cases has been visibly and functionally deteriorating, to such an extent that an urban crisis is said to be at hand.

THE URBAN CHALLENGE

Many of the metropolitan governments of Southeast Asia are now faced with an urban challenge of unprecedented proportions in their history of governance. From certain perspectives, it may even be argued that this challenge is more daunting than was faced in the developed countries at a comparable stage of development. Urbanization in the region, as in many parts of the developing world, has been racing ahead independently of industrialization and economic growth. An urban transformation measured in demographic, economic and social correlates cannot be said to have occurred in Southeast Asia as a whole (Yeung, 1976). The economic structure in many Southeast Asian countries is little modified from the traditional norm in which the highest proportion of the labour force is engaged in agricultural occupations. If the city-state of Singapore is excluded, the proportion of the labour force engaged in agriculture ranges from a low of about 55 per cent in the Philippines and Peninsular Malaysia to a high of about 80 per cent in East Malaysia, Cambodia and Thailand. Despite limited progress in grain output associated with the Green Revolution over the past decade, the remarkable upsurge in agricultural productivity and output that accompanied the urban transformation of the developed countries is still nowhere in sight in Southeast Asia. In the cities, too, there has been only a limited reorientation of the urban economy towards manufacturing industries. The combined result of the lack of basic changes in the economy is the persistence of relatively low annual per capita gross national products, which ranged in the early 1970s from a low of US$85 for Burma to a high of US$1,793 for Brunei (Yeung, 1976). As a consequence, urban functions are increasingly "involuted" (Armstrong and McGee, 1968) and dualistic economies, symptomatic of underdevelopment at large, are prevalent (McGee, 1970; Yeung, 1977). Unemployment and underemployment are becoming major developmental and social problems which confront the city governments (Oshima, 1967; Ooi, 1975). In part, these employment conditions result from the postwar population explosion and labour explosion, one following on the heels of the other (Yeh and You, 1971).

In spite of the absence of basic structural changes in the economy and restricted employment prospects, urban growth and urbanization continue to gain pace through considerable rural-urban migration and natural increase. The population dynamics of the region may be depicted by what Davis (1971) termed a combination of pre-industrial fertility and post-industrial mortality. Crude birth rates are generally over forty per thousand, but crude death rates are as low as less than ten per thousand in Singapore and Malaysia (You *et al.*, 1974:460). Cityward migration has also been triggered by war-related factors, as has been the case in Peninsular Malaysia (Sandhu, 1964) and Indochina (Goodman, 1973). In a different context, under the Second Malaysia Plan (1971–1975), *bumiputras* have been encouraged to move into the cities, with far-reaching repercussions for national development and inter-ethnic relations.

A consequence of government-induced rural-urban migration is the challenge posed, to varying degrees, to city governments in mediating among ethnic, religious and cultural differences inherited from a pattern of colonial development. In both the pre-colonial and colonial city, ethnic segregation was practised so that people of the same ethnic group but of varying socio-economic backgrounds tended to live in close proximity (Hodder, 1953). Occupational specialization along ethnic lines could often be identified. Under the impact of modernization and urbanization, Neville (1966) noted the weakened basis of residential localization and occupational specialization with ethnic affiliation. Lately, this undermining of ethnic identification with residence and jobs has steadily become more widespread. Evers (1975), for example, has suggested that increased residential segregation by socio-economic status rather than by race has occurred in the cities of the region. In place of the racial or ethnic group, social class denoted by income, wealth and occupation has gradually become a new criterion for residential separation. In a detailed study of residential mobility in Singapore, Teo (1976:55–56) has gathered evidence to indicate that a process of residential allocation by class or socioeconomic differences instead of ethnicity has been at play. If the above hypothesis can be fully substantiated, it is clear that profound changes are taking place in the spatial organization and urban ecology of Southeast Asian cities. In addition to the hitherto occasional civil disturbance springing from ethnic differences, city governments will have to alert themselves to a potential conflict based on class lines.

Finally, as a heightened sense of social justice is developed amongst the proletariat and the urban poor, the question of growth and equity has to be faced. The prevailing trend in many of the large cities is an ever-widening chasm between the urban rich and the urban poor. While the former increasingly indulge in conspicuous consumption, the latter are struggling for a life of subsistence in urban slums and squatter settlements. Additionally, the wider ecological relationship between city and countryside has to be reviewed critically since growing urban-rural imbalance may lead in the end to the demise of the cities themselves (Smith, 1976). All this requires difficult decisions on income distribution and equitable sharing if city governments are to experience evolutionary rather than revolutionary change.

In short, the urban challenge being faced by many urban governments in the region is how to keep the city economically vibrant and physically functional and growing in an orderly manner. Viewed against the general background of a plural society, persistent dualism, widespread urban poverty, a teeming population, a labour explosion, a sluggish economic transition and minuscule budgets, the challenge is indeed enormous. It is the task of city administrations not only to plan for day-to-day activities and sustenance, but also to plan with medium to longer-term perspectives for coming generations. With the exception of Singapore, almost every national and metropolitan government has to devise means and incentives to hold the farmers on the land so that an incremental urban improvement has a chance to be felt and a balanced national development strategy can be maintained. Given the urgency of the urban challenge, it is heartening to witness how, over the past few years, large city governments have responded in many ways befitting their political priorities and social philosophies.

A RANGE OF RESPONSES

The urban environment has come to such a state that many of the primate city governments have taken the view that if they do not act now, it might be too late in the future. Although the international marketplace has now made technology and know-how easily available to the developing countries at a price, it is the design of indigenous solutions to the urban problems which ultimately holds the key to success. Thus, the urban frontier in

Southeast Asia is at once one of challenge and of opportunity. It calls for imagination with innovative and appropriate solutions to meet country- and city-specific needs. Within the past ten years, at least five distinct approaches associated with each of the large city governments under review have been put into practice with varying degrees of success.

The survey begins with the primate cities of Jakarta, Manila and Bangkok which share the common attributes of rapid population growth with insufficient urban jobs and services to meet demands, harmful externalities of congestion and pollution, and a general overshadowing effect on their respective urban systems.

Jakarta

Despite a marked decline in Jakarta's annual rate of growth from 10.8 per cent in the 1950s to 4.6 per cent in the succeeding decade, its population reached 4.58 million in 1971. Over a million of the population was attributable to rural in-migration. A large proportion of the migrants cannot find jobs and an even larger percentage live without adequate housing, sanitation, or a pure water supply. Overall, 80 per cent of Jakarta's citizens live outside the reach of its basic public services and only 15 per cent have access to the city's water supply (Critchfield, 1971:89). In a desperate effort to stem the tide of in-migration, Ali Sadikin, the Governor of Jakarta, declared in August 1970 that the city would henceforth be a "closed city" to new jobless settlers. The declaration bestowed upon Jakarta the dubious distinction of being the first large Southeast Asian city to be "closed" to rural migrants. In-migrants are required to show evidence of employment and housing accommodation before they are issued with residence permits. They are further required to deposit with the city government for six months the equivalent of the return fare to the point of origin (Berry, 1973:100–101).

The drastic measure imposed by Governor Sadikin was intended primarily for its psychological impact rather than physically to prevent people from coming into Jakarta (Critchfield, 1971). The evidence to date indicates that the "closed city" policy has produced mixed results. On the one hand, Suharso et al. (1975) have suggested that there has been no noticeable diminution of the rate of growth from migration. An average of 648 migrants continued to enter Jakarta every day. On the other hand, Papanek (1975) has found that since a high "price" is attached to the residency card, the lowest income groups tend to ignore the card altogether, whereas others who need it would contribute towards bribery and corruption. While the policy has had some effect in slowing down the flow of migration to the city, those who remain in Jakarta are further pushed into poverty by the requirement and high cost of obtaining a residence permit. This outcome is not surprising since the policy has been complemented by other income-reducing policies, such as pedal trishaw-free zones and the elimination of pavement vendors. Furthermore, the policy of residence permits is counterproductive in another sense. It has led to the unintended effect of forcing some families to become full-time urban residents in Jakarta who would otherwise have remained rural inhabitants but working part-time in the city (Papanek, 1975).

Manila

Rural in-migration has likewise been a phenomenon of many years' standing in Metropolitan Manila, giving rise to a host of problems (Dwyer, 1964; Hollnsteiner, 1976). Perhaps more than any other primate city in Southeast Asia, Metropolitan Manila had been hampered in its planning and operational effectiveness until 1975 by a governmental system plagued by structural fragmentation, division of powers and boundary inflexibilities (Oamar, 1974). Within the metropolitan area there were no less than twenty-eight separate and distinct administrative units, each with guarded interests and overlapping responsibilities (Hollnsteiner, 1974:105). Metropolitan Manila was generally considered to consist of five cities and twenty-three towns, in four provinces, and under these conditions of political and administrative fragmentation, the delivery of basic urban services such as transportation, law and order, housing and flood control, remains sorely inadequate (Laquian, 1972). Quite clearly, for effective improvement in urban services and administration, political boundaries would have to be redrawn, while the governmental setup needs a basic restructuring so that metropolitan problems may be tackled in an area-wide fashion. Meanwhile, the metropolis keeps on growing and the gap between metropolitan problems and local government performance keeps widening (Oamar, 1974:7).

Since 1969 there have been at least twelve proposals advocating administrative reform for Metropolitan Manila, involving different permutations of administrative structure, area and cities covered and tax base (Pacho, 1974). The one that was finally adopted may be called a development authority approach, one of the four main approaches to metropolitan governance identified by De Guzman (1975). By Presidential Decree No. 824, the Metropolitan Manila Commission came into being on 28 February 1975. Four cities (Manila, Quezon, Pasay and Caloocan) and thirteen municipalities (Makati, Mandaluyong, San Juan, Las Pinas, Malabon, Navotas, Pasig, Pateros, Paranaque, Marikina, Muntinlupa, Taguig and Valenzuela) are integrated into a single administrative unit.

Thus constituted, Metropolitan Manila comprises a total population of 4.9 million which is projected to reach 6.2 million by 1980 (*Philippines Today*, 4, 1976:10). Established as a public corporation, the Commission can be seen as a supra-administrative layer superimposed upon the existing local government units. It is headed by a Governor, Mrs. Imelda Marcos, who was appointed by the President. She is assisted by a Vice-Governor and three Commissioners, each in charge of planning, finance and operations. For the first time in Metropolitan Manila, vital urban services and resources are integrated and coordinated under the jurisdiction of a unified entity. Recognizing that the physical survival of Manila was at stake, Mrs. Marcos set herself three priority problems requiring urgent solution—food control, public transport and traffic and garbage collection (Marcos, 1976). In order to decongest Manila, plans have been made to disperse institutions of higher learning, to decentralize industries, to build a new international airport and to relocate some piers. It is, however, too early to evaluate the extent of improvement in the quality of urban services resulting from the metropolitan reorganization. For Manila, however, the crucial first step in the right direction appears to have been taken.

Bangkok

The need for urban dispersion is nowhere more urgently felt than in Bangkok, the region's classic primate city which is thirty-four times the size of the second largest city, Chiengmai. Plans for decentralizing Greater Bangkok have been pursued along several fronts. Romm (1972:130–32) has reported a noticeable decentralization of industries, with attendant employment opportunities and new housing construction, beyond suburban Greater Bangkok. Similarly, most Bangkok universities have planned relocation beyond the metropolis. The Asian Institute of Technology, the English Language Centre, Kasetsart, Mahidol, Chulalongkorn, Thammasat and Silpakorn universities all have plans to relocate from the congested city area. The new Kasetsart campus is almost one hundred kilometres to the northwest.

In the meantime, the Greater Bangkok Plan is receiving a second amendment which is likely to alter the strategy of urban planning towards a decentralized structure, that is, to a polycentric pattern in preference to the existing monocentric plan. Government agencies such as the National Housing Authority are charting their course of development in accordance with this decentralized strategy. Among the many projects undertaken by the National Housing Authority, satellite communities complete with jobs are being planned at distances of ten to forty kilometres from the city centre.

While decentralization policies are being pushed ahead, policies to encourage regional growth and to reduce rural migration to Bangkok are largely fragmented and show few tangible results. Consequently, whether measures of dispersal of economic, educational and social activities will merely extend Bangkok's sphere of influence or be sufficient for secondary nodes of activities to sustain themselves remains to be seen. It is evident that what is needed for Thailand is not Bangkok-related expansion of development, but rather policies aimed at a more "balanced" distribution of future urbanization and the formulation of a national urban strategy, in which Bangkok is viewed in relation to the rest of the country and other urban centres are given sufficient opportunities to develop into important employment and cultural nuclei (Sakornpan, 1975:25). In any event, the formulation of a decentralized strategy of development focussed on Bangkok is a reflection of the official realization that the excessive concentration and agglomeration of economic, political and social life have come to a point of diminishing return.

Malaysia

Malaysian cities are far smaller than the primate cities discussed above, but they are confronted by problems of a different nature. Owing to a pattern of development dating from the colonial period, subsequent development of the country after independence in 1957 has not materially altered the imbalance between the *bumiputras* (indigenous peoples) and immigrant groups. There are significant differences in the pattern of population distribution, employment, business operation and control, and property ownership. The 1970 population census data for Peninsular Malaysia indicate that 85.1 per cent of the Malays lived in rural areas, whereas 47.4 per cent of the Chinese lived in towns. In other words, of the total urban population in 1970, Malays made up about one quarter and non-*bumiputras* constituted

71 per cent (Tajuddin, n.d.). In the major Malaysian cities, *bumiputra* property ownership is lower than their proportionate share of the population. In Kuala Lumpur, for instance, Malays constituted 24.9 per cent of the population in 1970 yet owned only 16.9 per cent and 7.3 per cent of the developed and undeveloped properties respectively (Ahmad, 1975). Traditionally, there is also the identification of ethnic groups with economic activities and specific location.

In the aftermath of the 1969 racial conflict, the Second Malaysia Plan (1971–1975) spelled out two explicit developmental objectives. One was to reduce and eventually to eradicate poverty by raising income levels and increasing employment opportunities for all Malaysians. The other was to restructure society by reducing and eventually eliminating identification of ethnic groups with economic activities. It is planned that by 1990, 30 per cent of the urban economy will be owned and managed by *bumiputras*. One of the operational strategies to achieve these objectives is through the process of urban development. Urban development is envisaged as a catalytic factor in uplifting *bumiputras* into a dynamic and industrial community. For this purpose, the Urban Development Authority (UDA) was created in September 1971 with the necessary legal, fiscal and manpower support for the task.

So far the bulk of the Authority's activities have focussed on Kuala Lumpur, but various urban development programmes are gradually being undertaken in other parts of the country. Basically, the Authority's development activities may be categorized into three types, primarily intended to enhance the business opportunities of *bumiputras* (Mustaffa, 1974). First of all, crash programmes make available already completed premises to *bumiputras*. Premises are identified, acquired at reasonable prices, and offered for sale or rent. Secondly, short-term programmes involve the reservation of business units under course of construction, the acquisition of equity shares in joint ventures and, by direct acquisition, the undertaking of land development. Finally, long-term programmes encompass large-scale comprehensive urban development and urban renewal projects, partnership with existing land owners and occupants, and joint ventures in which the Authority acquires up to 51 per cent of the paid-up capital.

The Urban Development Authority can now be regarded as one of the most important factors in shaping the pattern of urban development in Malaysia. During 1973 a total of M$9.8 million was spent on purchasing or leasing 253 business premises, seventy-one loans worth M$1.9 million were extended for renovating such business premises and M$23.6 million was provided for participating in seventeen joint ventures, in addition to other forms of support for indigenous business participation (*Annual Survey*, 1973). These activities are now gathering momentum in Kuala Lumpur and other Malaysian cities.

Singapore

This review of important urban policies would be incomplete without reference to some recent bold and innovative measures undertaken in Singapore. Many of the policy prescriptions practised in the city-state are often downgraded as being unique and therefore inappropriate for other large Southeast Asian cities, which invariably are linked to a rural hinterland. However, two recent policy decisions adopted in Singapore have potential application in other situations. These are the introduction of a battery of economic disincentives, with the aim of ultimately attaining zero population growth, and the use of a multiplicity of tax and fiscal measures in a concerted effort to curb private automobile ownership.

The stringent measures that have been brought to bear on private automobile are the response to a rapidly-worsening urban traffic situation. In the period from 1963 to 1973, the number of private automobiles more than doubled to 187,972. By 1974, more than 55 per cent of all registered motor vehicles were private automobiles. Although the government has been attempting to limit the growth of private automobiles over the past few years by increasing fuel prices, parking charges and road tax, the effects have not been entirely satisfactory. Thus more drastic measures were imposed in 1975 by raising levies on imported and locally assembled cars, up to 100 per cent for imported models, by increasing road taxes from 100 to 550 per cent as compared with pre-1972 levels, according to the engine capacity and by escalating parking charges. At the same time, public bus transport was improved. The most innovative and perhaps drastic of all policies was the decision to restrict entry of vehicles into the central city area during the morning peak hours, by applying what is called the "area licensing" scheme.

It is the first time such a traffic restricting scheme has been put into effect in a major city. Launched on 2 June 1975, the scheme delineates 620 hectares of the central city areas which are cordoned off as a restricted zone from 7:30 to 10:15 a.m. To be able to pass the twenty-two entry points to the city core, private automobiles not otherwise qualified under car-pooling exemption must purchase an area licence on either a monthly or a daily basis. In the hope of orienting the public to a new mode of commuting, fifteen car parks were built at the city fringe, with a capacity for 10,000 cars, complemented by a shuttle bus service. The so-called park-and-ride scheme, inaugurated on 16 May 1975 before the area licensing scheme was operational, has been a dismal failure. The excess parking facilities have yet to be used, although the shuttle bus service has now been integrated as a supplementary bus system serving the outlying housing estates (Chia *et al.*, 1975).

However, measured against the stated objectives, the area licensing scheme has been an immense success. When data showing the traffic entering the central city area during restricted hours in March and in August 1975 are compared, a reduction of 40 per cent is shown. For the most part, the scheme has been proceeding smoothly. Another positive aspect of the scheme is that the monthly sale of 7,000 area licences brought in a revenue of almost half a million Singapore dollars. Nevertheless, the 40 per cent reduction in traffic is much higher than the projected 20 to 30 per cent reduction and may raise the question of under-utilization of existing road capacity. Moreover, a secondary evening hour peak still remains and the enormous capacity of the fringe car parks has to be put to some use (Watson and Holland, 1976).

Booming rates of population growth affect practically every developing country and if economic progress is not to be whittled away by population increase, population control is imperative. The need to bring population growth under control is particularly incumbent on a city-state such as Singapore. Towards this end a series of economic disincentives, backed by political and social exhortations, have been put into practice over the last few years. Persistently, parents are encouraged to stop at two children. A fourth child in a family will be penalized by low priority in the choice of primary school, no income tax relief, high accouchement fees and no maternity leave for the mother. Concomitantly, new public housing alloca-tion criteria favour small families, subletting of public housing is permitted for families having not more than three children and abortion is legalized. The demographic target is to achieve a net reproduction rate of 1.0 from 1975 onwards. Zero population growth will be attained by 2030, when the population of Singapore will reach the neighbourhood of 3.5 million (Loh, 1976).

CONCLUSION

At the rates of growth shown in the introductory part of this chapter, most of the primate cities in Southeast Asia will become gargantuan urban agglomerations of ten million or more inhabitants by the end of this century (Hamzah, 1974). This trend is consistent with the pattern that is now emerging in other regions of the developing world (Cohen, 1976). If the beginnings of the workable solutions are not soon found, the prospect for urban Southeast Asia in the future cannot but be grim.

Davis (1975:83) was less than optimistic when he described Asian cities as follows:

> They are dense, inhabited by poorly educated and impoverished masses, yet growing rapidly under conditions of chronic resource scarcity; and they are strangers to the urban institutions that form the background of modern urbanization in the West. Under such conditions, democracy, private enterprise, and individual freedom seemingly produce chaos.

He further concluded that the path being taken by many Asian countries was "development without prosperity, urbanization without opulence, without sophistication, without urbanity" (Davis, 1975:85).

This dire prognosis should not deter Southeast Asian urban policy-makers from their determination to seek indigenous ways of coping with their problems. Clearly, Davis was using standards of opulence, sophistication and urbanity based on Western experience. By the same token, Asian administrators need to accept the fact that widespread urban poverty is going to be a continuing element for many years to come. Compared with Western cities, the majority of Southeast Asian cities will be characterized by greater poverty. To meet the problem squarely, the cities need to be designed for the poor, rather than to follow the prevailing mode of fitting the poor into cities basically designed for the moderately wealthy and the rich (Dwyer, 1972:52). This has policy and planning implications. From the viewpoint of policies, conscious efforts should be made to strive for practicable indigenous solutions. Some of the responses outlined in this chapter are examples of the innovation and imagination which must be continually refined and made flexible enough to meet changing conditions. Economic policies which have a large labour absorption capacity, such as those relating to the informal sector, can be fostered up to a point. In terms of planning, there is the need to revise and reorient planning expectations and methods. Economic growth for its own sake must be avoided. Aspirations for and a replication of the Western pattern of development and life styles are hardly the best choices for Southeast Asia. If high growth standards are scaled down to reasonable levels, urbanization may not be accompanied by "opulence, sophistication and urbanity," but it can at least be graced by satisfaction, fulfillment and a sense of purpose.

Urban Southeast Asia can now be considered at the crossroads. No road leads to Utopia, but one way leads to relative hope, the other to despair. It is vital that the right decisions are made at this time. The urban frontier is not only inviting with its challenge but it is also one laden with opportunities.

REFERENCES

Ahmad Indris Mohd. Noor. 1975. "Local Government and the Restructuring of Society." Unpublished paper presented at the National Seminar on Local Government, Kuala Lumpur, 30 June–4 July 1975.

Annual Survey of Malaysian Development Institutions. 1973. Kuala Lumpur.

Armstrong, W. R. and T. G. McGee. 1968. "Revolutionary Change and the Third World City: A Theory of Urban Involution." *Civilisation*, 18:353–78.

Arumainathan, P. 1973. *Report on the Census of Population, 1970, Singapore, I.* Singapore.

Berry, B.J.L. 1973. *The Human Consequences of Urbanization.* London.

Breese, G., ed. 1969. *The City in Newly Developing Countries: Readings on Urbanism and Urbanization.* Englewood Cliffs.

Chia, Lin Sien, *et al.* 1975. "Organization and Financing of Domestic Transportation in Singapore." Unpublished paper prepared for Asian Centre for Development Administration—Southeast Asian Agency for Regional Transport and Communication Development.

Cohen, M. A. 1976. "Cities in Developing Countries: 1975–2000." *Finance and Development*, 13(1):12–15.

Critchfield, R. 1971. "The Plight of the Cities: Jakarta—The First to 'Close'." *Columbia Journal of World Business*, 6(4):89–93.

Davis, K. 1969. *World Urbanization 1950–1970, Volume I.* Population Monograph Series, No. 4. Berkeley: Institute of International Studies, University of California.

————. 1971. "The Role of Urbanization in the Developing Countries." Paper read at the Rehovot Conference, Tel Aviv.

————. 1975. "Asia's Cities: Problems and Options." *Population and Development Review*, 1(1):71–86.

De Guzman, R. P. 1975. "Alternatives for Metropolitan Governance: The Case of Metro

Manila." *Local Government Bulletin*, 10(1):2–7.

Dwyer, D. J. 1964. "The Problem of In-migration and Squatter Settlement in Asian Cities: Two Case Studies, Manila and Victoria-Kowloon." *Asian Studies*, 2:145–69.

————. 1972. "Future (Urban) Shock." *Insight*, (May):49–52.

Evers, H-D. 1975. "Urbanization and Urban Conflict in Southeast Asia." *Asian Survey*, 15(9):775–85.

Goldstein, S. 1973. "The Demography of Bangkok: The Case of a Primate City." In *Population, Politics, and the Future of Southeast Asia*, ed. W. H. Wriggins and J. F. Guyot, pp. 81–119. New York.

Goodman, A. E. 1973. *The Causes and Consequences of Migration to Saigoon, Vietnam*. New York.

Goodman, A. E. and L. M. Franks. 1974. *Between War and Peace: A Profile of Migrants to Saigon*. New York.

Hamzah, Sendut. 1974. "Trends in Urban Development, With Special Reference to Southeast Asia." Speech read at the Annual Conference of Asia Foundation, Penang.

Hodder, B. W. 1953. "Racial Groupings in Singapore." *Malayan Journal of Tropical Geography*, 1:25–36.

Hollnsteiner, M. 1974. "The Case of 'The People Versus Mr. Urbano Planna y Administrator'." In *Development in the '70s*, ed. J. Hoyt, pp. 84–111. Manila.

————. 1976. "The Urbanization of Metropolitan Manila." In *Changing South-east Asian Cities: Readings on Urbanization*, ed. Y. M. Yeung and C. P. Lo, pp. 174–84. Singapore.

Laquian, A. A. 1972. "Manila." In *Great Cities of the World*, 3rd edition, II, ed. W. A. Robson and D. C. Regan, pp. 605–44. London.

Loh, M. 1976. " 'Beyond Family Planning' Measures in Singapore." Paper read at Inter-governmental Coordinating Committee, Southeast Asia Regional Cooperation in Family and Population Planning Workshop, Penang, 26–29 January 1976.

McGee, T. G. 1970. "Dualism in the Asian City. The Implication for City and Regional Planning." In *The Third International Symposium on Regional Development*, pp. 34–47. Tokyo.

McNicoll, G. and S.G.M. Mamas. 1973. *The Demographic Situation in Indonesia*. Honolulu.

Marcos, Imelda R. 1976. "A City of Man." Speech delivered at Rotary Clubs of Metropolitan Manila, 22 January 1976.

Milone, P. D. 1966. *Urban Areas in Indonesia: Administrative and Census Concepts*. Berkeley.

Munson, F. P. 1968. *Area Handbook for Cambodia*. Washington, D.C.

Mustaffa Mohd. Som. 1974. "Urban Development and New Economic Policy—USA Approach." Paper read at the SEADAG Seminar, Bali, 15–18 April 1974.

National Statistical Office. 1973. *1970 Population and Housing Census*. Bangkok.

Neville, W. 1966. "Singapore: Ethnic Diversity and Its Implications." *Annals of the*

Association of American Geographers, 56(2):236–53.

Oamar, F. V. 1974. "Approaches to Metropolitan Governance: Some Policy Considerations for Reorganization in Metropolitan Manila." *Local Government Bulletin*, 9(2):2–9.

Ooi, Jin Bee. 1975. "Urbanization and the Urban Population in Peninsular Malaysia, 1970." *Journal of Tropical Geography*, 40:40–47.

Oshima, H. T. 1967. "Growth and Unemployment in Singapore." *Malayan Economic Review*, 7:32–58.

Pacho, A. G. 1974. "Variations on the Metro Manila Reform Theme." *Philippine Journal of Public Administration*, 18(2):159–70.

Papanek, G. V. 1975. "The Poor of Jakarta." *Economic Development and Cultural Change*, 24(1):1–27.

Roberts, T. D., *et al.* 1969. *Area Handbook for Laos*. Washington, D.C.

Romm, J. 1972. *Urbanization in Thailand*. New York.

Sakornpan, C. 1975. "The Social Aspects of Low-Cost Housing." Bangkok. Mimeo.

Sandhu, K. S. 1964. "Emergency Resettlement in Malaya." *Journal of Tropical Geography*, 18:157–83.

Saw, Swee Hock. 1972. "Patterns of Urbanization in West Malaysia, 1911–1970." *Malayan Economic Review*, 17:114–20.

Smith, R. M. 1976. "Titling Toward the City." *Newsweek*, 17(May):9–15.

Suharso, *et al.* 1975. *Migration and Education in Jakarta*. Jakarta.

Tajuddin Mohd. Jali. n.d. "Urban Development and Restructuring of Society in Malaysia." Unpublished paper. Kuala Lumpur: Urban Development Authority.

Teo, Siew Eng. 1976. "Residential Mobility in HDB Flats and Private Housing in Singapore." Unpublished Ph.D. dissertation. Singapore: Department of Geography, University of Singapore.

Viloria, L. A. 1972. "The Manilenos: Significant Elites in Urban Development and Nation-building in the Philippines." In *The City As a Centre of Change in Asia*, ed. D. J. Dwyer, pp. 16–28. Hong Kong.

Watson, P. L. and E. P. Holland. 1976. "Congestion Pricing—The Example of Singapore." *Finance and Development*, 13(1):20–23.

Yeh, Stephen and You Poh Seng. 1971. "Labour Force Supply in Southeast Asia." *Malayan Economic Review*, 15:25–54.

Yeung, Yue-man. 1976. "Southeast Asian Cities: Patterns of Growth and Transformation." In *Urbanization and Counterurbanization*, ed. B.J.L. Berry. Beverly Hills. (Included in this book as Chapter 6.)

————. 1977. "Hawkers and Vendors: Dualism in Southeast Asia." *Journal of Tropical Geography*, 44:81–86.

You, Poh Seng, Bhanoji Rao and G. Shantakumar. 1974. "Social Policy and Population Growth in Southeast Asia." *International Labour Review*, 459–70.

8. The Dynamics of Growth and Decay
of Southeast Asian Cities

INTRODUCTION

At mid-century, Manila was a city of 1.78 million, 12.3 per cent of Indonesia's 76 million persons lived in urban places and about 13 per cent of Southeast Asia's total population of 173 million persons resided in towns and cities. Twenty-five years later in 1975, Manila had grown to a teeming metropolis of 4.97 million, Indonesia's population had augmented to 118 million of which 17.3 per cent lived in urban places, and the level of urban population in Southeast Asia had risen to 22 per cent or 72 million. These two sets of figures, randomly selected at different levels, serve to underline the rapidity at which urban growth has occurred in the third quarter of the present century. The period coincided with, in all probability, a historically unique era of cheap energy and moderate advances in food production through the Green Revolution, although employment opportunities remained limited in less-developed countries (LDC) cities in default of an industrial revolution. Cheap energy, food surpluses and sufficient employment are the three implied assumptions for the support of large urban agglomerations (Brown, 1976).

In spite of the rapid urban growth in Southeast Asia over the past three decades, it has remained one of the least urbanized regions in the world. Urbanization, independent of industrialization and economic growth, has given rise to a host of development problems for which answers are yet to be found. This chapter will be in three sections. First, the pattern of urban growth in Southeast Asia will be examined. It will be followed by a review of housing conditions and programmes, one of the intractable consequences of the process of rapid urban growth. Finally, several indigenous urban solutions are outlined and studied with a view to drawing guidelines for other Asian cities.

PATTERNS OF GROWTH AND DECAY

As the above-mentioned rates of urban growth might allude, Southeast Asian cities have in general witnessed booming rates of growth over the past three decades. The growth dynamism has been derived from natural increase, population transfer and boundary redefinition, subjects to be examined in this section. On the other hand, since urbanization is a relatively recent phenomenon in the region, its cities have not gone through the cycle of growth and decline. There are no ghost towns of any number or significance, which may be a feature of other sequence occupance in which towns rise and fall, for example, with the discovery and exhaustion of a mineral resource or the ascendance and obsolescence of a technology. Whatever decay which may be described of present Southeast Asian cities is found primarily in the large cities which, because of remarkably rapid population growth unmatched by infrastructural and other investments, have experienced a deteriorating urban environment (see Yeung, 1976, 1978).

In the twenty-five years between 1950 and 1975, Southeast Asia's urban population has almost tripled, from 23 to 72 million persons; in the next twenty-five years, it is projected to triple again, reaching 207 million by the year 2000 (Goldstein, 1978:4). The level of urbanization has increased from 13.4 and 22.1 per cent in 1950 and 1975 to 35.0 per cent in 2000. In other words, by the end of this century Southeast Asia will still remain one of the least urbanized regions. It will be below the average level of urbanization in LDCs at 40.8 per cent, much below the world average of 49.6 per cent and less than half of the rate reached in the more developed regions at 81.4 per cent (United Nations Population Division, 1975).

Not unlike other LDCs but in contrast to the more developed countries, Southeast Asia has experienced equally high birth rates of its urban and rural population (42.2 vs. 46.7 per 1,000) but urban mortality rates tend to be lower (16.2 vs. 21.1 per 1,000) (Table 8.1). The result has been an almost equally high rate of national increase in the urban and rural areas (26.0 vs. 25.6 per 1,000). However, because of the slightly highly rate of urban growth over rural growth, urbanization continues to increase, albeit in small increments. The slow rates of increase of urbanization, in fact, mask the very rapid urban growth which has widely occurred in the region. The recent pattern of urban growth in Southeast Asia does substantiate Davis's thesis that the urban revolution has a beginning and an end whereas urban

TABLE 8.1

Rates of Growth of Urban and Rural Populations, 1960
(rates per 1,000)

Region	Growth rate	Birth rate	Death rate	Natural increase	Population transfers*		Per cent urban growth due to rural-urban population transfers
					Rate	As per cent of natural increase	
Urban population							
World	32.7	27.7	11.6	16.1	16.6	104	51
More developed regions	24.0	20.1	8.9	11.2	12.8	114	53
Less developed regions	44.3	37.9	15.4	22.5	21.8	97	49
Southeast Asia	43.3	42.2	16.2	26.0	17.3	67	40
Rural population							
World	12.5	39.8	19.1	20.7	– 8.2	–40	—
More developed regions	–2.6	23.3	9.3	14.0	–16.6	–124	—
Less developed regions	16.5	44.1	21.7	22.4	– 5.9	–26	—
Southeast Asia	21.9	46.7	21.1	25.6	– 3.7	–14	—

Source: United Nations Population Division, *The Components of Urban and Rural Population Change: Tentative Estimates for the World and Twenty-Four Regions for 1960* (New York: United Nations, 1972).

From: S. Goldstein (1975:75).

* Population gains or losses from rural-to-urban migration within the region, inter-regional migration and rural-to-urban area reclassification.

growth can go on ad infinitum (Davis, 1965). The distinction between the
rates of urbanization and urban growth is crucial to an understanding of the
dynamics of the growth of cities in the region.

On account of the similarity in rates of urban and rural natural increase,
migration should conceivably be the main explanatory variable in the
differential pace of urban growth. As Table 8.1 shows, in 1960, 17.3
persons per 1,000 were accountable for the urban growth through migration, a movement representing at the same time a rural exodus of only 3.7
per 1,000. Rural-urban migration in Southeast Asia contributed only 40 per
cent to the total urban growth, leaving another 60 per cent to natural
increase. The implication to be drawn from this observation is that high
fertility has been the primary source of urban growth, to a degree which is
higher than other developing and developed countries. In the other regions,
it may be noted, the contributing factor of migration to urban growth ranged
from 49 to 53 per cent. Looked at from the other side, rural-urban migration
has not contributed much to lessening the population pressure in the rural
areas in Southeast Asia, either. Such transfers reduced rural growth by only
14 per cent.

Additional insights may be gained by comparing the role of migration to
urban growth over time. Goldstein (1975:83–84) estimated that during the
period from 1950 to 1960, migration resulted, on the average, in the annual
movement of 33.5 persons per 1,000 to urban places in Southeast Asia. By
1970–1975, the rate of net urban population transfer had declined by 30 per
cent to 23.4 per 1,000. On the other hand, the average annual number of net
urban migrants had increased from 778 thousand to 1.3 million in the two
stated periods. Similarly, because of the increasing population base, the
percentage of total urban growth ascribable to population transfer was also
lower in 1970–1975 than in 1950–1969, having declined from 57 to 47 per
cent of total growth. Thus by the early 1970s, migration became less
important as a factor of total urban growth.

The pattern of urbanization within the countries in Southeast Asia is
highly dissimilar (Table 8.2). Not only is the level of urbanization highly
variable, ranging from a low of 9.8 per cent in Laos to a high of 86.3 per
cent in Singapore, the average rate of urbanization is equally different.
Table 8.2 also presents some other key indicators which point to the wide
diversity extant in Southeast Asia. Taking the region as a whole, though,
Goldstein (1975) presented evidence of a strong relation between the level
of urbanization and the rate of urbanization. There is a vaguely discernible

TABLE 8.2
Selected Indicators of Urbanization and Social and Economic Development, Southeast Asia

Country	Per cent urban 1970[a]	Average rate of urbanization 1970–75[a]	Average annual urban migration rate 1970–75[a]	Gross national product (per capita) 1971[b]	Annual growth of gross domestic product (per capita) 1968–73[b]	Agricultural density per km^2 1965[c]	Annual rate of population growth 1970–75[a]	Energy per capita in kil. 1965[c]
Brunei	56.4	3.1	13.6	$1,370	3.4	—	1.9	—
Burma	19.9	3.2	27.8	80	2.0	162	2.4	47
Indonesia	17.5	2.7	23.9	80	4.2	595	2.6	111
Khmer Republic	19.3	4.5	39.3	130	−6.7	205	2.8	45
Laos	9.8	3.1	30.6	120	3.5	125	2.2	43
Malaysia	27.8	2.4	19.9	400	3.4	167	2.9	357
Philippines	33.6	2.2	16.5	240	3.1	289	3.3	209
Singapore	86.3	9.2	9.8	1,200	8.9	18,650	1.6	578
Thailand	15.0	2.5	24.5	210	2.2	289	3.3	110
Vietnam	15.1	3.2	28.2	160	2.7	632	2.1	—
Rank correlation among variables								
Per cent urban	—	−0.150	−0.729	+0.567	−0.033	+0.137	+0.079	+0.572
Rate of urbanization	−0.150	—	+0.663	−0.296	−0.250	−0.420	−0.588	−0.866

Sources: a. Based on data in United Nations Population Division, *Trends and Prospects in Urban and Rural Population: 1950–2000, as Assessed in 1973–1974* (New York: United Nations, 1975).

b. United Nations Economic and Social Council, *1974 Report on the World Social Situation*, Part One, January 1975, Table 2 (Mimeographed).

c. C. L. Taylor and M. C. Hudson, *World Handbook of Political and Social Indicators*, 2nd Edition (New Haven: Yale University Press, 1972).

From: S. Goldstein (1975:85).

trend (-0.150) for the more urbanized countries in the region to experience a lower rate of urbanization. By contrast, the relation between the level of urbanization and the rate of migration to urban places is much higher (-0.729), suggesting that rural-urban migrants are strongly attracted to urban places at low levels of urbanization in a country. Finally, the rate of urbanization and the rate of migration to urban places are highly and positively correlated (0.663).

An important characteristic of the urban growth in Southeast Asia is that increasingly, the large cities have assumed the biggest share of the population increase. As an indicator of the trend in favour of large cities, million-plus cities grew from two (Manila and Jakarta) in 1950 to nine (addition of Bangkok, Hanoi, Saigon, Rangoon, Singapore, Bandung and Surabaya) in 1970. The list will likely lengthen to sixteen by 1985, according to United Nations estimates. Using another way of highlighting the progressive concentration of urban population in these large cities, Goldstein (1975:77) indicated that such million-plus cities constituted in 1950 and 1970 about 13 and 32 per cent of the total urban population. By 1985, two out of every five urban dwellers will live in such urban places on the basis of a United Nations projection.

Finally, another factor of urban change is related to city boundary expansion together with new urban definitions used in the latest census. In Malaysia, for example, Pryor (1973) observed that large urban centres had grown so rapidly that by 1970, eight of the nine largest cities had a substantial proportion of their population overspilling the urban boundaries; almost all these cities had become underbounded. In part in response to this situation, Kuala Lumpur enlarged its city area in 1974 from thirty-seven square miles to ninety-four square miles, an increase of about 150 per cent. When city-area redefinition of such a magnitude has taken place, a city may even be renamed to emphasize its new identity, as Makasar in Sulawesi was thus renamed Ujung Pandang.

Turning to the problem of decay of Southeast Asian cities, the word "decay" is used in the qualified sense in reference to a physically and functionally deteriorating urban environment. This problem has stemmed from the fact that most of the large cities in the region were not built for the large population which they now accommodate. As service and infrastructural provisions lag hopelessly behind population growth, incessant pressure is built up on the severely strained urban fabric. Two examples from Jakarta and Manila will bring home this point.

In Jakarta, 40 per cent of the households depend solely on water vendors for their water supply at prices five times higher than the charges for piped water. The city has no water-borne sewerage system. Consequently, 80 per cent of Jakarta's residents live outside the reach of basic public services and only 15 per cent have access to the city's water supply (Critchfield, 1971:89). One explanation for the huge gulf between the demand and supply of urban services is the minuscule budgetary allocations in Jakarta. By way of comparison, Jakarta had in 1959 a municipal budget of less than 10 per cent of Singapore's, for a population which was twice as large (Hanna, 1960:5–6). Similarly, the sewerage system in Manila, constructed in 1909, was intended for a population of 220,000 to 440,000. There has been no notable improvement since although the present population of Metro Manila is about five million. Not surprisingly, therefore, in 1969 only 12 per cent of the population in Metro Manila was served by sanitary sewers.

A most visible sign of urban decay in most large Southeast Asian cities springs from the worsening traffic conditions. Most of these cities, originally built for foot and hoof, are ill prepared to such demands as generated by the sixfold increase of automobiles in Greater Bangkok between 1957 and 1969 (Romm, 1972:87) or the threefold increase in Singapore over the same period (Yeung, 1973:101). Traffic conditions have deteriorated to such a point that several city governments have applied a battery of economic and tax disincentives to curb private automobile ownership.

Still another manifestation of urban environmental decline is the general housing shortage and housing conditions, which the next section will focus specifically. Contributing to the trend of diminishing and rapidly deteriorating housing stock has been, at least for Singapore, the enactment of certain planning ordinance which had had the effect of restricting urban development. More particularly, the Control of Rent Ordinance was passed in 1947 and was in force until 1969 when decontrol of rent controlled premises was encouraged and facilitated through the enactment of another Act (see Yeung, 1973:29–38). The point of citing the rent control example in Singapore is not so much to question the wisdom of the original decision as to underscore the effectiveness or otherwise of planning legislation as a tool in effecting urban development (see also Willcox, 1978a). In this case, the legislation was upheld so long that it contributed to the gradual decline of the housing stock in the central city area until new public housing programmes and new planning legislation began to reverse the trend.

THE HOUSING CRISIS

Implicit from the preceding paragraph is the fact many of the urban dwellers in Southeast Asian cities live in slums. Indeed, a large proportion of the households in Jakarta (26 per cent), Kuala Lumpur (35 per cent), Metro Manila (35 per cent) and Greater Bangkok (30 per cent) was classified as slums and squatters in the early or mid-1970s. Over time, such proportions tended to increase. The shortfall of supply behind demand is so great and the level of housing provision so wanting that a housing crisis is said to exist.

Based on a recently completed IDRC-supported study, the selected indicators of housing conditions (Table 8.3) in Southeast Asia point to an overall picture of rather poor housing provision and services.[1] It should be noted that the figures are national averages which, with the exception of the city-states of Hong Kong and Singapore, have been adversely affected by the rural area, particularly with respect to the services available. With this caution, it is indicated that only a small fraction of the total housing stock in Indonesia and Laos is built of permanent material and only in Hong Kong and Singapore is a significant proportion of the housing stock found to be of permanent structure. Permanent structures, nevertheless, must not be equated with good housing conditions. In the early 1970s about 16 and 7 per cent of the population of around four million in Hong Kong lived in urban slums and squatter settlements respectively. Even in the case of Singapore, degenerating urban slums were a principal cause of overcrowding before the present large-scale public housing programme was launched in 1960. However, by 1970, Hong Kong and Singapore were able to achieve a measure of success in alleviating overcrowding, as the average number of persons per room index loads lowest in both city-states (Table 8.3). On the other hand, the figure of 3.0 persons per room for Indonesia borders on the lowest limit to indicate overcrowding recommended by the United Nations. Finally, less than half of the total households in Southeast Asia received piped water and electricity. Hong Kong and Singapore tower above the rest because of their predominantly urban characteristics, while

---

[1] The International Development Research Centre supported an eight-country study of low-cost housing in Southeast Asia between 1972 and 1975. The data on Hong Kong are included in this discussion as the situation is close to prevailing conditions in the region. Data on Sri Lanka are, however, left out. For the comparative study of this project, see Yeh and Laquian (1979).

TABLE 8.3
Selected Indicators of Housing Conditions in Southeast Asia, c. 1970

	Permanent dwelling units of housing stock (%)	Average number of rooms per housing unit	Average number of persons per housing unit	Average number of persons per room	Availability of piped water (%)	Availability electricity (%)
Hong Kong	88.3	3.04	5.90	2.17	86.1	—
Indonesia	5.8	1.50	5.30	3.00	—	—
Laos (Vientiane)	18.1	2.00	—	—	19.0	53.1
Peninsular Malaysia	—	2.30	6.10	2.70	47.5	43.7
Philippines	32.1	2.42	6.10	2.52	24.0	23.2
Singapore	63.7	2.64	6.64	2.32	90.6	91.8
Thailand	—	—	—	—	12.4	18.8

Source: IDRC-supported Southeast Asia Low-Cost Housing Study.

the other country figures have been pulled down by considerable urban-rural disparities. Considering the urban areas alone, Malaysia did not lag much behind Hong Kong and Singapore and, generally speaking, over half of the urban households in Thailand and the Philippines had piped water and electricity.

When the provision of services is focussed at the individual slum-squatter communities, the problem becomes magnified. Laquian (1979:57–58) observed that basic services like water supply, toilet facilities and garbage collection were woefully deficient. In the squatter community of Klong Toey in Bangkok, only 1.8 per cent of the households was able to get piped water, with the result that 67.5 per cent of the households had to buy water from vendors. Similarly, a study of Tondo in Manila revealed that 70 per cent of the inhabitants did not have any toilets in their homes. And only 23 per cent of the residents of the surveyed slum-squatter communities in Kuala Lumpur benefited from the government-run garbage collection service.

Deplorable may be the physical provisions of most of these slum and squatter communities, they provide the entrée for the majority of the rural in-migrants to a new life in the cities. Studies on these settlements reveal that close links are maintained between the rural and urban areas through circular and seasonal migration (Goldstein, 1978) and positive contributions are made by the inhabitants towards economic and social development despite the uninviting outlook of these habitats (Laquian, 1971). Taking into account the needs of these communities and the housing requirements arising from population increase and replacement, the IDRC study shows that for the next two decades at least, the housing needs for every Southeast Asian country, with the possible exception of Singapore, are enormous. As an illustration, for the period from 1970 to 2000, the Philippines would need annually 126,000 to 195,000 housing units in the urban areas. The annual need in both urban and rural housing units ranges from 304,000 to 463,000, or about 6.9 new dwelling units for every 1,000 inhabitants. The actual rate of production is only about two housing units per 1,000 inhabitants. Consequently, only 8 per cent of urban families can afford open market housing, 62 per cent can afford subsidized housing, and 30 per cent need social housing (Chander et al., 1979:48).

Although Singapore has been singularly successful in providing public housing to its masses (over 60 per cent so housed in 1979), it is a solution which other Southeast Asian countries will find most difficult and costly to implement. Instead, they have attempted a mix of alternatives aimed at enlarging and improving on the existing housing stock. As a sign of perhaps greater official commitment to housing investment, unified national bodies were formed in Indonesia, the Philippines and Thailand in the mid-1970s. A review of some of the experience may be instructive.

In Thailand when a new government came to power in 1975, housing was declared a national priority. The National Housing Authority's (NHA) Five-Year Plan (1976–1980) to construct 120,000 new housing units at an annual rate of 24,000 units was approved. However, the heavy government subsidies involved soon prompted the NHA to review the programme and decided quickly to veer towards greater emphasis on core housing, sites and services, and slum upgrading. The cost factor has been a major reason to change the emphasis of the programme so that at a much reduced rate of subsidy, the largest number of people can benefit from it. In 1980 another twenty-six slum areas in Bangkok are expected to be upgraded, bringing the total number of areas to fifty-seven and 15,000 households thus benefited. For this reason, the NHA projects have been able to reach a much larger number of low income households; 82 per cent of the target households earn less than 3,000 baht a month. Because of this re-oriented programme, the total cost to the government has been reduced in the five-year period from 3,466 to 1,500 million baht (Buranasiri, 1979).

The stress on social and economic mobility of the NHA programme in Thailand is shared by similar programmes in Indonesia. In the Urban Slum Improvement or Kampung Improvement Programme (KIP), a comprehensive approach is adopted in which physical improvements are complemented by social and welfare provisions, employment creation, cooperative movement and training programmes. With the assistance provided by the World Bank, UNICEF and UNEP, the programme is being mounted in six other large cities of Indonesia (Bandung, Surabaya, Semarang, Yogyakarta, Medan and Ujung Pandang) in addition to Jakarta. During the Third Five-Year Development Plan (1979–1983), this programme will be expanded to cover a total of 15,000 hectares in 200 towns affecting 3.5 million inhabitants. It will cost 45 billion rupiah to implement. Additionally, over the same Plan period the National Housing Corporation will construct 120,000 dwelling units in 100 towns, after completing 73,000 units in the previous Plan period (1974–1978) (Kartahardja, 1979).

Inasmuch as Malaysia recognized housing as an important tool for the attainment of the objectives of the New Economic Policy with its emphasis on restructuring society and eradicating poverty, it presents an example of potentially meeting the housing needs of the population. It was estimated for the Third Malaysia Plan (TMP, 1976–1980) that at least 515,000 dwelling units would be required for Peninsular Malaysia. As Jamal (1979) observed, at the end of 1978, some 313,944 units or 65 per cent of the original TMP target of 482,800 units were either completed or at various stages of implementation. The government was so encouraged by the result that an upward revision was made of the TMP target to 553,300 units. An important factor in this creditable progress was the greater ease with which housing loans have become available. Equally important, the greater contribution by the private sector, often in joint ventures with Federal and State organizations, particularly in meeting the needs of the lower income groups, is being realized.

URBAN SOLUTIONS

It is not only the field of housing in which solutions are being searched and experimented with in Southeast Asian cities. This section will also touch on several noteworthy approaches in dealing with urban problems (Yeung, 1978).

At the city level, one of the most drastic measures ever adopted to slow down metropolitan city growth in the region has been the imposition, since 1970, of the "closed city" policy to rural-urban migrants in Jakarta. In-migrants are required to show proof of employment and housing accommodation before they are issued with residence permits. They are further required to deposit with the city government for six months the equivalent of the return fare to the point of origin. Detailed account of the scheme has been described elsewhere (Yeung, 1978; Simmons, 1979). From all accounts the policy measure, applied now for almost a decade, has not been effective in fulfilling its original objectives. For one thing, it is too complicated a decree to implement and police in a large city. It has led, rather, to corruption, further hardship for the urban poor, and an increase of permanent in-migrants who would otherwise be seasonal or occasional migrants. This policy experience is cited to illustrate the desperate attitude with which some large city governments have viewed rural-urban migration. Equally important, it shows how ineffective and helpless a city government is in any attempt to physically stop in-migrants at the city gate. No matter how pressing the problems are besetting a primate city and how justifiable it may appear to redirect population growth to other urban/rural centres, any exercise of population redistribution, to be successful, must be carefully planned on a national scale and not carried out on a piecemeal basis.

Within individual city areas several innovative schemes designed at improving urban functions and use are deserving of wider attention. In the light of the common urban traffic problems mentioned earlier, Singapore's recent implementation of the Area Licence Scheme, in particular its impacts on various facets of urban life, merits study. In essence, the Scheme, instituted in 1975, delineates Singapore's central city area of 620 hectares as a Restricted Zone entry into which between 7:30 a.m. and 10:15 a.m. by private automobiles and taxis is subject to the payment of a licence fee. This fee may be paid either monthly or daily unless the vehicle is exempted under the car-pooling criterion. Holland and Watson (1978) have recently reported the direct and indirect impacts of the Scheme on urban life in Singapore. In direct impacts, it was found out that total traffic was reduced by 44 per cent during the restricted period, the evening peak (4 p.m. to 7 p.m.) changed very little, mean speeds within the Restricted Zone were 22 per cent higher during the restricted hours than during the evening peak, and car pools markedly increased. Indirectly, the Scheme accelerated the existing trend towards decentralization from the city centre, benefited wholesalers and retailers by an easier movement of goods in the central area during the morning when deliveries are made, and boosted the revenues of the bus company which in turn provided better service. In contrast, taxi operators have reported serious losses in business during the morning shift which are hard to be recouped later in the day. All in all, the Area Licence Scheme has simply attained its objectives of reducing congestion in the central city area, largely by inducing a shift towards public transport and car pools. Secondary positive effects include the increased ease of crossing streets for pedestrians, cleaner air and people's improved image of central Singapore. The success of the Scheme has so interested other city governments that modifications of the Singapore experiment for implementation are being seriously considered by planners from several Asian cities.

In recent years Southeast Asian cities, in consonance with the widely recurring trend in other parts of the world as well, has witnessed an astonishing appreciation of land values and property prices. During the period from 1962 to 1973 in Singapore, for instance, commercial prime land along thriving Orchard Road multiplied thirty-seven times in value and residential land in the popular Holland Road area jumped fifteen times in value (Motha, 1976:188). Despite a short period of decline in 1974–1975 coinciding with the minor world recession, the climb in land values in Singapore has since continued, most notably in 1979.

The quantum of increases in land values in Singapore may appear phenomenal but observations in the large cities in the region strongly suggest that the Singapore pattern is actually not atypical. Evers (1975) has noted that this pattern of development has come about because of the inherited urban land ownership structure and rampant land speculation. Land speculation goes hand in hand with economic development. Evers further noted that the urban elite has engaged in land speculation for lack of other investment opportunities and, most disturbingly, such speculative investment tends to be "institutional," that is between speculators rather than between the speculator and the ultimate user. This process of land speculation affects all parts of the city but in the rural-urban fringe where urban expansion is thus thwarted, the lower-income groups are adversely affected in their aspiration to own land. Even in a medium-sized town of Butterworth in Malaysia, land speculation has become a problem. Fortunately, land fragmentation has not proceeded far and most urban land is still suitable for redevelopment. Forming 23.9 per cent of the town's population, Malays owned only 9 per cent of the land. In contrast, Chinese constituting 58.9 per cent of the population owned 76 per cent of the land. Thus Goh and Evers (1978) recommended that measures should be taken to prevent further reduction of Malay ownership in Butterworth since much of the Malay-owned land was in the central urban area and probably subject to increasing pressure to sell. They also recommended against subdivision of urban land in the early stages of development.

How should city governments respond to the prevalent situation of urban land speculation with the associated deleterious consequences? Lim and Motha (1980) suggested that a coherent and coordinated land policy will be a positive step in the right direction. More specifically, in an attempt to curb speculative rises in property prices, the Urban Redevelopment Authority in Singapore announced in December 1979 a new tender system for redevelopment sites. Under the new system, a developer may pay in full the land price within 120 days after acceptance of the tender, or may opt for the existing practice in which 75 per cent of the land price may be paid by ten annual instalments (*Straits Times*, 21 December 1979). In Malaysia, a Property Gains Tax Act was passed in 1976 and has had the effect of dampening land speculation. In examining urban land policy in Malaysia in a more general context, Willcox (1978a, 1978b) drew attention to the practice that successive land laws had included provisions authorizing the imposition, at the time of alienation, of conditions on the use of land. Conditional land-titles, it is argued, can be a most serviceable legal instru-.ment for implementing any specific land policy. Willcox suggested the use of conditions on titles to land for a possible redress of the existing imbalance of urban land ownership among ethnic groups. Equally, it appears that a land-title system may serve another development objective of keeping land price increase in an orderly progression. The system may be "fashioned either for specific properties or for all properties of a particular description or geographic area" (Willcox, 1978a: 327).

As an answer to the same problem caused by land shortage and land speculation, an imaginative approach recently adopted by Taiwanese cities should be mentioned although they are outside the geographical purview of this chapter. The solution, by the process of urban land consolidation, was first pioneered by officials in Kaohsiung and was later applied with remarkable success in several cities in Taiwan (Pannell, 1974). Conceptually, it is a simple and straightforward process which involves the merging of a number of small, irregularly-shaped, fragmented land holdings into a larger unit.

> This collective, larger unit is then replotted and redivided on an equivalent, pro-rated basis into rectangular units. A certain amount of the original land is allotted to the state for roads and other public usages, and some of the land is sold to provide funds for the construction of capital improvements such as roads, drainage ditches and bridges. The result is planned, orderly development of the consolidation area and its transformation from an unplanned, often para-rural area into a systematically designed and developed urban landscape. (Pannell, 1974:114)

The obvious economic benefits to all parties concerned have been the main reason for the scheme's initial success and subsequent spread to other cities. It is a case of public-private cooperation in which the ones who suffer are squatters and those lessors having no legal rights to the land. This method of urban development bears closer study by planners in Southeast Asia for its potential application to their cities.

The above review of indigenous urban solutions is intended to be indicative of the need to search for answers to urban problems within the resources and setting of Asian societies of which cities form a part. It is hoped that this list of attempted solutions, both successful and not so successful, will lengthen in the future, and it is in the spirit of learning from each other that they can be perfected to serve purposeful developmental ends.

PROGNOSIS AND PROSPECT

In the light of the foregoing account on the patterns of growth and decay of Southeast Asian cities, their problems and some attempted solutions, what does the future hold for them in the next two decades? Hamzah Sendut (1974:3) offered the following prognosis:

> ... Jakarta, Bangkok and Manila especially shall attain a population by the year 2001 as large as that of the largest cities of the world at the present time; they are also projected to reach the New York–Tokyo–London size within the next quarter century. The growth rates of other towns are also known to be high and if continued along the present trend they can be expected to distort the hierarchy of towns within each country.
>
> The spread of towns as it persists presently in the respective countries of Southeast Asia also tends to thicken the networks of towns and create urbanized regions characterized by a high population density, a number of urban centres upon which public and private expenditures are focused and a hinterland without facilities for maintaining the basic minimum level of living.

Put differently, Hamzah's perspective of future urban Southeast Asia will continue along present trends in which the present primate cities will continue to grow unabatedly and urbanized regions will emerge as a salient feature of national development. The disquieting element of this prognosis is that the existing urban-rural disparities are not going to be bridged. On the contrary, an impoverished rural hinterland starved of the necessary public and private investment for self-sustaining development is envisaged.

Less optimistic about a unilinear pattern of urban development in Southeast Asia and in an effort to link present and future development trends, Lim (1976:5) presented another scenario:

> Notwithstanding the high concentration of resources in the urban centres, insufficient job opportunities are created for the continuous inflow of unskilled rural migrants ... urban development is often carried out at the expense of the urban poor. ... This is particularly obvious in the three major metropolises of Bangkok, Jakarta and Manila. The number of squatters is increasing at an alarming rate and will get progressively worse. Pollution and traffic jams are now serious hazards to health and safety, particularly for non-car users. If the present trend is to continue, it will lead to frequent unrest, gross administrative inefficiency and total breakdown in the functioning of essential urban services.

Quite clearly, in Lim's analysis the present large cities in the region have dangerously followed a path of development which is geared to the urban elite and which will experience serious problems if the trend is uncorrected. Indeed, given the present trend in resource distribution at the global level and, by and large, the absence of the three implied assumptions to support the growth and sustenance of large cities as referred to in the introduction of this chapter (Brown, 1976). Lim has argued for the need of an alternative urban strategy for Southeast Asia. In view especially of the continued escalating cost of energy, Lim foresees many advantages in the establishment of low resource urban centres. Among the more drastic measures in a re-orientation from present development practices, the strategy calls for severe restrictions in the use of private automobiles, a lowering of standards in urban infrastructural facilities, the reduction of air-conditioned buildings, the production of food within major urban centres, and a de-emphasis of the consumer culture. As Lim (1979) envisions, this alternative urban strategy will tend towards more social justice, more citizen participation, and the eradication of poverty and chronic inequality.

Given the recent trends in world urbanization and of interdependent development, it is probably correct to say that there are elements of truth in both prognoses for future Southeast Asian cities. Whichever pattern of development individual countries will follow, we certainly do not wish to see an increasingly improverished rural sector nor the breakdown of the large cities. What seems desirable at this stage of development in the region is a critical assessment of present urban growth and development trends against the background of national realities and international resource allocation. Since the region is generally well endowed in terms of natural resources and has achieved moderately high rates of growth (see Table 8.2 for indicators), the roles being played by the cities should be carefully examined and further strengthened in this development process.

REFERENCES

Brown, Lester R. 1976. "The Limits to Growth of Third World Cities." *The Futurist*, 6(10):307–15.

Buranasiri, Pree. 1979. "Bangkok's Low Income Housing Needs: An Overview of the Problems and Perspectives." Paper presented at RIHED's Housing as a Basic Need Seminar, 6–8 December 1979, Singapore.

Chander, R., *et al*. 1979. "Housing Conditions and Housing Needs." In Yeh and Laquian (1979), pp. 31–49.

Critchfield, Richard. 1971. "The Plight of the Cities: Djakarta—The First to 'Close'." *Columbia Journal of World Business*, 6(3):89–93.

Davis, Kingsley. 1965. "The Urbanization of the Human Population." *Scientific American*, 213(3):41–53.

Evers, Hans-Dieter. 1975. "Urban Expansion and Land Ownership in Developing Societies." *Urban Affairs Quarterly*, 11(1):117–29.

Goh, Ban Lee and Hans-Dieter Evers. 1978. "Urban Development and Landownership in Butterworth, Malaysia." *Journal of Southeast Asian Studies*, 9(1):28–49.

Goldstein, Sidney. 1975. "Urbanization and Migration in Southeast Asia." In *Population Change in the Pacific Region*, ed. Yunshik Chang and Peter J. Donaldson, pp. 69–92. Vancouver: Thirteenth Pacific Science Congress.

————. 1978. *Circulation in the Context of Total Mobility in Southeast Asia*. Papers of the East-West Population Institute, No. 53.

Hamzah Sendut. 1974. "Trends in Urban Development, with Special Reference to Southeast Asia." Speech read at the Annual Conference of the Asia Foundation, Penang.

Hanna, William A. 1960. "Bung Karno's Indonesia." *American Universities Field Staff*. New York.

Holland, Edward P. and Peter L. Watson. 1978. "Traffic Restraint in Singapore." *Traffic Engineering and Control*, 19(1):14–22.

Jamal Mohamed. 1979. "Housing Needs: An Overview of the Problems and Prospects in Malaysia." Paper presented at RIHED's Housing as a Basic Need Seminar, 6–8 December 1979, Singapore.

Kartahardja, Albert. 1979. "Housing Needs: An Overview of the Problems and Prospects in Indonesia." Paper presented at RIHED's Housing as a Basic Need Seminar, 6–8 December 1979, Singapore.

Laquian, A. A. 1971. "Slums and Squatters in South and Southeast Asia." In *Urbanizational and National Development*, ed. L. Jakobson and V. Prakash, pp. 183–203. Beverly Hills: Sage Publications.

————. 1979. "Squatters and Slum Dwellers." In Yeh and Laquian (1979), pp. 51–65.

Lim, William S. W. 1976. "Low Resource Urban Centres, with Special Reference to ASEAN Countries." In *City Planning Review*. Tokyo: City Planning Institute.

————. 1979. "An Overview of and Some Policy Guidelines to Low-Income Urban Housing in Third World Countries." Paper presented at RIHED's Housing as a Basic Need Seminar, 6–8 December 1979, Singapore.

Lim, William S. W. and Philip Motha. 1980. "Land Policy in Singapore." *Habitat International*, 4(4/5/6):499–504.

Motha, Philip. 1976. "Land Value Dilemma in Developing Economies, with Special

Reference to Singapore." In *Cities of Asia*, ed. John Wong, pp. 187–209. Singapore: Singapore University Press.

Pannell, Clifton W. 1974. "Urban Land Consolidation and City Growth in Taiwan." *Pacific Viewpoint*, 15(2):111–22.

Pryor, R. J. 1973. "The Changing Settlement System of West Malaysia." *Journal of Tropical Geography*, 37:53–67.

Romm, J. 1972. *Urbanization in Thailand*. New York: Ford Foundation.

Simmons, Alan B. 1979. "Slowing Metropolitan City Growth in Asia: Policies, Programs, and Results." *Population and Development Review*, 5(1):87–104.

United Nations Population Division. 1975. *Trends and Prospects in Urban and Rural Population, 1950–2000, as Assessed in 1973–74*. New York: United Nations.

Willcox, David L. 1978a. "Malaysia's System of Conditional Land Titles as a Potential Policy Instrument." *American Journal of Comparative Law*, 26(2):321–32.

————. 1978b. "New Planning Wine in Old Legal Bottles: The Case for Greater Utilization of Existing Legal Resources in Malaysia." *Urban Law and Policy*, 1:275–305.

Yeh, Stephen H. K. and A. A. Laquian, eds. 1979. *Housing Asia's Millions: Problems, Policies and Prospects for Low-Cost Housing in Southeast Asia*. Ottawa: International Development Research Centre.

Yeung, Yue-man. 1973. *National Development Policy and Urban Transformation in Singapore: A Study of Public Housing and the Marketing System*. Research Paper No. 149. Chicago: Department of Geography, University of Chicago.

————. 1976. "Southeast Asian Cities: Patterns of Growth and Transformation." In *Urbanization and Counterurbanization*, ed. Brian J. L. Berry, pp. 285–309. Beverly Hills: Sage Publications. (Included in this book as Chapter 6.)

————. 1978. "The Urban Environment in Southeast Asia—Challenge and Opportunity." In *Geography and the Environment in Southeast Asia*, ed. R. D. Hill and Jennifer M. Bray, pp. 17–33. Hong Kong: Hong Kong University Press. (Included in this book as Chapter 7.)

PART IV

City-States

9. Planning for High-Density Urban Centres: Lessons from Hong Kong and Singapore*

Statistics recently released by the World Bank (1979) on trends in world urbanization are indeed sobering for many administrators in the Third World. Between 1950 and 1975 the urban population in developing countries rose by some 400 million people. In relation to the total population, this is an increase from 20.6 to 31.1 per cent. The corresponding increase for South and Southeast Asia was 110 million, with an anticipated growth by the end of the century to a total of 600 million, or 35 per cent of the total population. In 1970, almost half of the thirty largest cities in the world were located in Asia and it is expected that by 1990 most of these will have populations in excess of 10 million each.

The import of the preceding paragraph is that it underlines the salience of Asian cities and their problems in the future. Many of these agglomerations, already beset with problems of housing shortages, unemployment, traffic strangulation, teeming slums and a deteriorating urban environment, are in search of more indigenous solutions instead of drawing inspiration from the West (Meier, 1970; Yeung, 1976, 1978). It is in this light that urban experience in Hong Kong and Singapore bears close examination. One may note the special circumstances under which economic transformations have been wrought since 1960 in both cities. Their present prosperity has been built upon a successful export-oriented manufacturing programme, which, in Hong Kong provided employment for 45 per cent of the labour force in 1976, and in Singapore provided employment for 27.2 per cent of the labour force in 1977. In recent years tourism has also become one of the top earners of foreign exchange. Whatever lessons Hong Kong and Singapore might have to offer clearly lie at the city level of high-density development with limited land resources. But given the tendency in many Asian countries to create special capital territory districts, the

---

*Co-authored with D. W. Drakakis-Smith.

administration and development of which are more closely linked to national rather than municipal goals, the experience of Hong Kong and Singapore are becoming increasingly important. The manner in which industrialization has occurred and housing provisions are made has been already analyzed, respectively, by Geiger and Geiger (1973), and Yeung and Drakakis-Smith (1982). It is the purpose of this paper to focus on a few of the most important facets of urban planning, the organizational framework and operational experience of which should be of interest and significance to other Asian cities. It is submitted that planning for high-density development is not only highly successful in the two city-states but its implications for other urban centres should be carefully evaluated.

THE PLANNING PROCESS

Hong Kong and Singapore have common beginnings as British colonies and until relatively recently, this has led to their emulation of the British model in the planning process and legislation. However, the last ten to fifteen years has seen some change in this situation. Singapore's urban transformation since self-rule in 1959 and independence in 1965 has been expedited by forward planning and several specific planning laws (Yeung, 1973:27–42). In Singapore the morphology of the central city area has been greatly influenced by Raffles' directives to differentiate that area adjacent to the two sides of the Singapore River according to ethnic segregation (Hodder, 1953). This early influence, while still discernible, is giving way to recent developments arising from public housing and urban renewal. At the nation-wide scale, however, the urban landscape has undergone rapid changes along lines that have been spelled out in the Singapore Master Plan, approved in 1958, and more recently, the Concept Plan which was approved in 1971 after years of study assisted by United Nations consultants (Fig. 9.1). Singapore's planning process has been treated in detail by Tan (1966) and Koh and Lim (1969), whereas Koenigsberger (1964) further advocated action planning within the framework of the Master Plan. What is being attempted here is to highlight the key organizational structure of the planning process.

A crucial feature of the planning process is centralization. This has come about in part in the absence of different layers of government and competing/overlapping administrative entities which often plague many city governments in Asia. In Singapore, the Minister of Law and National

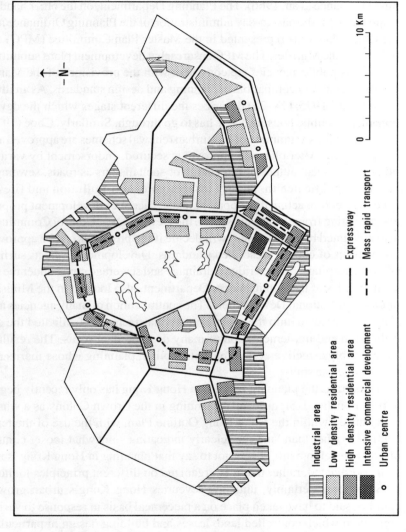

Figure 9.1: Singapore: Main Elements of the Concept Plan

Industrial area

Low density residential area

High density residential area

Intensive commercial development

o Urban centre

Expressway

- - - Mass rapid transport

N

0   10 Km

Development is responsible for physical planning and, under the Planning Ordinance, is empowered, *inter alia*, to sanction the Master Plan and additions and alterations thereof, to appoint the authorities to administer the Planning Ordinance (Tan, 1966). The Planning Department, on the other hand, is responsible for the day-to-day administration of the Planning Ordinance and the Chief Planner is represented in the Master Plan Committee (MPC) appointed by the Minister. The MPC ensures that development plans submitted by various public agencies are consistent with the provisions of the Master Plan and generally compatible in planning and design standards. As an illustration, Liu (1975:118–21) describes the different stages which the development of a public housing estate has to go through. Similarly, Choe (1975: 103–4) provides a summary of how urban renewal schemes are approved and implemented. After planning approval is secured, endorsement by various other government authorities in charge of such matters as roads, sewerage, drainage, public health, factory inspectorate, anti-pollution and fires is necessary before actual development takes place. For development proposals emanating from the private sector, the Development Control Committee, also appointed by the Minister, will decide if the proposals can be approved on the basis of certain prescribed standards. Development projects such as schools, hospitals, roads, bridges, drainage and sewerage come under the responsibilities of the Public Works Department, also located in the Ministry of Law and National Development. The centralization of many agencies and statutory boards within the same Ministry has tactically facilitated the co-ordination and implementation of many development plans. The result is a reasonably effective system of metropolitan planning whose merits are worthy of close study.

In contrast, the planning process in Hong Kong has only recently begun to be rationalized. Significantly, planning in the Crown Colony as a whole is organized within the Hong Kong Outline Plan, with the use of the term "outline" rather than "master" clearly indicating somewhat looser control of urban development. This is not to say that planning in Hong Kong is not well coordinated, rather that it is organized on different principles to those of Singapore. Certainly, until the seventies Hong Kong's urban growth could be said to have taken place on a piecemeal basis in response to varied legislation which controlled land, leases and building design in particular. The result of this planning by "ordinance" was the crowded inner metropolitan areas around Hong Kong harbour, in which inadequate open space, dilapidated tenements and congested streets all bear testimony to the lack of adequate controls (Fig. 9.2). Incredibly high-densities characterize much of the urban area which has been transformed from one of horizontal to vertical configuration since the 1960s.

During the succeeding decade it became incumbent upon Hong Kong to

Figure 9.2: Hong Kong: Diagrammatic Land-Use Zones

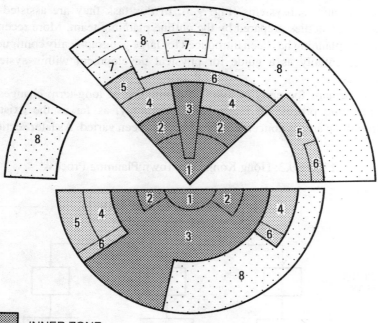

INNER ZONE
1. Central business districts, government and institutional uses
2. Tenements and commerce
3. Upper and middle income residential areas

INTERMEDIATE ZONE
4. Government housing estates
5. Inner "new towns"
6. Squatter settlements

OTHER ZONE
7. Outer "new towns"
8. Rural areas

revise its planning process, primarily because of the development settlement in the rural New Territories. This planning from scratch has demanded broader vision and tighter controls. The principles adopted have been
those of general systems analysis and in an attempt to break away from the
physical planning of the past, the concept of activity space has been adopted
(Pun, 1978). Colony-wide development strategy is thus contained within
the Outline Plan, within which district planners formulate town plans for
their particular subsystems (Fig. 9.3). In this task they are assisted by
background studies prepared by the outline planning team. More recently
structural planning has been introduced for large geographically contiguous
areas, essentially as a guide for physical development within systems
principles.

It is perhaps too early to assess the outcome of long-term changes in
the planning process in Hong Kong. Certainly, as far as the existing
metropolitan area is concerned, the effect has been varied. As later sections

Figure 9.3: Hong Kong: The Town Planning Process

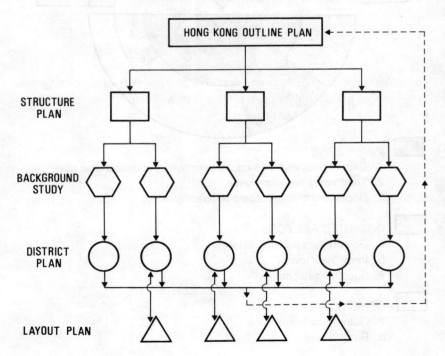

of this paper will show, the linkage component of the activity space concept has produced substantial change in transport systems. On the other hand, the pronounced shift in interest and emphasis from the old city to the New Territories has left the central tenement with little planning guidance and few positive goals. As a result the urban renewal scheme has deteriorated to a moribund state. In the New Territories, of course, the situation is somewhat different and there has been a determined effort to plan on the activity space principle and to establish a series of vertical channels in planning administration to link the bureaucracy with the people (Scott, 1979). However, some of the main problems appear to be with communication across the bureaucracy itself, although the New Territories Administration does try to act as a coordination body. As yet, it is perhaps too early to judge on success or failure.

PUBLIC HOUSING PROVISION

Next to food, shelter is the most important item of expenditure for almost all urban families in the Third World. In addition, it is an important generator of economic development, with new residential construction accounting, on average, for about 20 per cent of the fixed capital investment in most developing countries. Housing is also a major outlet for private savings and its construction operates employment at low foreign exchange costs (unless large imports of materials occur). In spite of these truisms, government housing investment in the Third World is almost uniformly low. As a result most of its burgeoning urban populations live in slums or squatter settlements, where basic facilities are poor and insecurity is high. Hong Kong and Singapore are obvious exceptions to this situation and the success of the two city-states in providing public housing to a large section of the population is frequently lauded as a model for the Third World. The Hong Kong experience has been studied by Drakakis-Smith (1979) and Wong (1978), and some of the more important Singapore studies are represented by Yeung (1973), Yeh (1975) and Hassan (1977). The two city-states are also comparatively studied by Yeung and Drakakis-Smith (1982). Both offer classic examples of the difference planning makes in high-density public housing.

In Singapore, after almost two decades of unabated efforts to promote public housing, 64 per cent or 1.5 million of the population were so housed in 1979. Four Five-Year Programmes have been nearly completed, bringing the total number of flats under the Housing and Development Board's (HDB) management in 1979 to 311,849. From the initial objective of meeting a housing crisis, public housing has gradually become a stabilizing force in society by providing many jobs in its construction, and through the popular home-ownership scheme. By 1979, 168,514 flats or 54 per cent of the total public housing stock were owner occupied. The HDB has been able to reduce the waiting time for both rental and purchased flats over the past few years, and in response to the changing complexion of the housing demand, standards are being continually upgraded, both in the size and design of individual flats as well as in the overall physical design of the estates (HDB, 1979). It is estimated that eventually 80 per cent of the Republic's population will live in public housing. Another noteworthy feature of the Singapore model is that public housing is closely linked to the goals of national development. One example is the recent change to untie the family size criterion from the list of qualifications for public housing. Until 1967 the minimum household size to qualify for public housing was five persons; it has since been reduced to two persons for any type of public housing. Indeed, with the national drive towards small family size it has become easier to be allocated public flats with small families.

Although Hong Kong successfully pioneered high-rise public housing as early as 1956, for a variety of reasons it has been less innovative than Singapore in meeting the housing needs of the populace. The very low standards which characterized the earliest estates persisted for some ten years and have continued to pose many problems for the colony's planners. Nevertheless, standards gradually improved from 1964 onwards and by 1979, more than four hundred thousand flats had been built by the government, housing over two million people or 45 per cent of the population.

It would be true to say that until the early 1970s Hong Kong had opted for quantity rather than quality, and there was a considerable difference in the standards of the flats produced by the four government-financed agencies involved in housing construction. In 1973–1974, however, these agencies were amalgamated into a single Housing Authority with the express purpose of housing 1.8 million in new homes over a ten-year period. The reorganization has not only eliminated unnecessary duplication of effort and competition for scarce resources but has also brought about a transformation in the planning, design and management of the new estates. Standards have risen rapidly since 1974 and are now comparable with the best in Singapore. As a result the recently introduced home-ownership programme has proved very popular, belatedly giving Hong Kong's middle class a sense of domestic identity.

Despite progress thus far, the housing situation remains very tight. It was hoped that the efforts made since 1974 would have enabled Hong Kong to break the back of its housing shortage and concentrate even more on quality. However, the massive influx of refugees from China and Vietnam during 1978 and 1979 has put the squatters population of the Crown Colony back to two hundred and fifty thousand, the same level it was twenty-five years ago when the housing programme began.

Nevertheless, Hong Kong and Singapore do provide important lessons for other Asian cities in the experience of their public housing policies. First, there may be a need for an initial sacrifice of standards in favour of a crash building programme, although these low standards must not persist for too long. Second, there are many benefits to be gained from centralizing the functions related to housing construction. Third, the government as the biggest landowner will facilitate land assembly at reasonable cost. Fourth, close links need to be forged between public housing policies and national development goals; although as we will see later these may not equate with social welfare objectives. Lastly, home ownership can help to establish stabilizing roots for newly urbanized families.

URBAN RENEWAL

Whilst many Asian cities are still struggling to improve the delivery of urban services and build up an urban infrastructure, Singapore is one of the few cities with a successful and efficient urban renewal programme. After the completion of preliminary studies by two United Nations teams in 1962 and 1963, an urban renewal programme was launched in 1966 under the wing of the HDB. Attention and efforts were focussed initially on the central city area, covering about 688 hectares or 1.2 per cent of the total land area of the island, which was to be renewed in a phased programme involving nineteen precincts. The Singapore example is a classic case of joint public-private participation. Apart from public projects to improve the social, economic and physical life in the central city area, the government progressively released land for private development through a competitive tender system after preparing the sites. Between 1967 and 1969, fourteen sites were released each year which were mainly devoted to hotels, luxury apartments and shopping-cum-office centres, respectively. These three sales accounted for an investment of S$500 million and provided employment for fifty thousand people. To allow for time in consolidation, no sites came up for sale in the next four years (Choe, 1975). The sale of sites was again offered in 1974 and at the seventh sale programme in 1978 overseas tenders were invited for the first time. At the latest (eighth) sale in 1980, the competition for prime land among foreign and local developers was unprecedented in enthusiasm and turnout.[1] By degrees, an increasing number of sites outside the central city area are being developed. In preparation for its expanded scope of activities, the Urban Renewal Department of the HDB was reconstituted as a statutory board called the Urban Redevelopment Authority since 1975. From its inception, an important reason for the success of the Singapore urban renewal programme has been the orchestration of redevelopment activities with resettlement, public housing and national development plans. Another positive factor has been the legislative powers bestowed upon the pertinent authority.

In contrast to Singapore, the fate of Hong Kong's urban renewal scheme has been very disappointing from all points of view. The area identified for renewal was, and is, undoubtedly one of the most congested and dilapidated districts in the colony, spanning as it does the original "Chinatown" of nineteenth-century Hong Kong. The initial Working Party Report was submitted in 1965 when a large section of Western District on Hong Kong Island was selected for comprehensive renewal, and a Pilot Scheme was commenced a few years later (Drakakis-Smith, 1976).

Unfortunately, the government has found it increasingly difficult to maintain its enthusiasm for urban renewal, largely as a result of the fact that the process appears to be too expensive. As a result, responsibility for the project has been pushed further down the bureaucratic scale and although large areas of the Pilot Scheme have been cleared, protracted negotiations between private developers and leaseholders have been allowed to drag on interminably. The Hong Kong Government has, in fact, confined its interest to structural improvement only, primarily roads and recreational space; it does not intend to construct any low-cost housing, although it has subsidized a small programme by the quasi-autonomous Housing Society.

---

[1]Bids were reported to be as high as S$2,000 per sq. ft. See *Straits Times*, 1 February 1980.

Consequently many residents have been forced out of the renewal district into either cheap government housing on the urban periphery or other tenements close by. The same situation also exists in Singapore (Western and Tan, 1973), and raises the question of how the success of renewal or rehousing programmes should be measured—a topic which will be discussed further in the conclusion to this paper.

Because of increasingly high-density developments concomitant with population growth and economic progress, the need for urban renewal has been growing rapidly in both city-states. In spite of Hong Kong's general *laissez-faire* policy, there has been no shortage of private initiatives or resources to continually renew the urban structure. In fact, in an attempt to strive towards a progressively higher-density target, it is not uncommon for urban projects not yet past their natural life span to be demolished in favour of developments of even higher density and greater economic return. It is thus not a want of ideas or enthusiasm, but rather the lack of a coordinated blueprint and government leadership, that has bedevilled the Hong Kong urban renewal programme. On the other hand, it is precisely because of the strong leadership assumed by the Singapore Government that its urban renewal programme has upgraded the quality and density of development to such an extent that an urban transformation can justifiably be said to have occurred (Yeung, 1973). Consequently the two programmes as exemplified in Hong Kong and Singapore do provide a sharp contrast in the style and efficacy of government planning notwithstanding their equally impressive results and pace of development.

URBAN TRANSPORT

Transportation plays a crucial role in urban development, linking residence and workplace, producer and consumer. As cities grow and become more prosperous the use of motorized transport has swelled enormously, and in many parts of the Third World automobiles have increased at rates two to five times those of the urban populations as a whole. On a global scale, whilst population increased by less than 20 per cent in the period from 1967 to 1970, the number of automobiles more than doubled. Most of the automobiles in developing countries are concentrated in large cities. These may have a smaller vehicle to people ratio compared to the typical Western city but because of their overall population size, often have higher absolute numbers of automobiles. In many Third World cities this situation has created huge problems of congestion and pollution, the solution of which has placed tremendous financial burdens on cities with pressing alternative problems. Moreover, the policies adopted to date have served only to increase the road capacity for automobiles. In particular, such policies have not always led to greater efficiency, especially for the urban poor whose modes of transport, such as pedicabs, have often been prohibited from the main roads.

The high cost of systems giving priority to the automobile has in recent years led to an intensive search for alternative policies: two main options have emerged. The first is a more effective transport pricing system in which road users, particularly those who are motorized, are made to bear an appropriate share of the costs they place on society as a whole; the second revolved around a more sympathetic and supportive attitude towards non-conventional, sometimes non-motorized, modes of transit. In Hong Kong and Singapore, where limited space has intensified an already acute transportation problem, a wide range of attitudes has influenced the planning responses and many administrators in the rest of Asia are keeping a close watch on the situation in the city-states to see how effective each measure is.

Of the two, Singapore has been more rigorous in its attempts to control the growth of, and the difficulties posed by the expansion of private car-ownership. As in many other Asian cities, Singapore has tried several tax and fiscal disincentives over the past few years to dampen the rise of automobile ownership and, in particular, the entry of vehicles into the city centre during rush hours. None of these measures has really worked to satisfaction, so much so that an innovative, if not drastic, policy has been put into practice since 1975 which effectively restricts the movement of vehicles into the city core during certain hours.

Called the "area licensing" scheme, it delineated 620 hectares of the central city area which are cordoned off as a restricted zone from 7:30 a.m. to 10:15 a.m. To be able to pass the twenty-two entry points in to the city centre, private automobiles not otherwise qualified under car-polling exemption must purchase an area licence on a monthly or a daily basis, hence the term congestion price. From all indications, the scheme has been widely acclaimed as a success. During the restricted hours in March and August 1975, the traffic entering the central city recorded a 40 per cent reduction. Happily, the implementation of the scheme is now routine and generally free from major problems. What is more, the monthly sale of

7,000 area licences brought an additional revenue of almost half a million Singapore dollars to government coffers (Watson and Holland, 1976). These direct impacts of the new policy may extend to an accelerated trend towards decentralization from the city centre as well as an easier movement of goods in the restricted area by wholesalers and retailers. Furthermore, a recent study has shown that indirect benefits accruing to the scheme include the increased ease of crossing streets, cleaner air and an improved image of central Singapore (Holland and Watson, 1978). Given certain adaptations to suit local conditions, the application of this scheme to other Asian cities is far from an impossibility.

Hong Kong, with only 625 miles of roadway, faces even thornier problems of urban transport. With a concentrated urban area, high level of business and economic activity, and low private automobile ownership,[2] conditions seemed favourable for the operation of rapid mass transit of some form in Hong Kong. Soon after the politically motivated riots in 1967, the mini-bus operation became legalized in the urban area. Whilst it has alleviated the congestion in the buses and trams, it aggravates the overloading of the overall traffic density. The cross-harbour tunnel, opened in 1972 and now carrying ninety-two thousand vehicles a day between Kowloon and Victoria, has shortened the travel time between many points across the harbour. However, for many planners and administrators the greatest hope of improvement in urban transport lies in the underground railway, the first stage of operation of which was opened for service in late 1979. For Hong Kong, "the problem is not to find passengers for the transit vehicles, but to find enough transit vehicles to accommodate those desiring to ride" (Smith, 1969:125). Hong Kong has thus joined the ranks of Tokyo, Osaka, Nagoya, Seoul, Pyongyang and Peking in being served by a subway network in Asia. Hong Kong's system is one of the most modern in the region whose reception and operation, particularly its pricing and subsidy policy, will be watched with interest by urban planners in many other Asian cities.

The more recent crisis related to fossil fuel supplies has added a new

---

[2] Automobile ownership is considerably lower in Hong Kong than in Singapore. In 1977 there was one automobile for 36.7 persons in Hong Kong and one for 17.1 persons in Singapore. However, patronage of motorized public transport was equally high, accounting for 78.3 and 67.3 per cent of the trips in Hong Kong and Singapore, respectively.

dimension to transport planning in Asia. Not only is there a concern to improve the linkages between "action space" and control pollution, but also a
desire generally to reduce the overall consumption of imported oil. In this respect, Hong Kong, with its greater commitment to a wide range of public
transport, seems better placed than Singapore where dependence on the private automobile is still very high. Even so, Hong Kong has begun to impose
more punitive controls on its vehicle population, and is seriously considering
the introduction of a restricted access scheme for its central districts. However, in both cities fuel consumption is still rising rapidly and the less healthy
urban centres of Asia may have to look elsewhere for more useful transportation policies, particularly if the urban poor are to benefit directly.

THE URBAN ENVIRONMENT

While housing, renewal and transportation are critically important components in planning programmes for high-density living, they cannot and must
not be pursued in isolation from one another or without consideration
for their effect on the city as a whole. In Singapore it has been argued
by architect-planners, such as Tay (1969, 1979) and Lim (1973), that the
single-minded pursuit of economic growth and the pace of urban change
have been needlessly rapid and that some planning practices and instruments should be carefully examined before they are widely applied. They
have, for example, questioned the wisdom of rigid zoning according to
classified usages, road construction to maximize vehicular accessibility to
the central area, and indiscriminate increase in the plot ratio and density.
They have also argued for the introduction of low-rise, high-density public
housing to complement the high-rise, high-density developments since
1960. At a more general level, the rapidity with which the city core, which
encompasses the most colourful and well-defined sections of Chinese settlements, commonly called the Old and New Chinatowns, is being torn
down by urban redevelopment programmes has continued to attract pleas of
conservation from concerned observers both in Singapore and abroad. This
is where value judgements come in, because from many Asian perspectives
Singapore is a veritable garden city.

   In Hong Kong, too, there has recently been a growth of interest in the
environment. This is largely discussed in terms of "balanced community
growth," a concept which is difficult to define and which tends to have

different meaning for different sections of the community. In the metropolitan area, it is interpreted in terms of facilities—the amount of open space, the availability of health services and the like. These are, of course, the quantifiable aspects of the social planning process. On the other hand, the more subtle elements of urban environmental balance, such as the conservation of architecturally interesting building, receive scant support. Perhaps this is inevitable in space-conscious Hong Kong but it is nonetheless depressing to see the cynical way in which inconvenient aspects of environmental planning are sacrificed to "progress."

One respect in which Hong Kong differs from Singapore and perhaps has more in common with other Asian cities, is in the problem rapid growth has posed for the adjacent rural areas. This theme was very prominent in the symposium held in the colony on Geography and the Environment in 1976 (Hill and Bray, 1978), and since this date a determined effort has been made to control the deprivations of urban sprawl in terms of both agriculture and recreational activities. In this latter case, the new system of country parks has been established throughout the "New Territories," not only to maximize the recreational use of open space but also to ensure vital water-catchment areas suffer minimal damage.

To the extent that both Hong Kong and Singapore are high energy consumers, even for fundamental needs, the pattern of recent changes in energy use together with growing energy demands does add a significant dimension to the management of the urban environment. As Newcombe has elaborated elsewhere in this volume, the shift from solid fuels to liquid petroleum fuels was almost complete in Hong Kong by 1971. Between 1971 and 1978, energy use increased at an annual rate of 6.8 per cent whilst energy imports grew by an astonishing 64 per cent. A conservative estimate projected a five-fold increase in energy use by the year 2000. Clearly at such an accelerated rate of energy consumption, the problems posed to a high-density urban environment in heat stress and air pollution are grave, not to mention the high costs in the procurement of the fuel supplies. The biggest challenge faced by Hong Kong and Singapore would, therefore, be the search for alternative patterns of organization and production which would allow a reduction in energy consumption without affecting the quality off life. In this respect, conservation, a higher government profile in energy management, improvement in building regulations and management, and lower energy consumption strategies, are some of the policy options that must be seriously pursued.

DISCUSSION

The foregoing account of some important aspects of planning in Singapore
and Hong Kong as high-density urban centres has been necessarily brief
and cannot do justice to either the scope of the problems or the attempted
solutions. However, it has been the contention of this paper that although
many of the problems faced by the two cities may have local peculiarities,
they frequently mirror situations towards which many Asian cities will
move in their continued efforts to achieve greater economic development
and urban efficiency. On the other hand, it is clear that planning does
not take place within a social vacuum and that all developments must
be evaluated in terms of the benefits they bring to the society concerned. This raises the important question, posed earlier, of how success is
to be evaluated and which criteria should be used to measure "urban
efficiency."

It must be very tempting for planners and administrators from other
Asian cities to return from visits to Singapore and Hong Kong thinking that
they have "seen the future and it works." Indeed, the two cities do "work"
considerably better than most, including those in Japan. Perhaps the most
important criterion for estimating the degree of success lies in the extent
to which the benefits of prosperity have filtered down to the poor. As
discussed by Chau elsewhere in this volume, Hong Kong and Singapore are
slowly moving towards greater income equality, in complete contrast to
most other cities in the Third World. Whilst many radicals would question
whether the relative position of the poor has improved to any great extent,
there is no doubt that the lower echelons of society are better off in Hong
Kong or Singapore than in most other Asian cities. On the other hand, it is
appropriate to question the motivation behind such egalitarian trends because it is clearly political rather than welfare considerations which have
moulded government policy in this respect.

Whilst the general well-being of the urban poor is undoubtedly tied to
overall economic growth, the distribution of benefits is closely linked to the
various planning programmes geared to the exceptional high-density conditions found in the two city-states. This is most evident in housing and in this
respect, Hong Kong and Singapore seem to have achieved a great deal for
the low-income groups. However, in both cities government housing programmes have been pursued primarily for economic or political objectives
rather than those of social welfare (Buchanan, 1972; Drakakis-Smith,

1979). From a strictly national perspective, the Singapore housing programme is regarded as a notable success. Yeh, for example, cites the geographical redistribution of the population, the political stabilization of the economy, and general economic well-being as important consequences (Yeh, 1979). The social benefits tend to be played down somewhat and several surveys have failed to reveal widespread enthusiasm amongst HDB residents for the changes that relocation has brought. Moreover, as few surveys of those who have refused public housing have been undertaken, it is difficult to assess the real impact of public housing on the poorest elements in Singaporean society. Certainly within the estates, satisfaction correlates closely with economic status (Hassan, 1976).

The increasing middle-income bias in housing programmes, which is characteristics of both cities, is also reflected in transportation policies. This is particularly true of Hong Kong where the pro-automobile schemes of road improvement, such as elevated freeways, favour the car-owning household at the expense of the living environment of the poor. The mass transit system, too, will bring little benefit to the lower-income families unless costs are heavily subsidized. Given these circumstances, the benefits of the Hong Kong and Singapore experience must be carefully evaluated, because they may not always accrue to the most needy groups in society. However, this might not concern planners in the rest of Asia who may well perceive the main objectives for controlled urban growth to be economic or political rather than social. If this is the case, then Hong Kong and Singapore clearly offer desirable models to follow; but if it is not, and let us hope that this is so, then the lessons from the two cities must be assessed very carefully. This perhaps poses the most crucial dilemma—growth for whom?

Finally, apart from the above considerations of the primary beneficiaries of the planning strategies adopted, the experience of Hong Kong and Singapore in their relative success in coping with large populations on severely limited land is likely to be increasingly relevant to other large urban centres in Asia. Considering their comparatively strong economic position and exceptional geographical setting, solutions and policies which have evolved in the two city-states will probably have to be adapted for maximum effectiveness in other situations. All the same, the store of practical experience in the planning for high-density urban centres will be of value to more cities faced with similar problems in the future.

REFERENCES

Buchanan, I. 1972. *Singapore in Southeast Asia*. London: G. Bell and Sons.

Choe, F. C. 1975. "Urban Renewal." In *Public Housing in Singapore: A Multi-Disciplinary Study*, ed. S.H.K. Yeh, pp. 97–116.

Drakakis-Smith, D. W. 1976. "Urban Renewal in an Asian Context." *Urban Studies*, 13(3):296–306.

————. 1979. *High Society: Housing Provision in Metropolitan Hong Kong from 1954 to 1979*. Hong Kong: Centre of Asian Studies, University of Hong Kong.

Geiger, T. and M. Geiger. 1973. *Tales of Two City-States: The Development Progress of Hong Kong and Singapore*. Studies in Development Progress, No. 3. Washington, D.C.: National Planning Association.

Hassan, R. 1976. "Public Housing." In *Singapore: Society in Transition*, ed. R. Hassan. Kuala Lumpur: Oxford University Press.

————. 1977. *Families in Flats: A Study of Low Income Families in Public Housing*. Singapore: Singapore University Press.

HDB. See Housing and Development Board.

Hill, R. D. and J. M. Bray, eds. 1978. *Geography and the Environment in Southeast Asia*. Hong Kong: Hong Kong University Press.

Hodder, B. W. 1953. "Racial Groupings in Singapore." *Malayan Journal of Tropical Geography*, 1:25–36.

Holland, E. P. and P. L. Watson. 1978. "Traffic Restraint in Singapore." *Traffic Engineering and Control*, 19(1):14–22.

Housing and Development Board (HDB). 1979. *Annual Report 1978–1979*. Singapore.

Koenigsberger, Otto. 1964. "Action Planning." *Architectural Association Journal*, pp. 306–12.

Koh, T.T.B. and W.S.W. Lim. 1969. "Planning Law and Process in Singapore." *Malaya Law Review*, 11(2):315–44.

Lim, W.S.W. 1973. "The Impact of Economic Development on the Physical Environment of Singapore." *The Developing Economics*, 11(4):409–15.

Liu, Thai Ker. 1975. "Design for Better Living Condition." In *Public Housing in Singapore: A Multi-Disciplinary Study*, ed. S.H.K. Yeh, pp. 117–84.

Meier, Richard L. 1970. "Exploring Development in Great Asian Cities: Seoul." *Journal of Association of Institute of Planners*, 36(6):378–92.

Pun, K. S. 1978. "Planning for Environmental Balance: A Theoretical Study of the Hong Kong Situation." In *Geography and the Environment in Southeast Asia*, ed. R. D. Hill and J. M. Bray, pp. 323–45.

Scott, Ian. 1979. "Administrative Adaptation and the New Towns Policy in Hong Kong." Port Moresby: Waigani Seminar on Urbanization, University of Papua New Guinea. Unpublished paper.

Smith, Wilbur S. 1969. "Mass Transportation for Hong Kong." *Ekistics*, 27(159):124–30.

Tak, Kheng Soon. 1969. "Housing and Urban Values—Singapore." *Ekistics*, 27(158):27–28.

————. 1979. "The Architecture of Rapid Development." *School of Architecture Journal*, 1(1):5–11. Singapore: University of Singapore.

Tan, Jake Hooi. 1966. "Metropolitan Planning in Singapore." *Australian Planning Institute Journal*, 4(3):1–9.

Watson, P. L. and E. P. Holland. 1976. "Congestion Pricing—The Example of Singapore." *Finance and Development*, 13(1):20–23.

Western, J. S., P. D. Weldon and Tsu Haung Tan. 1973. "Poverty, Urban Renewal and Public Housing in Singapore." *Environment and Planning*, 5:589–600.

Wong, L.S.K., ed. 1978. *Housing in Hong Kong: A Multi-Disciplinary Study*. Hong Kong: Heinemann.

World Bank. 1979. *World Development Report 1979*. Washington, D.C.

Yeh, S.H.K., ed. 1975. *Public Housing in Singapore: A Multi-Disciplinary Study*. Singapore: Singapore University Press.

————. 1979. "Residential Mobility and Public Housing." In *Migration and Development in Southeast Asia*, ed. R. J. Pryor, pp. 165–74. Kuala Lumpur: Oxford University Press.

Yeung, Yue-man. 1973. *National Development Policy and Urban Transformation in Singapore: A Study of Public Housing and the Marketing System*. Research Paper No. 149. Chicago: Department of Geography, University of Chicago.

————. 1976. "Southeast Asian Cities: Patterns of Growth and Transformation." In *Urbanization and Counterurbanization*, ed. B.J.L. Berry, pp. 285–309. Beverly Hills: Sage Publication. (Included in this book as Chapter 6.)

————. 1978. "The Urban Environment of Southeast Asia: Challenge and Opportunity." In *Geography and the Environment in Southeast Asia*, ed. R. D. Hill and J. M. Bray, pp. 17–33. (Included in this book as Chapter 7.)

Yeung, Yue-man and D. W. Drakakis-Smith. 1982. "Public Housing in the City States of Hong Kong and Singapore." In *Urban Planning Practice in Developing Countries*, ed. J. L. Taylor and D. G. Williams, pp. 217–38. Oxford: Pergamon Press.

10. Cities That Work: Hong Kong and Singapore*

INTRODUCTION

Situated 2,583 kilometres apart on the Asian Pacific rim and serving their respective geographic regions, the city-states of Hong Kong and Singapore are frequently paired in development, scholarly and planning circles. Hardly two cities so separated geographically are cited more often in the same context because of their numerous similarities. Both cities are widely known for their successful socioeconomic transformation in recent decades, yet it was achieved through different planning approaches and political philosophies.

Parallels between Hong Kong and Singapore may be drawn on many planes. Both are city-states of compact size[1] whose modern history began as British colonies in the nineteenth century. Similarly short of natural resources, except for their harbours, both depended heavily on entrepôt trade as their economic base until the 1950s. They have since developed into export-oriented manufacturing economies of world stature. The majority of their population is Chinese, noted for their Confucian ethics and social cohesiveness. The per capita gross domestic product of both cities ranks the highest in Asia after Japan. Most important, from the viewpoint of urban development, Hong Kong and Singapore are fascinating case studies because their urban policies have been painstakingly designed and successfully implemented. Many urban planners and policy-makers from developing countries visit the city-states and come away with the conviction that they have seen the future and it works.

*The helpful research assistance of Miss Yvette Luke Ying at the Centre for Contemporary Asian Studies, in the preparation of this chapter is gratefully acknowledged.
[1] The total areas of Hong Kong and Singapore are 1,064 and 602 square kilometres, respectively.

To have entitled this chapter "Cities That Work" may have been presumptuous, as no city can claim to be fully efficient. In view of the urban predicament in which many developing countries have found themselves, however, it is instructive to compare the development experiences of Hong Kong and Singapore. This chapter first analyzes the developmental context in each city that makes it possible for urban policies to be formulated and carried out, then examines urban housing and transportation as two facets of urban development policies, and finally offers concluding observations about some of the problems that have yet to be solved and prospects for the future.

THE ALCHEMY OF SUCCESS

The success that Hong Kong and Singapore have enjoyed in their urban policies is premised upon several contextual factors, the first of which is political stability. Anachronistic because it is still a British colony, Hong Kong has experienced few political upheavals. Only three major riots have rocked the territory in the postwar period—in 1956, 1966 and 1967. Through political co-option, many local Chinese leaders have been absorbed into the power structure through membership in the councils. Many others serve in consultative and advisory capacities at various governmental levels, while still others are bestowed honours. The real and day-to-day governing power lies in the hands of the civil service, headed by the chief secretary, under the direction of the governor. Hong Kong is said to be an "administered city," governed by "departmentocracy" (King, 1981:133). It has forty government departments, providing employment in 1983 to 173,788 civil servants, a phenomenal increase compared with 17,500 in 1949 and 60,286 in 1963 (Hong Kong, GIS, various years). It has been argued that the large public bureaucracy has contributed to political stability through the absorption of the potentially "discontented" into the governing machinery (King, 1981:134). To these factors may be added international power politics and the political apathy of the Chinese, both conducive to political stability in the territory (Lau, 1981:209). A delicate equilibrium of political forces has been achieved in which a centralized, powerful and administratively capable bureaucracy has been able to target and complete development projects. To combat the problem of rampant corruption, which had plagued the public bureaucracy and the private sector for many years, the Independent Commission Against Corruption was established in 1974.

Political leadership has been a critical factor in Singapore's economic and social progress since self-rule in 1959 and independence in 1965. The People's Action Party, which has been in power since 1959, has built its political platform on its record of economic and social achievements. It was again returned to power in the December 1984 general election, although the opposition parties were able to win two of the seventy-nine seats. Singapore's political stability has been noteworthy in a region often shaken by political turmoil, but it was accomplished through sometimes ruthless subordination of opposition. Since 1959 Singapore has forsaken *laissez-faire* policies in favour of what has been described as the elite and the interventionist approach, which is efficient, pragmatic and top-down (Chen, 1983:20). National development in independent Singapore has been characteristically project-oriented, carried out by statutory boards that numbered more than ninety in 1982. The demanding approach to urban governance has been well summed up by Prime Minister Lee Kuan Yew:

> Everything works [here], whether it is water, electricity, gas, telephone, telexes. It just has to work. And if I am not satisfied, as often as not, the chief goes. And I have to find another chief. Firing a chief is very simple, getting one who will do the job better, that is different (Stockwin, 1984:2).

A second factor in the rapid economic growth of Hong Kong and Singapore has been their successful development policies. Despite their different political philosophies and leaderships, the two cities have achieved equal distinction as export-manufacturing bases, financial centres and tourist destinations. In 1983 Hong Kong's domestic exports amounted to HK$104,405 million (Hong Kong, GIS, 1984:20).[2] With one of the largest industrial economies in Asia, Hong Kong is by far Asia's ranking territory in terms of per capita value of manufacturing production; it is followed by Singapore, Taiwan and South Korea.[3] Sustained high economic performance has led to a per capita GDP increase of more than eleven times in two decades, from

---

[2]In 1985 US$1 was converted to approximately HK$7.80 at a pegged rate. By comparison US$1 was traded for approximately S$2.2.

[3]Their respective per capita figures were US$815, $446, $258 and $220. The fifth ranking country was the Philippines, with only US$85 (Sit, 1983:179).

HK$2,382 to $30,240 (Hong Kong, CSD, 1984:8). The buoyant economy permits the government to spend the lion's share on social services such as education, medical care, public housing, social welfare and labour training. In fiscal year 1982–1983 the government spent 42 per cent of the total recurrent budget outlay of HK$20,498 million on these services (Hong Kong, GIS, 1984:284). Hong Kong is now the third largest financial centre in the world. In 1982, 2.6 million tourists visited Hong Kong, each spending an average of HK$3,137 (Hong Kong, CSD, 1983:84–85).

In almost every aspect cited above, Singapore rivals Hong Kong. Economic, social, demographic and other indicators for the two city-states are compared in Table 10.1.

A third factor in the success of Hong Kong and Singapore is that they have both evolved efficient and flexible planning processes and approaches to achieve urban development. In Hong Kong the primary legislation to facilitate urban planning is the Hong Kong Town Planning Ordinance, enacted in 1939 and subsequently modified several times. It is an admirably short document consisting of only eighteen sections, but it is effective, easy to interpret, especially suitable to the highly intermixed urban land-use pattern prevailing in the territory, and flexible to meet rapidly changing circumstances (Pun, 1983). The overall long-term planning document is the Colony Outline Plan of 1972, in 1979 retitled the Hong Kong Outline Plan. As early as 1958, when considering a plan for the district of Ma Tau Kok, the governor-in-council agreed that mixed zoning should be used out of fear of heavy compensation in the case of land acquisition through the traditional zoning approach. For similar reasons, the secretariat decided against blanket adoption of statutory planning in 1959 (Bristow, 1984:229–30). Two committees—the Town Planning Board and the Land Development Policy Committee—are principally responsible for land-use planning in Hong Kong. Thus essential policy-making is centralized within the committee hierarchy, and operational departments implement the committees' decisions (Bristow, 1984:173). Consequently, a great deal of urban planning takes place outside the statutory planning mechanism in the form of district plans or "action plans." These departmental plans, which are constantly amended to reflect changing socioeconomic conditions, can be revised through administrative procedures rather than the more complicated requirements stipulated in the ordinance (Pun, 1983). The ordinance does provide for citizen participation in the town planning process and stipulates that draft plans be exhibited for public inspection for two months, a period considered adequate for ensuring democratic contributions. Two recent developments are worthy of note as attempting to improve coordination between government departments. In 1982 responsibility for all land matters were brought under a single authority, the director of lands. The unified department coordinates all aspects of land administration—surveying, planning, land sales and development, and legal matters. In the same year, however, the previously centralized planning functions of the government were subdivided. With the reorganization of planning functions, the Central Planning Office is now responsible for planning standards, structure and statutes; strategic planning remains with the Strategic Planning Unit in the Lands and Works Branch; and action planning in the existing urban areas has been transferred to the Urban Area Development Organization, whereas that of the rest of the territory is gradually being shifted to the New Territories Development Department (Pun, 1984:68). It remains to be seen if the reorganized administrative structure is a real improvement.

In Singapore urban planning had a more definite start, at least in the central area, through Sir Stamford Raffles's directives in the nineteenth century to segregate the area adjacent to the two sides of the Singapore River according to ethnic group (Hodder, 1953). At the national level the urban landscape has undergone rapid changes along lines that were spelled out in the Singapore master plan, approved in 1958, and more recently the concept plan, which was approved in 1971 after years of study assisted by United Nations consultants. Singapore's planning process has been treated in detail by J. H. Tan (1966) and Koh and Lim (1969); Koenigsberger (1964) has advocated action planning within the framework of the master plan.

A crucial feature of the planning process is centralization. The minister of law and national development is responsible for physical planning and, under a planning ordinance enacted in 1959, is empowered, among other things, to sanction the master plan and additions and alterations thereof, and to appoint the authorities to administer the planning ordinance. The planning ordinance and other related ordinances enacted subsequently provided the necessary legal framework for the urban transformation that has occurred in Singapore since self-rule (Yeung, 1973:27–42). The Planning Department is responsible for the day-to-day administration of the planning ordinance, and the chief planner is represented on the Master Plan Committee (MPC) appointed by the minister. The MPC ensures that development plans submitted by various public agencies are consistent with the provisions of the master plan and generally compatible in planning and

TABLE 10.1

Key Development Indicators: Hong Kong and Singapore, 1960, 1970 and 1983

Indicator	Hong Kong			Singapore		
	1960	1970	1983	1960	1970	1983
Economic						
GDP[a] (in millions) at current market prices	HK$6,050 (1961)	HK$21,879	HK$205,427	S$2,150	S$5,805	S$35,171
Per capita GDP[a] at current market prices	HK$1,910 (1961)	HK$ 5,526	HK$ 38,664	S$1,306	S$2,798	S$14,057
Percentage of labour force in manufacturing	39.9% (1961)	39.4%	36.1%	14.2% (1957)	22.0%	27.8%
Percentage of women in labour force	36.8% (1961)	42.8% (1971)	47.4%	21.6% (1957)	29.5%	45.7%
Unemployment rate	1.3% (1961)	4.5% (1971)	4.5%	4.9% (1957)	6.0%	3.3%
Consumer Price Index[b]	33.4	44.7	143.2	55.2	61.5	130.8
Tourist arrivals[c]	163,700	927,256	2,775,014	90,100	521,700[c]	2,853,600
Demographic						
Total population size	3,075,300	3,959,000	5,313,200	1,646,400	2,074,500	2,502,000
Percentage of population under 20 years of age	46.1% (1961)	47.9% (1961)	33.5%	53.0%	50.7%	35.5%
Percentage of population over 60 years of age	4.8% (1961)	6.5%	10.8%	4.0%	5.7%	7.5%
Dependency ratio[d]	77.3% (1961)	69.4% (1961)	45.1%		72.8%	43.1%
Crude birth rate per 1,000 population	36.0	20.0	15.7	37.5	22.1	16.2
Crude death rate per 1,000 population	6.2	5.1	5.0	6.2	5.2	5.3
Natural growth rate per 1,000 population	30.0	14.9	10.7	31.3	17.0	10.9

Social

Total population in public housing	357,340	1,436,000	2,186,300	149,800	717,800	1,926,000
Percentage of population in public housing	11.6%	36.5%	41.5%	9.1%	34.6%	77.0%
Percentage of school-age children (6–17) in school	83.2% (1961)	86.1%	94.4%	—	76.7% (1972)	88.2%
Persons per registered doctor	3,072	1,819	1,130	2,573	1,522	1,060
Divorces[e]	52	215	3,446	574	219	2,136 (1982)
Criminal offences against persons and property per 10,000 population	37	66	147	78	68	121

Others

Telephones	108,799	583,200	2,050,000	59,722	161,310	923,000
Telephones per 1,000 population	35.4	147.3	379.0	36.3	77.8	368.9
Private automobiles	31,507	92,884	200,923	63,344	142,568	202,092
Population per automobile	97.6	42.6	26.4	26.0	14.6	12.4
Traffic fatalities	189	381	336	155	287	297
Traffic injuries	7,695	13,179	21,638	5,736	9,932	10,819

Sources: Variously derived official statistics.
Notes: a. GDP in 1983 is preliminary for Singapore and revised preliminary for Hong Kong.
b. Base year for Hong Kong: 1979–1980 = 100. Base year for Singapore: 1977–1978 = 100.
c. Includes arrivals by air and sea (but not land).
d. Calculated as the population under 15 and over 65 years of age divided by the population 15–64 years old.
e. Only Supreme Court figures available for Hong Kong in 1960 and 1970.

design standards. Liu (1975) describes the various stages through which the development of a public housing estate must go, and Choe (1975) provides a summary of how urban renewal schemes are approved and implemented. After planning approval is secured, endorsement by various other government authorities in charge of such matters as roads, sewerage, drainage, public health, factory inspection, antipollution and fire prevention, is necessary before actual development takes place. For development proposals emanating from the private sector, the Development Control Committee, also appointed by the minister, decides if they meet prescribed standards. Such development projects as schools, hospitals, roads, bridges, drainage and sewerage come under the responsibility of the Public Works Department, also located in the Ministry of Law and National Development. Thus the same ministry has direct or indirect control over many agencies and statutory boards, and this arrangement has facilitated the coordination and implementation of many development plans. The result is a reasonably effective system of metropolitan planning.

The fourth factor that lends support to the urban transition in Hong Kong and Singapore is their geography. Although both city-states are small, size has not been an inhibiting factor for their economic and urban development (Dwyer, 1965). By necessity, rather than by choice, the urban ecology of both cities has evolved into high-rise, high-density living that has its merits (Yeung, 1977). Pun (1984:66) argues that high-density vertical urban development has the advantages of minimizing urban encroachment into the countryside, facilitating the provision of services, maximizing convenience, and maximizing the use of scarce land resources. Even though high-rise structures are more costly to build and maintain than low-rise buildings, it is argued that the overall costs to the community are lower. Administratively, the small size of Hong Kong and Singapore necessitates only one level of government,[4] thus avoiding the bureaucratic redundancy and competition that often saddle multilevel administrations. The limited area of each city is more than compensated for by its strategic location in relation to dynamic and growing regions, Hong Kong vis-à-vis southern

---

[4]Although power is heavily concentrated in the central government, Hong Kong has recently evolved a three-tier administrative structure consisting of (1) the executive and legislative councils, (2) the urban council and district administration, and (3) the district boards.

China and Singapore vis-à-vis Southeast Asia. Moreover, Hong Kong and Singapore are no longer burdened by massive rural-to-urban migration. In Singapore in-migration ceased to be a major cause of population growth during the postwar period. Hong Kong, however, has had to deal with successive waves of migrants from China and, in the 1970s, from Vietnam. Only since the abandonment of the "touch-base" policy in 1980 has population inflow from China become more controlled. In any event, because they lack a large rural hinterland, both city-states can concentrate their resources, financial or otherwise, on urban and national development.

Finally, having a resourceful and industrious population has been a primary asset in the development experience of both Hong Kong and Singapore. Nevertheless, both administrations have taken the view for some time that if left uncontrolled and unguided, population growth would easily whittle away whatever gains in living standards that economic growth may bring. By 1983 the vital statistics of the two city-states were very similar (Table 10.1).

Singapore's official policy of controlling population growth is implemented through an intensive family planning programme and comprehensive policy measures, including legal abortion, liberalized sterilization, and incentives and disincentives relating to maternity benefits, accouchement fees, tax reduction, allocation of public housing, and primary school registration. From a postwar high of 3.23 children per woman in 1957, the gross reproduction rate fell every year to a low of 1.02 in 1975. Thus in merely eighteen years Singapore effected a demographic transition, achieving replacement fertility for its population of 2.25 million (Chen and Fawcett, 1979; Saw, 1980).

Similarly, Hong Kong's fertility decline was assisted by the efforts of the Hong Kong Family Planning Association, initially a private initiative that later turned into a government programme. Hong Kong, however, has no territory-wide population policy linked to social and economic policies. All the same, the family planning programme, together with self-motivational factors, accounted for rapid decline of the birth rate from 39.7 births per 1,000 in 1956 to 19.7 per 1,000 in 1971. A study undertaken by the Hong Kong Family Planning Association in 1967 and 1972 found an inclination towards smaller families as evidenced by the increasing use of contraception among women between ages 15 and 44—from 44 per cent in 1967 to 54 per cent in 1972 (HKFPA, 1975:39).

PUBLIC HOUSING

Against the background of unsuccessful mass housing in cities of many developing countries, Hong Kong's and Singapore's conspicuously effective policy of housing a vast proportion of the population through the use of public funds has attracted widespread attention. Their comparative experience in this achievement has been analyzed elsewhere (Yeung and Drakakis-Smith, 1974, 1982). It will suffice for this chapter to highlight some of the salient elements of that experience and recent policy changes.

Public housing in Hong Kong originated in 1953 when a large squatter fire in the district of Shek Kip Mei forced the government into providing emergency resettlement housing. As measured by quantitative yardsticks and low cost, the resettlement housing achieved notable success in providing shelter to a large number of people within a short period, especially in the uncertain political climate of the 1950s. Resettlement housing has been criticized as being a central component of public housing whose standards have been too low for too long. The peak of resettlement housing was reached in the period from 1963 to 1967, when more than 20,000 units were constructed annually. When the Ten-Year Housing Programme began in 1973, some 234,059 resettlement housing units were already completed, providing shelter to over one million inhabitants.

Resettlement housing, especially Marks I and II, is the lowest grade of public housing, built to abysmal standards with communal kitchens and toilet facilities. Better-quality public housing became available through a low-cost housing programme in 1964 and from the Housing Authority and the Housing Society. All these types of public housing were provided with little coordination between them until 1973, when the separate programmes were amalgamated into a unified and reconstituted Housing Authority. At the same time, an ambitious programme to house 1.8 million people was announced for the period from 1973 to 1982. Unfortunately, early bureaucratic restructuring problems, the world recession triggered by the oil crisis and the gradual depletion of developable urban areas caused the building programme to slow down until the late 1970s. During the ten-year period only 220,527 units were completed, housing about one million inhabitants, which represent quite a shortfall from the original target. Nonetheless, the longer-term programme sets Hong Kong on the path to a public housing policy noted for its progressive outlook and widened participation.

The first significant policy shift was spatial. Since 1973, when the urban area had reached a saturation point, public housing has been constructed primarily in the new towns of the New Territories. In large new towns like Shatin and Tuen Mun, as much as 70 per cent of the population is expected to live in public housing estates. These towns are planned to high architectural, aesthetic, and service standards and are supposed to be self-contained and socially balanced. The latter two goals are not fully attained, however, and self-sufficiency in employment is difficult to achieve (W. T. Leung, 1983; Yeh and Fong, 1984). Despite the public's initial reluctance to live in the new towns away from the city, the attraction of superior living conditions and a much shorter waiting time for housing (three to four years as opposed to eight or nine years in the more central localities) quickly overcame this hesitancy, resulting in accelerated population decentralization. By 1984 as much as 36 per cent of the housing stock and 37 per cent of the tenants were located in the new towns (Hong Kong, HKHA, 1984a) (see Fig. 10.1). During 1971–1981 fully half of the population increase was due to the growth of new towns. Those towns are poised for even faster development, given improved transportation links via a recently modernized and electrified railway system and a light rail system that is under construction. Their land holdings also rest on a more certain future as a result of the recent Sino-British accord over the governance of Hong Kong when Great Britain's stewardship of the territory ends in 1997.

Although public housing has already benefited 2.4 million people, or 45 per cent of Hong Kong's population, in a second major policy shift the government has been making determined efforts to help still larger numbers of people whose housing needs are acute. For instance, the income ceiling for rental housing has been progressively raised. In 1984 the family income ceiling for public housing ranged from HK$4,500 for a three-person family to HK$6,800 for a ten-person family. Even though public housing is designed for families of three or more persons, provision is being made for single- and two-person families to apply (HKHA, 1984b). Since 1979 the elderly have also been given special privileges in the allocation of public housing. The waiting time for couples or for three unrelated individuals over 60 years old is less than two years. This policy has proven to be popular, and in 1984 at least 1,000 elderly persons benefited from it. For those waiting for public housing, shared space between two or more families is no longer calculated as part of the allowable space per adult. All these measures are designed to broaden the base of participation in public housing.

Figure 10.1: New Towns and Public Housing: Hong Kong, c. 1984

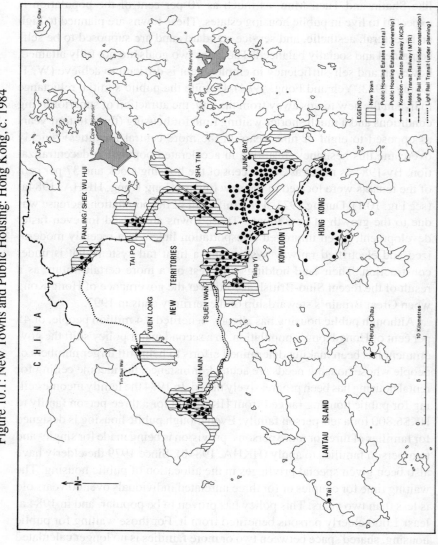

LEGEND:
● New Town
● Public Housing Estates (rental)
▲ Public Housing Estates (ownership)
▪▪▪ Kowloon – Canton Railway (KCR)
▪▪▪ Mass Transit Railway (MTR)
▬▬▬ Light Rail Transit (under construction)
▪▪▪▪ Light Rail Transit (under planning)

A third policy change related to the public housing measures has been the introduction of home ownership, through the Home Ownership Participation Scheme (HOS) in 1978 and the Private Sector Participation Scheme (PSPS) in 1979. By 1984, 12,600 HOS and PSPS units had been sold to public housing tenants: The government has been encouraging ownership by gradually raising the income ceiling for those eligible to purchase public flats, among other measures. In 1984 the family income was raised to HK$7,500 per month. Recent sales of such flats have been reported to be many times oversubscribed (HKHA, 1984a).

In a fourth move, as public housing is being more widely accepted and demanded, the government has been redeveloping the early resettlement housing that was built to unacceptably low standards. In 1984 Shek Kip Mei Estate, the first public housing estate, which had housed 62,000, was redeveloped for 34,000 inhabitants. Redevelopment of all such substandard estates is expected to be completed by 1990. As part of the redevelopment, single-room flats are being replaced by flats that can be partitioned into one to three bedrooms (HKHA, 1984a).

To cope with the city's 500,000 squatters, a Squatter Area Improvements Division was set up in 1982, signifying a more positive approach to squatter rehousing and redevelopment. The government has earmarked funds to improve the living conditions in the squatter areas and includes them in its development plans. The authorities plan to reduce the squatter population by at least half within five years (HKHA, 1984b).

Finally, the government's commitment to housing has continued to be given high priority, occupying one-third of the total public capital expenditure and 10 per cent of annual recurrent expenditure, well above the 5 to 6 per cent generally recommended for developing countries. The government subsidizes public housing programmes by providing free land for both rental and home ownership projects. As of 1983 this subsidy amounted to HK$12,002 million (Hong Kong, GIS, 1984:115–16).

In Singapore, although public housing efforts go back as early as 1927, its present successful public housing development began in 1960 with the establishment of the Housing and Development Board (HDB). In 1985 the Fifth Five-Year Building Programme was completed. In 1984, 1.97 million inhabitants, or 78 per cent of the total population, were beneficiaries of the programme, making Singapore one of the best-housed countries in the world. Since 1970, when the backbone of the housing shortage was broken, Singapore's efforts have been geared towards increasing housing quality and ownership. Some of these trends are likely to persist.

In 1964 the HDB set up the home ownership scheme, which soon became popular. It was facilitated in 1968 by a policy to allow the use of Central Provident Fund (social security) contributions towards down payments and monthly payments. With increasing affluence in Singapore, since 1970 the tendency of new applicants has been to buy rather than to rent public flats. By 1984, persons applying to buy flats outnumbered those applying to rent flats by more than five to one, and 297,243 flats had been sold, more than twice the number of rental properties under HDB's management (Singapore, HDB, 1984). Thus Singapore is fast becoming a nation of homeowners.

Accompanying the preference for home ownership has been a desire for improved quality in public housing. In 1966 a design and research unit was established in the HDB with the objective of improving planning and physical designs to upgrade living conditions in public housing estates. Aware of the need to promote individual identity in such estates, the government recently supplemented its neighbourhood planning principle with precinct planning, which is to be further refined by cluster planning. Each cluster would comprise three to four blocks of flats containing 400 to 500 dwelling units (HDB, 1984:6). Newer flats have varied heights and architectural styles, a far cry from the monotonous slab blocks that characterized the construction of the 1960s.

With higher-quality housing come higher prices. Rising costs have resulted in part from the competition between the HDB and the private sector for the construction industry's labour force. Successive projects emanating from the Urban Redevelopment Authority have added to this competition. Many building materials have to be imported, at ever-increasing costs. As the cheaper land around the city's periphery has been exhausted, land prices have likewise risen. Consequently, in 1973 rents and prices of HDB flats rose after remaining stable for more than a decade, and they have since risen again several times. By 1984 a three-bedroom flat cost between S$36,300 and S$56,000, depending on the locality, and the most expensive executive flat in the inner urban area cost S$161,900 (HDB, 1984:87). Public housing under the home ownership scheme is no longer cheap, but it is still competitive with and superior to its counterpart in the private sector.

As public housing is increasingly built for home owners, the early considerations of proximity to the city centre and rentals relative to family income have become less critical. For over ten years construction efforts have concentrated in peripheral new towns located as far as 25 kilometres from the city centre (Fig. 10.2). The locations of the new towns are consistent with the concept plan of 1971 for the long-term development of the city-state. As these new towns are being developed, residents increasingly are feeling the strains of commuting to the urban area. Traffic congestion was an important reason for the recent decision to build a mass rapid transit system. As the new generation of public housing estates has more owner occupants and is more self-contained, the government is giving more attention to professional estate management. A social transformation is said to be in progress with the creation of planned communities (Lim *et al.*, 1983).

URBAN TRANSPORTATION

Hong Kong and Singapore are crowded and bustling cities in which people, vehicles and activities vie for space. In two decades (1961–1981) Hong Kong's population increased by 53 per cent to 4.2 million, while the number of automobiles soared almost sevenfold to 211,556. In 1980 Singapore's population totalled 2.4 million, an increase of 42 per cent over two decades, and the number of automobiles was 364,829, more than triple the number in 1960. Thus in both city-states automobile ownership increased much faster than population growth, and Hong Kong and Singapore have experienced the same traffic congestion that is so common in cities of developing countries. Nevertheless, the traffic situation has improved greatly in both Hong Kong and Singapore in recent years. Both cities have managed to extract a semblance of order out of traffic chaos by adopting policies that make motorists bear a price for using the roads and by offering alternatives to private automobile transportation.

In Hong Kong public transport is cheap and well patronized. It is served by a wide variety of transport modes: bus, tram, peak tram (cable tram up to Victoria Peak), minibus, taxi, maxicab, ferry and hydrofoil. High-density usage at almost any time of the day means that public transportation is efficiently and profitably run. For Hong Kong, "the problem is not to find passengers for the transport vehicles, but to find enough transit vehicles to accommodate those desiring to ride" (Smith, 1969:125). Several recent developments are worthy of note.

First, after two decades of government indecision towards major transport commitments, a cross-harbour tunnel was finally opened in August

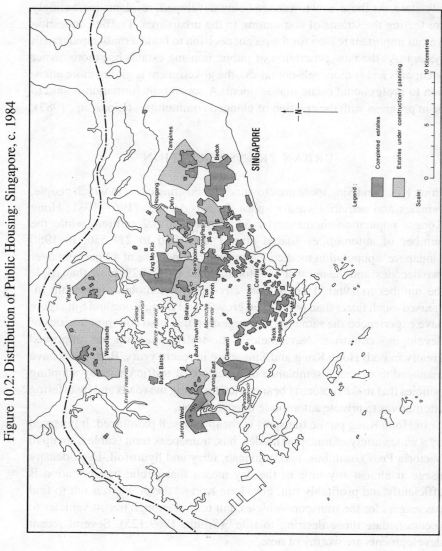

Figure 10.2: Distribution of Public Housing: Singapore, c. 1984

1972 which greatly increased the convenience of travel across the harbour. Cross-harbour service by the bus companies and minibus operators has since prospered and continued to proliferate between ever-increasing paired destinations. The tunnel has reduced the volume of passenger traffic on the cross-harbour ferries (C. K. Leung, 1983:251) and has made it possible to cross the harbour regardless of adverse weather.

Even more dramatic in its effects on the ease of movement within urban Hong Kong was the opening in 1979 of a mass transit railway. That system has been gradually expanded and has already affected land values and travel patterns in the territory. The opening in October 1979 of the first line of 15.6 kilometres, linking the central district under the harbour with Kwun Tong, an industrial town in east Kowloon, was followed in 1982 by a 10.5 kilometre extension to Tsuen Wan, another industrial satellite beyond west Kowloon. A third line along the northern shores of Hong Kong Island was partially opened in mid-1985 and completed in 1986, when another 13 kilometres were added. The new subway found instant success, for in 1981 the first line carried 223 million passengers (Hall, 1984:210).

The popularity of the mass transit railway was recently enhanced by a parallel improvement of the Kowloon-Canton railway serving the fast-growing towns of the New Territories. In 1983 the railway completed its programme of electrification and double-tracking, and with the purchase of completely new rolling stock it has been able to handle the increasing traffic between the urban area and the new towns and beyond, to the special economic zone in Shenzhen across the border in China. A connection between the two railway systems was completed in 1983 at Kowloon Tong, and a cross-system ticket system became operational in 1984. In the multi-centred, interlinked metropolis that is emerging with the development of the new towns, the two systems have contributed to the assessment that Hong Kong has "perhaps the most modern and efficient public transport system of any of the great cities of the world" (Hall, 1984:210). The government has also decided to build a light rail transit linking Tuen Mun and Yuen Long in the northwestern New Territories (Fig. 10.1). Construction of this transit system was completed in 1988 and has since been put into service.

Finally, recent increases in automobile ownership and horrendous traffic jams prompted the government to adopt a series of traffic limitation strategies. In 1982 it adopted a package of fiscal measures, including a doubling of the registration tax paid by the first owner, a threefold increase in annual

licence fees, and a 70-cents-per-litre rise in the duty on light oils. The aim
was to restrict the annual increase of automobiles to less than 5 per cent. For
fear that these measures may be insufficient, the government has been
pursuing what is called an electronic road-pricing system, which involves
the installation of camera-sensitive plates under each automobile to record
for subsequent charge to the road user its passage through controlled points
where congestion is to be minimized. The system, although successfully
tested in its technical and operational aspects, has been shelved in the face
of fierce opposition from within the community (Fong, 1984).

In Singapore urban traffic management was a thorny problem until the
government introduced an area licensing scheme for automobiles in June
1975. The government also advocated voluntary restraints, such as stag-
gered working hours and car pooling, and adopted more stringent measures
to curb the rapid growth of automobile ownership, including steep increases
in the annual road tax (1974 and 1975), a preferential registration fee to
induce owners of old automobiles to take them off the road, higher parking
charges and a surcharge on old cars.

The public bus system was rationalized and improved with the formation
of the Singapore Bus Service Ltd. in late 1973, and new services and bus
lanes were created. A park-and-ride scheme was introduced in urban fringe
areas to induce drivers into riding public transport to the city, but it was not
effective and was subsequently abandoned.

The most innovative measure for regulating traffic has been the area
licensing scheme, the first large-scale traffic control scheme of its kind in
the world. It is designed to limit traffic within the 620 hectares constituting
the central city by cordoning them off as a restricted zone between 7:30
a.m. and 10:15 a.m. The zone is manned at twenty-nine entry points, which
can be passed without a fine only by qualified company-owned automobiles, taxis carrying four or more passengers, and other cars having daily or
monthly licences. Licence rates are highest for company-owned vehicles
(S$10 daily or S$200 monthly). The sale of these licences brings in substantial revenue for the government. An analysis of traffic flows between
March and August 1975, immediately before and after the scheme was
introduced, revealed a 40 per cent reduction of traffic in the restricted area
(Watson and Holland, 1976). A more recent study (World Bank, unpublished data) found that a more or less consistent level of traffic reduction
(36 per cent during the peak morning hours) has been attained. Car pooling
has become more common since the scheme was introduced; by May 1983,

44 per cent of inbound automobiles had at least four passengers. Finally, the scheme has stabilized afternoon traffic congestion within the restricted area. Thus, the first road-pricing scheme has met all its objectives.

Notwithstanding its success in managing surface traffic in Singapore, the government finally became convinced of the need for a mass transit railway, in view of the city's rapid economic development and increasingly decentralized population, and it therefore commissioned a mass transit feasibility study in 1972. The system eventually approved for implementation was an expanded version of the consultants' recommended alternatives (C. H. Tan, 1976:81). Under construction now, it consists primarily of two lines, one running east and west between Tampines and Jurong, and another running south and north to the new towns of Ang Mo Kio and Yishun. The lines converge at the busy Orchard Road corridor. The system will be 66.8 kilometres long and have forty-two stations, fifteen of them underground. Estimated to cost S$5,000 million, construction is expected to be completed by 1992, when 1 million passengers a day can be carried. The first stage of the system will open in 1988 and accommodate 370,000 passengers daily (Singapore, GPO, 1984:146).

PROBLEMS AND PROSPECTS

Owing to efficient policy-making and implementation, urban services work generally well in the two city-states, but success brings its own challenges and problems. With their growing affluence, Hong Kong and Singapore are beginning to face the kinds of problems that characterize cities in developed countries.

A Hong Kong study reveals that the populace there no longer regards lack of basic physical services to be a general problem, in contrast to many other Asian cities (Lau, Kuan and Ho, 1983). It seems apparent that what is needed in the high-density living environment is better delivery of various social services.

One change in both Hong Kong and Singapore is that the extended family has been weakened to such an extent that not all aged are looked after by their children as they were in the past. Thus care for the elderly in an aging population is likely to emerge as a social issue of greater precedence. Likewise, with the tide of rising expectations, the needs of youth—training, jobs, recreation, crime and drug prevention, political participation, and so on—are claiming the attention of policy-makers and administrators. As the two societies become more modern and complex, innovative solutions appropriate for a population with strong Chinese roots must be found for their social and economic problems.

Hong Kong and Singapore are vulnerable to a variety of external influences. Until 1984, when China and Great Britain reached an agreement about Hong Kong's status after 1997, the date when Britain's lease on the territory is due to expire, uncertainty over Hong Kong's political future caused an economic downturn, a moratorium on large-scale projects, and shaken confidence there. Even in the best of political climates, a small margin of error in planning may result in economic imbalances that take time to rectify. An example of this occurred in Singapore in the late 1970s, when the government undertook several large-scale urban renewal projects in anticipation of an increase in tourism. When the projected increase turned into a decrease, many hotel rooms and apartments and a great deal of over-built office space were left vacant. Property prices accordingly dropped a reported 20 to 30 per cent (Spence, 1985; *WKYP*, 1984).

An Australian study in the mid-1970s concluded that Hong Kong and Singapore, like most cities of the Western world, are locked into a set of economic processes that demand increasing energy resources, even for fundamental needs. The study found that Hong Kong's energy consumption was growing at approximately 9 per cent per year (Icamina, 1980). But its dependence on imported fossil fuels should be minimized in the future because Hong Kong's utility company and China agreed in early 1985 to build a nuclear power plant at Daya Bay, some 50 kilometres from Hong Kong. Hong Kong is providing 25 per cent of the capital and will buy 70 per cent of the electricity expected to be available from the first reactor in 1991. This is the first large-scale joint venture between China and Hong Kong since the Sino-British accord of 1984 (Chan, 1985). Unfortunately, the recent nuclear disaster in Chernobyl, USSR, triggered the largest public controversy in 1986, focussing on the construction plan at Daya Bay.

1984 proved to be a critical year for both Hong Kong and Singapore. For Hong Kong, the historic signing of what is widely regarded as the best possible accord between China and Great Britain concerning the future of Hong Kong restored public confidence and rejuvenated the economy. Plans are being made for Hong Kong's transition to a special administrative region in July 1997, under the formula of "one country, two systems." There is likely to be wider participation in urban policy-making, given the current trend towards more representative government in Hong Kong. With the question of the political future between Hong Kong and China settled, Hong Kong appears set again on a course of rapid development. Besides the Daya Bay nuclear power plant project, plans for the city include a second cross-harbour tunnel at the eastern extremity of the harbour and the construction of a light rail transit system in the New Territories. In the broader perspective, Hong Kong's potential for further development has never looked better. Its prospects have improved to develop in tandem with a much enlarged geographical hinterland stretching to Guangzhou and beyond to the Pearl River Delta and South China.

The year 1984 similarly can be regarded as a watershed for Singapore. It saw the People's Action Party returned to power with diminished popular support and the transfer of power from Lee Kuan Yew and his colleagues to a second generation of leaders. Although Lee remains prime minister, the younger leaders will be assuming greater power and have declared a more open and responsive approach to urban governance. In the short run the economic imbalance adumbrated earlier will have to be corrected, but development policies are unlikely to shift from their established course.

In an updated study of world cities, Hall (1984:212) flatteringly described Hong Kong as "one of the most dynamic, the most exciting and above all the most forward-looking great cities of the world." If present-day Singapore does not fit this description, it has the potential to do so should its politicians and planners strive towards that end.

REFERENCES

Bristow, Roger. 1984. *Land-use Planning in Hong Kong: History, Policies and Procedures*. Hong Kong: Oxford University Press.

Census and Statistics Department (CSD). 1983. *Hong Kong Monthly Digest of Statistics*. December. Hong Kong: Government Printer.

—————. 1984. *Estimates of Gross Domestic Product 1966–1983*. Hong Kong: Government Printer.

Chen, Peter S. J., ed. 1983. *Singapore Development Policies and Trends*. Singapore: Oxford University Press.

Chen, Peter S. J. and Janes T. Fawcett, eds. 1979. *Public Policy and Population Change in Singapore*. New York: The Population Council.

Choe, Alan F. C. 1975. "Urban Renewal." In *Public Housing in Singapore*, ed. Stephen

Yeh, pp. 97–116. Singapore: Singapore University Press.

Dwyer, D. J. 1965. "Size as a Factor in Economic Growth: Some Reflections on the Case of Hong Kong." *Tjidschrift voor Economische en Sociale Geografie*, 56(5):186–92.

Fong, Peter K. W. 1984. "The Electronic Road Pricing System in Hong Kong." Centre of Urban Studies and Urban Planning, University of Hong Kong. Mimeo.

Government Information Services (GIS). 1984. *Hong Kong 1984*. Hong Kong.

Hall, Peter. 1984. *The World Cities*. 3rd ed. London: Weidenfeld and Nicolson.

Hodder, B. W. 1953. "Racial Groupings in Singapore." *Malayan Journal of Tropical Geography*, 1:25–36.

Hong Kong Family Planning Association (HKFPA). 1975. *Silver Jubilee. Hong Kong*.

Hong Kong Housing Authority (HKHA). 1984a. *A Review of Public Housing Allocation Policies: A Consultative Document*. Hong Kong.

————. 1984b. *Annual Report 1983/84*. Hong Kong.

Housing and Development Board (HDB). 1984. *HDB Annual Report 1983/84*. Singapore.

Icamina, Paul. 1980. "The Things That Keep Hong Kong Ticking." *South China Morning Post*, 25 January.

Information Office, Ministry of Culture (IOMOC). 1984. *Singapore 1984*. Singapore.

King, Ambrose Y. C. 1981. "Administrative Absorption of Politics in Hong Kong: Emphasis on the Grass Roots Level." In *Social Life and Development in Hong Kong*, ed. Ambrose Y. C. King and Rance P. L. Lee, pp. 127–46. Hong Kong: The Chinese University Press.

Koenigsberger, Otto. 1964. "Action Planning." *Architectural Association Journal*, pp. 306–12.

Koh, T.T.B. and W.S.W. Lim. 1969. "Planning Law and Process in Singapore." *Malayan Law Review*, 11(2):315–44.

Lau, Siu-kai. 1981. "Utilitarianistic Familism: The Basis of Political Stability." In *Social Life and Development in Hong Kong*, ed. Ambrose Y. C. King and Rance P. L. Lee, pp. 195–216. Hong Kong: The Chinese University Press.

Lau, Siu-kai, H. C. Kuan and K. F. Ho. 1983. *Leaders, Officials, and Citizens in Urban Service Delivery: A Comparative Study of Four Localities in Hong Kong*. Occasional Paper No. 1. Hong Kong: Centre for Hong Kong Studies, The Chinese University of Hong Kong.

Leung, C. K. 1983. "Urban Transportation." In *A Geography of Hong Kong*, ed. T. N. Chiu and C. L. So, pp. 246–63. Hong Kong: Oxford University Press.

Leung, W. T. 1983. "The New Towns Programme." In *A Geography of Hong Kong*, ed. T. N. Chiu and C. L. So, pp. 210–27. Hong Kong: Oxford University Press.

Lim, Kok Leong, *et al.* 1983. "Management of Singapore's New Towns." In *A Place to Live: More Effective Low-Cost Housing in Asia*, ed. Y. M. Yeung, pp. 49–64. Ottawa: International Development Research Centre.

Liu, Thai Ker. 1975. "Design for Better Living Conditions." In *Public Housing in Singapore*, ed. Stephen Yeh, pp. 117–84. Singapore: Singapore University Press.

Pun, K. S. 1983. "Administrative and Legal Aspects of Urban Planning in Hong Kong." Mimeo.

————. 1984. "Urban Planning in Hong Kong." *Third World Planning Review*, 6(1):61–78.

Saw, Swee-Hock. 1980. *Population Control for Zero Growth in Singapore*. Singapore: Oxford University Press.

Sit, V.F.S. 1983. "Industry in Limited Space." In *A Geography of Hong Kong*, ed. T. N. Chiu and C. L. So, pp. 177–87. Hong Kong: Oxford University Press.

Smith, Wilbur S. 1969. "Mass Transportation for Hong Kong." *Ekistics*, 27(159):124–30.

Stockwin, Harvey. 1984. "Hong Kong and the Singapore Lesson." *South China Morning Post*, 2 September, p. 2.

Tan, Chwee Huat. 1976. "Measures to Improve the Transport System in Singapore." In *Focus on Transportation*, ed. Rex Toh, pp. 71–82. Singapore: Prinmore Printing Co.

Tan, Jake Hooi. 1966. "Metropolitan Planning in Singapore." *Australian Planning Institute Journal*, 4(3):1–9.

Watson, P. L. and E. P. Holland. 1976. "Congestion Pricing—The Example of Singapore." *Finance and Development*, 13(1):20–23.

WKYP. Wah Kiu Yat Po, 28 October 1984.

Yeh, Anthony G. O. and Peter K. W. Fong. 1984. "Public Housing and Urban Development in Hong Kong." *Third World Planning Review*, 6(1):79–94.

Yeung, Yue-man. 1973. *National Development Policy and Urban Transformation in Singapore: A Study of Public Housing and the Marketing System*. Research Papers No. 149. Department of Geography, University of Chicago.

————. 1977. "High-rise, High-density Housing: Myths and Reality." *Habitat International*, 2(5/6):587–94.

Yeung, Yue-man and David Drakakis-Smith. 1974. "Comparative Perspectives on Public Housing in Singapore and Hong Kong." *Asian Survey*, 14(8):763–75.

————. 1982. "Public Housing in the City States of Hong Kong and Singapore." In *Urban Planning Practice in Developing Countries*, ed. John Taylor and David Williams, pp. 217–38. Oxford: Pergamon Press.

PART V

Thematic Perspectives

11. Third World Urban Development: Agency Responses with Particular Reference to IDRC*

INTRODUCTION

This chapter is divided into three parts. First, it will analyze the recent urbanization trends in the Third World and highlight some of the major problems being faced by policy-makers and residents in the light of accelerating urban growth without commensurate resources to deal with it. These problems will worsen in the foreseeable future given trends in population growth and concentration.

The second part of the chapter documents the nature and scope of assistance provided by donor agencies historically. It is stressed that despite the urgency of problems in many Third World cities, the major thrust of the international assistance has rarely been directed specifically to the urban sector. There have been some favourable recent developments, but it is argued that these are far from keeping with the pace of urban change and the real needs in these cities.

The third section of the chapter focuses on the evolution of urban research support by the International Development Research Centre (IDRC), leading recently to the establishment of an Urban Policy Programme. Research support will be analyzed by region and subject, and intended future directions will be described. The paper concludes with an introspective review of the IDRC approach and of recent mechanisms to strengthen research capacity in developing countries.

*Co-authored with Francois Belisle. The views expressed in this paper are the authors' and they do not necessarily coincide with those of International Development Research Centre.

THIRD WORLD URBANIZATION

One of the world's most critical development problems that has emerged in recent decades is the unprecedented growth of cities in developing countries (Gilbert and Gugler, 1981). While the total population in the Third World is growing rapidly, the urban population is growing twice as fast. As a result, more people now live in Third World cities than in the cities of the developed countries. This trend is expected to continue over the next several decades, with Third World urban population steadily increasing from 29 per cent to 41 per cent of the total population of those countries between 1984 and 2000, thus exacerbating the serious urban problems that exist today (UN, 1983).

Lima, Cairo and Calcutta are examples of the urban crisis in the developing world. Lima's population increased from 600,000 in 1940 to over five million today, fully one-quarter of the nation's population. The city's housing and service infrastructure is deplorable, and there are growing numbers of people living in conditions of abject poverty. Over one-third of the city's population lives in some 400 recent low-income settlements on the outer urban rim. Only half of the households in these settlements have water and electricity indoors; schools are very few, hospitals non-existent. The slums of straw huts have spread everywhere on the barren, sandy ground and up on the rocky hills surrounding the city. Pollution is high and crime widespread. Cairo now has 12 million inhabitants, up from one-half million at the turn of the century. In some areas of the city population density reaches 800,000 per square kilometre. Water shortages are regular events; huge traffic jams occur daily; and industrial pollution levels in some areas are several times higher than what is considered dangerous. Calcutta, with a population of 10.2 million, is perhaps the most extreme example of the Third World's urban crisis. Over two-thirds of the city's population earn less than US$8 a month and live in one-room houses. An estimated 600,000 have no home and literally live and die in the streets.

In the now developed countries urbanization occurred slowly over centuries and with limited communication and transportation facilities, and was intimately linked to industrialization and improvements in agricultural productivity. In developing countries urbanization is occurring under very different conditions (Beier, 1976). The urban explosion has taken place over the past few decades as a result of very high rates of both natural population growth and rural-urban migration. Migrants have access, however constrained, to modern communications and transportation.

Finally, Third World urbanization is not closely related to industrialization or increases in agricultural productivity, hence the large proportion of the urban labour force that seeks to survive in a myriad of low-productivity service and handicraft occupations called the informal sector.

Contemporary urbanization in the developing world may be examined by comparing levels and trends of urbanization among and within the three major regions—Asia, Latin America and Africa. This geographical approach highlights the major difference at the aggregate level between Latin America on the one hand and Asia and Africa on the other (Table 11.1). Latin America's population, which is the smallest of the three regions but enjoys a per capita income more than twice as high as that of Asia or Africa, is 65 per cent urban as compared to 27 per cent in either Asia or Africa. There are, of course, very substantial differences within each of these regions. For instance, Northern Africa is three times as urbanized as Eastern Africa; Southwest Asia is twice as urbanized as the rest of Asia; and temperate South America (the highly developed Southern Cone) is significantly more urbanized than the rest of Latin America—in fact, it is more urbanized than North America or Western Europe (although differences in the definition of "urban" may account for some of the differential).

Moreover, this approach masks the sometimes wide variation among countries in pace and patterns as well as levels of urbanization. In Latin America, for example, generally the higher the level of urbanization, the lower the rate of urban population growth. There are, however, a few exceptions to this rule, such as Venezuela, which has very high levels of both urbanization (83 per cent) and urban population growth (4.2 per cent). Urbanization patterns also vary considerably from one country to another. For instance, Brazil and Colombia have well-developed urban systems comprising several large and intermediate cities, whereas Jamaica, Costa Rica and Argentina are dominated by primate cities.

Another approach to examine urbanization in developing countries, followed by the World Bank, is to group countries according to per capita income levels and compare urbanization or their characteristics. The World Bank aggregates statistics into low-income economies (up to US$400 per capita income), broken down into China and India on the one hand and other low-income countries on the other; middle-income (US$400–1,700) and upper middle-income economies (US$1,700–6,000); and finally high-income oil exporters. This classification scheme, because it groups countries on the basis of economic development level and not spatial contiguity, reduces in many cases the variance among countries on particular variables.

In all income categories urban population growth has been much faster than total population growth during the period 1960 to 1981. Typically, the urban population grew yearly by more than 4 per cent while total population grew by around 2.5 per cent. The high-income oil exporting countries (Libya, Saudi Arabia, Kuwait and the United Arab Emirates) constitute a special case. Able to import labour from Asia and elsewhere, these countries experienced total population and urban population growth rates of over 4 per cent and over 8 per cent per year, respectively, during that period.

Also highly revealing is the fact that, high-income oil exporters excepted, it is the 32 low-income economies (India and China excluded) that have registered the highest average annual rate of urban population growth in the

TABLE 11.1
Population Indices for Developing Countries

	Population estimate (m) mid-1983	GNP per capita (US$) 1981	Annual natural population increase (%)	Urban population (%)
Developing countries	3,519	728	2.1	29
Developing countries (excl. China)	2,496	916	2.4	33
Africa	513	783	3.0	27
Northern Africa	120	1,165	3.1	42
Western Africa	155	681	3.1	22
Eastern Africa	146	305	3.1	14
Middle Africa	58	483	2.7	30
Asia	2,730	968	1.9	27
Southwest Asia	108	3,865	2.6	53
Middle South Asia	1,011	251	2.3	22
Southeast Asia	382	663	2.1	24
East Asia	1,229	1,396	1.4	29
Latin America	390	2,063	2.3	65
Middle America	100	1,953	2.7	61
Caribbean	31	—	1.8	54
Tropical South America	216	2,065	2.4	65
Temperate South America	44	2,578	1.5	82

Source: Population Reference Bureau, *World Population Data Sheet* (Washington, D.C., 1983).

world, both in the 1960s (5.4 per cent) and in the 1970s (5.3 per cent). Moreover, the rate has hardly decreased in the 1970s compared with the 1960s, which indicates that in the world's poorest countries rapid urbanization is far from over. The fact that the most rapid urbanization occurred in the world's poorest countries is the clearest evidence that urbanization in the developing countries is unrelated to economic progress or opportunity. Indeed the poorest countries experienced an average annual growth in per capita GNP of only 0.8 per cent between 1960 and 1981, in contrast to an average annual growth of population of 2.5 per cent over the same period. Rapid urbanization has therefore accompanied economic deterioration in those countries; in particular it has not accompanied industrialization as had historically been the case in the now developed countries.

In the middle-income countries, the rate of growth of the urban population has also been very high and has not undergone a drastic decline from the 1960s (4.3 per cent) to the 1970s (4.1 per cent). In fact the decline is hardly more considerable than that in total population growth in those countries. Both population growth and urbanization are expected to remain high in the period from 1980 to 2000.

As a result of such rapid urban growth, urban population as a percentage of total population has increased rapidly between 1960 and 1981 from 17 per cent to 21 per cent in the low-income countries (from 12 per cent to 20 per cent if China and India are excluded), from 24 per cent to 33 per cent in the lower middle-income countries, and from 45 per cent to 63 per cent in the upper middle-income countries. However, because the primarily rural low-income countries account for two-thirds of the developing countries' population, the urban population today is as a whole only 29 per cent of the total population in the Third World as compared with 70 per cent in the industrialized world. Third World urban population is nonetheless expected to increase to 41 per cent by the year 2000.

The number of Third World cities of over 500,000 persons has increased dramatically from 109 in 1960 to 276 in 1980, of which 114 are in China and India alone. The proportion of urban population living in these cities has increased from about one-third to over one-half during the same period. In general, the growth of each developing country's largest city has been more rapid than in the other cities, as a result of particularly heavy rural migration towards those centres. This is true of the low-income and lower middle-income countries where the proportion of urban population in the largest city increased from 25 per cent to 28 per cent, and from 27 per cent to 32 per cent, respectively, from 1960 to 1980; however, it is only marginally true in the upper middle-income countries. In general, therefore, urban primacy has increased over the last two decades, with all of the characteristic problems of large cities. Such problems are particularly acute in the developing world's largest cities such as Mexico City, Sao Paulo, Shanghai, or Cairo (Misra and Dung, 1983), and whereas only six of the world's 20 largest cities were in the developing world in 1950, 17 of them will be there in the year 2000, each one with more than 11 million people (Table 11.2).

It is difficult to imagine that some cities would reach their projected size, particularly in view of physical constraints, such as lack of available space and water, and the inadequate technological and financial resources to

TABLE 11.2
Twenty Largest Agglomerations in the World,
Ranked by Size, 1950 and 2000

Rank	1950	Population (m)	2000	Population (m)
1	Greater New York	12.3	Mexico City	31.0
2	London	10.4	Sao Paulo	25.8
3	Rhein/Ruhr	6.9	Tokyo/Yokohama	24.2
4	Tokyo/Yokohama	6.7	Greater New York	22.8
5	Shanghai	5.8	Shanghai	22.7
6	Paris	5.5	Peking	19.9
7	Greater Buenos Aires	5.3	Rio de Janeiro	19.0
8	Greater Chicago	4.9	Greater Bombay	17.1
9	Moscow	4.8	Calcutta	16.7
10	Calcutta	4.4	Jakarta	16.6
11	Greater Los Angeles	4.0	Seoul	14.2
12	Osaka-Kobe	3.8	Greater Los Angeles	14.2
13	Milan	3.6	Greater Cairo	13.1
14	Mexico City	3.0	Madras	12.9
15	Greater Philadelphia	2.9	Manila	12.3
16	Rio de Janeiro	2.9	Greater Buenos Aires	12.1
17	Greater Bombay	2.9	Bangkok/Thonburi	11.9
18	Detroit	2.8	Karachi	11.8
19	Naples	2.8	Delhi	11.7
20	Leningrad	2.6	Bogota	11.7

Source: United Nations, *Patterns of Urban and Rural Population Growth, 1950–2000* (New York: United Nations, 1979).

overcome them. For example, how could Mexico City's population reach 31 million by the year 2000? With 17 million people now, the city is regularly afflicted with huge traffic jams, water shortages and dangerous levels of air pollution. Such a projection implies an annual population increase of almost one million.

To sum up, in most Third World cities jobs fall far short of supply, basic urban services are deficient and insufficient, poverty is widespread, and management is antiquated (Linn, 1983). Masses of people are under—or unemployed and live in crowded conditions without adequate provision of water, electricity and other basic services. In very large cities the situation is especially acute because their growth is unprecedented in the history of developing countries. Yet all projections suggest that in Third World cities the situation is likely to get worse before it ever gets better (Bedvioer, 1984). The task at hand is gargantuan, and the need for increased international assistance is clear (Beier *et al.*, 1976).

THE AGENCY RESPONSE TO URBANIZATION

Although the rate and scale of Third World urbanization began to command the attention of international assistance agencies as early as the 1950s, it is difficult to document the nature of this assistance except in broad terms, largely because assistance often is not categorized as urban, even if the urban areas benefit from it. In addition, one can only derive an approximate idea of the amount that accrues to urban areas when the assistance is categorized into research, training, action programmes and so on. What will be attempted in this section is an approximate profile of the nature and range of assistance that donor agencies have provided towards urban development in the Third World, emphasizing, without any claim to comprehensiveness, the changed orientations of this assistance. Any budget figures quoted are intended as indicative of the support extended.

Assistance programmes of any import took shape only in the 1960s when the United Nations system of agencies was amongst the early ones to respond to the new needs. The United Nations Industrial Development Organization (UNIDO), for example, has been interested in the impact of industrial investment on urban growth, and the World Health Organization (WHO) has supported projects on urban infrastructure, particularly water supply. The United Nations Development Programme (UNDP) also has been active in urban-supporting pre-investment studies. However, the most active agency in urban-oriented assistance within the UN family was the Centre for Housing, Building and Planning (UNCHBP) of the Department of Economic and Social Affairs. It was set up in 1965 to serve as a focal point for conducting assistance activities in the specified fields as well as to coordinate these activities with other UN agencies. As can be seen in Table 11.3, much of the assistance is focussed on housing and infrastructure, a pattern which was to persist with the heightened interest of other assistance agencies towards the urban sector in the early 1970s.

Much of the assistance provided by the UN agencies was in the form of technical assistance (with some training), pre-investment studies and capital assistance. The last-mentioned was especially important when the financial assistance agencies oriented their loan programmes to urban development in the less developed countries (LDCs) in the 1970s, although the Inter-American Development Bank (IDB) had been active in this field earlier than the World Bank and the Asian Development Bank (ADB). Between 1961 and 1975, IDB provided some US$500 million in fifty-six loans for projects in such fields as potable water, electric power, industry, education, transportation, communication and tourism that had either a direct or indirect bearing on the welfare of the people in urban areas. It might be mentioned that competition for capital assistance among LDCs has had an inhibitive effect on the development of a less expensive infrastructure technology more consistent with local conditions. Often, authorities in LDCs prefer high-cost urban technologies under the mistaken impression of a high level of external capital assistance being available. This choice is likewise frequently reinforced by externally funded pre-investment studies that are of little practical value in that they do not relate to actual development conditions or to implementation capacity.

The response by international assistance agencies up to the late 1960s may be described as one which failed to strive towards a conscious effort to evolve a coordinated urban approach well integrated with other development sectors. Despite the increasing recognition of the importance of urbanization in the development process, neither the donors nor the recipients were able to pinpoint the critical pressure points of urban development. Certainly with the UN family of agencies urban assistance was provided without clear reference to any established strategy. One general criterion was a balanced coverage of member countries. The emphasis adopted by the UN agencies was clearly sectoral, with only scant attention given to

TABLE 11.3
Urban Related Programmes by International Assistance Agencies

Agencies	Physical urban planning	Regional urban system	Housing	Infra-structure	Urban econ. growth	Urban trans-port	Urban poverty	Urban admin. finance	Urban land policy	Info. prov.	Training
United Nations											
UNCHBP (1965)	*		*								
HABITAT (1978)	*		*	*						*	
UNDP				*	*					*	
UNIDO				*	*						
UNEP (1972)			*	*	*	*	*			*	
UNICEF				*							
UNCRD (1971)	*	*		*	*			*		*	
WHO				*							
ILO											
Banks											
IRBD (1972)	*		*	*	*	*	*	*	*	*	
ADB (1976)	*		*	*							
IDB				*							
Others											
USAID (1969)				*						*	
FF										*	*
OAS											*

Dates indicate either time of creation of agency or time when active urban assistance began.

inter-sectoral and spatial dimensions of development. A UN publication (UNCHBP, 1969:55) summed up the position well at the end of the First Development Decade:

> Similarly, among the international agencies, the urban problems tend to fall into the interstices between the interests of agencies devoted primarily to health, education, industrialization or farming. What is lacking is the sense of process of interrelation, of a general crisis gathering most grievously in the urban sector where more and more of the world's people will eventually be living.

Indeed, as the world entered the Second Development Decade in 1970, an impending urban crisis in the Third World was beginning to be felt in many quarters. Exhortations such as those of Robert McNamara (quoted below) found a more familiar ring in development circles.

> The cities of the developing countries are the centres which ought to serve as the basis of both industrial growth and social change. Instead, with a growing proportion of their inhabitants living at the margin of existence, and the quality of life deteriorating for all, the cities are spawning a culture of poverty that threatens the economic health of entire nations. Historically, violence and civil upheaval are more common in cities than in the countryside. Frustrations that fester among the urban poor are readily exploited by political extremists. If cities do not begin to deal constructively with poverty, poverty may well begin to deal more destructively with cities.

To match these urgent messages with a concrete assistance programme, McNamara set up within the World Bank in 1972 a multi-pronged anti-urban-poverty programme focussed on the developing world. This urban programme has now developed into one of the largest and best funded assistance programmes covering almost every aspect of urban development (Table 11.3). A shorthand description of this programme may refer to two components. First, at the country level, national spatial development revolving around the principal determinants of growth is emphasized. Second, at the city level, urban transportation, housing and social services are the three sectors given special attention. The urban programme has not benefited the urban elite, as was initially feared, but rather has aimed at increased efficiency and evolving programmes and services affordable by the urban poor and replicable in many situations. By early 1972, 46 per cent of the Bank's total lending to LDCs comprised projects in the urban areas. Ten years later in 1981, a total of sixty-two projects worth US$2,014 million had been approved (for a statement of the World Bank's funding activities see Cohen, 1983). They covered the fields of shelter, urban transport, integrated urban development and regional development in different parts of the developing world.

The thrust on the alleviation of urban poverty similarly distinguishes other recent urban assistance programmes by other agencies, most notably the United Nations Children's Fund (UNICEF), the United States Agency for International Development (USAID), the Asian Development Bank (ADB) and the International Labour Office (ILO).

UNICEF has developed a programme of assistance seeking to research children and women of the urban poor in developing countries, with a focus on basic urban services. UNICEF's Executive Board recognized and reaffirmed in 1982 the need to attach a higher priority to the problems of the urban poor in its programme of cooperation. Emphasis was to be placed on childhood malnutrition, the situation of women, pre-school and day-care services, responsible parenthood and family planning, abandoned and disabled children, and the provision of adequate sanitation facilities. In 1982 basic urban services programmes were active in forty-three countries and were being expanded into another twenty-four. UNICEF has thus continued to become more active in urban development and committed to finding cost-effective solutions to programme planning and delivery. Its total expenditure increased by 63 per cent from US$183 million in 1978 to US$289 million in 1982.

USAID can be accredited with various urban-oriented research activities centred on the Third World during the 1960s. It collaborated with the Department of Housing and Urban Development, Division of International Affairs, in commissioned research and international conferences. An example of the former is Charles Abrams' *Squatter Settlements: The Problems and the Opportunity* (Washington, D.C., 1966). USAID was also the co-sponsor of one of the largest international conferences of its kind, the Pacific Conference on Urban Growth held in Honolulu in May 1967. The conference report (Kaplan, 1968) brought together many viewpoints which are still of value to this day. Finally, USAID through its funding to the Asia Society in New York indirectly supported research and scholarly exchange on a variety of development-related subjects. As far as urban research is concerned, the Southeast Asia Development Advisory Group (SEADAG), funded by the Asia Society, sponsored regular meetings with commissioned papers through the Urban Development Seminar series. The Group was most active in the late 1960s and early 1970s.

With USAID the Office of Urban Development under the Bureau for

Development Support (DS/UD) was established in 1969. Its programme on the dynamics and consequences of Third World urbanization was divided into four clusters: regional development, employment and productivity, urban finance and management, and urbanization in national development. The first cluster of activities was fully developed by 1980, while the other three sectors began operation in 1978 and 1979. It may be stated that the urban programme is geared towards USAID policies and priorities in keeping abreast of the urban and regional aspects of development; providing technical support to field missions and other units in the agency; and engaging in selected research and development to strengthen agency and developing country capabilities in addressing the problems and opportunities of rapid urbanization. The implicit emphasis in these three objectives of the programme appears to be on a service responsibility to existing policies and programme priorities of USAID itself. Only limited resources are provided for building up research capabilities in developing countries. In support of four programme clusters, the yearly allocation has decreased in the period from 1978 to 1980 from US$2.7 million to US$1.3 million. For the year 1981 the budget slightly rose, however, to US$1.7 million.

In 1982, however, the Office of Urban Development was discontinued. The large city-oriented projects were undertaken by USAID's Housing Office. The remaining interests in urban development regarding regional development and employment were reorganized under the Office of Multisectoral Development under the directorship of Human Resources (pers. comm.). It would appear that with this reorganization of activities and administration relating to urban development in the Third World, USAID has chosen a more diffuse approach. Assistance may bear on urban areas but it is hidden by USAID's internal organizational labels.

Finally, USAID has provided considerable support through the Housing Guaranty Programme for helping developing nations address their shelter problems. Since the Programme's inception in the early 1960s, US$1.6 billion has been spent in Housing Guaranty loans for projects in forty-four nations. Every year USAID has provided about US$150 million for low-cost housing activities as compared to about US$300 million from the World Bank. For any single loan made by USAID the annual limit is US$25 million (Chanda pers. comm.).

ADB began its assistance to urban development as such in 1976 with the establishment of an Urban Development Division with two staff members. It was a limited effort geared to Asia's specific urban problems. In the 1980s the Division doubled its staff to four urban specialists. It has been active in Indonesia, Korea, Malaysia, Thailand and Hong Kong. Lately it has been trying to broaden activities in Bangladesh, Pakistan, the Philippines and India. Capital assistance provided has amounted to sizeable investments, but there has been no research component in any of the loans (pers. comm.).

The significant contributions of ILO to urban-oriented assistance in the Third World must be noted. In particular, the World Employment Programme (WEP) should be underlined as ILO's main contribution to the International Development Strategy for the Second United Nations Development Decade. Funding for the programme amounted to US$0.14 million per year since 1974, in addition to donor contributions for research of approximately US$1 million since 1971 (pers. comm.). A recent ILO publication summarized the programmes as follows:

> The overall objective of the WEP is to persuade policy makers to include productive employment creation among the major goals of economic development policy and to assist governments in formulating strategies to attain this goal. Its specific aims are to identify particular policies and measures to improve the employment situation in the developing countries, and to help those countries to implement such policies and measures. Four principal means of action have been developed to this end: regional employment teams; comprehensive and exploratory country employment missions; regional employment teams for Africa, Asia and Latin America and the Caribbean; country employment teams; and an action-oriented research programme.

Of the seven fields identified under WEP for research and action activities, the urbanization and employment project is of particular interest. The project is in three phases. First is a survey of the nature and scope of existing urban employment problems in Asia, Africa and Latin America. The second phase consists of a series of field case studies to assess the dimensions of urban employment. The third phase will draw policy conclusions and recommendations, and specify policy instruments. So far, the project has generated a sizeable literature on urban employment in the Third World which can be divided into two groups. First is a set of analytical and policy-oriented studies on urban development and employment in a number of large cities in the Third World. The second group is a set of reports on the project's urban informal sector field surveys carried out in a wider, but somewhat overlapping, set of large- and medium-sized Third World cities.

On the question of assistance support by geographic regions it may be noted that Latin America, the most urbanized developing region, has been better supported than any other region. The Organization of American States (OAS), with its Division of Urban Development, within the Department of Social Affairs, and IDB are largely devoted to assistance in Latin America. OAS has supported two urban training centres: the Inter-American Programme for Urban and Regional Planning (PIAPUR) in Lima and the Inter-American Information Service in Bogota. IDB has provided development assistance in such fields as housing, investment strategies, urban planning and community facilities. Moreover, USAID has an active Latin American Bureau that supports urban projects in the region.

Among the agency programmes reviewed so far, the USAID programme is more research-oriented than others despite its technical assistance and related components. In the wide-ranging World Bank urban programme research and evaluation frequently go hand in hand with capital assistance. Some of the best and exhaustive reviews on the current status of certain urban subjects have been produced by the World Bank. In general, it may be observed that research is a weak link in the urban assistance programme under review.

When attention is turned to research-oriented donor agencies, one is struck by the surprising lack of an urban focus in their programme. The Rockefeller Foundation has organized its staff in eight divisions. Research and training activities are, however, organized in nine programmes. None of these focuses specifically on Third World urbanization, but two of them Equal Opportunity and Quality of Environment, are concerned, respectively, with minority, youth and employment problems, and water quality and other aspects of environmental planning, in urban America. In the Education for Development Programme, there is a small investment in training for public-sector management. This appears to be the only direct urban involvement in LDC cities.

In contrast to Rockefeller, the Ford Foundation's (FF) programme activities are so designed that there is a separate international programme aimed at assistance to LDCs. Four programmes are arranged for this purpose: agricultural and rural development, economic and social policy, education, and population. Again, a specific focus on urban problems in the Third World is lacking, although some projects intersect with the urban sector. In addition, FF has supported research in urban and regional planning at Torcuato Di Tella Institute in Buenos Aires, and it should be noted that it has been the principal source of external support for the development of social sciences in Latin America. Since the large-scale and highly useful International

Urbanization Survey (fourteen country studies and four thematic reviews) in the early 1970s, direct involvement by FF in urban development research in LDCs has waned to insignificance until the early 1980s.

Under the Foundations' present president Franklin A. Thomas, there has been since 1981 a major reorganization with Urban Poverty and the Disadvantaged being the largest and most prominent of the six new programmes. It was allocated US$43.5 million for the year 1982–1983, with a primary focus on the reduction of urban poverty in the United States. However, as much as 35 per cent of the funds may be spent in developing countries. The Urban Poverty Programme is subdivided into several subsections: Physical, Economic and Social Revitalization; Public Secondary Schools; Welfare/Underclass; Research and Evaluation; Fair Start; Youth Employment; and Refugees and Migrants. Some of these are operative in the regional offices in developing countries. For example, in the Middle East and North Africa Office based in Cairo, US$0.57 million was spent on support of Urban Poverty activities in 1982, only second to Rural Poverty and Resources. Thus FF appears to have chosen to become more active in urban development research and related activities in the Third World through its network of regional offices (pers. comm.).

In like manner, the Swedish Agency for Research Cooperation with Developing Countries (SAREC) has, since its inception in 1975, provided programme support under four themes, none of which directly concerned with urban problems in LDCs. Research cooperation is targeted to four subjects; development theory and development economics, health and nutrition, agriculture and rural development, and technology and industrialization.

Finally, reference must be made to the UN Habitat Conference on Human Settlements in 1976 held in Vancouver, which, more than any single gathering, was instrumental in bringing to world attention and that of many policy-makers, the urban predicament in the developing world. It is too much to expect that the international assistance agencies would respond with a coherent and coordinated game plan as a consequence of this historic meeting. However, the conference at least provided the opportunity for them to understand the need for and attempt a better coordination of their programmes. More important, most national governments and assistance agencies began to recognize the value of the integration of sectoral policies into a comprehensive human settlements programme. One major consequence of the conference was the creation in Nairobi in 1978 of the Habitat Centre for Human Settlements, which subsumes the functions of

UNCHBP. Relatedly, the former UN Committee on Housing, Building and Planning has been transformed into the Commission on Human Settlements, with a concomitant expansion of membership from twenty-seven to fifty-eight countries. Many governments and assistance agencies look with anticipation to the new Centre and Commission for guidelines for a concerted attack on urban problems in the Third World.

If the above review of agency programmes towards the urban sector conveys a sense of urgent need for increased commitment, it should be realized that urban allocations are dependent primarily on a shifting of priorities within the agencies rather than on the sudden availability of untapped resources. In this light a reordering of priorities, nationally and internationally, is necessary if the assistance agencies are to devote a greater share of their attention and resources to Third World cities. It is towards the gap in urban research support that IDRC's Urban Policy Programme is purposefully oriented.

URBAN RESEARCH SUPPORT BY IDRC

As the majority of the Third World population still resides in the countryside, IDRC's support has from the outset been geared to the welfare of rural people. As rural development cannot be fully understood without reference to changes in society at large or in the urban areas, the now defunct Rural-Urban Dynamics Programme of the Social Sciences Division sought to understand the interrelationships between the rural and urban segments of society in the development process. The projects it supported furthered the understanding of the processes of modernization and change as they occurred in both the urban and rural areas. Moreover, the programme in its concern for policy intervention supported applied social science projects which evaluated actual development policies and strategies. In its five years of operation as of the end of 1976, it was the most active programme in the Division, having supported over fifty projects which can be classified into four groups viz. migration; the social and economic aspects of increasing agricultural production; marketing of agricultural goods from rural to urban areas; and basic urban services (housing, sites and services, transport).

With the exception of the last-mentioned cluster of projects specifically dealing with the urban area, many of the projects were concerned with rural-urban linkages. In terms of the number of projects, the second group was most important and the focus was clearly rural. The large number of projects in the sector later justified a separate programme unit, Economics and Rural Modernization, when Rural-Urban Dynamics ceased to exist. The other unit, Development Management, which was an offshoot of Rural-Urban Dynamics, funded many projects which were largely concerned with urban phenomena.

Accommodation of rural-urban migrants in Third World cities was an important focus of the previous Rural-Urban Dynamics Programme, as attested to by the many projects which the Division supported. The project on low-cost housing, low-cost transport, hawkers and vendors, and sites and services stemmed to a large degree from the concern of how to better accommodate and serve the large number of migrants to the cities. By the end of 1976, more than Can.\$3.6 million worth of projects had been supported by IDRC in the urban field, broadly defined, with about Can.\$2.5 million spent on Asia, as compared with less than half of that amount for Latin American and far less for Africa. The regional concentration on Asia up to that time had been a function of the strengths and interests of the staff in addition to the justification that Asia has the largest number of cities and the biggest urban population among the developing regions.

The period 1976 to 1980 saw staff changes in the Division and hence a transitional phase in which support for urban research in developing countries did not flow from established programme priorities. However, in 1980 what was soon to become an independent Urban Policy Programme began to take shape, built upon the foundation of considerable urban research investment by IDRC in the earlier years and a wide network of previously supported researchers and institutions in developing countries. Staffed by two full-time professionals at the Head Office, the programme ensured a minimum of overlap with other existing programmes and identified the following five specific themes on which research was encouraged. These emphases in fact continue to be the backbone of the programme.

Firstly, the critical need for improvement in urban services in developing countries is recognized. True, in recent years, development banks have increased their lending to strengthen infrastructure and services in cities. The effectiveness of these services and the extent to which they help improve the living conditions of the urban poor, however, need to be evaluated.

The main objective of projects supported in this field is to improve the delivery, access and effectiveness of urban services for the urban poor.

Research on services related to the basic needs of urban dwellers, such as transportation, sanitation and waste disposal are supported. Evaluative studies, which usually include the collection of primary data, assess the success and failure of existing programmes and make appropriate policy recommendations. Networks of research institutions and individuals having a common interest in this subject are developed or consolidated. For example, the following have been supported: a five-country network project on participatory urban services in Asia; a study of low-cost transport modes in South Asia; and studies on waste management, sanitation and health in Korea, Tanzania, Mozambique and Sudan.

Low-cost housing and food market studies, in particular, continue to receive support. In the former, evaluative case studies that analyze the lessons learned from different approaches to low-cost housing are supported. In the latter, support is provided to projects that improve understanding of food market operation in general and of better ways to serve the poor in particular. Housing studies that have been supported include a six-country network evaluating housing cooperatives in Latin America; a large study in the Philippines; and several independent projects in Africa and Latin America, with several smaller city studies including Bangkok, Manila and Cairo.

Secondly, research on the management of urban growth is encouraged. One key factor in the inability of many urban governments in developing countries to respond effectively to rapid urbanization is the lack of appropriate institutions. Institutions capable of managing the increasingly complex tasks concomitant with urban growth and change have not evolved in many instances. Their viability is inevitably linked to management methods, which are often in need of reform. The problem of managing rapid urban growth is especially acute in Africa, where several projects designed to analyze and strengthen urban institutions have been supported.

Thirdly, studies on the informal sector and small-scale enterprises are being supported. The informal sector consists of a wide range of economic activities characterized by low productivity, rudimentary methods of production, a high ratio of labour to value of production, and small amounts of capital investment—and thus, low income for those who work in them. Such activities usually absorb most of the rapidly growing labour force. Informal activities are generally not registered or supervised by the government. The vast majority of workers in them are not eligible for social security and other government benefits, and are not organized into cooperatives or protected by labour unions. The informal sector in Third World cities provides a livelihood for a large part of the population. In spite of its importance, it remains largely an enigma to Third World social scientists and policy-makers. The programme has sponsored a five-project network on various aspects of the informal sector in Latin America, and it has co-sponsored a series of projects on handicraft industries in Asia.

Fourthly, exploratory studies related to urban-regional relations have been supported. Primarily they seek to evaluate the role of cities in national and regional development, identify policies affecting urban growth and regional development, and analyze the flow of capital, goods and services between city and countryside. These studies depend largely on the analysis of existing secondary data, and they probe possible new directions for policies intended to reduce urban poverty. Under this category, projects supported included studies of urban development policies in Colombia; rural-urban mobility and employment in Southeast Asia; industrial and regional planning in Egypt; and the regional socioeconomic impacts of export processing zones in Asia.

Fifthly, IDRC supports studies evaluating the efficiency of public programmes aimed to reduce poverty and improve the living conditions of the low-income population. Third World cities are characterized by enormous social disparities and, for some years, various levels of government have designed and implemented a wide range of programmes to improve the standards of living of their low-income population. Yet these have often not been evaluated thoroughly. Studies in this category include a three-country evaluation of poverty-eradication programme in Asia and an analysis of programmes for the urban poor in Recife, Brazil.

Finally, the Programme supports, in addition to the above themes, exploratory studies on other topics that may receive more funding in the future. Topics that might fall under this head include the problem of increasing food production in Third World cities; the evaluation of policies to decrease urban unemployment; the impact of urban expansion on surrounding agricultural lands; changing land-use patterns in and around cities; and household adaptive strategies.

Funding for urban projects has steadily increased from less than Can.$0.5 million in fiscal year 1980–1981 to over Can.$1.5 million in 1984–1985. During that period a total of 63 projects have been supported by the Urban Policy Programme at a cost of Can.$4.8 million. They were evenly spread among the developing regions, with 22 projects in Asia, 21 in Latin America and 20 in Africa (Table 11.4). In terms of allocation of

TABLE 11.4
Funding for Urban Research by IDRC, 1980–1984

Themes	No.	(%)	Value (Can.$)	(%)
Urban services	29.5	(46.8)	2,220.6	(46.3)
Housing	8.5	(13.5)	680.0	(14.2)
Food	8	(12.7)	590.0	(12.3)
Sanitation and health	4	(6.3)	190.6	(4.0)
Transportation	1	(1.6)	154.0	(3.2)
Other	8	(12.7)	606.0	(12.6)
Management of urban growth	7	(11.1)	622.7	(13.0)
Informal sector and small-scale enterprises	10	(15.9)	573.4	(11.9)
Urban-regional relations	6	(9.6)	427.4	(8.9)
Evaluation of poverty-redressal programmes	4	(6.3)	239.3	(5.0)
Other	6.5	(10.3)	713.8	(14.9)
Total	63	(100.0)	4,797.8	(100.0)
Average value of project			76.2	
Region				
Asia	22	(34.9)	1,849.9	(38.5)
Latin America	21	(33.3)	1,706.9	(35.6)
Africa	20	(31.8)	1,240.9	(25.9)
Total	63	(100.0)	4,797.7	(100.0)

N.B. Includes two cooperative projects.

funds, the three regions received 38.5 per cent and 25.9 per cent of the funds, respectively. The topical distribution of funds shows that projects on various aspects of urban services delivery account for almost half of both the total number of projects supported and the total funds spent, the other half being spread over the other topics discussed above (Table 11.4). There has been a deliberate effort to spread the funds evenly among the regions and to reach non-metropolitan research institutions. The first objective has been achieved and there has been moderate success in reaching the second.

Research projects are developed primarily by indigenous researchers, with IDRC officers playing an advisory role. Research projects are the property of recipient institutions, and although IDRC may be able to assist in a variety of ways to realize the research objectives and to disseminate the study results, it is up to the researchers to bring these to the attention of policy-makers in their countries. It is for this and other reasons that urban research priorities for IDRC support have been identified after dialogue with researchers in developing countries. It is believed that it is in this way that IDRC can most effectively assist Third World institutions and re-searchers in their attempt to study crucial urban problems. The priorities are reviewed critically and continually and are in fact modified as the Pro-gramme expands.

Although the bulk of support to developing countries is for research projects, other means of support are nonetheless actively pursued. From 1980 to 1984 more than Can.$0.2 million has been allocated in support of project development activities, meeting and consultancies. The Programme also supported training activities through grants to institutions of excel-lence. For instance, in 1983 and 1984, through the International Geograph-ical Union (IGU) Working Group on Urbanization in the Developing Countries, successful one-month training workshops were organized in Penang, Malaysia, on the theme of Third World urbanization and the household economy. The primary objective was not only to advance re-search in the chosen theme of critical enquiry, but also to train a cadre of junior researchers who will be able to carry out independent research. A similar group training initiative is being discussed for possible support in Latin America. Besides supporting the IGU Working Group, IDRC funds a network of human settlement researchers in central and southern Africa. Support is provided through the Mazingira Institute based in Nairobi, Kenya, which organizes regular meetings and publishes a newsletter.

Another support mechanism that permits researchers in Canada and in developing countries to work cooperatively on urban problems in the Third World has been made possible by funds provided by the Cooperative Programme set up recently at IDRC. Two projects are worthy of note. One is jointly undertaken by researchers at the University of British Columbia and Universiti Sains Malaysia on household responses to socioeconomic changes resulting from industrialization through free-trade zones in Penang. Another is a collaborative project focussed on the evaluation of urban growth management in East and West Africa involving the University of Toronto and seven countries both from francophone and anglophone Africa.

Finally, through IDRC's in-house publication facility, research findings are often published for the benefit of a larger audience. To date, more than twenty country and comparative monographs have been published on a range of subjects related to urban development in the Third World.

CONCLUSION

Rapidly accelerating urbanization in developing countries has been, and will continue to be, a major event on a global scale. The problems engendered by more rapid growth of urban populations than the existing urban resources can cope with have called for the search for innovative measures rather than conventional strategies developed in advanced economies. The speed, magnitude and nature of Third World urbanization contrast with the past experience of developed countries. In the absence of any ready-made solution, there is a clear need for international assistance to the economically disadvantaged countries so that urban problems and poverty can be alleviated if not solved.

The chapter has shown that the availability of assistance from donor communities has not kept pace with the increasing saliency of Third World urbanization and attendant problems over the past three decades. There is a plethora of international assistance agencies, but only relatively recently has assistance been provided specifically for urban development in developing countries. The survey of agency responses pointed to research as the weakest link in the assistance to Third World urban development.

In this context of scarce research resources for Third World urban development, IDRC has since its creation in 1970 regularly channelled a small proportion of its funds for support of urban research in developing countries. The IDRC style of operation is responsive, in that research projects are conceived, developed, implemented and disseminated by developing-country researchers, with financial and professional support from IDRC. One of the criteria for support from IDRC is that a research project should have regional relevance and wide applicability. Thus, IDRC has often helped its recipients examine their problems from a regional perspective. Participants in these projects learn through doing together and share a great deal of experience.

With the recent establishment of an Urban Policy Programme within the Social Sciences Division, IDRC has come some way in recognizing the increasing importance of Third World urban development and the need for research into urban issues. A wide range of projects have been supported over the past four years and it is expected that support will continue to expand in future. The paper noted several recent mechanisms that have become available to strengthen research capacity in developing countries. These include cooperative research between Canadian and Third World scholars and group training. IDRC's contribution will continue to help developing countries in their search for innovative ways to come to grips with their ever-daunting problems.

REFERENCES

Beier, George J. 1976. "Can Third World Cities Cope?" *Population Bulletin*, 31(4).

Beier, George, *et al*. 1976. "The Task Ahead for the Cities of the Developing Countries." *World Development*, 4(5):363–409.

Bouvier, Leon F. 1984. "Planet Earth 1984–2034: A Demographic Vision." *Population Bulletin*, 39(1).

Cohen, Michael A. 1983. *World Bank Lending for Urban Development, 1972–82*. Washington, D.C.: The World Bank.

Gilbert, Alan and Josef Gugler. 1981. *Cities, Poverty, and Development: Urbanization in the Third World*. New York: Oxford University Press.

Linn, Johannes F. 1983. *Cities in the Developing World: Policies for Their Equitable and Efficient Growth*. New York: Oxford University Press.

Misra, R. P. and Nguyen Tri Dung. 1983. "Large Cities: Growth Dynamics and Emerging Problems." *Habitat International*, 7(5/6):47–65.

United Nations, Population Division. 1983. "Urbanization and City Growth." *Populi*, 10(2):39–50.

12. Travelling Night Markets in Singapore*

INTRODUCTION

In many rural areas of the world, periodic markets and fairs constitute a familiar landscape feature closely bound up with transportation technology, levels of living and methods of economic organization (Allix, 1922; Hodder, 1961; Skinner, 1964; Spencer, 1940; and Yang, 1944). In the city there are normally enough static marketing elements to discourage the existence of periodic markets. Indeed, many scholars believe that urban retail units represent the end product in an evolutionary process from mobile to static modes (Berry, 1967:111–14). For instance, Hodder (1971) and Scott (1970: 127–41) suggest two paths periodic markets can take in their development: shops and specialized wholesale daily markets. Much of the literature deals with periodic markets in a rural context; Singapore's travelling night markets are explicitly urban phenomena and therefore are of special interest and significance, particularly as they display a distinct cycle of periodicity. A similar orderly system of periodic markets is also found in Mexico City (Pyle, 1970, 1978).

There have been several recent surveys related to travelling night markets in Singapore (Nanyang University Geographical Society, 1973; Lim, 1973),[1] and in 1970 the author conducted a comprehensive survey of

*I wish to extend my sincere thanks to students of the Geography Department at the University of Singapore for their active participation in my survey of night markets; to the Geographical Society of Nanyang University for the release of night market customers data; and to Mrs. Charlotte Lim for the use of unpublished survey data on market operators.

[1]The Nanyang survey was conducted in late 1971 by the Geographical Society of Nanyang University. The survey covered 1,689 customers in six markets: Jalan Jurong Kerchil, St. Michael's Market, Jalan Bukit Ho Swee, Pesiarian Keliling, Telok Kurau and Tanglin Halt (Fig. 12.1). Charlotte Lim's hawker study included a national sample

night markets (Yeung, 1973:7). This chapter is concerned especially with the mechanics of the present night market system, and with their spatial and temporal distribution. In addition, the origins of the system will be discussed and a typology of the markets will be presented.

ORIGINS OF *PASAR MALAM*

Although they are now widespread, travelling night markets (or *pasar malam*, as they are called locally) are a relatively recent phenomenon (Fig. 12.1). Despite the early operators' knowledge of periodic markets in China, Singapore's system seems to be an independent development, more in keeping with local conditions than as the result of conscious transfer of techniques. Chao (1962) noted that the first night market was started in 1953 in Jalan Kayu by a group of enterprising hawkers whose mode of operation had hitherto been associated with opera troupes and followed their itinerant performing schedules. Higher profits connected with hawking at these opera sites spurred the pioneers to look for a more dependable clientele than that attracted by erratic performing schedules. Early night markets were explored in Sembawang and the Keppel Harbour area, where not only fewer shops existed in relation to the population but, perhaps more importantly, weekly markets were scheduled to coincide with the pay day of the workers in the military establishments in the vicinity.

Growth of night markets initially was slow. At this incipient stage the *pasar malam* were nurtured by indigenous and expatriate employees of the military bases in different parts of the island. Growth became more rapid with the beginning of the present phase of accelerated public housing construction in 1960. The development in the early 1960s of public and private housing estates, in which shopping facilities were insufficient to meet demands, contributed to the mushrooming of night markets at this stage. By 1962 the basic framework of the present system of night markets had crystallized, with forty *pasar malam* operating in different parts of the island in a week. Markets established later tend to fill the interstices of a

---

of 1,128 hawkers, 44 of whom were *pasar malam* operators. Lim's survey results are being incorporated into a Master's dissertation in Sociology at the University of Singapore.

pattern already formed, and many gravitated towards the western Alexandra-Queensway corridor where substantial population increases associated with public housing have since taken place. Not all of the original forty market sites are shown in Figure 12.1 as more than ten sites have since been abandoned or resited. Many of those abandoned market sites are in close proximity to the new sites that have subsequently been opened. This serves to underline the limited maximum range of many *pasar malam*, a feature related to the role and nature of the markets themselves.

Figure 12.1: Travelling Night Market Sites in Singapore

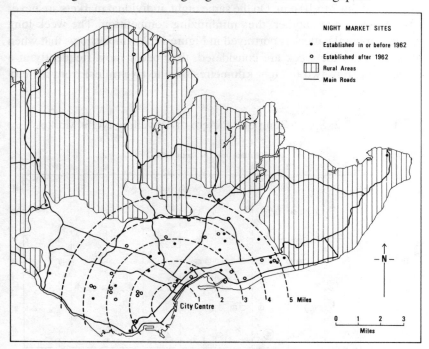

NIGHT MARKET SITES

• Established in or before 1962
○ Established after 1962
▥ Rural Areas
— Main Roads

City Centre

1 2 3 4 5 Miles

– N –

0 1 2 3
Miles

THE PRESENT SYSTEM OF *PASAR MALAM*

There are sixty-six recorded night markets in Singapore: several usually operated with less than ten stalls, and fifty-seven markets were covered in the author's night markets survey (Yeung, 1973). The survey recorded a total of 4,853 stalls and 8,787 hawkers; the mean number of stalls, functions and hawkers were 86, 22 and 156 respectively. *Pasar malam* vary considerably in size and, to a lesser degree, in function. In size, they range from an agglomeration of less than ten stalls to over 200. In all cases, however, the markets operate well below capacity which is fixed by the number of licences issued and pitches marked. Hawkers pay a licence fee on the basis of the number of occupied unit pitch each measuring three by one metres, and each operator can occupy as many as four units.

The system of travelling night markets is characterized by a regulated cycle of about eight markets per night, with the peak trading period stretching from about 7 to 10 p.m. On the same night, individual markets are never sited close to one another, thus minimizing competition. The week-long spatio-temporal pattern is portrayed in Figure 12.2, which shows that when all markets in the week are considered, they occur most frequently at a distance of from two to eight kilometres (one to five miles) from the city

Figure 12.2: Spatio-Temporal Pattern of Travelling Night Markets

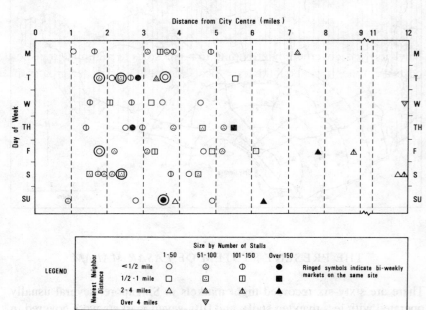

centre (i.e., within the urban area, Fig. 12.1). Within this zone, markets meeting on the same night rarely are more than one kilometre (half a mile) apart, and in many cases spatial separation is considerably less. Market size also varies considerably, with the smallest and some of the largest markets being found here. Nevertheless, in the more outlying and rural area, markets not only tend to be larger; beyond the eleven-kilometre (seven-mile) limit, the nearest[2] markets are without exception, the farthest apart as well. The markets occur in closer proximity to each other in centres of population concentration. Markets are held on new sites on each night of the week, and only where exceptionally favourable conditions prevail are markets held on the same site more than once a week.

The preference for unique sites on different days of the week to repeated use of the same site is a consequence of an at once self-imposed and self-regulating mechanism. Chao (1962) reported that in the cases of at least four sites, attempts were made to operate for a second night; quarrels ensued when business in the first night declined, and latecomers were persuaded (sometimes coerced) to look for a new site. This is consistent with an observation made by Yap (1972:35) who recently found that the locus of hawker mobility in relation to other *pasar malam* can be identified by groups. *Pasar malam* operators trading in rural centres do not usually choose public housing sites for other nights' activities. In addition, Yap noted that the choice of market sites (at least for a significant proportion of hawkers) was governed by proximity to home so as to minimize transport costs and time. In general, the less "local" the night market, the greater the distance travelled and the mobility of hawkers. Urban markets are thus characterized by typically short-distance movements of their operators, whereas the converse is true of rural markets.

In the present system, the cycle of periodicity among the market sites is complete in one week. Night markets occur every night of the week but, judged by the number of markets and stalls (Fig. 12.2) and, by inference, the level of activity, Wednesday and Sunday nights are, in relative terms, the slack evenings of the week. In a sample of *pasar malam* operators, Lim (1973) found that more hawkers traded every night of the week than those

---

[2]"Nearest" is used here in a strictly spatial sense, with no reference to time of meeting. The nearest market can be any market meeting on any night.

who reported not selling in any night of the week. She also found that in three nights of the week, Monday, Tuesday and Wednesday, more hawkers took a rest than in the other nights.

As Table 12.1 indicates, the majority of the stalls in night markets are manned by one hawker (42.0 per cent) or two hawkers (40.1 per cent), with a progressively smaller proportion of the stalls operated by up to five or more hawkers. The dependence on one or more operators seems to vary with the nature of stalls; eating places have the largest proportion of single operators, whereas for the clothing and personal furnishing group stalls with two hawkers predominate. This latter group ranks first in total number of stalls, with 2,644 of 4,853 (55 per cent). The remaining four retail categories have an approximately equal number of stalls, ranging from 10 to 12 per cent of the total. However, service functions are conspicuous by their absence, and there are only three stalls in this category. This observation distinguishes Singapore's travelling night markets from the rural periodic fairs and markets referred to earlier, in which service and social

TABLE 12.1

Business Functions by Stall Size in Singapore's *Pasar Malam*

Functions	Stalls by number of hawkers							No. of hawkers
	1	2	3	4	5	5+	Total	
Retail								
Eating places	327	146	33	10	3	0	519	773
Food	211	225	96	35	12	6	585	1,185
Clothing and per-								
sonal furnishings	978	1,146	381	97	29	13	2,644	4,956
Personal needs	265	198	52	4	0	0	519	841
Household goods								
and furnishings	255	231	80	13	4	0	583	1,029
Services								
Fortune telling	3	0	0	0	0	0	3	3
Total								
Number	2,039	1,946	642	159	48	19	4,853	8,787
Per cent	42.0	40.1	13.2	3.3	1.0	0.4	100.0	

Source: Author's night markets survey.

(and occasionally political) activities loom large. It would appear that in Singapore, *pasar malam* have a rather specific and well-defined role to play: that is, they fill a lacuna in the marketing system which static retail elements have not adequately served. This role seems to be remarkably consistent throughout the year; thus, Lim (1973) found that all of her sample of *pasar malam* operators were engaged in selling the same line of goods at any time of the year, with little adjustment to meet seasonal demands. In their present form and under the prevailing social conditions, night markets do not perform any social function of significance.

Yeung (1973:120–30) has substantiated the short maximum range of Singapore's *pasar malam*. This seems to be related to generally high levels of urban transport costs and to the predominance of low-order goods for which the demand is elastic. Conversely, the minimum range is large. Night markets in the urban area often operate in areas of medium to low population density with medium to high socioeconomic status. Thus, despite high levels of disposable income, there is no sustaining demand from low population densities for a market to operate more frequently than once a week. The limited maximum range of goods in *pasar malam* is underscored when it is noted that since the relocation of Tanglin Road Market in early 1971 from its former thriving Wednesday meeting along Orchard Road a stone's throw away, business is reported to have declined.

NIGHT HAWKERS AND CUSTOMERS

Pasar malam are run almost exclusively by Chinese operators, and even with those participants from other ethnic groups, Chinese dialects still form the lingua franca in most transactions. The multi-lingual ability of *pasar malam* operators was also emphasized by Chao (1962). Educational attainment of most night hawkers tends to be low: the majority completed only primary education in the Chinese stream, and only a relatively small number received any secondary education (Chao, 1962). Related no doubt to the historical development of night markets, both Yap (1972) and Lim (1973) found that over 70 per cent of the operators were of at least five years' standing in their business; there have been very few entrants to the system in recent years.

The Nanyang survey reveals that the six sampled *pasar malam* attracted, on the average, 3,000 customers (Yap, 1972:12). As there were an average of 82 hawkers per *pasar malam*, it is estimated that every hawker had about

400 customers.[3] Although not all of these people would buy, the number of potential customers is still very large. However, this potentially large clientele is not reflected in the level of earnings by each stall: Lim's data indicated that 66 per cent of the sampled operators reported net earnings of between S$4 and S$12 (US$1 = S$2.50) per night per stall. There is, of course, a high probability that the high earners are included in the minority and that operators may under-report their profits.

The night markets survey results agree well with other observations on the functions of *pasar malam* and consumer behaviour: Lim's data showed that *pasar malam*, from the standpoint of the operators, was primarily a local marketing institution (Lim, 1973), with most customers coming from the immediate neighbourhood. The proportion of regular customers is moderately high, with 32 per cent of the operators reporting 25 per cent of their business with regular customers. The notion of a local clientele is reinforced by the results of the Nanyang survey which show that half of the customers come from within two kilometres (one mile), arriving principally on foot (72.3 per cent). In addition, 64 per cent of the interviewed customers stated that they did not visit any other *pasar malam* apart from the one they were patronizing. The modal frequency of attendance was weekly (47.8 per cent), followed by fortnightly (27.8 per cent) and monthly (14.2 per cent). Thus, almost half of the customers regularly use the weekly cycle.

The dominance of Chinese operators is matched by an overwhelming Chinese participation in patronage. The Nanyang survey reveals that 93 per cent of the *pasar malam* clientele was Chinese, although the sex distribution favours females (in contrast to the dominance of male operators): 58.5 per cent female compared with 41.5 per cent male. Most customers came from the younger age groups: just over half of the customers were between 15 and 25 years of age, and over 80 per cent were below 35 years of age. In this respect customers resembled operators. Many of the customers spent over two hours in the *pasar malam*, but the modal length of stay was 1 to 1½ hours (37.2 per cent). Most visitors are moderate spenders, as suggested

---

[3]It should be noted that since the Nanyang survey included only six markets, these statistics are representative of only the surveyed markets. The author's night markets survey (see also Yeung, 1973) suggests that the average figures in the Nanyang survey were reduced by the smaller markets surveyed; the mean hawker numbers in the two surveys are, respectively, 156 and 82.

by over half of them spending from S$1 to S$20 per month. To some extent, this explains the rather low level of operators' income.

A TYPOLOGY OF *PASAR MALAM*

The discussion so far has been concerned with the entire system, and has not focussed on individual markets. Yap (1972) performed a classification of fifty-nine markets using a number of variables, and arrived at a typology of six market types.[4] The characteristics of the six groups are summarized in Table 12.2, which is discussed below.

Type I: Non-local market

This group represents the *pasar malam* phenomenon, comprising the largest number of markets whose major characteristic is an exceedingly high proportion of the operators living outside the Postal District[5] in which the *pasar malam* occurs; operators often travel long distances to reach market sites. Most hawkers sell *general merchandise* items and the smallest number belongs to the *drinks* group. Multiple-pitch stalls are well represented.

The thirty markets of this group are widely distributed geographically, occupying sites ranging from near the city centre to the rural area (Fig. 12.1). Whereas rural markets cater largely for daily necessities, *pasar malam* in the more central localities depend on lower prices and convenience to attract customers. Although twenty-one of the thirty markets were established before 1962, this group of markets appears the most attractive to new operators to enter the *pasar malam* system. This is implied by the highest proportion of traders having less than one year of experience.

---

[4]This was a twenty-stage linkage tree analysis, using twenty variables in seven groups (Yap, 1972:7–8). They were average age; sex; degree of "localism"; percentage of hawkers with means of transport; years of hawking experience; number of stalls occupied; and kind of goods sold. It should also be noted that because of different research methodologies, there is a slight discrepancy in the number of markets in the Yap and Yeung studies. Yap collected data from hawker files on fifty-nine markets, fifty-five of which tally with those in Yeung's night markets survey (see also Yeung, 1973).

[5]The Republic of Singapore is divided into twenty-eight Postal Districts. The relationship of place of residence and market sites is the basis upon which "local" markets are differentiated from "non-local" markets.

TABLE 12.2
Summary of Characteristics of *Pasar Malam* Types

Market type	I	II	III	IV	V	VI	Total
Number of markets	30	11	9	5	3	1	59
Mean number of hawkers	98	77	61	88	9	107	82
Mean number of stalls	221	172	116	172	15	231	178

Markets (%)
Commodities

General merchandise	85.0	79.3	84.1	87.1	46.5	89.3	82.1
Food	6.7	8.8	6.3	4.9	28.9	3.9	7.9
Drinks	2.4	4.2	5.3	3.3	8.3	1.0	3.5
Fruits	5.8	7.7	4.2	4.6	16.3	5.8	6.4

Stall size (%)

1 Pitch	28.1	36.3	36.9	34.8	84.5	23.4	33.9
2 Pitch	35.5	35.7	41.4	40.0	11.8	46.7	35.8
3 Pitch	27.4	20.7	14.0	18.8	3.7	20.6	72.4
4 Pitch	9.0	7.3	7.6	6.4	0.0	9.3	7.9

Operators

Mean age (years)	39	39	41	40	39	38	39
Sex* (%): Male	80.3	81.15	76.19	73.91	88.17	80.37	79.63
Female	19.7	18.84	23.80	26.08	11.82	19.62	20.36
"Non-local"	86.29	59.49	24.17	59.28	39.17	40.56	66.35
"Local"	13.70	40.50	75.82	40.71	60.82	59.43	33.64
With owned transport	55.09	57.01	56.80	43.39	63.81	47.66	54.18
Without owned transport	44.91	42.99	43.19	56.60	36.18	52.33	45.81
Years of experience: 1	1.4	0.5	0.7	0.4	0.1	0.0	1.5
2	7.3	7.7	9.9	8.4	3.7	2.8	7.9
3	6.7	5.1	5.1	4.4	2.5	9.3	5.9
4	7.5	6.1	4.6	9.4	5.5	9.3	6.9
5+	77.1	80.6	79.4	77.4	88.1	78.5	77.8

Source: Yap (1972:13).
*Percentage totals may not sum to 100.0 due to rounding.

Type II: Average market

The eleven markets of this group are concentrated in five Postal Districts. Whereas the proportion of "local" operators is higher than that in Type I markets, stall size does not seem to differ significantly. It suggests that the scale of operation and "local" character are not necessarily linked. Many of the characteristics of Type II markets are close to the national average, hence the designation.

Type III: Local or HDB[6] market

Located exclusively in public housing estates, the nine Type III markets are confined to only Postal Districts 3 and 12. They were all developed after 1962, in response to local shopping demands. The proportion of "local" operators is unusually high and, in contrast to Type I and II markets, Type III markets tend to be smaller in terms of both stall size and total number of hawkers and stalls. The average age of the operators is marginally higher than that in other groups, which is consistent with the general observation that the older the age of operators, the more "local" the market.

Type IV: Female operator market

Like Type III markets, the five markets of this group are all sited in HDB estates. However, since they are not in areas with the highest densities of hawkers, the "local" tendency is not pronounced. Two features appear to set these markets apart from the other groups: the highest incidence of female participation and the largest proportion of operators without owned transport. As with type III markets, the stalls are generally small.

Type V: Withering or male operator market

Longest established in terms of operators' experience and distinctly "local," the three Type V markets appear to be on their way to decline if not disappearance. Table 12.2 indicates the highest proportion of male

---

[6]The Housing and Development Board (HDB) is a statutory body responsible for, among other things, the development of public housing in Singapore.

participation, small stalls and a distribution of commodities weighted heavily towards food and fruits.[7]

Type VI: Tanglin halt market

If it were not for the high percentage of "local" operators, this market could be grouped under Type I market. Stalls are generally big and deal mostly in general merchandise.

The implication to be drawn from this classification of *pasar malam* is that the mobility of operators and, by implication, the "local" tendency, is a function of the operators' sex, age, ownership of transport and commodities traded. Operators engaged in the sale of general merchandise and fruits exhibit much greater mobility than food sellers who are quite restricted in their movements. The relationship between types of goods sold and market sites seems clear: in higher-income or European districts, general merchandise stalls, by virtue of their greater appeal, prevail. In contrast, *pasar malam* operating in lower-income areas devote greater attention to food items. It is useful to order the available information about *pasar malam* in this way, but such a classification does not clarify the interrelationship of the markets, especially those which pertain to the timing and spacing of meetings.

SPATIO-TEMPORAL ANALYSIS OF *PASAR MALAM*

Such authors as Stine (1962), Hay (1971) and Smith (1971a, b) searched for explanations of linkages between temporal periodicity and locational spacing, but a general theory of periodic markets with wide applicablity is yet to be propounded. As a step towards that goal, Fagerlund and Smith (1970) suggested an admirably simple working hypothesis, that proximity in space implies separation in time. They proposed that spatial and temporal competition are complementary, and that markets located close to each other in space will be separated by longer time intervals, and *vice versa*. This section will examine this hypothesis using data from Singapore's *pasar*

---

[7]This suggests that a *pasar malam* is sustained by stalls specializing in general merchandise, not by those selling food and fruit items, which appeal more to the impulsive buyer.

malam.[8] Measurements were taken from each of the fifty-seven travelling night markets (Yeung, 1973) to the nearest market meeting on the same night, on pre- or post-adjacent nights, pre- or post-adjacent nights plus one night, and on pre- or post-adjacent nights plus two nights. The mean distances are recorded in Table 12.3.

TABLE 12.3
Temporal and Locational Spacing of Singapore's Night Markets
(kilometres)

	Temporal separation (nights)			
	Same	Adjacent	One night	Two nights
By market group				
All markets	3.36	1.98	2.17	2.20
Rural markets	7.39	7.35	8.11	9.46
Urban markets	2.85	1.35	1.43	1.29
By night of week				
Monday	3.57	1.53	2.04	1.27
Tuesday	2.27	1.13	1.13	1.13
Wednesday	4.15	2.56	2.48	2.43
Thursday	2.85	1.16	1.26	1.40
Friday	4.07	2.38	2.77	2.59
Saturday	2.93	3.03	3.30	4.25
Sunday	3.88	1.75	1.50	1.74

Source: Author's night markets survey.

It is readily apparent that while the hypothesis is generally applicable, there are conspicuous anomalies. Whereas, for instance, the average spacing values for all markets and urban markets conform roughly to the postulated regularities, the rural markets do not. Rural markets whose meetings are separated by one and two nights are (comparatively) widely spaced "on the ground." Several reasons can be advanced in explanation. Firstly, there are only six rural *pasar malam* in Singapore (Fig. 12.1), and

---

[8]An expanded version of this part of the chapter has been presented in Yeung (1974).

they provide anything but uniform coverage of the rural areas. Moreover, even temporal spacing is incomplete: no rural market occurs on Mondays or Tuesdays. Frequently, urban markets were used in the measurement of distances to nearest markets, accounting in part for the large mean distances and inversion of locational spacing of markets at one and two nights apart.

A second reason relates to the existence of factors extraneous to the night market system. The *pasar malam* operate within fairly restricted spatial and functional limits, and since they have to compete with static and day-time mobile marketing units, they are never allowed full authority in locational choice, particularly in the urban area. In other words, within the locational constraints imposed by population densities and different forms of business competition, *pasar malam* must seek out the interstices of the demand surface inadequately filled. To compensate for the relative lack of influence in choosing locations, they can more readily regulate temporal periodicity and schedule meetings the most efficient way. The self-correcting mechanism helps to rectify inefficiencies arising from excessive competition through too close temporal and locational spacing. Finally, the use of linear instead of functional distances may also contribute to the disparity between empirical results and theoretical norms.

When the temporal and locational spacing of markets is analyzed by nights of the week, the results do not approximate more closely to the anticipated regularities. In fact, the hypothesis is confirmed in about half of the cases: distances separating nearly all nearest markets on adjacent nights are shorter than for those on the same night. However, when markets at one and two nights remove are considered, almost all mean distances are anomalous. With the exception of Tuesday and Wednesday markets, all markets on other nights are at greater distances apart as compared with adjacent-night markets.[9] The considerable variation in every set of distance measurements may reflect uneven population distribution and other competing marketing facilities. On the basis of the evidence adduced, it appears that the articulation of locational spacing is more difficult than temporal control in the system.

Identification of nearest neighbours with respect to the same scheme of temporal spacing yielded more encouraging results, and Table 12.4 indicates that with the exception of Saturday markets, markets on every

---

[9]The standard deviations for all distance measures are very high, often as large as or even exceeding the mean, and caution in interpretation is in order.

other night have a great majority of (spatially) nearest markets at one and two nights remove. That almost an equal number of nearest markets is spaced at one and two nights apart serves to show that while there must be a break of one complete night before shopping demand re-emerges, the difference between a separation of one and two nights is apparently immaterial. In a clearer way, therefore, the nearest-market analysis does give support to the notion that spatial and temporal competition are qualifiedly complementary in the system of *pasar malam*.

TABLE 12.4
Nearest Market by Temporal Separation and Nights of Week

	Nights of week							
Temporal separation	M	T	W	Th	F	Sat	Su	Total
Same night	0	0	0	0	0	4	0	4
Adjacent nights	1	1	3	2	3	1	1	12
One night	1	3	3	4	3	2	4	20
Two nights	6	4	1	2	4	3	1	21
Total	8	8	7	8	10	10	6	57

Source: Author's night markets survey.

CONCLUSION

It has been the purpose of this chapter to document the phenomenon of travelling night markets in Singapore, but it is also appropriate to raise several points of a more general theoretical and policy nature (Yeung, 1974). At the present time, there are insufficient urban periodic market systems documented to judge whether the operation of such systems can be explained in similar terms to those which apply to their rural counterparts. The Singapore case, however, does provide several points of departure.

The policy implication to be drawn from this study is that there appear to be two alternatives at the disposal of the city administration with respect to mobile marketing elements. One is an active strategy, in which the authorities have a decisive say in matters of the location and number of stalls and hawkers, etc. An example of this approach is Singapore's recent decision to relocate street and stall hawkers into landscaped and sanitary hawker centres. The alternative is the present system of *pasar malam*, in which the government plays but a passive role. Initially, the government exerted a minor influence on the mechanics and planning of night markets; assessment of market viability and site selection was left entirely to individual hawkers, almost invariably on a trial-and-error basis, and the government exercised greater control only after the market had started to function. The public roles are limited to the licensing of hawkers, resiting of markets when and where there is need, and policing of the market area. The experience of *pasar malam* in Singapore suggests that, given a tolerant and benign official attitude and the existence of a pool of energetic entrepreneurs, a marketing innovation can evolve.

There has recently been a noticeable decline in the fortunes of some *pasar malam*, associated apparently with the British military pullout and the departure of attendant personnel. It is perilous to speculate whether the present marks the beginning of an end of this heretofore successful institution, but the heyday of the system seems gone beyond recall. That dynamism still remains in the system is reflected in the beginning of booming *pasar malam* recently in Jurong, the industrial town in west Singapore. The *pasar malam* has been legalized on Wednesday nights in Jurong, although trading activities are carried out on many other nights of the week as well. This recent development is reminiscent of the extraordinary growth of the system in the early 1960s, when rapid development of residential estates contributed substantially to the expansion and consolidation of the system. In view of the resilience of the *pasar malam* system, and given the fact that many new towns are being developed by government authorities, the *pasar malam* should have an assured future barring official intervention to the contrary.

REFERENCES

Allix, A. 1922. "The Geography of Fairs: Illustrated by Old-world Examples." *Geographical Review*, 12:532–69.

Berry, B.J.L. 1967. *Geography of Market Centres and Retail Distribution*. Englewood Cliffs: Prentice-Hall, Inc.

Chao, Syh Kwang. 1962. "The Phenomenon of the Travelling Night Market: A Study of Its Origin, Growth and Organization." Singapore: Unpublished Academic Exercise

(Social Work), University of Singapore.

Fagerlund, V. G. and R.H.T. Smith. 1970. "A Preliminary Map of Market Periodicities in Ghana." *Journal of Developing Areas*, 4:333–47.

Hay, A. M. 1971. "Notes on the Economic Basis for Periodic Marketing in Developing Countries." *Geographical Analysis*, 3:393–401.

Hodder, B. W. 1961. "Rural Periodic Day Markets in Part of Yorubaland." *Transactions of the Institute of British Geographers*, 29:149–59.

—————. 1971. "Periodic and Daily Markets in West Africa." In *The Development of Indigenous Trade and Markets in West Africa*, ed. Claude Meillassoux, pp. 347–58. London: Oxford University Press for the International African Institute.

Lim, Charlotte. 1973. Personal communication.

Nanyang University Geographical Society. 1973. Personal communication.

Pyle, J. 1970. "Market Locations in Mexico City." *Revista Geografica*, 73:59–69.

—————. 1978. *"Tianguis*: Periodic Markets of Mexico City." In *Periodic Markets, Hawkers, and Traders in Africa, Asia, and Latin America*, ed. Robert H. T. Smith, pp. 132–41. Vancouver: Centre for Transportation Studies, University of British Columbia.

Scott, P. 1970. *Geography and Retailing*. London: Hutchinson University Library.

Skinner, G. W. 1964. "Marketing and Social Structure in Rural China." *Journal of Asian Studies*, 24:3–43.

Smith, R.H.T. 1971a. "West African Market-Places: Temporal Periodicity and Locational Spacing." In *The Development of Indigenous Trade and Markets in West Africa*, ed. Claude Meillassoux, pp. 319–46. London: Oxford University Press for the Internaitonal African Institute.

—————. 1971b. "The Theory of Periodic Markets: Consumer and Trader Behaviour." In *Pre-conference Publication of Papers, Canadian Association of Geographers, Waterloo*, pp. 183–89.

Spencer, J. E. 1940. "The Szechwan Village Fair." *Economic Geography*, 16:48–58.

Stine, J. H. 1962. "Temporal Aspects of Tertiary Production Elements in Korea." In *Urban Systems and Economic Development*, ed. F. R. Pitts, pp. 68–88. Eugene: University of Oregon School of Business Administration.

Yang, C-K. 1944. *A North China Local Market Economy*. New York: Institute of Pacific Relations.

Yap, S-K. 1972. *The Spatial Analysis of Pasar Malam in Singapore* (in Chinese). Singapore: Graduation Exercise (Geography), Nanyang University.

Yeung, Y. M. 1973. *National Development and Urban Transformation in Singapore: A Study of Public Housing and the Marketing System*. Research Paper No. 149. Chicago: Department of Geography, University of Chicago.

—————. 1974. "Periodic Markets: Comments on Spatial-temporal Relationships." *Professional Geographer*, 26:147–51.

13. Urban Agriculture in Asia: A Substantive and Policy Review*

Urban agriculture, if approached in a systematic way, can provide important amounts of food for those who need it most—the urban poor. (Wade, 1983:28)

INTRODUCTION

By the end of this century, 52 per cent of the world's population, compared with 42 per cent in developing countries, will live in cities. Between 1980 and 2000, the "million" cities in the Third World will be augmented by 593 million inhabitants. Then, of the thirty largest urban agglomerations in the world, twenty-one will be located in developing countries by 2000 (Hauser and Gardner, 1980). One implication that may be drawn from these sets of figures of everincreasing number and size of cities in developing countries is that larger urban populations have to be fed every year. In the case of Asia, in which 58 per cent of the world's population live on only 29 per cent of its arable land, feeding the urban masses is at once a problem and a challenge.

Traditionally, urban size bears a close relationship to the food it is able to procure from its hinterland. With efficient and cheapening transportation in modern times, cities have increasingly drawn on food sources from faraway places, with the ability to pay becoming a determining factor. Given this tendency, many large cities have become vulnerable as more countries are unable to feed themselves and fewer countries produce exportable surpluses (Newland, 1980:12). In Asia, where most of the urban growth has concentrated in metropolitan areas, the problem of food availability and access is becoming more acute. In these urban centres uneven distribution of incomes, the prevalence of poverty, diminishing

*Sincere thanks are due to Eric Kwok Chin of the Centre for Contemporary Asian Studies for his research assistance. Drs. Francois Belisle, Isabel Wade and Ernesto Pernia kindly assisted by providing bibliographic material.

farmlands, inefficient distribution systems and rising expectations have all contributed to increasing critical problems of food supply and distribution, particularly as they affect the urban poor (Pernia, 1983:30).

Indeed, surveys of food prices in five developing countries showed that city dwellers paid between 10 and 30 per cent more for their food than rural dwellers. A recent World Bank study maintained that as many as 360 million inhabitants of Third World cities suffer from chronic calorie deficits. Five out of every six urban families in India typically spend 70 per cent of their income on food (Newland, 1980:13–15). Even in relatively prosperous Kuala Lumpur, between 45 and 50 per cent of total household expenditure in the city goes to food, or twice the proportion on such expenditure in the United Kingdom (Jackson, 1979:6). Consequently, the lower-income groups in cities of Asia are often worse off nutritionally than their rural counterparts.

This chapter is divided into several parts. It will examine food supply problems in Asian cities and the state of urban agriculture, highlight present production patterns, present six city case studies, discuss policy issues and review implementation strategies. The chapter will be concluded on a prospective look to the future.

PROBLEMS OF URBAN AGRICULTURE

For purposes of this chapter, urban agriculture is defined as the practice of food production within the urban and peri-urban area. Ganapathy (1983:2) used the term to include formal cultivation of crops, fruits and vegetables, forestry, parks, gardens, orchards, animal husbandry, fuel wood plantation, aquaculture and related activities. It is assumed that the supply of food grains and staples will have to depend on more distant sources, but ideally a city should supply a large proportion of its needs in vegetables, fruits, livestock and fish. Although there are cases of success of cities in self-providing some of these foods, most Asian cities have not devoted the needed attention or devised appropriate policies to harness their food-production potential. What are the major problems and points of tension?

First of all, as an inevitable result of urban growth/sprawl, urban fringe farmland has been disappearing fast. In Taipei, for example, such farmland used to provide 70 per cent of the vegetables consumed by the city's population. By 1974, this proportion had already declined to 30 per cent because of reduction of agricultural holdings in the face of urban expansion (Wade,

1984:27). Similarly in South Korea, a total of 1,016 square kilometres of agricultural land has been converted to non-agricultural uses during the past ten years, and a similar amount of agricultural land will be lost to urban expansion as predicted by the Second National Comprehensive Development Plan (Song and Lee, 1984:10). In Beijing, too, the relative rural affluence resulting from the recent shift to a family-based, market-oriented farm system has led to an upsurge in new home construction at the expense of a heavy loss of scarce cropland. As a compromise, planners in Beijing have encouraged peasants to construct two-storey homes (Brown, 1985:26).

The loss of fertile farmland is accompanied by considerable vacant or under-utilized land in the urban area that has become inaccessible for various reasons, including speculation. Despite the space limitations, the urban poor still engage whatever land they can find in limited agriculture, producing a much smaller proportion of the food they consume compared with rural inhabitants. The highest proportion of subsistence production to the total household consumption expenditure is 18 per cent in East Jakarta (Evers, 1981:94), as opposed to 7.7 per cent in Metro Manila (Bulatao-Jayme, 1981:17). To a large degree, therefore, the nutrition of the urban poor depends on sufficient food being available at the marketplace at prices they can afford. They must pay, as well, for inefficiencies in storage, handling, processing and promotion of different commodities (Newland, 1980:15).

To some planners and administrators, agriculture in an urban setting is not a compatible activity. Economists tend to treat the many benefits that may be accrued from urban agriculture as "externalities." Investment in urban agriculture in Asia thus has been low. In fact, urban agriculture never figures in the master plans of Indian cities. On the contrary, urban agriculture is viewed as backward in these development plans and is to be minimized (Ganapathy, 1983). By the same token, virtually all development assistance in the spheres of agriculture and forestry has been confined to rural programmes. This neglect of urban agriculture is paradoxical inasmuch as the technology and research in these fields can be easily applied to urban areas. Moreover, most of the Asian scientists with skills useful in urban agriculture are city-based in universities and scientific institutes (Wade, 1981:7).

The impediments to urban agriculture are many. These have been summed up by Di-castri et al. (1981) as the lack of the following: overall policies and goals, information systems to collect and process information, managerial skills, multi-level coordination, understanding of the aspirations of local people, and democratic participation. In addition, there are problems relating to sectoral administrative structures and funding patterns not conducive to urban agriculture. Furthermore, scientists, planners and managers are isolated from each other and cannot devote their collective energies to improving food production in the cities.

Finally, it should be mentioned that as Asian countries become more developed economically, they tend to become increasingly import-dependent in food. Singapore, Japan, South Korea, and recently Malaysia, exhibit this tendency of greater import dependence, in contrast to Bangladesh, India, Pakistan, Indonesia and Thailand, which still depend on domestic supplies. This is a reflection of a country's shifting comparative advantage from agriculture to industrialization as it moves up the economic ladder (Pernia, 1983:15–17). The increasing import-dependent tendency also mirrors changing food tastes of the population as it improves in purchasing power. All these changes have direct implications for agricultural supply, farming practice and choice of crops. They certainly have an influence on the development of urban agriculture.

PRESENT PRODUCTION PATTERNS

As a general description of urban agriculture in developing countries, Smit (1980:499) has characterized it in relation to rural agriculture as having the following characteristics: higher productivity per unit of space, low capital per unit of production, low energy consumption, low marketing cost, and special fish and fruit. An urban agriculture technology exchange among developing countries experiencing rapid urbanization would offer great benefits, but this is not practised. Instead, urban agriculture in Asia has been largely pursued, with a few exceptions, in a piecemeal and uncoordinated fashion. Nevertheless, several commonalities may be distinguished.

First, the importance of fish in the food basket of Asian cities is widespread. For most countries in Asia, particularly in East and Southeast Asia, fish often represents more than half of the animal protein intake. In South Korea and Indonesia, nearly 70 per cent of the animal protein intake comes from fish. Although most of the fish is derived from capture in marine and freshwater, increasingly aquaculture assumes greater importance. For instance, aquaculture provides almost 50 per cent of the food fish in China, and correspondingly 9.2 per cent and 10.1 per cent in Indonesia and the Philippines. In the latter two countries, aquaculture grew by over 50 per cent during the 1970s. In China, pond-fishing has been practised for untold generations and in certain Chinese cities over 90 per cent of the food fish originates from this source (Bardach, 1984). An effective ecological cycle of mulberry-dyke-fish-ponds has been perfected in the Pearl River Delta of South China, providing a steady supply of fish to the urban areas (Zhong, 1980).

Secondly, there has been a noticeable trend in many countries over the past two to three decades, in response to changing food consumption patterns, to divert from traditional food grain production to cash crops and livestock products. This trend has been especially apparent in countries that have experienced rapid economic growth, such as South Korea (Song and Lee, 1984:8), Japan (Gallagher, 1975), Hong Kong (Wong, 1983) and Taiwan. In Japan, which became self-sufficient in rice production for the first time in 1966, efforts have since been made to overcome the problem of overproduction in this commodity. A rice production adjustment policy was thus put into effect in 1971, whereby the government would provide subsidies to farmers who refrained from growing rice and used their paddy fields for other crops. This policy directly accounted for the decline of the value of rice as a proportion of all agricultural production from 63 per cent in 1965 to 36 per cent in 1972. In contrast, over the same period the share of livestock and vegetables/fruits rose from 14 to 26 per cent, and from 17 to 24 per cent, respectively (Gallagher, 1975:5). Even in socialist Shanghai, a 60-per cent income gap between growing vegetables and grain has posed a strong inducement to switch to the higher-value crop, in particular since the adoption of a responsibility system in farming in the late 1970s. Higher yields in Shanghai have also permitted diversification. Higher overall production of grain, cotton and vegetables was realized from 90 per cent of Shanghai's arable area in the 1970s, compared with 95 per cent in 1957, thus enabling the cultivation of other important crops such as rapeseed (Ash, 1981:211–13).

Thirdly, excepting a handful of Chinese and Indian cities, urban forestry for fruit production is a rare phenomenon in Asia. The experience of Bangalore in South India is probably worthy of scrutiny and possible replication. In that city a large number of street trees are grown by the Department of Horticulture. A quarter of these trees bear fruit, with many providing food for animals at the same time. The potential of many trees like Eucalyptus, Subabul, Mahua, Neem, Mango, Jamun and Tamarind for multiple use in Indian cities is equally to be considered for other Asian cities (Ganapathy, 1983). Here the concept of social forestry may be introduced, as the situation in Calcutta is such that many trees also bear fruit but they are located on private property (Smit, 1980:503).

Fourthly, wherever it is practised in Asia, urban agriculture can be very intensive and highly successful. Skinner (1981:215–34) reported that in six large Chinese cities visited, well over 85 per cent of the vegetables consumed by the urban population was produced within the bounds of the municipality. Vegetable production, highly structured spatially, has evolved as part of the traditional ecological complex tied to pig breeding, and recycling of night soil and rubbish produced by the urban population for application to vegetable fields. In Guangzhou, up to nine crops a year may be grown sequentially on a single field. In Hong Kong, six crops of cabbage a year is not uncommon. Likewise, Karachi, where rains are never heavy and fluctuate widely from one year to another, takes advantage of its dry river flood plains to produce half of the city's fresh vegetables (Smit, 1980:503). The high productivity of small and marginal spaces in urban agriculture has been so well demonstrated that Ganapathy (1983:9) reported that a six square metres space can produce all the vegetable needs for a family of four for a year.

Fifthly, many Asian countries have been promoting the practice of home gardens with different degrees of success. So far, most of these efforts have been directed towards the rural areas, with a beginning having been made to extend the movement to urban areas. The campaign has been variously called "Green Revolution Campaign" and "Project Compassion" in the Philippines, the Saemaul Undong (New Community Movement) in South Korea, and linked to a "Green Book" in Malaysia to encourage local food production. Indonesia has also adopted the micro-horticulture approach as a long-term solution in the fight against the widely prevalent vitamin A deficiency. Similar programmes are also being implemented in Thailand, Sri Lanka, Bangladesh and other Asian countries (Yang, 1982:135).

To sum up this section about present patterns, it may be said that urban agriculture has been evolving rapidly in response to changing demand and supply characteristics. Despite the lack of planning and government support in some Asian cities, many have produced food effectively within their spatial confines. Other cities have enjoyed a great deal of policy guidelines and capital injection to promote food production within the urban area. Individual city situations are so variable that it will be instructive to examine a number of Asian cities which have developed different approaches to urban agriculture and are faced with different problems.

SELECTED CITY PROFILES

Six city profiles are presented to highlight varying approaches and degrees of success in urban agriculture in Asia. These profiles include the city of Shanghai, an example of highly articulated rural-urban relationships leading to a high level of self-sufficiency in essential foods; Lae in Papua New Guinea, which is noted for a comprehensive city-wide food and fuel self-reliance programme; the dilemma of conflicting demands posed by rightful landowners and entrenched farmers on land that have for decades been used to produce food on Penang Island for Georgetown; the city-states of Hong Kong and Singapore that have vigorously pursued urban food production in an intensive and scientific manner; and a successful but shortlived community garden programme that was implemented in Barrio Matalahib, Metro Manila.

Shanghai

Although Shanghai was able to feed its inhabitants of three million as early as in the 1930s, with food drawn from a 100-kilometre radius based on pre-industrial technology (Murphey, 1953), it was largely over the past three decades that Shanghai, along with many large Chinese cities, has refined and systematized food production in its municipal region of eleven million. This process has been facilitated by a ten-fold expansion of the city boundaries in 1958 to 6,000 square kilometres. Apart from the inclusion of large farming areas in the Shanghai Municipality, two other factors have contributed to increased food production in the municipal region.

One is the transfer of the control of production, distribution and marketing food from diverse operating units to the Shanghai Municipal Government. All growing and marketing of food followed centrally-planned agricultural policies for the area involving officials at the city, county and farm levels. A unified, coordinated regional food system has superseded the fragmented, individual decisions of many rural and provincial authorities (UNICEF, 1984:24). In order to overcome the lack of linkages between rural supply and marketing cooperatives, Shanghai has recently allowed communes and production teams to transport and sell their produce directly (within certain boundaries). The establishment of cross-province companies (or *kuasheng gongshi*) has also greatly facilitated the flow of agricultural goods to the city and industrial goods to the countryside (Hawkins, 1982:15).

Another factor accounting for enhanced agricultural productivity is the modernization of farming achieved via mechanization, electrification, water-conservancy work and the large-scale provision of modern inputs. A direct outcome of these improvements in farming practices is the intensification of cropping patterns. The traditional two crops began to be intensified to three crops. By 1965, over 33,000 hectares of farmland were supporting three crops a year, and by 1973, almost 60 per cent of the suburban grain area was planted under three crops a year (Ash, 1981:210).

Figure 13.1 shows that Shanghai Municipality, like other large Chinese cities, is organized into two zones for purposes of urban agriculture. The nearby suburbs (*neichiao*) refer to the inner zone immediately surrounding the built-up area, and the outlying suburbs (*waichiao*) include all the other counties beyond but within the Municipality. Under this ecological arrangement, the inner zone produces vegetables year round destined for the main urban area. Thus most vegetables are produced within ten kilometres of their point of sale, and within ten to fifteen hours of their being harvested (UNICEF, 1984:25). This zone provides 76 per cent of the vegetables consumed in the city, a percentage lower than some Chinese cities, because only 16 per cent of the cultivated land within this zone is devoted to vegetables, again much lower compared, for example, with Guangzhou's 28 per cent (Skinner, 1981:230, 244). In the outer zone of seasonal fields, coarse, hardy crops such as white onions, garlic, ginger, chili pepper, carrots and turnips are grown.

Shanghai has adopted methods such as intercropping and overplanting to increase production and to ensure sufficient supplies. It has also taken measures, such as advance purchasing and a combined contract (purchase of primary and subsidiary products), to maintain stable and generally low prices. Consequently, the Chinese concept of urban self-sufficiency in food has, by and large, been translated into reality. Shanghai is totally self-sufficient in vegetables, most of the grains, and significant proportions of pork, poultry and other foods. In fact, it exports surplus grains and vegetables to other cities and provinces and operates a variety of food processing plants (UNICEF, 1984).

Lae (UNICEF, 1984)

During the period of the sixties and seventies, the city of Lae in Papua New Guinea experienced exceptionally rapid growth. The city grew by 16 per cent per year in the period from 1966 to 1971, and reached a total population of 52,000 by 1980. Rapid urban and population growth have their toll in widespread destruction of forested lands surrounding the city, a heavy dependence on imported food supplies representing over a quarter of the total food

Figure 13.1: Spatial Arrangement of Urban Agriculture in Shanghai

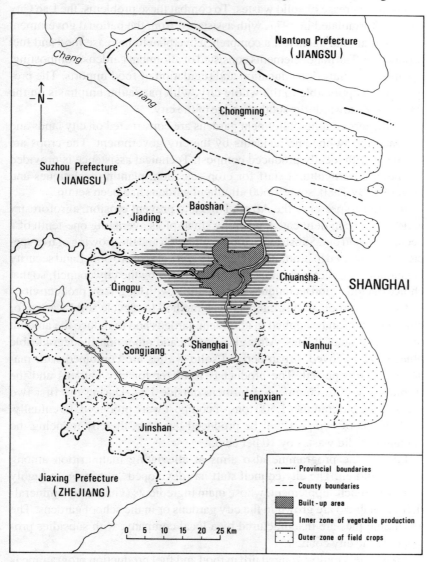

After W. Skinner (1981).

consumption, high unemployment and underemployment, malnutrition, and a massive increase of solid wastes. To combat these problems, the Lae City Council formulated in 1977, with assistance from the national government and international agencies, a comprehensive plan to increase food and fuel production. The major elements consisted of allotment gardens, composting, agroforestry, nutrition education and regulation of food imports. The programme is applicable to the whole city, with particular emphasis on the Atzera Hills towards the southern edge of the city.

As the term implies, allotment gardens are constructed on city lands and assigned to low-income residents by the city government. The crops are fertilized with locally produced compost. Technical assistance is provided by the city horticultural staff for crop selection, planting techniques and such like. By 1980, some 1,500 allotment gardens had been set up.

In order to preserve the Atzera Hills and prevent erosion, agroforestry zones have been delineated, whereby small plots averaging one-tenth of a hectare are laid out. Subsistence food production and the growing of tree species are combined to promote soil fertility and prevent erosion. Land security is guaranteed by leases and use permits granted by the city council, so that choice of cultivation techniques is compatible with long-term productivity.

Compost production is intended as a method to recycle solid wastes for nutrients that can be applied in allotment gardens and to reduce the amount of wastes at landfill sites. After glass, metal and other non-biodegradeable objects are removed, urban-derived solid wastes are combined with manures and composted. The product is fertilizer for city gardens and the surplus is sold to commercial farmers outside Lae. During the first two years of the programme, 1,500 tons of compost were produced. Eventually, 11,000 tons of compost will be produced per year, thereby reducing the amount of solid wastes by 10 per cent.

Finally, the programme also aims at alleviating malnutrition among school children. The city council staff has developed "nutripies," a highly nutritious lunch supplement, whose main ingredients (vitamin and mineral-rich vegetables) are grown in the city gardens or in the school gardens. The appetizing pies are manufactured by a local company, with subsidies provided by the city council.

Thus, Lae's multi-pronged urban food and fuel production programme is one of the most comprehensive and extensive the world has witnessed, and should be noted for the interrelatedness of its components and the many improvements on the well-being of the citizens.

Penang (Tan, 1983)

After many decades as a flourishing commercial centre in the Malay Penin-
sula, Penang found its fortunes gradually on the wane in the postwar period.
By 1969, when its free-port status was withdrawn by the federal government, Penang had reached a point of stagnation. Because of lagging agriculture and declining commerce, unemployment reached 15 per cent in 1970.
In order to raise the economy out of the doldrums, the state government
adopted a strategy of industrialization, signalled by the establishment in
Penang in 1972, of the first two of eight free-trade zones in Malaysia.

As a result of these developments, a structural change has been progress-
ing rapidly. In the ten years from 1970 to 1980, the share of agriculture in
the gross domestic product of Penang fell from 19.5 per cent to 11.9 per
cent, while that of manufacturing rose from 12.7 per cent to 24.3 per cent,
to become the leading source of revenue for the State. In the process of
progressive shrinkage of the agricultural sector, it has been estimated that
acreage under agriculture in Penang is being halved every ten years. The
result is a deleterious impact on the state of market gardening. Of the 35
licensed vegetable farms within the city limits of George Town, 13 licences
were cancelled during the past five years.

Market gardening is carried out primarily in two areas, viz. Thean Teik
Estate and Relau-Bayan Lepas, in addition to pockets found in George
Town itself (Fig. 13.2). More than half of the 158 vegetable farms surveyed
in 1983 planted only vegetables, while the remainder combined vegetable
growing with livestock raising and growing of horticultural plants. Monthly
incomes of the farming households are low to moderate, with half of them
earning less than M$500 (about US$200) a month. Acreage planted in
vegetables has never amounted to more than one per cent of agricultural
land, but had fallen sharply by 30 per cent from 939 acres in 1966 to 656
acres in 1974. For the whole State leafy and fruit vegetables fell by a further
8 per cent between 1977 and 1981. Nevertheless, the 1983 survey revealed
that vegetable farms on the island produce approximately 9,000 million
tons of produce a year, or 750 million tons per month. This meets about
one-third of the vegetable requirements in Penang, with the balance of
15,000 million tons imported from Peninsular Malaysia.

The looming crisis of urban agriculture came into the open in 1978,
when conflicting positions between rightful landowners and de facto farmers of Thean Teik Estate became polarized. The 350-acre first-grade grant

Figure 13.2: Location of Agricultural Activities in Penang

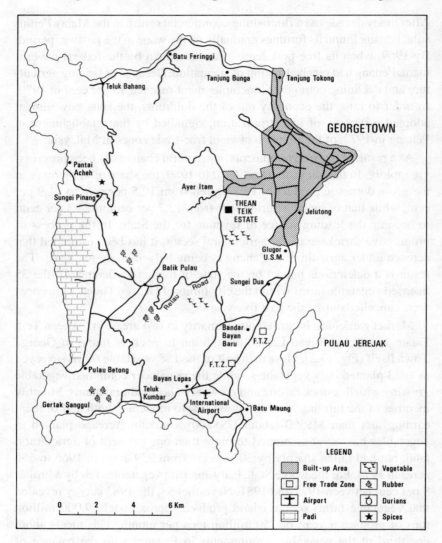

land was owned by the Leong San Tong Khoo Kongsi, a registered society
of clansmen formed in 1834. From the outset, farmlands were rented out to
farmers whose diligence and labour over seventy years have converted
dense jungle land into productive vegetable gardens. Some residents in the

estate have made their livelihood off the land for four generations and constitute part of the 520 households in the area with a total population of two thousand. On a daily basis, Thean Teik Estate supplies Georgetown with about 12,000 katis (about 7.7 tonnes) of vegetables and significant quantities of fruits. There is also supplementary production of poultry and livestock. In April 1978, the trustees of the Leong San Tong Khoo Kongsi and Perumahan Farlim, a housing development corporation, entered into a joint venture agreement to develop Thean Teik Estate into a housing estate. The plan called for the construction of two thousand houses and shophouses in the estate. Offers of compensation to rehouse the residents in high-rise flats (apartments) plus cash awards for loss of crops and farmlands have not been taken up by the farmers. A series of confrontations between the farmers and the developer led to one woman farmer being killed and newspaper headlines about the deadlock. The problem, which is still unre-solved, underlines the difficulty of resolving conflicting claims of the legal rights of ownership and a community's right to survival. It also portrays the dilemma many other Asian cities may have to confront in the legal claims to redevelopment at the expense of urban agriculture.

Hong Kong

With a population of five million in a small area (1,060 square kilometres), Hong Kong distinguishes itself in urban agriculture by using only 10 per cent of its total area to produce 45 per cent of the fresh vegetables, 15 per cent of the pigs and 68 per cent of the live chickens consumed by its population (Wade, 1981:7). This is even more surprising considering the fact that 40 per cent of its 10,000 hectares of agricultural land was aban-doned or laid waste in 1979 because of restriction of conversion of agricul-tural land to other uses (Wong, 1983). Thus, the apparent irony in this city-state is the continual and accelerating trend of abandoned farmland along with the unmistakable move towards greater specialization, intensifi-cation and modernization in urban agriculture.

Vegetable growing and fish ponds occupied 31.1 per cent and 18.2 per cent, respectively, of all the agricultural land use in 1979, and constituted by far the two most important types of food commodities produced by area. Over 60 kinds of vegetables are grown by Hong Kong farmers, essentially on a year-around basis. As a reflection of mechanization and capitalization, 2,400 rotary cultivators and 1,350 sprinkler units were in use on vegetable farms in 1977 (Sit, 1981:136). In contrast, paddy cultivation has dwindled to insignificance, from occupying 9,450 hectares or 70.3 per cent of the agricultural land in 1954 to a mere 40 hectares or 0.4 per cent in 1979 (Wong, 1983:162). Paddy cultivation has declined precipitously because of its relative unprofitability and the continued exodus of villagers to the urban area in Hong Kong or overseas. Paddy cultivation, along with field crops, is now confined to the relatively remote areas of off-shore islands and the border area, with the more accessible lowlands of Yuen Long, Kam Tin and Sheung Shui District given to vegetable fields and fish ponds (Sit, 1981:136). In a sense, a spatial pattern of an inner and an outer zone comparable to the Chinese cities, as described earlier, may be identified.

Pond-fish culture is an important source of food in Hong Kong, having developed very rapidly in recent years but now increasingly subject to encroachment from urban development. Two types of fish farming prevail: polyculture of Chinese carps, tilapia and grey mullet, integrated with animal husbandry; and monoculture of carnivorous fish, such as the snakehead and catfish. Some 300 monoculture farms operate in Hong Kong with yields ranging from 60 to 74 tons per hectare, compared with 1,100 polyculture farms producing 25 tonnes per hectare. Fish farming is viable on account of improved yield rates and a premium price being paid for live, freshwater fish (Wong, 1983).

Intensive livestock farming is indicative of the need to modernize continually the agricultural sector in Hong Kong. Chicken raising thus transformed itself from subsistence production in 1949 to a commercial scale with a total chicken population of 6.7 million in 1979. At present over a quarter of the chicken farms raise over 10,000 birds. Technological improvements, development of local breeding stock and availability of feed at reasonable prices have together contributed to the growth of the chicken-raising industry. Similarly, pig-farming has become more modern and larger in scale, with a steady but definite tendency towards fewer and bigger farm units. The number of pig farms decreased therefore from 13,700 in 1968 to 5,238 in 1979 (Wong, 1983:173). Newcombe (1977:193) calculated that 130,000 tonnes of food wastes from restaurants and food processing plants are effectively used every year for feeding pigs. This is a most remarkable use of recycled wastes which otherwise would be difficult to dispose of. From the standpoint of nutrient flow, he even cautioned against the trend to promote beef as a prestige food in Hong Kong as well as in other Asian cities. Pig and poultry raising, it is emphasized, maintains the capacity of the existing food system to recycle food wastes back into human food.

Singapore

Like Hong Kong, Singapore is a city-state with a relatively large population of 2.5 million on a small area of 602 square kilometres. Urbanization and industrialization have transformed the landscape and elevated the economy to almost a developed country status over the past two decades. Correspondingly, agriculture has declined in importance, certainly in terms of area occupied and employment provided, but not in efficiency or contribution to self-sufficiency in food demands. Indeed, the Republic is self-sufficient in pork, poultry and eggs with a surplus of eggs and chickens for export. Singapore also grows 25 per cent of its vegetables consumed by its population, and has a thriving specialized industry of orchids, primarily for export. These achievements have been realized through a programme of modernization and commercialization under the guiding hand of the government.

In the face of rapid urban and industrial growth, agriculture has had to make significant adjustments. The first has been the loss of agricultural land. During the 1960s, approximately 520 hectares of land were required annually for public housing and industrial development, often at the cost of fertile farmland. New town development, as prescribed by the Ring Concept Plan of 1971 for the long-term development of the Republic, made further inroads on dwindling arable land. Singapore's cultivated land decreased from 13,160 hectares in 1965 to 10,595 hectares in 1979 (Humphrey, 1982:152–55). The resettlement programme for the farmers spanning the period from 1957 to 1975 eased some of the pains, but major realignments needed to be made if agriculture was to remain a viable economic sector against the background of rapid economic growth.

The government policy towards agriculture in Singapore is premised upon three objectives: a high degree of self-sufficiency, no subsidies, and the development of a large-scale, modern and a fully commercial type of farming business. Recent changes in pig farming, the leading agricultural activity, reflect these policy directions. While the number of pigs grew, the number of pig farms drastically declined: the average number of 44 pigs per farm in 1970 increased to 158 in 1979 (Tempelman and Suykerbuyk, 1983). The Ponggol Pig Farming Estate, located in northeast Singapore with some 1,000 hectares of land and a capacity to house 750,000 pigs, exemplifies the direction the government plans for agriculture, namely intensive production employing high levels of technology and mechanization.

Next to pig farming is the production of poultry and eggs which, unlike pig farming, is still expanding. Between 1971 and 1980, the number of chickens increased by 29 per cent per year, from 24.7 to 31.9 million. The widespread introduction of new and more productive poultry breeds is an indication of technological progress in this activity.

Vegetable cultivation, largely of the leafy varieties, remained quite stable in annual production at around 35,000 tonnes per year, despite a declining farm area. In 1980 only 267 hectares of cultivated area was under vegetable crops. High yields have been maintained through a higher intensity of land-use by the adoption of multicropping methods, hydroponics and short-growing varieties. There is also the trend towards a smaller number of farmers and a larger scale of operation in crop farming (Tempelman and Suykerbuyk, 1983; also Cheng, 1976).

Specialized and intensive farming schemes are developed, as well, for orchids, aquarium fish and mushrooms. The key to Singapore's agricultural activities is economic and rational use of limited land resources. Emphasis is placed on a few activities for which high productivity is reached by economies of scale, modern inputs and intensification. Urban agriculture in Singapore is a model of maximization of economic return through selective emphasis with central planning and policy intervention.

Metro Manila

Three developments are worthy of note in a discussion of urban agriculture in Manila. The first is to mention one of the objectives of the agricultural policy in the Five-Year Philippine Development Plan (1983–1987) that would stimulate the growth of food production, with special emphasis on food products for the nutritionally at-risk and deprived population groups, including many in Metro Manila (Herrin et al., 1984:26). Secondly, the Philippine government has recently been encouraging food production within the urban area by providing home garden areas around new low-income housing, including multistorey housing estates constructed in Metro Manila (Wade, 1984:28). Thirdly, in order to encourage food production, even in the centre of Metro Manila, President Marcos issued a declaration obliging owners to cultivate idle, unused lands, or, with landowner's consent, giving people the right to cultivate land in an owner's absence. The same rule applied to public lands that adjoin streets or highways under certain conditions (Bulatao-Jayme *et al.*, 1981:20).

However, a community garden programme in Barrio Matalahib in Quezon City within Metro Manila is most notable for its initial success and lessons to be learned. It began in June 1980 in a 1.5 hectares "battle ground" or "no-man's land" between two squatter communities. With the help of the local police, university technical assistance and the professional advice of a community group called the Earthman Society, the project was proven to be a success. Throughout 1981, the gardens produced abundant crops of mustard, sweet potato greens, kangkong, eggplants and other nutritious leafy vegetables, meeting 80 per cent of the needs of the 400 families of Barrio Matalahib. Vegetable buyers and curious visitors came from other parts of Metro Manila to see how squatters produced their own food in the city. Unfortunately, in 1981 the government sold the land occupied by the Matalahib Gardens to a private developer. By mid-1982 the gardens had been abandoned and the area was cordoned off.

The message that is clear from the Matalahib experiment is that given land, organization and official blessings, the poor would seize any opportunity to produce their own food in the city, and they usually excel at it. The experience also demonstrated that without any assurance of land tenure, any investment in time and resources in home gardens within the urban area is at risk. Finally, Jamir (1983) even suggested that this example of urban agriculture may be seen as a vehicle to solve social problems in urban areas. Prior to the implementation of the garden programme in Barrio Matalahib, the area was plagued by gang fights, malnutrition and other problems. A semblance of social order prevailed during the period when the experiment was in progress.

POLICY ISSUES

One of the most important issues governing agriculture, including that practised in the urban area, is the pricing policy. Here a wide range of pricing policies may be noted depending on the country/city situation.

In Indonesia, for instance, the price of rice is used as a price leader in the economy, so that any efforts towards economic stabilization have to be premised upon an adequate supply of rice. One way of coping with a rice deficit is to raise the price of rice because, contrary to popular worry, cross-price elasticities between rice and other staples are high. Indonesians consume significant amounts of cassava in their diet, thus prompting the suggestion of a policy framework in which non-rice staple production is to be increased. What counts in the final analysis is to find policy measures that provide more incentives towards higher yields (Sigit et al., 1984).

In the case of the Philippines a ceiling price for rice is maintained by the National Food Authority (NFA) through holding an adequate buffer stock. At the same time, a floor price is maintained making it attractive for farmers to increase production. The combination of these two price mechanisms enables rice to be available to consumers in adequate supplies and at reasonable prices. The success of these pricing mechanisms obviously hinges on the effectiveness of the procurement precedure and the maintenance of a buffer stock (Herrin et al., 1984).

Similarly, in Japan, the price of rice is linked to food security and subject yet to another set of policies. Since 1945 rice distribution has been a government monopoly, with a commitment to buy all the rice that could be produced at a price artificially fixed each year in accordance with the provisions of the Food Control Law. The artificial high price of rice was initially designed to induce production and to win rural votes. When overproduction became a problem, a rice production adjustment policy had to be implemented in 1971 (Gallagher, 1975).

Every now and then retail food prices in a city become too high, and pressure is then exerted on the government to act. Public intervention, in response to such pressure and often of a short-term and misguided nature, is inclined towards lower retail prices by decree. The effect of such policy intervention is the creation of a black market at the retail level, and decreased production on the farm. It has been suggested that the determination with which governments have kept down the prices paid to farmers for basic food grains in developing countries has been attributed as one of the main causes of the 1973–1974 world food crisis (Mittendorf and Abbott, 1979:27). One economist even ventured so far as to assert that if farmers of developing countries had received the same prices for food grains as those prevailing on world markets, there would have been no world food problem. In the same vein, Wade (1984) observed that systems of price supports and excise taxes hold down prices paid to rural producers in developing countries in order to maximize the revenue gained upon resale in the international market. The proceeds may go to finance food imports which are consumed primarily in the cities.

To keep down rising retail prices for food, some governments have set up direct state marketing enterprises supported by public funds. They buy and sell in competition with the private sector. These state enterprises are set up to maintain food prices at low levels, particularly under conditions of serious inflation (Mittendorf and Abbott, 1979:27).

In still other situations, city governments may set up a two-price system, with the objective of protecting lower-income consumers from high prices of food. Such a system usually involves a large part of the supply of basic food commodities delivered to a single government-controlled assembly and wholesaling agency committed to the programme. There must also be some means of distinguishing lower from higher income consumers. In India, a dual-price system has been run by the Food Corporation of India for many years in the cities. There are no less than 50,000 fair prices shops in India's 3,000 urban places (Ahmad and Singh, 1981). Similar programmes with two sets of consumer prices have been in operation in Sri Lanka, Bangladesh, Pakistan and other Asian countries.

Even in socialist cities like Shanghai, devising a rational price structure for vegetables has proven to be difficult. The approach adopted to regulate the price according to the seasonality of production, aimed at the elimination of glut and shortages, has not entirely met its objectives. It encouraged the emergence of "capitalist tendencies," whereby members of the production team manipulated supplies for improving their team income. Consequently, attempts at price adjustments failed to stabilize vegetable prices but led instead to more severe price fluctuations (Ash, 1981:214).

The second policy issue—food security—is closely connected to the questions of pricing policies already discussed above. Food security concern is often addressed at the national level and, as several country examples about the price policy for rice already indicated, there is a policy relating to rice production in most Asian countries since it is the main staple. Many a development plan includes self-sufficiency in rice production as a stated goal. Pernia (1983), however, cautioned that considerations of food security at the national level may lead to complacency if food availability is shown to be adequate in gross national or per capita terms. Subnational, location- or group-specific instabilities must be taken into account. It is also stressed that as urbanization generates different food demands and tastes, food security should include non-staples and other types of food besides food grains.

A third policy concern is whose responsibility it is in urban agriculture.

At least for Indian cities, Ganapathy (1983) argued that the State alone is not sufficient to promote urban agriculture. Decentralization and local control commitment are essential if it is to succeed. Community participation holds the key to success, with the role of professionals, like agricultural engineers, plant breeders and agronomists, much subdued. Technology should increase in step with social organization of production and distribution. Gathapathy (1983:8) concluded that "an important policy goal in urban agriculture is to develop a contextually relevant optimal balance of power between community, state and the market place."

Of course, State support for research and development, extension and provision of inputs, and encouragement of local planning, are critical factors to successful urban agriculture. Most important, the State can act as an arbitrator between conflicting uses of urban space. Given high land prices in the urban area and many demands on limited land resources, Ganapathy (1983) argued, again using Indian cities as examples, that urban agriculture cannot be economical on a large scale. Yet it is important for the urban poor that land made available to them should be based upon a needs-use logic. The problem of access to land is a critical factor for urban agriculture but one which land-use planning and policy-making do not often address, especially from the standpoint of the urban poor.

Fourthly, food for the city has to be purposefully planned and certain policy options exercised in view of ever-growing urban populations and their food requirements. The examples of Hong Kong and Singapore already showed how they decidedly chose to pursue a narrower scope of agricultural activities but on a highly commercial, intensive and scientific basis. However, for most other cities, the suggestion of integrated planning of city food-shed development should be needed (Bardach, 1982). The large Chinese cities are probably the best examples which can be carefully studied for the lessons they might yield. Three particular policy goals of the Chinese approach may be noted. First, it is planning for the integration of the funding and management aspects of agriculture, industry and commercial enterprises. Second, productivity is increased through integrated improvements in educational, scientific and technical skills. Third, Chinese food planning for the city includes an objective to reduce the gap between the city and the countryside, and between industry and agriculture (Hawkins, 1981:15).

The last policy issue is whether to take a holistic approach to urban agriculture, viewing it, in other words, as part of total urban development itself. If this approach is adopted, many policy implications would follow.

Under this approach the State promotes research and controls countervailing market forces. Producers' cooperatives, neighbourhood associations, citizen groups and voluntary organizations are to be promoted. Measures such as incentives, subsidies and tax rebates are used to promote urban agriculture. Public education and awareness of the purpose and usefulness of producing their own food must be better supported. Some of the development assistance with respect to agriculture and related fields ought to be spent on the urban area.

IMPLEMENTATION STRATEGIES

Policy issues having been reviewed, it remains here to examine what possible strategies may be pursued to enhance urban agriculture in Asia. As a starting point, one must recognize that serious obstacles still exist to impede progress in this direction. The more serious physical constraints include limited water supplies, the decline in production space, severe air pollution and poor land quality. To these are added social and political barriers, such as overly rigid laws prohibiting the production of small livestock within city limits, the threat of a growing taste for imported, packaged foods posed to urban self-reliance, and difficulties in land tenure and land speculation (Wade, 1984:29).

One strategy that can be more actively developed in Asian cities is greater reliance on recycling urban biological wastes through hand cultivated "mini-farms" that can be maintained with low investment and operating costs. In this respect, Chinese cities have developed a very productive urban recycling agricultural technology that has lasted for centuries to this day. In the year 1900, of the 16 cities in the world exceeding one-half million population, eight were in China (Smit, 1980:503). The Chinese way of biological recycling is also practised in such cities as Hong Kong, Singapore and other Asian cities where significant proportions of the Chinese population reside. It was observed earlier that huge amounts of food waste are recycled every year to maintain a large pig population in Hong Kong (Newcombe, 1977).

Other organic wastes, such as sewage, can also be recycled for purposes of aquaculture. A good example is Calcutta, where in the wetlands, fish is raised using self-purified sewage (Ghosh and Furedy, 1983). The use of human waste for renewing fertility of vegetable farms is an age-old practice in China. Even as late as the 1950s in Hong Kong, up to 77 tonnes per hectare of human waste was applied to agricultural land (Newcombe, 1977:194). This practice is still employed in China, although some large Chinese cities have reportedly used chemical fertilizer in place of human waste. It may be noted that in terms of overall energy expenditures in the production of equivalent amounts of food, aquaculture of the low to medium cost type (such as carp, mullet, tilapia and milkfish) requires only a fraction of what is required in animal husbandry (Bardach, 1984:18).

In land-scarce cities such as Hong Kong and Singapore, a relatively new farming technique oblivious to soil conditions has become popular. Called hydroponics, the method relies on scientifically controlled mixtures of plant nutrients and water to be supplied to vegetables and fruits as these are required. On the same amount of land, multiple tiers of vegetables and fruits can be grown, thus increasing production levels several times. The potential for this technique to be applied to other Asian cities is bright provided it is accompanied by heavy capital outlay, technical knowhow and management skills.

Another broad policy sphere that warrants attention with respect to improving supply of food in Asian cities relates to the distribution and marketing system. In many Asian cities lower prices of essential foods can be provided through the regular market system in at least four ways: construction of new wholesale markets and supply centres designed to reduce traffic congestion and facilitate better handling methods; promotion of vertical linkages between enterprises along the marketing channel to reduce costs; public provision of services to support those engaged in food distribution; and provision of practical training programmes adapted to the requirements of managers and the staff of distribution enterprises (Mittendorf and Abbott, 1979:29). It was further observed that at the wholesale level, most wholesale markets in Asian cities were built many decades ago and are unable to handle the present volumes and traffic. In Hong Kong, for example, Tse (1974) found out that most of the supply centres of vegetables, fruits, dry goods and other types of food are located on the western side of Victoria Harbour centred around Cheung Sha Wan, Sham Shui Po, Kennedy Town and Western, with the result that there is a great deal of cross-town traffic leading to higher food prices for population centres in the eastern parts of the territory. Apart from wholesale and retail markets, considerable proportions of both the raw and cooked food in Asian cities move through hawkers and vendors. The contributions of hawkers in food distribution in Southeast Asian cities have been reviewed by McGee and Yeung (1977). In support of this statement,

Lam (1981) discovered that between 20 and 25 per cent of household food expenses was spent on food consumed outside the home in cities of Peninsular Malaysia.

A survey of urban agriculture in Asian cities pointed to a range of techniques that have led to more intensive use of available land space to produce more food. In Hong Kong, a system of catch cropping is practised, involving the growing of a vegetable crop between the harvest of the second crop of paddy in November/December and the transplanting of the first crop of paddy in the following April/May period. This is to maximize land that would otherwise lay fallow (Wong, 1983:167). In Shanghai a practice of replacing vegetable plots taken over for other uses with equivalent new plots was implemented in 1980, when unusually wet and cold weather, combined with a pest attack, decreased vegetable production. A tendency of converting vegetable plots to other uses was discernible. In this way, the danger was averted and land devoted to vegetable production did not decrease (Hawkins, 1981:26–27). In order to ensure an adequate supply of food, Shanghai, too, maintained a strategy of overplanting. Acreage would be overplanted by 10 to 30 per cent, depending on the crop, with varying times of delivery. Although this practice is used on limited acreage, it can only succeed where food processing enterprises agree to absorb the over-supply, leaving the remainder for animal fodder (Hawkins, 1981:28). Another farming technique increasingly used in Chinese cities, following established practice in Japan and Korea, is to use vinyl plastic covers and structures to protect early spring plantings against late frost. This method also helps in the control of plant diseases, and is especially employed for growing frost-vulnerable crops such as tomatoes and lettuce. Extensive areas of subdued reflection seen from plane windows during landings and take-offs at the airports of large East Asian cities in the mid-latitudes, attest to the widespread adoption of this farming method.

Further to the specific techniques aimed at higher food production, several more general practices can be applied to the same purpose although these are not urban-specific. The most important is the need to increase acreage under food production, a topic to be dealt with below. Other important factors that will materially increase production are the application of fertilizers, adoption of high-yielding varieties, and a more reliable and adequate supply of water. The use of machinery, however, will not be a critical factor to boost production as land is limited in urban areas.

Finally, possibly the most important consideration in extending urban agriculture is to increase land used for food production. To start with, idle and unused land within the urban area should be so used; the example of Manila, involving a Presidential directive, is a step in the right direction. Realistically, however, the search must concentrate on small and marginal spaces that may be found in many Asian cities. Such areas may include reinforced rooftops, balconies, backyards, transportation right of ways, institutional grounds, and, even on a temporary basis, parks, cemeteries and palace grounds. If hydroponics are used as a method to produce food, even baskets, tin cans, plastic bags and other containers can be used where no land is really needed (Bulatao-Jayme *et al.*, 1981:20). Of course, this is a far cry from the commercial hydroponics farms found in Singapore and Hong Kong.

PROSPECTS FOR THE FUTURE

The foregoing review of the state-of-the-art and policy issues in urban agriculture in Asia clearly shows that the proposition for Asian cities to feed themselves is not an impossibility. Many cities have succeeded in producing large quantities of food for their inhabitants, while others are struggling with means to increase production. Urban agriculture is not simply an experiment. "From rooftops to fishponds, the possibilities for making Asia's cities more self-reliant are limited only by our failure to recognize the potential of the urban ecosystem and to utilize it" (Wade, 1984:29).

Indeed, many factors are conducive to increased food production in Asian cities. Many of the inhabitants are themselves recent migrants from the rural areas. They have brought with them useful agricultural skills that can easily be applied to food production in the cities should they be presented with the opportunities. Many of them also bring, as well, the spirit of community participation that can be useful in community-based urban agriculture. Parallels may be drawn to the provision of urban services by people themselves in Asian cities (Yeung, 1985). If many of the implementation strategies discussed earlier can be applied, there are excellent prospects of increased food production within and on the outskirts of most Asian cities. Some even believe that intensive urban agriculture could produce at least two-thirds of the food needed in most Asian cities (Wade, 1981). The future prospects of food for Asian cities are summed up below by Meier (1981:40):

It is evident that provision of food and water will be increasingly difficult for the expanding Asian cities, and will probably be the crucial factors in maintaining and improving the quality of life in cities. Security of supplies to enable survival through periods of drought and famine will force many modifications in the structure of the cities.

The resultant picture that comes to mind is a new kind of garden city that sets aside places for efficient animal feeding, reprocessing the wastes, and fish ponds that are likewise equipped. Green spaces are allocated throughout the city for trees and vines that produce the fruits, while garden plots and streamlined hydroponics facilities produce the vegetables. Thus, the city with the help of its own reprocessed wastes, produces its own perishable foods, the most prized components of the local cuisines.

The staples, which provide the bulk of the calories in the diet, are imported from the most economic producers, anywhere in the world. The grain, sugar, pulses, cooking oil, and spices are stockpiled in granaries and warehouses in quantities, sufficient to overcome uncertainty in supply. They are transformed by the food processing industries into packaged items available in the shops.

Meier's garden city of tomorrow is certainly a model to which most Asian cities would aspire. In fact, elements of the described scenario are already present in some Asian cities of to-day, notably in Singapore, Hong Kong and large Chinese cities. The success of these cities should be carefully studied for possible lessons that can be applied elsewhere. In fact, there is a real possibility of the transfer of techniques in urban agriculture from one country/city to another. The exchange of experience among cities in Asian cities can only lead to a speedier diffusion of technology and knowledge, learning about common problems and ways to avoid them, and ultimately increased food production within cities.

On the other hand, one must not underestimate the obstacles that still impede progress in urban agriculture in Asia. Among the issues reviewed, the land question is one of the most difficult to resolve. One may suggest land reform similar to what rural areas have experienced, but there are strong vested interests one has to contend with in the urban setting. The challenge to seek innovative ways to resolve these difficulties is real to policy-makers, planners and citizens at large. Based on the experience of many Asian countries in the postwar period, one of the factors contributing to sustained increase in the quality of life has been the higher rates of food production compared with rates of population increase. If Asian cities are to maintain and raise their levels of living, they must not let population growth overrun their within-city food production capacity. Increased food production in Asian cities is a realizable goal, but the road to this policy objective is strewn with technical, financial and administrative obstacles, which most city governments will find a challenge to overcome.

REFERENCES

Ahmad, Aijazuddin and Anjani K. Singh. 1981. "Public Food Distribution Systems in Indian Cities." Paper presented at the Fourth Inter-Congress of the Pacific Science Association, Singapore, September.

Ash, Robert. 1981. "The Quest for Food Self-Sufficiency." In *Shanghai: Revolution and Development in an Asian Metropolis*, ed. C. Howe, pp. 188–221. Cambridge: Cambridge University Press.

Bardach, John E. 1982. "Food and Energy Problems of Third World Cities." Paper presented at the Conference on Urbanization and National Development, East-West Center, Honolulu, January.

————. 1984. "Fish in the Food Basket of Asian Cities." Unpublished paper. Honolulu: Resource Systems Institute, East-West Center.

Brown, Lester R. 1985. "Reducing Hunger." In *State of the World*, ed. L. R. Brown *et al.*, pp. 23–41. New York: W. N. Norton.

Bulatao-Jayme, Josefina, *et al.* 1981. "Poor Urban Diets: Causes and Feasible Changes." Paper presented at the Fourth Inter-Congress of the Pacific Science Association in Singapore, September.

Cheng, Siok-Hwa. 1976. "The State of Agriculture in Singapore: A Survey Based on the 1973 Agricultural Census." *Journal of Economic Development & Social Change in Asia*, 1(1).

Di-castri, F., *et al.* 1981. "The Man the Biosphere Programme as an Evolving System." *Ambio*, 10(2–3).

Evers, H. D. 1981. "The Contribution of Urban Subsistence Production to Incomes in Jakarta." *Bulletin of Indonesia Economic Studies*, 17(2):89–96.

Gallagher, Charles F. 1975. "Japan and the World Food Problem." *Fieldstaff Reports* (American Universities Field Staff, Asia), 22(1).

Ganapathy, R. S. 1983. "Development of Urban Agriculture in India: Public Policy Options." Paper presented at the Urban Agriculture Seminar, International Development Research Centre, Singapore, July.

Ghosh, D. and C. Furedy. 1983. "Ecological Traditions and Creative Approaches to Urban Waste Reuse: Lessons from Calcutta." Paper presented at the International Conference on Ecological Aspects of Solid Waste Management, The Chinese University of Hong Kong, December.

Hauser, Philip M. and Robert W. Gardner. 1980. "Urban Future: Trends and Prospects." In *Population and the Urban Future*, pp. 9–80, an international conference, Rome, September. Sponsored by UNFPA.

Hawkins, John N. 1981. "Shanghai: An Exploratory Report on Food for the City." Paper presented at the Fourth Inter-Congress of the Pacific Science Association, Singapore, September.

Herrin, A. N., M. F. Montes and R. Florentino. 1984. "Food, Fuel and Urbanization in the Philippines." Paper presented at the Working Group Meeting on Food, Fuel and Urbanization in Asia, Nihon University, Tokyo, May.

Humphrey, John W. 1982. "The Urbanization of Singapore's Rural Landscape." In *Too Rapid Rural Development: Perceptions and Perspectives from Southeast Asia*, ed. Colin MacAndrews and Chia Lin Sien, pp. 334–66. Athens, Ohio: Ohio University Press.

Jackson, James C. 1979. "Daily Fresh Food Markets in Greater Kuala Lumpur." *Pacific Viewpoint*, 20(1):1–32.

Jamir, Nap C. 1983. "The Short Happy Life of Matalahib." Paper presented at the Urban Agriculture Seminar, International Development Research Centre, Singapore, July.

Lam, Timothy T. F. 1981. "Food for the City: The Role of the Informal Sector." Paper presented at the Fourth Inter-Congress of the Pacific Science Association, Singapore, September.

McGee, T. G. and Y. M. Yeung. 1977. *Hawkers in Southeast Asian Cities: Planning for the Bazaar Economy*. Ottawa: International Development Research Centre.

Meier, Richard L. 1981. "Qualities of Life and Foods for the City." *Proceedings of the Fourth Inter-Congress, Pacific Science Association* (Singapore, September), pp. 37–41.

Mittendorf, H. J. and John Abbott. 1979. "Provisioning the Urban Poor: The New Challenge in Food Marketing Systems." *CERES*, 12(6):26–32.

Murphey, Rhoads. 1953. *Shanghai: Key to Modern China*. Cambridge, Mass.: Harvard University Press.

Newcombe, Ken. 1977. "Nutrient Flow in a Major Urban Settlement: Hong Kong." *Human Ecology*, 5(3):179–208.

Newland, Kathleen. 1980. *City Limits: Emerging Constraints on Urban Growth*. Worldwatch Papers 38.

Pernia, Ernesto M. 1983. "Implications of Urbanization for Food Policy Analysis in Asian Countries." Unpublished paper. Honolulu: Resource Systems Institute, East-West Center.

Sigit, Hananto, K. Wirosuhardjo and Prabowo. 1984. "Food, Fuel and Urbanization in Indonesia: A Review of Evidence and Research Proposal." Paper presented at the Working Group Meeting on Food, Fuel and Urbanization in Asia, Nihon University, Tokyo, May.

Sit, Victor F. S. 1981. "Agriculture under the Urban Shadow." In *Urban Hong Kong*, ed. V. Sit, pp. 125–40. Hong Kong: Summerson Eastern Publishers Ltd.

Skinner, G. William. 1981. "Vegetable Supply and Marketing in Chinese Cities." In *Vegetable Farming Systems in China*, ed. D. L. Plucknett and H. L. Beemer, Jr., pp. 215–80. Boulder, Colorado: Westview Press.

Smit, Jac. 1980. "Urban and Metropolitan Agricultural Prospects." *Habitat International*, 5(3/4):499–506.

Song, Byung-Nak and Lee Tae-Il. 1984. "Country Report: Republic of Korea." Paper presented at the Working Group Meeting on Food, Fuel and Urbanization in Asia, Nihon University, Tokyo, May.

Tan, Pek Leng. 1983. "Endangered Species: The Urban Farmer in Penang." Paper presented at the Urban Agriculture Seminar, International Development Research Centre, Singapore, July.

Tempelman, G. J. and F.J.J. Suykerbuyk. 1983. "Agriculture in Singapore." *Singapore Journal of Tropical Geography*, 4(1):62–72.

Tse, F. Y. 1974. "Street Trading in Hong Kong: Part II—Spatial Economy." Hong Kong: Social Research Centre, The Chinese University of Hong Kong. Mimeo.

UNICEF. 1984. "Urban Examples: For Basic Services Development in Cities." June. Mimeo.

Wade, Isabel. 1981. "Fertile Cities." *Development Forum*, September.

————. 1983. "Cracks in the Concrete." *UNICEF News*.

————. 1984. "Can Asia's Cities Feed Themselves?" *Asia 2000*.

Wong, C. T. 1983. "Land Use in Agriculture." In *A Geography of Hong Kong*, ed. T. N. Chiu and C. L. So, pp. 161–76. Hong Kong: Oxford University Press.

Yang, Y. H. 1982. "A Neglected Food Resource: Home Garden." Unpublished paper. Honolulu: Resource Systems Institute, East-West Center. Mimeo.

Yeung, Y. M. 1985. *Provision of Urban Services in Asia: The Role of People-Based Mechanisms*. Occasional Paper No. 78. Hong Kong: Department of Geography, The Chinese University of Hong Kong.

Zhong, Gongfu. 1980. "Mulberry-Dyke-Fish-Pond on the Zhujiang Delta—A Complete Artificial Ecosystem of Land-Water Interaction" (in Chinese). *Acta Geographica Sinica*, 35(3):200–208.

14. Provision of Urban Services in Asia: The Role of People-Based Mechanisms*

INTRODUCTION

Over the past forty years the pursuit of accelerated economic growth by the market economies of Asia, especially in urban areas, has posed many problems for city governments. The problem of delivering adequate urban services to low-income communities is growing ever more acute.

At the global level, the problem of deteriorating basic services for cities in Third World countries was a major theme of the United Nations Habitat Conference held in Vancouver in 1976. Worldwide attention was drawn to the plight of the urban poor in developing countries, exacerbated by difficulties in providing basic services. The work and assistance related to the current concepts of basic needs (ILO) and basic services (UNICEF) can be regarded as parallel efforts geared to the improved access and provision of urban services for the stated group of population.

In almost every developing country in Asia, the gap continues to widen between the demand and supply of urban services to low-income communities. The problem includes both physical services such as water provision, garbage collection and disposal, fire protection, and human waste disposal, and social services such as health care, child care, recreation and education. The gradual realization of the ineffectiveness of a "service delivery" model (i.e., government-provided services) has promoted experimental and innovative efforts to mobilize people's resources towards improving the urban living environment.

*The data on which this paper is based come primarily from a five-country comparative study called Participatory Urban Services in Asia, funded by the International Development Research Centre (IDRC) of Canada from 1980 to 1984. I am grateful to the participants of the project and T. G. McGee for use of the data, wise counsel and ideas. Any errors of representation and interpretation are entirely mine.

The underlying rationale of these experimental approaches is to make use of community resources for the delivery of basic physical and social services. These pioneering attempts require new organizations and mobilization, usually taking the form of participatory, self-help, cooperative, self-sustaining and community-based styles of management characterized by popular participation. A corollary assumption is that a minimum of government involvement is required. Whether they arise from the government, the private sector, or the community itself, the distinguishing feature is that they will reduce public transfers and thus free public capital for other developmental investments.

It may be argued that any programme designed to reduce public transfers to low-income communities is "antisocial"—the government merely abdicates its responsibility to provide basic services to the urban poor. This argument must be tempered by the reality that urban service provision is more often than not unevenly distributed, skewed in favour of high-income communities. A queuing system of some kind is usually at play, where, for lack of political clout, interest articulation and appropriate organization, low-income communities are served last. Under these circumstances it is a pragmatic strategy for the urban poor to organize to deliver the needed services to themselves, preserving indirectly scarce capital for the government to pursue other developmental purposes that might also benefit them. It thus appears that the ideological question is related as much to the definition of participatory services as to the beneficiaries of these services.

From the standpoint of the government, participatory services may be beneficial in several ways. First of all, increased popular participation will reduce the costs of social transfers, thereby enhancing the government's ability to pursue development options. Secondly, people-based programmes can potentially provide the government with needed information on the socioeconomic characteristics of the inhabitants. Thirdly, the existence of participatory service organizations will likely help the government identify community leaders who can help both the community and the government in realizing their respective goals.

On the other hand, as viewed by low-income communities, participatory urban services will provide physical and welfare needs, even at a rudimentary level, that otherwise would not be available. In the process of organizing for such services, the socioeconomic structures of the community are strengthened, giving rise to a sense of community and neighbourliness that is often weakly developed in urban areas. Moreover, even with very small subsidization by the government to carry out participatory urban services, many income opportunities for low-income communities may be created.

Within many parts of rural Asia, self-help and community participation have been age-old traditions whereby people have satisfied a wide range of functions and needs (Ahmad and Hossain, 1978; Ban 1977; Ratnapala, 1978). With increasing urbanization, economic growth, and the entry of more and more people into the wage labour force, the time available for participatory activities has been decreased. The state and the private corporate sector at various levels (national, regional and city) have come to play an increasing role in service delivery. A top-down service delivery model is almost universally accepted instead. But where the state suffers from lack of funds or administrative inefficiency, provision of services becomes inadequate and worsens over time.

So ubiquitous has been the state's role in service delivery that much of the literature and research on this subject in developed countries has focussed upon the theme of returning control or at least some form of control of the delivery of basic services to the community level. This goal is accomplished through increasing community access to and control of the political process (Bish, 1979; Harlan, 1977). Citizen involvement with an accent on neighbourhood and local government services is encouraged (Lovrich and Taylor, 1976; Zimmerman, 1972). The influence of intermediary groups on urban service delivery is recognized (Jones, 1981). Decentralization and citizen participation are especially advocated in the sphere of social services (Rein, 1972).

The developing countries of Asia, however, present a different set of circumstances. First of all, the role of the state is much more powerful and the possibility of communities clamouring for urban services through the recourse of political parties is limited. Then, urban populations have been growing at twice the national average, leading to a situation, in large cities in particular, of already heavily strained services falling far behind demand. The situation is further compounded by the ever increasing proportion of population in low-income communities, many of whose inhabitants are close to the poverty line. Many of these inhabitants are also migrants from the rural areas who have brought with them the tradition of self-help and community participation. Given this background and the severely limited financial resources of city governments for development projects and service provision, the ecological environment is conducive to a wide range of people-based mechanisms to deliver some of the needed urban services.

THE COMPARATIVE STUDY

Over the past few years experimental approaches to the delivery of basic urban services have been carried out in at least five Asian countries, namely, Hong Kong, Indonesia, Republic of Korea, Malaysia and the Philippines. These countries are marked by different economic, social and cultural conditions. Recently, they took part in a joint project which attempted to share these experiences and evaluate the success and failure of the various programmes.

In Hong Kong intermediate organizations, traditionally acting as mediators between the government and the public, have evolved new functions and structures founded on modern principles so that urban needs can be better met and urban services more efficiently delivered. Membership in these new organizations is based on the real need for certain urban services rather than on former ascriptive ties such as clans or communities. They have grown in response to factors such as increasing urban density, diminution of social welfare funds from non-governmental sources and decentralization of the population. Activist residents' associations and mutual-aid committees are examples of such new organizations in the rapidly changing urban ecology of Hong Kong.

Despite considerable physical improvement in some urban communities in the several large Indonesian cities through the internationally assisted programmes of sites-and-services and kampung improvement, it has been observed that the emphasis has been on infrastructural improvement at the expense of social services. However, community-based efforts, both formally and informally organized, have tended to meet part of the gap in social services. These include improvements in education, recreation, health and other related needs. Considering the time-honoured spirit of *gotong-royong* (self-help), it is believed that a more significant role of community-based urban services can be promoted.

The Saemaul Undong (New Community Movement), in the Republic of Korea, based on the principle of self-reliance and applied in rural areas since the early 1970s with immense success, was extended to the cities in 1975. The rationale of its application to urban areas is the fact that many municipal governments have been unable to respond adequately to the demand for urban services. Neighbourhood self-help organizations arising from the Urban Saemaul Movement have taken over many functions such as road construction, installation of sewerage lines and extending piped water to large cities. In the small towns, a town regeneration programme, including the rehabilitation and reconstruction of housing and shops, is in progress.

Under the New Economic Policy, Malaysia has also been pursuing an intensive industrialization programme. A Free Trade Zone has been established in Bayan Lepas, Penang. The new industrial labour force in a new urban environment has experienced specific service problems and needs. An important programme designed to cater to the recreational and educational needs of the 30,000 young workers in the area has been the three-year Young Workers' Community Educational Project (YWCEP), initiated in 1975 under the auspices of the Federation of Family Planning Associations, Malaysia. It provided a wide range of community-based activities for the mostly female worker who come from the rural areas. The pilot project confirmed the need for a continual and more comprehensive community development project.

Finally, in the Philippines the demonstrable inability of the large city governments to provide most urban services has led to a search for systems other than the "service delivery" model. Recent efforts have sought approaches which can be described as cooperative management with greater dependence on resources from the popular sector (community). A recent study conducted in the community of Leveriza in Manila has provided some promising leads in this approach to people-based urban services.

Since 1980, five teams from these countries have been participating in an international study which is intended to provide important policy-relevant information on the development and operation of a range of basic urban services based on the principle of self-help. The choice of the five countries was guided by the mix of social-cultural conditions under which different types of participatory mechanisms have evolved.

The overall objective of the study is to gain a better understanding of the development and provision of basic urban services through different mechanisms of self-help in a range of Asian cities at different levels of economic development and of varied sociocultural backgrounds. Specifically, each country study will:

1. identify and describe the existing range of urban services and their structural arrangements, with an emphasis on participatory mechanisms;
2. analyze and compare the various mechanisms utilized in the

generation and delivery of services through self-help;

3. evaluate the effectiveness of varying forms of self-help service delivery;
4. draw policy implications for planners and city administrators; and
5. train young Asian researchers through participation in the project.

In view of the different societal conditions under which participatory urban services systems have emerged, the research design devised for each of the participating countries is geared to the local circumstances.

In Hong Kong four communities have been selected for investigation by virtue of their maximum variation in living conditions and modes of interaction between the government, intermediate organizations and the local people. The four study areas are, respectively: Sai Ying Poon, an old traditional neighbourhood on Hong Kong Island; Tuen Mun, a growing new town in the western New Territories; Tai Hang Tung, a residential area planned and built by the government to accommodate those too poor to afford "adequate" housing; and Kwun Tong, a large and established industrial community in eastern Kowloon.

In Indonesia six kampungs, four in Jakarta and two in Ujung Pandang, have been chosen to correspond to variations in ethnic origin and homogeneity, distance from the city centre, access to transportation and employment, and past government policies. Where possible, the effect of internationally assisted programmes in some of the kampungs will also be taken into account.

For the Korean study, three dongs, or typical municipal administrative units, have been identified. These include two dongs in Seoul (Sangge Dong and Changsin Dong) and one dong in Sungnam (No. 4 Dong), about 15 kilometres from Seoul. A dong varies in area from 2 to 4 square kilometres, and in population from 15,000 to 30,000. These dongs were chosen for their ongoing activities under the Urban Saemaul Undong.

The Philippine research design is most comprehensive and ambitious since it will cover nine low-income communities in three cities of varying sizes. Three study areas, each defined by spatial and ecological factors, have been selected in three different regions of the Philippines, namely, Metro Manila, Cebu and Davao. The three low-income communities from each city have been identified in an area near the city centre, located in a "zone of transition" within the urban periphery.

The Malaysian study is of Bayan Lepas in Penang, where the corporate sector with employment in export-oriented industries is important. The YWCEP programme, designed for young female workers in the area, has been carefully evaluated. In addition, a complementary inquiry has been done on the urban services in the Weld Quay area, which has a flourishing informal sector.

MAJOR FINDINGS

The five teams have met in Hong Kong, Manila, Penang and Seoul since the project was launched in 1980, and have shared their experiences. The last meeting was held in Seoul in March 1984, when policy-makers, in addition to researchers, were invited to discuss the results of the study in a mutually beneficial manner. To date, country results are available for Hong Kong (Kuen et al., 1983; Lau et al., 1983), Indonesia (Karamoy and Dias, 1983), Republic of Korea (Park, 1982) and the Philippines (Ramos, 1983), while the comparative volume was published recently (Yeung and McGee, 1986). Thus, only a synopsis of the country results will be highlighted here.

Hong Kong

In Hong Kong, 278 local officials and leaders and 191 local leaders were interviewed. The results confirm that participatory urban services under-taken in the four study areas are varied, but largely limited to services of a social nature, such as Keep Hong Kong Clean, an anti-crime campaign, and recreational activities. They were considered successful because they elic-ited the support of the residents. The attitudinal context of this range of successful participatory urban services was, however, somewhat ambigu-ous. While local officials were generally in favour of giving more power to the citizens through participatory projects, they also feared that unfulfilled expectations might cause the situation to go out of control. Consequently, when given the choice between expanding governmental activities and resources or mobilizing and organizing citizens for self-help, only 30 per cent of the officials preferred the latter option.

Similarly, the results of the interviews with local leaders are quite varied. Generally, they favour greater participation by the citizens in self-help activities and approve of their growing awareness of the potential of these activities to improve their welfare. Without an autonomous power base, the local leaders do not feel entirely successful in mobilizing citizens to support their cause, and yet they are highly instrumental in organizing residents to cooperate with the government. Thus, half of them preferred the expansion of governmental activities and resources to mobilizing citizens as the appropriate strategy for solving local problems.

The Hong Kong study included a special investigation of the roles of Mutual Aid Committees (MACs) which have been effective in mitigating crime rates in high-rise buildings and in performing other functions. However, the ambiguous objectives of MACs and the lack of interaction between local leaders and residents have prevented their development into powerful vehicles for delivering a range of basic services. It must be recognized that at Hong Kong's present stage of development, it is not so much a question of infrastructural deficiency. The question is centred around the quality and cost of services, and the trade-off between physical and social services. The need for the latter services has yet to be better articulated by the residents.

The study pointed to the lack of organic linkage and interaction between officials and residents mediated by local leaders. This structural problem has been an inhibiting factor to better urban service delivery. One important finding from the study was the need to involve local leaders in a greater role in decision-making and resource allocation if the present system is to improve. The study offers a number of policy recommendations as an improvement on existing practices.

Indonesia

The Indonesia study focussed on urban service delivery in six kampungs in Jakarta and Ujung Pandang. The Jakarta study covered four *Rukun Warga* (neighbourhood units) or RW, the closest territorial expression of a kampung, in Kebon Kosong, Rawa Badak, Jelambar and Kayu Manis, located in four different parts of the city. In Ujung Pandang the two kampungs studied were Maecini and Layang, which have enjoyed improved services since 1971. The six locations were identified as part of a *kelurahan* (district), the lowest administrative unit in urban Indonesia. It is headed by the *lurah*, who is an appointed official, and most of the governmental basic services are provided through him and his staff. However, such services were found to be wanting, not only because of insufficient financial resources to meet all deserving needs but because the bureaucratic structure of the district was incapable of responding to the felt needs with its typically top-down approach.

The study nevertheless revealed, as well, a well-developed informal leadership structure in the RWs. Such leadership has been highly valued and has been responsible to a large extent for enriching the social lives of the residents. A wide variety of group activities, largely on a voluntary basis, was found. They organized and mobilized the residents to engage in activities relating to income generation, social welfare, health, kampung maintenance and security patrols. These activities are seen as critical for many of the urban poor to survive in a large city like Jakarta. For many reasons, the poorer families have found it difficult to relate their problems and needs to the formal leaders (the *lurah* and his staff) whose organized activities are seen at best as only marginal to their real needs. The head of the RW is regarded as a true leader by the people.

Within the formal structure, the *lurah* coordinates all programmes which have been "channelled downwards" from the various government departments. He coordinates these activities through what is called Organization of Community Security or the LKMD. For the most part, these are social activities aimed at fulfilling the basic needs of certain groups, such as the social welfare of different types, youth, religion, economic activities, education and health. The utilization levels of these governmental services are low, however, fewer than half of the respondent families availed themselves of them. The residents were generally more responsive to social activities organized by the informal leaders who appeared better able to perceive their needs. This pattern of patronage of urban services might suggest a problem of structural poverty, since the low-income groups, by refusing to take part in activities outside their immediate reference group, became further entrenched in their existing precarious conditions as a result of inaction.

Another important finding from the study is that the needs and problems facing each kampung are different. In Rawa Badak it is clean water, but it is unemployment and crime, especially among the youth in Jelambar. As long as the government continues "delivering" packages of services, it is unlikely that the residents will be able to improve their living standards significantly. People should be given more opportunity to take part in decision-making and in setting their own priorities.

To the extent that the respondents did not know of the availability of government initiated programmes and services, the study pointed to the need for closer interaction and discussion between kampung residents and *kelurahan* staff. The idea of benefiting the higher-income groups failed as a strategy for allowing the benefits to "trickle down" to the poorest groups. Finally, in view of the varying needs and problems of each kampung, the study advocates a greater scope for each *kelurahan* to set its own priorities. In reality, the districts are quite different from each other and the approach of "delivering" one package of services without a built-in mechanism allowing for local differences is problematic.

Republic of Korea

A study of 1,244 households samples from communities in Seoul, Daejeon, Iri and Sungnam has been completed. Six of these communities are in Seoul, which is by far the largest city in the Republic of Korea. The household survey yielded the information normally expected of low-income communities whose residents have mainly migrated from the rural areas.

The profile of the survey community is that it is overcrowded and suffers a serious shortage of essential facilities. About 40 per cent of the residents expressed dissatisfaction with both the amount of living space and the quality of housing. Water supply is satisfactory (93 per cent are supplied), although reliability is questionable. Only about one-third of the residents expressed dissatisfaction with garbage disposal, manure disposal and disinfection service. Difficult and narrow access roads increase fire hazards in the community, but police service is deemed acceptable. When required, most residents seek medical help in the vicinity despite the lack of sufficient services. A high degree of neighbourliness prevails, as many of the residents turn to neighbours for assistance in livelihood and family problems.

Unlike some other communities, most families are not trapped in the area for purely economic reasons. Twenty per cent of the families earned sufficient income to be able to afford alternative accommodations in other residential areas. They chose to live in the area because the low rents relative to their income released resources for other priority purposes, such as education for the children, a balanced diet, decent clothing and adequate medical care.

Under Saemaul Undong, as many as sixty different types of self-help projects were found to be active in the study areas. They range from physical improvements in housing and basic urban services to improvements in economic and cultural life. Most residents reported having had experience in twenty different self-help projects within the various programmes in one community.

Housing improvement at first proceeded on an individual basis, confined at first to replacing fragile materials with durable structures. After the Saemaul Undong was initiated, cooperative housing improvement schemes were introduced, including structural repairs and total redevelopment. Where legal occupancy status has not been accorded to the residents, only partial improvement is possible. In such cases Saemaul Undong facilitates group action since a great deal of work impinges on multiple house ownership. In communities where legal occupancy status has been conferred, housing improvement can be very substantial. New housing, indeed modern apartments, can be constructed.

In Jayang Dong, a study community, for example, the makeshift houses were redeveloped into apartment houses. First the residents set up a community credit union to pool savings which allowed residents to finance purchase of part of the land which they illegally occupied. Then a committee of fifteen members was constituted which was empowered to approach the municipal government for legal permission to build and to be assisted financially. A housing loan of 3 million won (US$7,200) for each eligible family was extended. As a result of these efforts, what was once a substandard housing area has been transformed into a modern residential area.

Malaysia

The study covered 632 respondents from Weld Quay and Bayan Baru areas. The former is a predominantly Chinese area near the waterfront in a well-established part of Georgetown, Penang; the latter is a newly developing township providing export zone facilities for assembly factories employing predominantly young Malay female workers drawn from the rural hinterland. The two study areas typify working conditions and relationships of the informal and formal sectors. The contrast in the two working environments is important because, while the former is associated with many traditional Chinese small-scale industries, the latter is a product of the emerging proletarianization process which has been proceeding apace in Malaysia with its recent rapid industrial development through export processing zones.

The demographic and economic profile from the survey data more or less conforms to our notions of workers in the formal and informal sectors. The formal sector tends to draw workers from younger age groups, with higher educational attainment, having a migrant background, and who have obtained jobs by formal application. Directly related to the nature of the work, formal sector workers reported much higher incidents of complaints/symptoms than their informal counterparts.

Survey results show that formal sector workers tend to be better provided with facilities through their companies. Workers are generally aware of these facilities and utilization rates are high. But other types of services which cater more to the overall development and education of workers are poorly developed. The data are being analyzed to draw out the comparison of services available to the workers from the two different employment sectors.

Apart from this structured comparison of young workers, the Malaysia study also includes an earlier evaluation of the Young Workers Education Project (YWEP). The evaluation in this project attempts a need-goals analysis, a programme audit and a goals achievement analysis. The target group is located in Bayan Baru, which is the project centre. A comparison of the YWEP in Bayan Lepas and other self-help community projects in Weld Quay will be illuminating as regards the factors which contribute to the success or failure of non-governmental delivery systems.

Philippines

Although the original sampling frame for the Philippine study allowed for nine study areas, eventually only seven were chosen from Metro Manila, Cebu and Davao, the three largest cities in the country. A total of 1,197 respondents were interviewed in an attempt to obtain information on the basic urban services that were available to the low-income communities.

The survey results from the three cities are emphatic that basic services available to the study communities are very poor. In the three cities studied, only 15 per cent of the households have direct water supply, 22 per cent have no toilets in their households, 45 per cent resort to open dumping of garbage on vacant lots or into bodies of water, and 37 per cent do not have metres installed for measuring consumption of electricity.

The Metro Manila households surveyed rank highest in supply of electricity and in disposal of garbage. About seven out of ten households have metres for electricity, and 42 per cent of the households use dump truck service for disposal of garbage. The communities surveyed in Cebu have the best water supply and toilet facilities. One in five households has direct water supply, and only 12 per cent of the households lack toilet facilities. Finally, Davao scores lower than the other two cities in terms of almost all indices, an indication perhaps of the influence of city size despite the common feature of low-income communities surveyed in all three cities.

The population is growing faster than the municipal budget available for service delivery, and a progressive deterioration of basic services provided in Manila is obvious. Even years after the Metropolitan Manila Commission was created in 1975, the delivery of basic urban services was found to be still wanting and ineffective. Almost every basic service—water supply, flood diversion, sewerage, waste disposal, fire prevention, health care, housing and electric supply—saw no marked improvement in recent years. The conclusion drawn from a study of urban management in Metro Manila is that improvement of service delivery appears to have to go beyond organizational and management reform. The study advocates a basic re-orientation of attitudes, both on the part of the bureaucrats and the people themselves for whom the services are intended.

Reorientation of the bureaucrats must begin with a sharpening of their awareness of the needs of the communities. They must first understand the problem of the community by immersing themselves in the actual problems confronting the people. This has to be followed by regular visits so that good relationships with the residents can be established. To be effective, any development programme affecting the residents ought to draw on their views in order that formulated objectives can specifically and operationally address community problems. All this leads to the idea of partnership between the reoriented bureaucrats and community residents in delivering any specific service. Community leaders, discovered through formal or informal networks, are critical if any service project is to succeed.

To test the above ideas concretely, a cooperative management model is proposed to enlist greater participation from the people. The model consists of six elements, namely, environment, receptors, government, community, planning machinery and effectors, and was applied tentatively in one study area in Metro Manila for different services. The model has yet to be rigorously tested before it can be concluded that it is a departure from existing service delivery models.

COMMON THEMES

Since neither the country studies together nor the countries themselves are strictly comparable, a rigorous set of findings would be presumptuous. This section will, however, identify the salient themes that have recurred in these case studies.

In the organization of participatory urban services, one critical question is to identify the geographic and demographic unit for functional efficiency. Is there a minimum threshold size at which urban services can be effectively organized by the people themselves? Are existing administrative units viable surrogates for this purpose? In the studies in Indonesia and the Philippines, the lowest administrative units, namely the *kelurahan* and the *barangay*, are organic entities within which urban services are organized. They are convenient building blocks for extending or organizing urban services because they possess an effective leadership. In the Republic of Korea, the present organization of participatory urban services is undertaken at the dong level. The study concluded, however, that this unit is too large to be effective as a functional unit. At this level, it is particularly difficult to create a sense of social cohesiveness among the residents. Yet the lower level of administrative unit—*tong* or *ban*—is considered too small. Consequently it is proposed that two or three *tongs* should be unified as a superior functional unit which, if adopted for implementation, will entail massive reorganization of service delivery within the urban areas of the Republic of Korea. In the case of Hong Kong, a ready association of geographic and administrative districts has produced convenient units around which to organize participatory services. There are eighteen such districts in Hong Kong, but they are already heavily used. More popular participation in improvement of urban services may make it necessary to subdivide them further, an act that would depend on the political climate and the articulation of needs by the populace. When the felt need for services is location-specific and clearly spelled out, small functional units can often be highly effective. For example, to combat the problem of crime, countless Mutual Aid Committees, usually on the basis of a block of high-rise flats, have been successfully established and run in many parts of the territory.

As participatory urban services are people-based, it is not uncommon to find that strong leadership and successful delivery are positively related. Such leadership may be formal or informal. Krus na Ligas, one of the study communities located in Diliman in Metro Manila, has six types of formal organizations, and five informal groups, all with their own leaders. Leadership structures are especially well developed in the barangay. This extensive network of leadership within an urban community in the Philippines is greatly preferred to another system in the Indonesian kampungs in which leadership is centralized in the *lurah*. The *lurah* is the appointed head of the local LKMD (Organization of Community Security), the basic unit for delivering community services. With the responsibility of implementing service programmes so heavily centred on one individual, the likelihood of ineffective delivery is so much greater. Similarly, dong leaders in Urban Saemaul Undong are appointed. Installed leadership is necessary when there is a shortage of competent leaders in the community. In Hong Kong, on the other hand, most of the leaders were drawn from voluntary associations, and their relationship with government officials is quite different. Perhaps the most important finding to emerge from all the country studies is that leadership is the most critical factor in the success of any participatory urban service. Many studies identified weaknesses in present leadership, such as lack of dynamism, inadequate training and poor communication skills. Almost every case study pointed to the need and ample room for improvement of leadership qualities, if participatory urban services are to further improve. In this respect, several studies recommended better training for leaders, both formally and informally. In passing, it may be mentioned that in the urban kampungs of Indonesia activities organized by housewives are frequently well participated in and successful. This shows not only the important role of women in many community activities, but the existence of a pool of potential informal leaders in these communities.

One of the main responsibilities of leaders in urban communities, it was argued, is to help residents articulate their needs for services in a more effective and organized way. In the study of kampungs in Indonesia, for example, the government package of services does not reach the lowest socioeconomic groups. The real needs and problems of the community at large are quite different from those provided by the government programmes. A similar situation is found in Penang, where government programmes have been slow to react to the needs and problems of young workers. As a result, they have to turn to a host of non-governmental organizations which have been far more successful in identifying and meeting the needs of a new work force. In the Mutual Aid Committees in Hong Kong, the ambiguity of objectives together with the lack of close interaction between local leaders and residents has led to the failure of felt needs to be articulated. It was concluded that participatory services would prosper if these were geared to the genuine needs of the citizens.

Different perceptions of the needs of an urban community by the residents, as opposed to an external delivery organization, bedevil many well-intentioned efforts, and result in low rates of participation and success. Effective leadership in an urban community contributes to a solid identification of needs, a search for consensus, and an enlarged ability to respond to community needs. This was achieved to some degree in the community management cycle in the study communities in the Philippines.

The studies also offer some insight into the nature and scope of activities on which community participation should focus. The Korean study concluded that the activities pursued in the urban communities under study were not diversified enough to cater to a broad spectrum of needs. In part, this is the consequence of a governmental bias which tends to favour community-wide and basic physical services at the expense of socioeconomic services specific to individual communities. The study advocated a shift of activities towards improving the household economy and income generation, along with cultural activities. In a similar vein, the Indonesian study strongly suggested a more accurate need assessment within individual kampungs before any decision is taken to implement urban services. The present programmes being implemented in these communities were initially developed for rural areas and are therefore not sensitive to the heterogeneity of the urban population. It was suggested that the main problems in the kampungs were unemployment, housing and capital accumulation. Government or community programmes must recognize these needs and design programmes and activities that will alleviate the immediate needs. Finally, in the study of urban communities in the Philippines, the most critical shortages of services were in water, sanitation facilities and garbage disposal. These should be high priority concerns in any attempt to improve the living environment.

Successful articulation of needs and choice of activities for community participation depend on the availability of information. Ideally, information should flow freely among four different levels—individual, household, community and state—so that the strategies can be adopted to meet the socioeconomic needs of each urban community. In the country studies, different mechanisms have been developed to facilitate the flow of needed information. In Hong Kong, the District Board meetings are occasions when major changes affecting the urban community can be discussed and decided. In the barangays in urban Philippines, well developed formal and informal leadership structures have been most useful in promoting effective communication among the actors in question. Consequently, a participatory management model could be developed which depended on the active contribution of all actors, in particular the community and the government, for the improvement of basic services. Other things being equal, the more information flows among the four different levels, the more likely effective urban service delivery will be.

One issue that is implicit in all the country studies concerns the success and failure of the mechanism of participatory urban services. Measurement of success is extremely difficult across nations given the diverse socioeconomic and cultural settings. But there are generalizable elements of success and failure in almost all the mechanisms used. Befiting their own country situations, different methods have been chosen to respond to highly similar problems. Some of the plausible criteria that may be used to measure success include the reach of services in the community, the extent of participation, visible physical improvement and qualitative changes in daily life, among others. The study did not specifically design indicators to measure success, but the detailed country findings should provide the basis on which approximate degrees of success can be measured along the suggested dimensions.

POLICY RECOMMENDATIONS

Since all of the country studies addressed policy relevant concerns in different situations, specific and detailed policy recommendations were presented.

The first is that participatory urban services depend on people's active involvement if they are to succeed. The most practical recommendation flowing from that finding is to expand residents' awareness of the need and scope of such activities and their essential roles in bringing these to fruition. The more the people can be involved in all stages of services provision, including planning, implementation and evaluation, the better will be the service provided. This multiple-stage process entails the identification of needs, the search for consensus, a free flow of information, community involvement, and monitoring and assessment of results. The Philippine model in this study appears to come closest to this ideal.

Community and self-help services cannot be organized overnight. A step-by-step and incremental process of mobilization and organization, on the basis of the Hong Kong experience, is seemingly a sound approach which can be recommended for other countries similarly interested in community activities.

In almost every study, a mismatch between residents' needs and actual programmes was perceived. Most recommend that service delivery agencies should examine the hierarchy of needs. Some are essential, others supplementary; some are basic and economic, others cultural and social; some are production-oriented, others consumer-oriented. Upon a clearer identification and verification of needs, almost every community can consider a shift or broadening of existing programmes and activities. It is therefore recommended that governments further expand their community development programmes.

The studies were unanimous about the critical factor of leadership for effective participatory urban services. Leaders have to be identified, trained and nurtured. Wherever possible, leaders must be trained and educated to acquire the necessary skills and qualities. In the Urban Saemaul Movement, for instance, leaders need a knowledge of technical procedures in order to perform certain tasks. Residents, similarly, need to be educated and trained as a majority of them are too poorly educated to comprehend the complexities of existing bureaucratic procedures.

A case in point is in the kampungs in Indonesia, where the intricate bureaucracy surrounding the *kelurahan* has inhibited most residents in the lowest socioeconomic groups from articulating their needs through the *lurah*. The studies recommended more flexible, decentralized responses to expressed needs within existing institutional structures. This strategy may involve devolution of authority to local administrative offices, or setting up of new institutions such as the non-governmental organization in Penang.

In the same spirit of greater local autonomy, the studies recommended that where relevant, government financial assistance should be accompanied by only broad guidelines such that the community can set its own priorities in what services to provide. The Hong Kong study recommended going one step further and incorporating community groups in the allocation of financial resources in the annual budgeting process.

From a policy point of view it is possible to recognize a cluster of policy priorities for governments and another set for local communities. For governments in the region there is clearly a need to improve the following aspects of urban service delivery systems:

1. information on urban service needs;
2. flexibility in developing urban delivery systems reacting to the scale of community organization and need priorities;
3. quality and training of leaders and administrators involved in urban service delivery schemes;
4. understanding of existing community resources;
5. willingness to involve a wide spectrum of community resources, including non-governmental organizations (NGOs), political parties and religious organizations already active in urban areas; and
6. coordination of institutional responses to urban service delivery which are often spread out among a plethora of departments.

For urban communities the policy options are rather different, for they must develop more effective means to: (a) communicate their needs to the government; (b) develop new participatory activities; and (c) create more community awareness of their needs. It is particularly with respect to the poorer inhabitants of these Asian cities that the need to develop these responses is most crucial. It is these groups that have the least economic capacity to satisfy these needs. It therefore seems necessary to suggest policies which increase community control over their resources. In such propositions there is often a delicate balance between government paternalism and community activism which can only be resolved in each city situation. Clearly this is a crucial area for further policy information and formulation.

The results of the five studies certainly emphasize that governments are not unaware of the need to improve urban service delivery programmes. Nor for that matter are urban communities unaware of their needs. The problem is how to develop effective responses. This is both a challenge and a necessity for it is clear that the growth of urban centres in these countries is inevitable and the need to deliver urban services will not disappear. To this extent all governments face similar problems and need to learn from their common experiences of being increasingly dependent on people-based resources to deliver urban services for the improvement of the lives of the urban poor.

REFERENCES

Ahmad, Q. K. and M. Hossain. 1978. *Development through Self-Help: Lessons from Ulashi*. Dacca: Bangladesh Institute of Development Studies.

Ban, S. H. 1977. *Saemaul Udong: The New Community Movement in Korea*. Seoul: Korea Development Institute.

Bish, Robert. 1979. "Public Choice Theory for Comparative Research on Urban Service Delivery." *Comparative Urban Research*, II(1):18–26.

Harlan, Hahn, ed. 1977. *People and Politics in Urban Society*. Beverly Hills: Sage Publications.

Jones, B. D. 1981. "Party and Bureaucracy: The Influence of Intermediary Groups on Urban Public Service Delivery." *The American Political Science Review*, 75:688–700.

Karamoy, Amir and Gillian Dias. 1983. "Community Based Delivery of Social Services in Indonesia: Case Study in Jakarta and Ujung Pandang." Jakarta: Institute for Social and Economic Research, Education and Information (LP3ES). Mimeo.

Kuan, Hsin-chi, Lau Siu-kai and Ho Kam-fai. 1983. *Organizing Participatory Urban Services: The Mutual Aid Committees in Hong Kong*. Occasional Papers No. 2. Hong Kong: Centre for Hong Kong Studies, The Chinese University of Hong Kong.

Lau, Siu-kai, Kuan Hsin-chi and Ho Kam-fai. 1983. *Leaders, Officials, and Citizens in Urban Service Delivery: A Comparative Study of Four Localities in Hong Kong*. Occasional Papers No. 1. Hong Kong: Centre for Hong Kong Studies, The Chinese University of Hong Kong.

Lovrich, N. P., Jr. and G. T. Taylor, Jr. 1976. "Neighbourhood Evaluation of Local Government Services: A Citizen Survey Approach." *Urban Affairs Quarterly*, 12:197–222.

Park, Soo-young. 1982. *Urban Services for the Poor: The Case of Korea* (in Korean). Seoul: Korea Research Institute for Human Settlements.

Ramos, Exaltacion C. 1983. "The Delivery of Basic Services in Three Selected Philippine Urban Centres: Implications for a Participatory Management Model." Manila: Integrated Research Centre, De La Salle University. Mimeo.

Ratnapala, N. 1978. *Sarvodaya Movement: Self-Help Rural Development in Sri Lanka*. Essex, Connecticut: International Council for Educational Development.

Rein, Martin. 1972. "Decentralization and Citizen: Participation in Social Services." *Public Administration Review*, 32:687–700.

Yeung, Y. M. and T. G. McGee. 1986. *Community Participation in Delivering Urban Services in Asia*. Ottawa: International Development Research Centre.

Zimmerman, J. F. 1972. "Neighbourhoods and Citizen Involvement." *Public Administration Review*, 32:201–210.

15. Livelihoods for the Urban Poor: Case for a Greater Role by Metropolitan Governments

INTRODUCTION

Over the past four decades or so rapid urbanization and attendant urban poverty in developing countries have been persistent and deepening concerns confronting planners and policy-makers at the city, national and international levels. Between 1950 and 1975, cities in these countries grew annually at 5 per cent—twice the national rate, but the urban poor within them grew two or three times as fast as the urban population as a whole. Consequently, over 250 million urban dwellers in developing countries are severely deprived, without reasonable access to minimal nutrition, safe water, minimal sanitation, and basic education and shelter. At an estimated increase of 15 to 18 million persons per annum, urban dwellers living in these deplorable conditions will exceed 600 million by the year 2000 (Jaycox, 1978:10). The explosion of the urban poor may be translated into an enormous challenge, if not a mounting burden, for the countries concerned in striving for socioeconomic progress as well as political stability. Only recently has policy and development attention been devoted, nationally and internationally, to the problem.

Yet, willy-nilly, over 550 million people had been absorbed by the cities in the developing world during the period 1950 to 1975, and another 1.2 billion people will have to be similarly absorbed by the year 2000 (Jaycox, 1978). To be more explicit, Farbman (1981:44) reported that between 1980 and 2000, 782 million new jobs will need to be created. The United Nations also estimated that between 1975 and 2000, the labour force in all the developing countries will rise by 75 per cent, or by 2.7 per cent a year (ILO, 1977:19). How can the inhabitants of these cities find jobs? Will future inhabitants be able to find jobs?

THE INFORMAL SECTOR

The answer to the first question lies in the fact that, in the absence of anywhere close to sufficient factory jobs to meet demands, most cities in the developing world have depended on what is widely known as the informal sector (IFS) to absorb surplus labour. The concept of the IFS as opposed to the formal sector (FS), popularized by Hart (1973) and subsequently adopted by the International Labour Office (ILO) in its assistance programme, can be traced to the dualistic model, with such dichotomized concepts as modern and traditional, and firm-centred and bazaar (Geertz, 1963). The IFS may be characterized in many ways but Sethuraman (1981:17) has defined it as follows:

> It consists of small-scale units engaged in the production and distribution of goods and services with the primary objective of generating employment and income to their participants notwithstanding the constraints on capital, both physical and human, and know-how.

Sethuraman reported that urban employment in the IFS in many developing countries ranged between 20 and 70 per cent. In Jakarta, for instance, the size of the IFS in 1967 in terms of employment was estimated to be around 435,000, or 41 per cent of the total employed. The bulk of the jobs provided in the IFS lay in the service sector, accounting for 27 per cent of the IFS employment, engaging 117,000 persons. The other major sectors were trade, transport and construction, manufacturing, and agriculture in descending order of importance (Sethuraman, 1976:127–29).

Quite clearly the predominance of service provision within the IFS is related to the abundance of labour and low requirements in terms of skills, education and capital for entry. In fact, Hart (1973:69) has identified a wide range of both legitimate and illegitimate informal income opportunities within Third World cities. The socioeconomic structures of these cities are such that there are certain markets within which the IFS can sustain itself and thrive. Such markets exist because the FS cannot reach them (e.g., repairs, services, tailoring, etc.), does not find enough incentive to enter (e.g., duplication of imported spare parts on a small scale), finds the labour intensive and expensive (e.g., garbage collection), and deliberately seeks the cooperation of the IFS through subcontracting (Sethuraman, 1981:39).

These diverse markets of the IFS are reflected in the heterogeneous composition of those who participate in its activities. In a study of hawkers in Southeast Asian cities, it was discovered that there was considerable variation in the socioeconomic and demographic background of those engaged in the trade. While hawking was a source of quite handsome returns to some, it was a refuge occupation to others. Hawking was taken up by both long-term residents as well as relatively new migrants to the city. Hawkers also ranged widely in age (McGee and Yeung, 1977). The diversity and scale of the IFS means that unless policies are purposefully designed and funded, it is particularly difficult for governments to affect its activities either positively or otherwise. Empirical evidence has indicated that macroeconomic policies aimed at increasing urban employment have largely failed to trickle down to the IFS and the urban poor (Linn, 1983:38). As a result, these macroeconomic policies will not, in themselves, provide the jobs needed by the urban poor, nor help them in breaking the vicious circle of poverty.

Since the mid-1970s, the adoption of development strategies focussed on basic needs and the urban IFS has gained currency in some quarters with resultant changes in the patterns of consumption and production. Although the provision of basic needs services can improve the quality of life in the short term, it does not necessarily lead to the creation of a more dynamic economy in which employment opportunities are provided for the poor. This does not preclude, however, the devising of measures designed to gradually improve the system of services which are within the ability of the poor, and the country as a whole, to pay (Richards and Thomson, 1984:27–38). Indeed, there are possibilities for both service provision and employment creation to be combined in the same project, as exemplified in the Kampung Improvement Programme (KIP) in Indonesia.

Despite the large labour absorptive capacity of the IFS, a persistent question that is raised is whether it is evolutionary or involutionary growth. In this respect, it is noteworthy that an increasing number of economists have taken the view that IFS activities are "productive," using provision of employment to the poor as a criterion of productivity. It is further argued that only the introduction of value judgements regarding the nature of output would lead to the notion of IFS activities being considered unproductive, superfluous, or undesirable (Linn, 1983:40). This more sympathetic assessment of the IFS appeared to have emerged in the early 1970s, as the World Bank and other international assistance agencies began to realize the severity of the problem of urban poverty in developing countries. In fact, recent studies have agreed on the efficient manner in which a range of useful and important services and goods are provided in Third World cities—housing (Drakakis-Smith, 1981; Yeung, 1983), transport (Ocampo, 1982), food distribution (Smith, 1978; Bath, 1983), waste recycling (Furedy, 1986; Pollock, 1987) and so on.

Notwithstanding the important contributions IFS activities have made towards city life in the developing countries, they are subject to many discriminatory policies and negative attitudes on the part of administrators. Restriction of their activities may stem from taxation, fines, licensing, or locational measures. In general, the greatest problems of the self-employed are exploitation by merchants and middlemen; limited access to credit, raw materials, and markets for their goods and services; and low incomes (Sebstad, 1982:252). For small-scale enterprises, five specific problems have been mentioned: limited access to credit, limited markets, limited space for industrial establishment and expansion, limited access to material supplies, and limited levels of technology and organization (OUD, 1981:A8–10). In Indian cities, Singh and de Souza (1980:123) have reported that IFS has been virtually ignored by those concerned with urban policy and planning. This situation is not peculiar to Indian cities, as IFS activities generally do not figure in the master plans of most Asian cities.

INTERVENTION EFFORTS

One of the most effective ways of overcoming the above listed difficulties faced by the IFS is the design of intervention strategies that will assist its activities. In fact, as the main cause of poverty is the severely limited income from gainful employment, a practical objective is linked to policies aimed at increasing employment and wages, particularly through small-scale enterprises which require less capital to create jobs. In these intervention strategies, the experience to date, at different levels, is noteworthy.

At the international level, the massive assistance programme of the World Bank towards the urban sector since 1972 must be considered. The generation of nonfarm employment opportunities at low capital cost is a major component of its urban poverty programme and probably the most difficult to achieve. This urban poverty programme has two mutually reinforcing thrusts: (1) to create productive nonfarm employment opportunities in much greater numbers than would otherwise take place; and (2) to develop programmes to deliver basic services to the urban poor on a very large scale, at standards which they, and the economy, can afford (Jaycox, 1978:12). Underlying the objective of the urban strategy is the increase of the absorptive capacity of towns and cities in the face of their growing labour force.

By 1981, sixty-two projects were approved which amounted to US$2,014 million in lending. Although the projects are broadly categorized into four types (shelter, urban transport, integrated urban and regional development), it was recognized that job creation would be an important component of these lending activities. Indeed, many projects used credit, training, organization, marketing and other forms of assistance to encourage the creation of small enterprises, thereby increasing urban employment. To be more specific, more than half of all urban projects supported by the World Bank have included measures intended to support small businesses as a means of improving employment opportunities in urban areas. It must be recognized that even as late as 1982, the employment objectives had not been fully achieved, for project-level reasons as well as conceptual problems (Cohen, 1983).

In addition to the urban assistance programme, the World Bank has channelled not inconsiderable resources to the support of small-scale enterprises (SSEs), specifically in the nonfarm sector. These are recognized as more capable of generating more jobs per unit of investment than do larger firms. They would form an effective policy plank in an attack on poverty. Lending is through conventional development finance companies (DFCs) and includes projects in construction, transportation, trade, repair facilities, personal services and other activities. Between 1972 and 1976, DFC projects totalled approximately US$2,200 million, of which only about US$100 million was explicitly for SSEs. However, by 1981, lending for SSEs had soared to US$300 million, representing 30 per cent of the DFC commitments. The policy guiding the World Bank approach to this cluster of economic activities may be summed up thus:

> SSEs should not be promoted indiscriminately through the developing world, but in some places, employment and income opportunities for the urban poor can be improved through the use of coordinated credit and technical assistance and without sacrificing efficiency (Gordon, 1978:12).

The United States Agency for International Development (USAID) through the Office of Housing and the Office of Urban Development (OUD) has mounted two projects, both noted for their contributions to increasing urban livelihoods in developing countries. The first is the Integrated Improvement Programme for the Urban Poor (IIPUP), designed as multifaceted, integrated interventions to address the underlying causes of poverty. The programme seeks to reach segments of the population who are outside the regular credit markets or urban services delivery systems. Shelter is viewed as central to improving the welfare of the urban poor, but other types of assistance encompass small-scale enterprises, informal adult education, environmental sanitation and so on. Comprehensiveness and integration are two principal characteristics of IIPUP. The former is premised upon the notion of multiple and interdependent needs of the poor that can be included in a proper programme design, whereas the latter is intended to reduce duplication of services and improve efficiency. The project design is elaborately detailed and the approach of integrated urban development has been tested in projects supported in India (Ahmedabad), Honduras, Indonesia (KIP), Kenya and Zambia (OUD, 1981).

The second project that was started by the OUD with USAID support in 1978 is the Programme for Investment in the Small Capital Enterprises Sector (PISCES). The programme provided direct assistance to the smallest businesses within the IFS where capital start-up was minimal, from a few dollars to one or two hundred dollars. Under the programme, many projects in all developing regions, including India and the Philippines in Asia, were supported. The programme shows that it is possible to effectively assist the smallest businesses of the IFS. Projects assisted large numbers of businesses with initial loans ranging from US$12 to US$300, with very high payback rates between 90 and 99 per cent. Other projects helped the poorest enter the urban job market to start hawking with loans of as little as US$100. Apart from its effective reach of target groups, the programme demonstrated significant positive impacts on the family and the community. An important finding is that credit was seen by beneficiaries as the most important and often the only input that mattered to their businesses (Farbman, 1981).

A third group of efforts designed to alleviate mass poverty and unemployment in developing countries stems from the ILO, in particular its World Employment Programme launched in 1969. This is a large-scale programme involving many countries in all major developing regions and sustained over many years. The programme has produced a large number of monographs, based mainly but not exclusively on individual city case studies, in which the role of the IFS is affirmed as playing a significant role in labour absorption in cities in developing countries. There is another practical dimension to the programme, in that it included pilot projects and country missions by which expert advice on employment matters would be provided. The pilot projects, in Bombay and French-speaking African countries, for example, explored possible approaches within the limitations of national capacities, but emphasized, like the World Bank projects, the goal of replicability so that the solutions could be applied on a wide scale (Sethuraman, 1981:208).

Turning to intervention strategies at the national and city levels, they are more closely interwined but, even so, coordination of policies between these two levels sometimes proves difficult. In the long run, national policies are likely to provide the driving force for solving the urban employment problem in developing countries. The Malaysian example of setting national targets of eradicating poverty, in the form of the New Economic Policy in 1971, is a classic case attesting to national determination and purpose. Under this broad national policy, urban poverty eradication can be tackled through strategies formulated at the city level.

For many years since 1945, developing countries have generally attempted to emulate, without success, the experience of developed countries in coupling urbanization with industrialization. Even without industrialization, however, rapid urbanization has characterized developing countries in the postwar period. National investment policies have often favoured capital over labour, with the result that over time the problems of urban unemployment and underemployment intensify. The failure of the benefits of macroeconomic policies to trickle down to the urban poor has been generally acknowledged (Linn, 1983:42; Sethuraman, 1981:33). Recent modification of the industrialization policy by capitalizing on the labour surplus situation in developing countries has been the development of export processing zones. Despite the modest success of this development strategy in generating growth and employment, its full impact on the host countries is yet to be carefully assessed.

As regards IFS development, Sethuraman (1981:42) has argued that it must form an integral component of the national development plan, noting its contributions to the labour force for different sizes of cities. Similarly, Richardson (1984:23–24) hypothesized that the share of the IFS in total urban employment increased with decreasing city size. A recent study by Costello and others (1987) has reaffirmed the vital role that the IFS has played in the economy of medium cities in Indonesia and the Philippines.

As far as the urban poor is concerned, national policies in developing countries have primarily not benefited them directly. On the contrary, McGee (1979:65) perceives the present policy process to be working against the interests of low-income populations:

> For the moment, it seems that the greatest burden the Third World urban poor have to carry is the governmental elites who purport to be representing their interests, but instead are really collaborating with the overall processes in "peripheral capitalist societies" which are encouraging the persistence of poverty and preventing any radical redistribution of income.

When intervention strategies are carried out at the city level, the livelihoods of the urban poor are directly and indirectly affected. While individual Asian cities have a certain latitude to evolve their own policies, it should be remembered that many derive their authority from the central government. In the administration of cities, one of the major problems being faced is the lack of funds. Bangkok, Jakarta, and even Tokyo, to cite only three cases, have had problems of insufficient municipal finance to provide essential services. Bangkok, for example, has only four taxes coming under the Metropolitan Administration, with property, land and cars grossly undertaxed. As a result, the average revenue of the city government was only one-third of the national average (Yeung, 1985:37–38). To make matters worse, planners and administrators, influenced by visions of the modern Western city, often adopt measures that are detrimental to the interests of the urban poor. Becak-free zones in Jakarta, removal of squatters from central Manila to the suburbs, and strict control of street hawking in many Asian cities are examples of policies that inadequately balance ecological concerns against viable alternatives for the economically disadvantaged groups. As some students of urbanization would argue, cities in developing countries are planned for the rich, with the interests of the poor relegated to secondary importance.

Given the urban policy bias in favour of the rich, the poor have taken upon themselves the task of improving their welfare by providing better services (Yeung and McGee, 1986) and enhancing economic opportunities. An example of the latter is the Self Employed Women's Association (SEWA) in Ahmedabad, located in Gujarat, Western India. Formed in 1971, SEWA is a trade union of over five thousand poor women workers, many of them illiterate. Its members include women in a wide range of self-employed traders, such as vegetable vendors, hand cart pullers, carpenters, wastepickers and so on. After more than a decade of operation, SEWA is widely recognized as one of the few and most successful organizations of poor women workers in the world. The union succeeded in stabilizing and increasing incomes (a bank was formed), initiating social security programmes, developing skills among members, providing the opportunity for social interaction, and making policy-makers aware of the needs of the poor. In short, it is a developmental and organizational effort that has enhanced access to raw materials, markets, credit, training and other productive resources (Sebstad, 1982). The association notably increased the material resources of a subgroup of the urban poor and would qualify for Richards and Thomson's (1984:23) criterion of a useful programme. Linn (1983:60) went even further, while relating national and city-level intervention strategies, by suggesting that:

> If progress is to be made in solving the general problem of urban poverty and the employment problem in particular, action must be taken on all possible fronts. This implies that concerted action is necessary at both the national and city level regarding labor demand, labor supply, and labor market imperfections, in the form of both general and urban poverty-oriented employment policies.

POVERTY-REDRESSAL PROGRAMMES

Concerted action between the national and city level is indeed essential not only to employment generation policies for the poor but to a whole range of strategies aimed at poverty-redressal in general. This line of action rests on the notion of a direct attack on poverty to improve the lot of the urban poor, playing down the trickling-down effects of economic growth on this population group. The cynics of development studies may argue that, short of intervention at the society level, entailing radical structural changes affecting all social groups, poverty-redressal policies are at best piecemeal palliatives providing temporary relief. In any event, various types of anti-poverty programmes have been in effect in Asian cities, structured both by the nature of activity and varying geographical scales. This section will briefly report three recently completed studies, all funded by the International Development Research Centre (IDRC) of Canada, carried out in different societal settings in Asia.

The first study (Viloria et al., 1983) was focussed on Metro Manila, where problems of poverty had been sharpened under the New Society of former President Marcos, particularly during the latter part of his administration. Guided by the principles of equal opportunities and access, a total of 116 poverty-redressal programmes, including fifty-seven on a nationwide scale, were identified. The rest of the programmes operated on the metro/city-wide as well as barangay scales. The programmes were organized around eleven basic needs that were considered necessary for wholesome living standards. The study attempted to identify the government agencies involved in the programme and to examine existing delivery mechanisms for the programmes and how they facilitated or hindered effective delivery. The study discovered that among problems encountered in delivering the programmes were insufficient funds, bureaucratic red tape, administrative inefficiency and lack of cooperation among agencies. An interagency council was recommended for creation to improve service delivery. The projects most preferred by depressed Metro Manila barangays are mainly of an income-generation and employment-creation nature. In the fifteen barangays under study, an average of 68 per cent of the residents availed of poverty-redressal programmes, with food and nutrition programmes and medical services being the most popular. Residents did not utilize the programmes because they were fee-charging, absent from the locality in which the people resided, or poor in service. Also, the residents did not know enough about requirements and procedures, had no time to queue, or had found alternative services. Generally speaking, people are dependent on the government for community needs but are quite self-reliant in solving their family problems. On the perception of poverty, 58.7 per cent or 599 households considered themselves poor subjectively, whereas by actual incomes compared with established criteria, only 29.2 per cent could be defined poor objectively. Not surprisingly, therefore, more than half of the households considered Metro Manila to be offering more opportunities for economic improvement in comparison with their home towns. The study concluded that the degree of awareness of the programmes was directly related to the rate of utilization of the programmes. In order to improve utilization rates, it would be necessary to better inform the target beneficiaries. Yet, insufficient funding for the programmes resulted in officials having to wait for referrals and walk-in clients instead of reaching out to the target groups. The study recommended that services and programmes be prioritized so as to ensure that they would be able to make a community-wide impact. The alternative is to spread benefits thinly to benefit a wider population. The study also urged avoidance of duplication of programmes and efforts. Pooling of resources and manpower would be required to mount a plan for uplifting the urban poor, which should be measured not simply by how many people are serviced, but by the degree to which these people have improved their socioeconomic situation after being supplied with certain material or nonmaterial resources.

The Republic of Korea is a country of rapid economic growth but the government has not neglected the welfare of the economically disadvantaged. Anti-poverty programmes have been organized in five spheres, viz., income subsidy, health maintenance, housing, education and employment. In a study of three separate low-income areas in Seoul (Ro and Oh, 1985) with a sample size of 1,000, the first three most favoured programmes were living cost assistance (34 per cent), educational expense assistance (27.6 per cent) and house improvement (9.5 per cent). On the quality of the programmes, 43 per cent rated them as poor, 32.5 per cent rated them good, and 24.6 per cent rated them fair. Part of the problem was due to the relative lack of official commitment, for 61.3 per cent of the officials interviewed felt that the programmes had received a low priority from the government. In 1982, 88 billion won (US$1 = 780 won) was spent on the income subsidy programme, representing 1.4 per cent of the total government budget, designed to benefit 33,400 inhabitants or 0.9 per cent of the total population. The low priority and budget assigned to anti-poverty programmes appeared inevitable given the country's massive defence budget. With respect to programme performance, the study revealed that it was positively related to organizational factors such as job satisfaction, programme officials' ability/responsibility, interagency communication, interaction between policy-makers and administrators, and the organizational hierarchy and flexibility. To improve the effectiveness of anti-poverty programmes, the study emphasized the need for formal and informal channels of interaction and communication between programme officials and the residents, between policy-makers and implementators, and between different programme agencies to be developed and improved upon. In order to win wide support for the programmes, the general public should be made aware of the process of policy formulation and how the organization of the programmes works. The study concluded with a recommendation that the government should establish a system with which to monitor and evaluate the performance by programme, agency, region and the type of target population.

The third study (Fong, 1984) is one on urban poverty in Malaysia, limited to four metropolitan centres in Penang, Kuala Lumpur, Kota Bahru and Johore Bahru. It attempted to construct profiles of urban poverty in these four urban areas and to evaluate how poverty-eradication programmes were implemented. The approach to poverty eradication differs from Metro Manila and Seoul, as it is designed to be spatially differentiated. In the rural areas, poverty eradication concentrates on target groups, such as rubber smallholders, oil palm smallholders, paid farmers, fishermen and estate workers; industrial estates created in rural areas, with the aim of bringing industrial employment to these places; and labour recruitment from rural areas for urban industrial establishments. In the urban areas, alleviation of poverty is pursued through low-cost housing provision, squatter upgrading, income generation (handicrafts, small-scale industries, etc.), "integrated" development (delivery of primary health care services with family planning, kindergarten, etc.), and community-based activities such as self-help projects and garbage disposal. Although poor urban households in Malaysia increased from 85,900 in 1970 to 97,900 in 1983, in relative terms the incidence of poverty sharply decreased from 21.3 per cent in 1970 to 11.1 per cent in 1983. The above poverty eradication programmes can be said to have attributed, in part, to the decline.

The study covered 2,000 households drawn from the three major ethnic groups in 100 poverty-stricken areas in the four metropolitan areas of Malaysia. It provided a detailed account of the economic conditions, education, health and fertility, and access to public services in the urban areas. A major finding is that the manner in which poverty-eradication programmes are structured, organized and implemented in the urban areas would have a strong impact on the socioeconomic status of the urban poor. The importance of the programme staff in inspiring the urban poor to be self-confident and self-reliant was emphasized. The study concluded with a number of policy recommendations, including implementation strategies to improve socioeconomic conditions in urban poverty areas in the immediate, medium and long term.

Although the three studies adopted rather different methodologies to deal with individual poverty-redressal programmes, several generalizations may be made, especially about the Metro Manila and Seoul study, which had more in common. First of all, it is clear that the degree of awareness among the citizens in the programme and their utilization rates are closely linked. That being the case, the need to increase publicity and awareness by the agencies concerned is urgent. Then, the problem of insufficient funding for the programmes is a serious one, reflecting the country's and city's priority in economic growth or other social programmes. It is thus necessary to prioritize services and target groups in a situation of limited resources. Thirdly, functional duplication of efforts is a general problem but one that especially bedevilled Manila's numerous programmes. This calls for a comprehensive approach to mounting these programmes, with built-in monitoring and evaluation. Finally, the organizational factors are closely related to programme performance. Given the generally low educational levels of the target groups, the organizational structure should be simplified, cost-effective and designed in such a way that the programmes can be easily used by, and identified with, the needs of the target population.

MEASURES TO HELP

While the poverty-redressal programmes represented urban as well as rural efforts in tackling poverty problems in many ways, what other special measures can metropolitan governments introduce with the purpose of improving the livelihoods of the urban poor? This section attempts to review possibilities which may be grouped under several headings for convenience of discussion.

Firstly, the government should refrain from negative actions that will directly or indirectly threaten the livelihoods of the urban poor. McGee (1979), for instance, reported that after Jakarta was declared a "closed city" in 1971, military units had been organized into controlling teams whose task was to destroy squatter settlements, arrest hawkers who infringed regulations and remove illegal migrants. Many city governments still regard IFS activities as outside their administrative and planning framework and have discouraged these activities through fines, imposed standards, ecological controls and the like. The siting of public facilities with little or no regard for the location or needs of the urban poor will result in a situation whereby the economically disadvantaged groups have to pursue their livelihoods at increased inconvenience and costs. Examples of policy measures detrimental to the interests of the urban poor spring from the failure of administrators and planners to recognize the economic contributions of the urban poor to their city and from the fact that these people pursue activities that are at variance with their concept of a modern city. Both notions are, of course, erroneous but they are very difficult to change.

The second group of measures refer to positive policies that will directly or indirectly benefit the livelihoods of the urban poor. In respect of the IFS, studies cited in this chapter showed that credit availability was a critical factor in assisting the activities concerned to sustain themselves, and expand. Lending procedures and policies should thus be adjusted to take into account the needs and absorptive capacity of the participants in the sector (Sethuraman, 1981:203). Lending instruments, if properly and purposefully applied, can have the further effect of upgrading the scale of enterprises. When this is realized the traditional and peculiar markets of the IFS, already outlined earlier, is not only strengthened but expanded. Needless to say, the metropolitan government is often in a position to assist or discourage IFS activities with recourse to ecological controls. For instance, central city car parks may be allowed to be turned into hawker centres at night, a supportive measure which may be contrasted with the resiting of a squatter colony to the urban fringe. A more indirect policy measure is to reorient the educational goals of the city. In Jakarta, it has been observed that there are too many general educational establishments and too few vocational training establishments (Sethuraman, 1976:139). Even if the educational system cannot, in the short term, be adjusted to this need, vocational counselling and skills training can be specifically built into development projects associated with the IFS. Many of the above policy measures point to the desirability of reorienting development strategies and restructuring socioeconomic relationships, in particular between the formal and informal sectors. Most of the positive policy measures are designed to increase the opportunity for IFS enterprises to expand, to transfer technologies, to foster linkages between the two sectors, and to narrow the productivity gap between the two.

Thirdly, there are several policy measures that metropolitan governments may, through a change of attitude initially, rather than an infusion of funds, focus attention on—to address some neglected needs of the urban poor. In respect of the IFS activities, many are still unprovided for, in the legal sense, and thus operate outside the ambit of law. Where these activities are useful, efficient and within the limits of law, such as street food selling, changes should be made in the present system to incorporate them into the overall structure. In addition, female participation in the IFS in most Asian countries, with the exception of the Philippines, appears small. Despite their smaller representation, women make significant contributions to the welfare of the urban poor, particularly if they are also heads of households. The special needs of women should be provided for, if not directly by government, at least through indirect encouragement of new institutions. The example of the SEWA in Ahmedabad, India, referred to earlier, is an eminent case of positive action. Here, income generation projects are organized by providing skills training, facilitating access to raw materials and markets, and assisting in the formation of cooperative production units.

Finally, urban management itself bears scrutiny in its effects on the livelihoods for the urban poor. Richards and Thomson (1984:249) maintain that urban management in developing countries is not responsive nor perhaps wants to be responsive to the needs of the urban poor. The main difficulties appear to lie in readjusting the planning and implementation of urban projects and programmes to make them more sensitive to basic needs satisfaction. Government hierarchy and bureaucracy are further obstacles to improved urban management. A more optimistic view is advanced by Sethuraman (1981:203) who suggests that positive policies in favour of the IFS can be effected by suitable changes in the prevailing master plans for cities. Such changes will not only meet the environmental objectives but also facilitate the IFS's physical access to various markets that is viewed as one of the critical determinants of income inequality. However, to increase the absorptive capacity of cities in developing countries, Linn (1983:57) advocates a comprehensive approach to improving urban management. The approach involves control of central city congestion (as in Singapore), improved public utility services and road infrastructure at cost-covering charges, a streamlined administration of local taxes and regulations, and provision of a wide variety of marketing facilities, all within the purview of urban management.

CONCLUSION

This chapter has reviewed some important empirical evidence that pertains to coping with the aggravating problem of urban poverty in developing countries. At every level under review, only relatively limited progress has been achieved in the light of the enormity of the problem and the immensity of the resources that would be required. True, this modest success should be seen in the context of how recently attention has been drawn to the necessity of improving the lives of the urban poor. Nonetheless, one cannot help reaching the conclusion that many of the efforts devoted to poverty alleviation smack of something that attacks the symptoms rather than the causes of economic deprivation. The study of poverty-redressal programmes in three Asian countries threw into sharp relief the need for greater determination of national and city governments to sharpen the focus of these activities if they were to succeed. The question of setting priorities among competing demands is relevant, so is the perennial debate of the trade-off between economic efficiency and social equity.

This chapter examined the arguments in favour of a greater role that can be played by metropolitan governments to enhance their labour absorptive capacity. The experience in developing countries revealed the considerable constraints which these governments are confronted with in their attempts to combat poverty and create jobs. Given the increasing connections between these national economies and the process of world accumulation, it is more likely that metropolitan governments will improve the livelihoods of the urban poor if they can work in concert with national and international bodies.

Two questions were raised at the beginning of this chapter. The first, concerning the manner in which inhabitants of cities in developing countries find their present livelihoods, was hopefully answered in the previous sections. The second was a speculative one relating to the ability of future inhabitants of these cities to find jobs. Of course, this question cannot be adequately answered. The degree of satisfaction of livelihoods for the urban poor is dependent on the success of job creation and poverty eradication at different levels. In view of recent development trends, economically as well as demographically, it does not seem probable that the urban poor in the developing countries have any basis to look forward to a much brighter tomorrow.

REFERENCES

Bath, Gerald A. 1983. *Street Foods: Informal Sector Food Preparation and Marketing.* Iloilo City: Equity Policy Center.

Cohen, Michael A. 1983. *Learning by Doing: World Bank Lending for Urban Development, 1972–82.* Washington, D.C.: The World Bank.

Costello, Michael A., Thomas R. Leinbach and Richard Ulack. 1987. *Mobility and Employment in Urban Southeast Asia: Examples from Indonesia and the Philippines.* Boulder and London: Westview Press.

Drakakis-Smith, D. W. 1981. *Urbanisation, Housing and the Development Process.* London: Croom Helm.

Farbman, Michael, ed. 1981. *The PISCES Studies: Assisting the Smallest Economic Activities of the Urban Poor.* Washington, D.C.: Office of Urban Development, Agency for International Development.

Fong, Chan Onn. 1984. "Urban Poverty in Malaysia: Its Profile in Four Metropolitan Centres." Kuala Lumpur: Faculty of Economics and Administration, University of Malaya. Unpublished report submitted to IDRC.

Furedy, Christine. 1986. "The People Who Set in the Way: Changing 25 Values in Urban Waste Management." *Water Science Technology,* 18:121–28.

Geertz, Clifford. 1963. *Peddlers and Princes: Social Change and Economic Modernization in Two Indonesian Towns.* Chicago: University of Chicago Press.

Gordon, David L. 1978. *Employment and Development of Small Enterprises.* Sector Policy Paper. Washington, D.C.: The World Bank.

Hart, K. 1973. "Informal Income Opportunities and Urban Employment in Ghana." *Journal of Modern African Studies,* 11(1):61–89.

International Labour Office (ILO). 1977. *Employment, Growth and Basic Needs: A One-World Problem.* New York: Praeger Publishers.

Jaycox, Edward. 1978. "The Bank and Urban Poverty." *Finance and Development,* 15(3):10–13.

Linn, Johannes F. 1983. *Cities in the Developing World: Policies for Their Equitable and Efficient Growth.* New York: Oxford University Press for the World Bank.

McGee, T. G. 1979. "The Poverty Syndrome: Making Out in the Southeast Asian City." In *Casual Work and Poverty in Third World Cities,* ed. Ray Broomley and Chris Gerry, pp. 45–68. New York: John Wiley and Sons.

McGee, T. G. and Y. M. Yeung. 1977. *Hawkers in Southeast Asian Cities: Planning for the Bazaar Economy.* Ottawa: International Development Research Centre.

Ocampo, Romeo B. 1982. *Low-Cost Transport in Asia: A Comparative Report on Five Cities.* Ottawa: International Development Research Centre.

Office of Urban Development (OUD). 1981. "Integrated Improvement Program for the Urban Poor: An Orientation for Project Design and Implementation." Washington, D.C.: Agency for International Development. Mimeo. 2 volumes.

Pollock, Cynthia. 1987. *Mining Urban Wastes: The Potential for Recycling.* Worldwatch Paper 76. Washington, D.C.: Worldwatch Institute.

Richards, P. J. and A. M. Thomson, eds. 1984. *Basic Needs and the Urban Poor: The Provision of Communal Services.* London: Croom Helm.

Richardson, Harry W. 1984. "The Role of the Urban Informal Sector: An Overview." *Regional Development Dialogue,* 5(2):3–40.

Ro, Kong-Kyun and Oh Sang-Bong. 1985. "Poverty Redressal Programs in Korea: Current Status and Evaluation." Seoul: Management Research Center, Ewha Women's University. Unpublished report submitted to IDRC.

Sebstad, Jennefer. 1982. "Struggle and Development among Self Employed Women." A Report on the Self Employed Women's Association, Ahmedabad, India, for Office of Urban Development, Agency for International Development. Mimeo.

Sethuraman, S. V. 1976. *Jakarta: Urban Development and Employment*. Geneva: International Labour Office.

————, ed. 1981. *The Urban Informal Sector in Developing Countries: Employment, Poverty and Environment*. Geneva: International Labour Office.

Singh, Andrea Nenefee and Alfred de Souza. 1980. *The Urban Poor: Slum and Pavement Dwellers in the Major Cities of India*. New Delhi: Manohar Publications.

Smith, Robert H. T., ed. 1978. *Market-Place Trade: Periodic Markets, Hawkers, and Traders in Africa, Asia, and Latin America*. Vancouver: Centre for Transportation Studies, U.B.C.

Viloria, Leandro A., *et al.* 1983. "Study of Poverty Redressal Programs in Metro Manila." Quezon City: Institute of Environmental Planning, University of the Philippines. Unpublished report submitted to IDRC.

Yeung, Y. M., ed. 1983. *A Place to Live: More Effective Low-Cost Housing in Asia*. Ottawa: International Development Research Centre.

————. 1985. *The Great Cities of Eastern Asia: Growing Pains and Policy Options*. Occasional Paper No. 69. Hong Kong: Department of Geography, The Chinese University of Hong Kong.

Yeung, Y. M. and T. G. McGee, eds. 1986. *Community Participation in Delivering Urban Services in Asia*. Ottawa: International Research Centre.